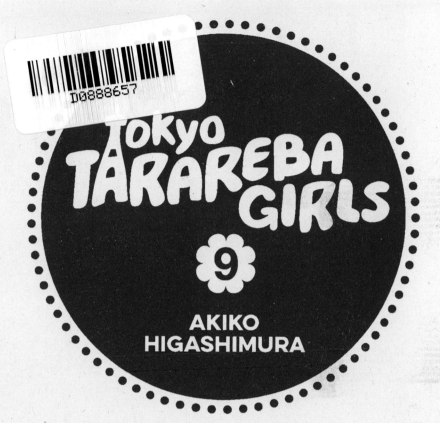

Tokyo
TARAREBA
GIRLS

9

AKIKO
HIGASHIMURA

TODAY'S RECOMMENDATIONS

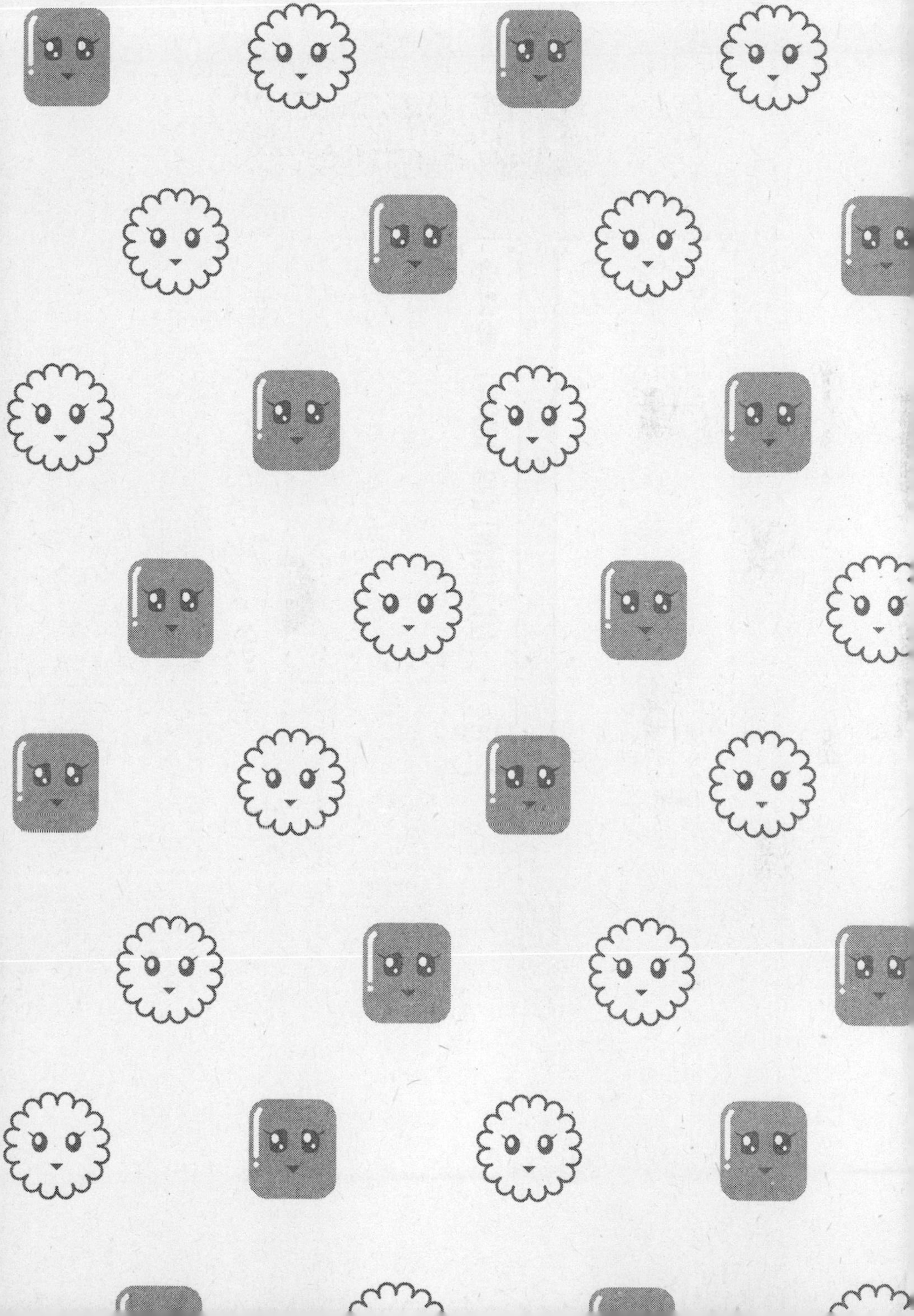

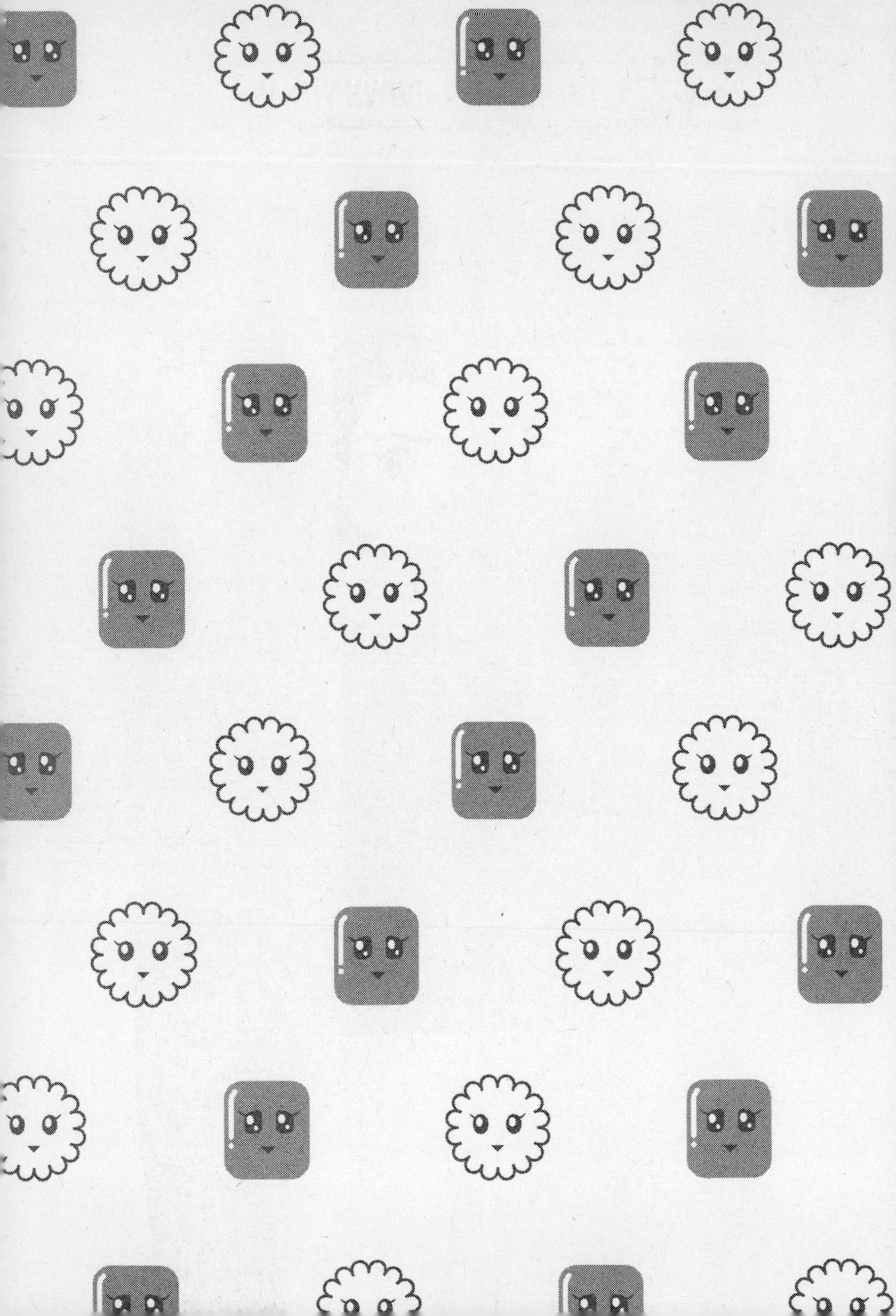

ACT 28 THE BROKEN-DOWN WOMAN

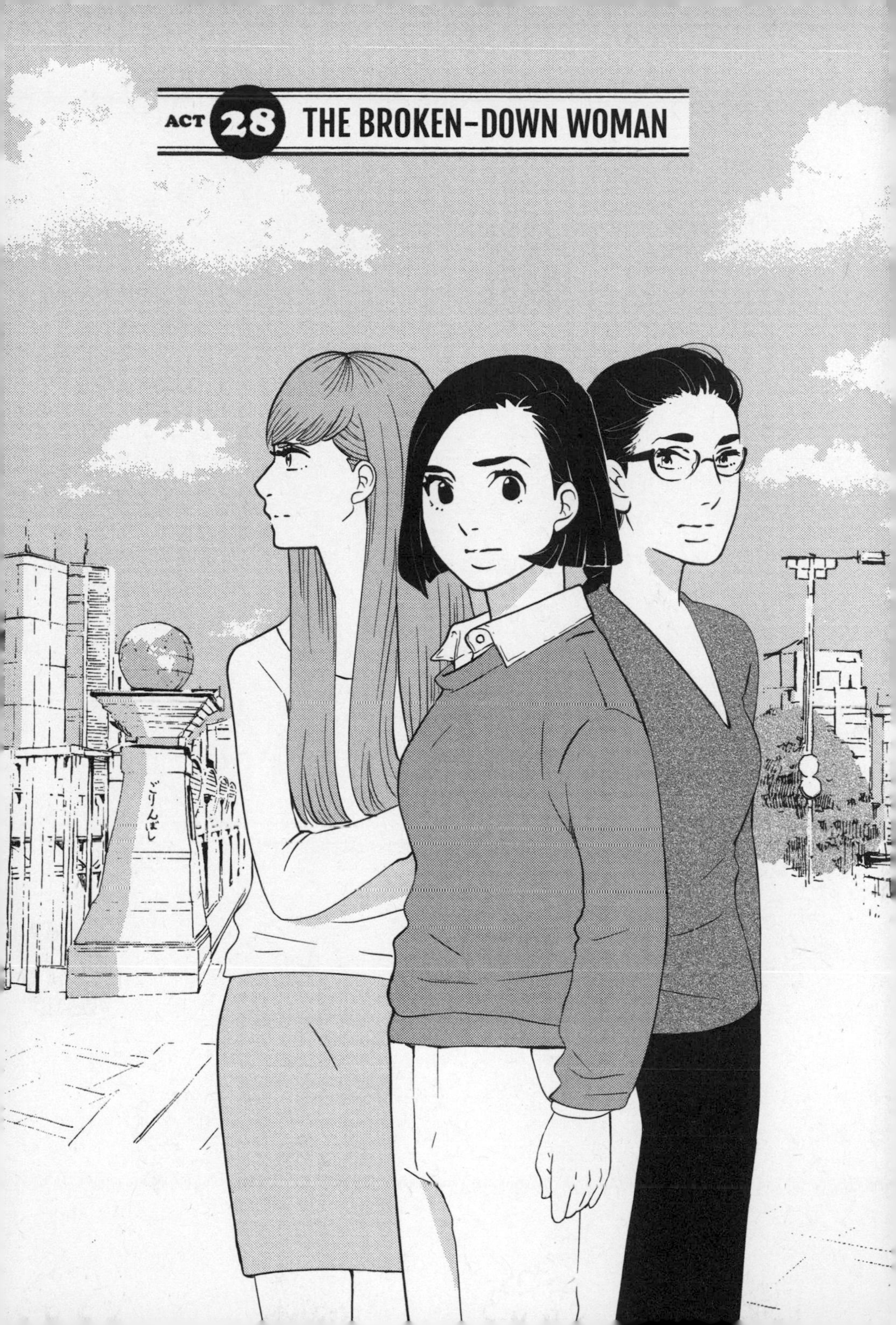
ごりんばし

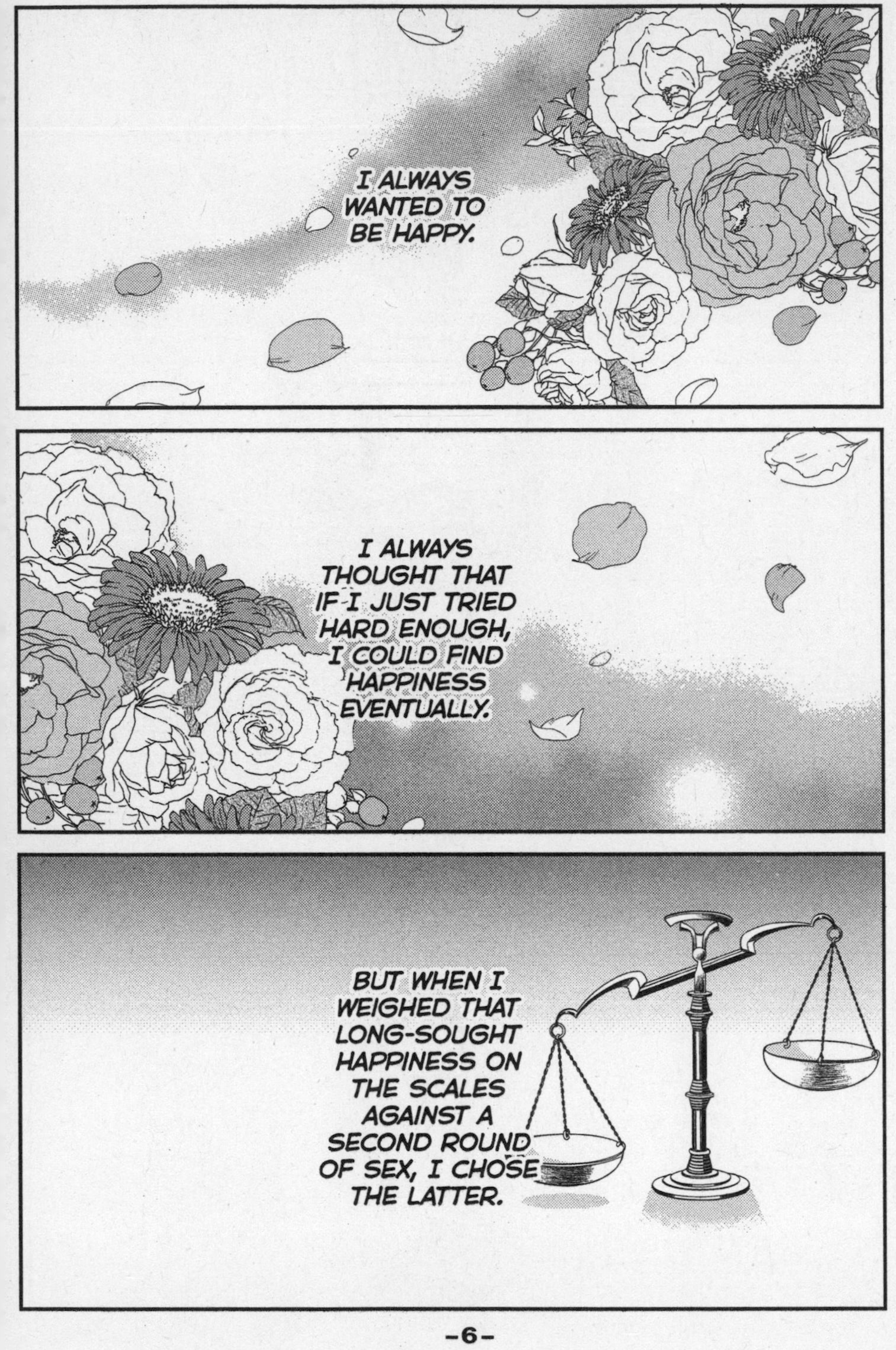
I ALWAYS WANTED TO BE HAPPY.
I ALWAYS THOUGHT THAT IF I JUST TRIED HARD ENOUGH, I COULD FIND HAPPINESS EVENTUALLY.
BUT WHEN I WEIGHED THAT LONG-SOUGHT HAPPINESS ON THE SCALES AGAINST A SECOND ROUND OF SEX, I CHOSE THE LATTER.

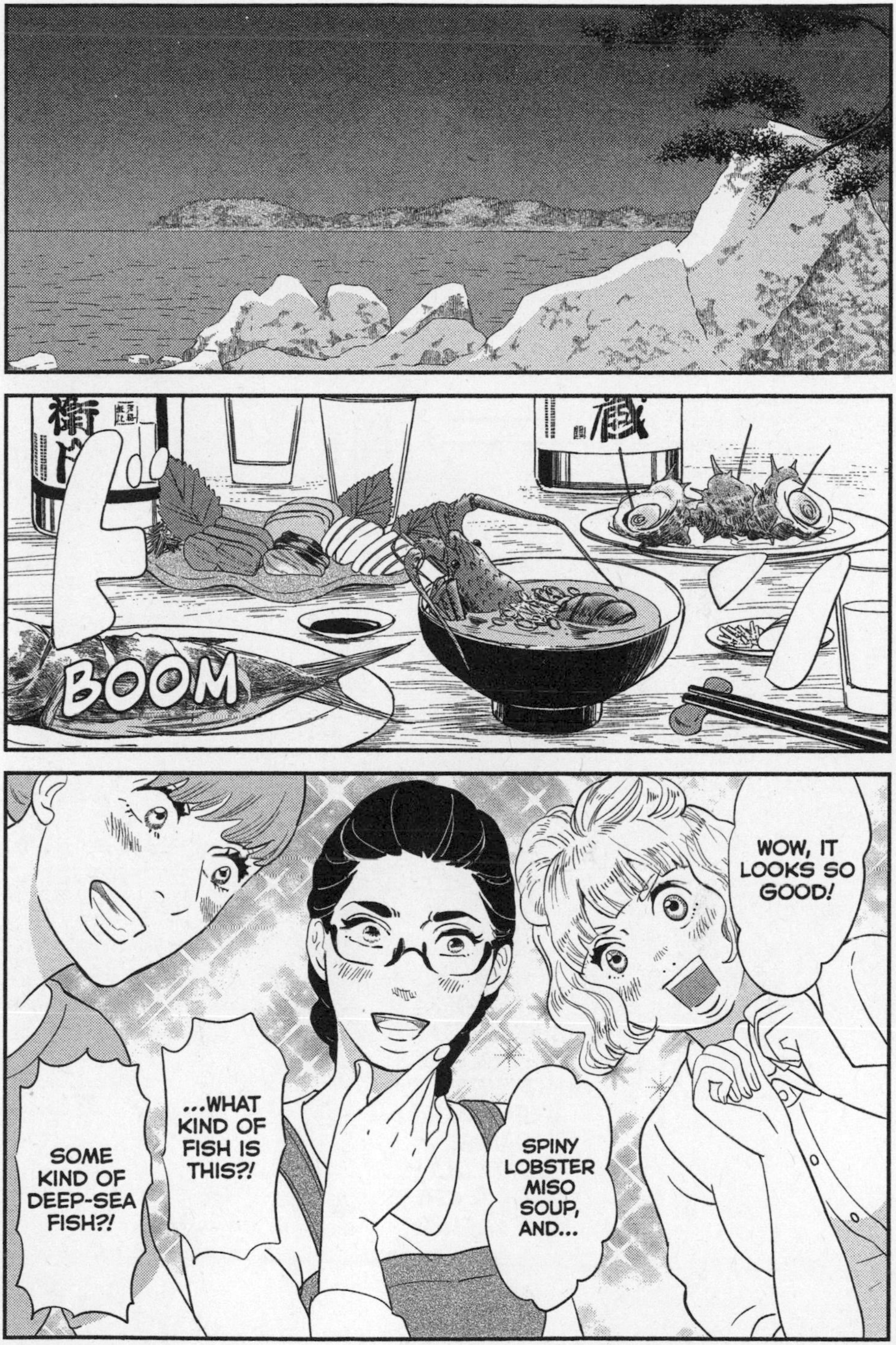
BOOM
WOW, IT LOOKS SO GOOD!
SPINY LOBSTER MISO SOUP, AND...
...WHAT KIND OF FISH IS THIS?!
SOME KIND OF DEEP-SEA FISH?!

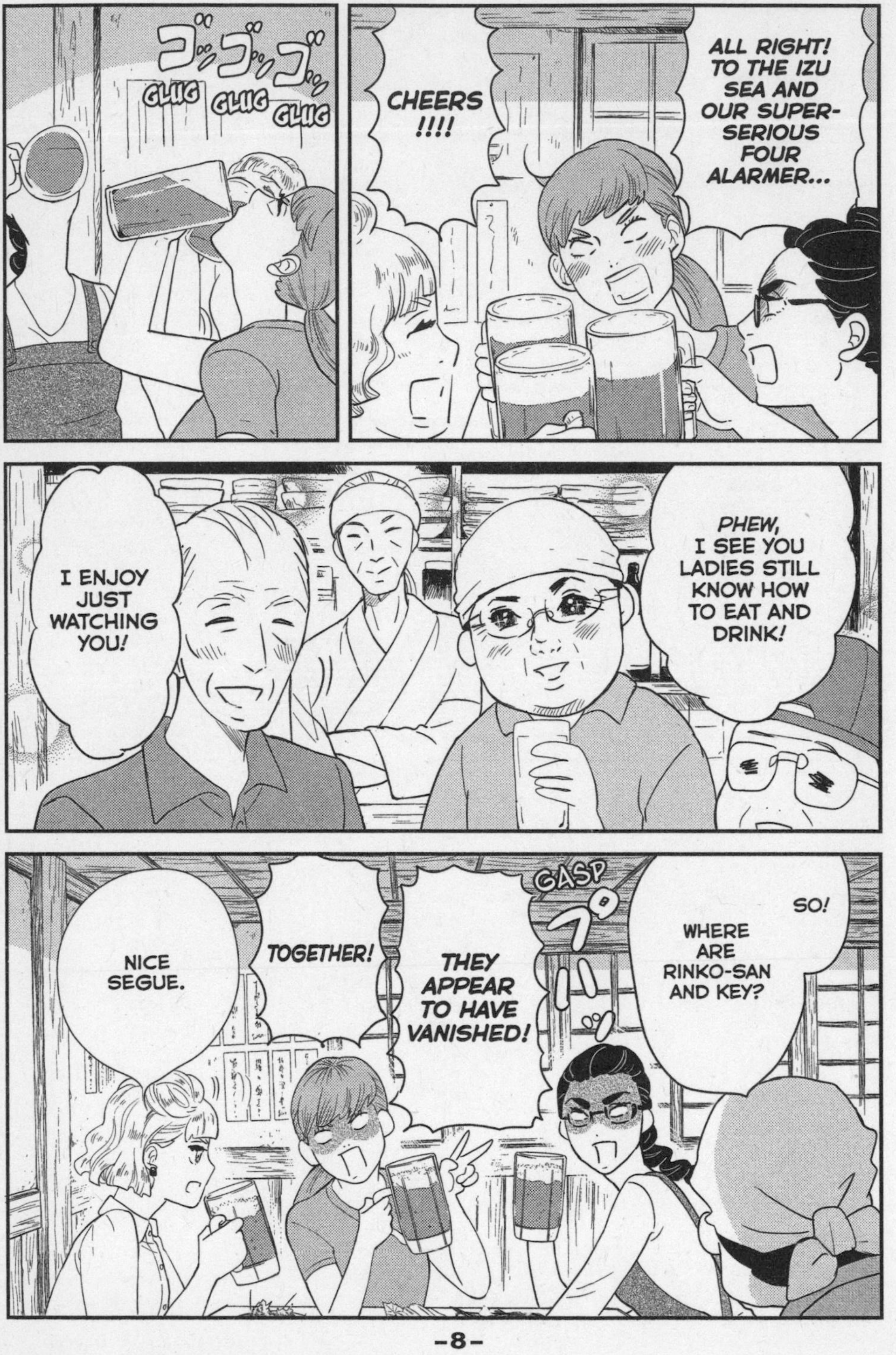
ALL RIGHT! TO THE IZU SEA AND OUR SUPER-SERIOUS FOUR ALARMER...
CHEERS !!!!
ゴッゴッゴッ
GLUG GLUG GLUG
PHEW, I SEE YOU LADIES STILL KNOW HOW TO EAT AND DRINK!
I ENJOY JUST WATCHING YOU!
SO!
WHERE ARE RINKO-SAN AND KEY?
GASP
プッ
THEY APPEAR TO HAVE VANISHED!
TOGETHER!
NICE SEGUE.

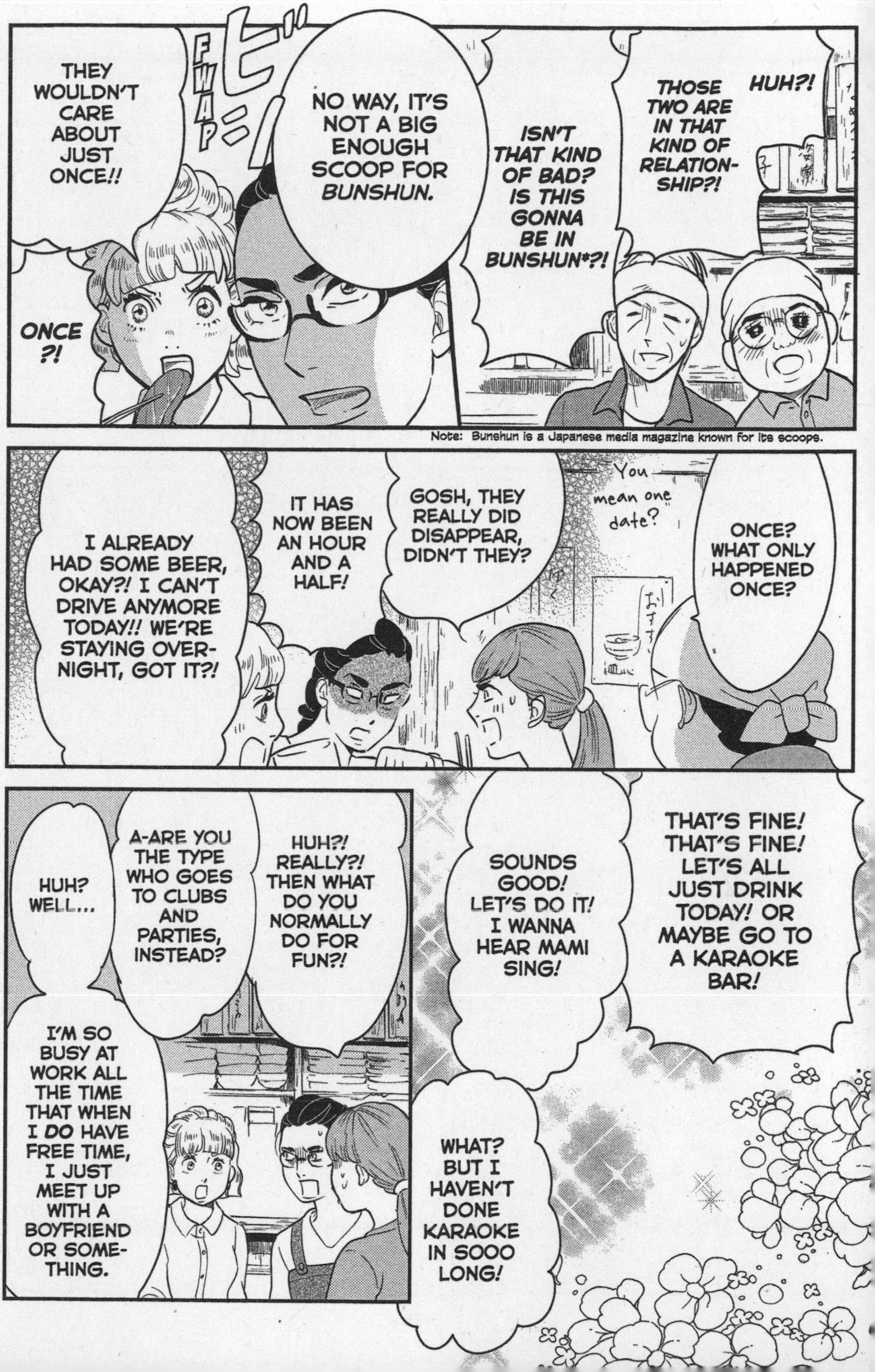
HUH?!
THOSE TWO ARE IN THAT KIND OF RELATIONSHIP?!
ISN'T THAT KIND OF BAD? IS THIS GONNA BE IN BUNSHUN*?!
NO WAY, IT'S NOT A BIG ENOUGH SCOOP FOR BUNSHUN.
FWAP
THEY WOULDN'T CARE ABOUT JUST ONCE!!
ONCE?!
Note: Bunshun is a Japanese media magazine known for its scoops.
ONCE? WHAT ONLY HAPPENED ONCE?
You mean one date?
GOSH, THEY REALLY DID DISAPPEAR, DIDN'T THEY?
IT HAS NOW BEEN AN HOUR AND A HALF!
I ALREADY HAD SOME BEER, OKAY?! I CAN'T DRIVE ANYMORE TODAY!! WE'RE STAYING OVER-NIGHT, GOT IT?!
THAT'S FINE! THAT'S FINE! LET'S ALL JUST DRINK TODAY! OR MAYBE GO TO A KARAOKE BAR!
SOUNDS GOOD! LET'S DO IT! I WANNA HEAR MAMI SING!
WHAT? BUT I HAVEN'T DONE KARAOKE IN SOOO LONG!
HUH?! REALLY?! THEN WHAT DO YOU NORMALLY DO FOR FUN?!
A-ARE YOU THE TYPE WHO GOES TO CLUBS AND PARTIES, INSTEAD?
HUH? WELL...
I'M SO BUSY AT WORK ALL THE TIME THAT WHEN I DO HAVE FREE TIME, I JUST MEET UP WITH A BOYFRIEND OR SOME-THING.

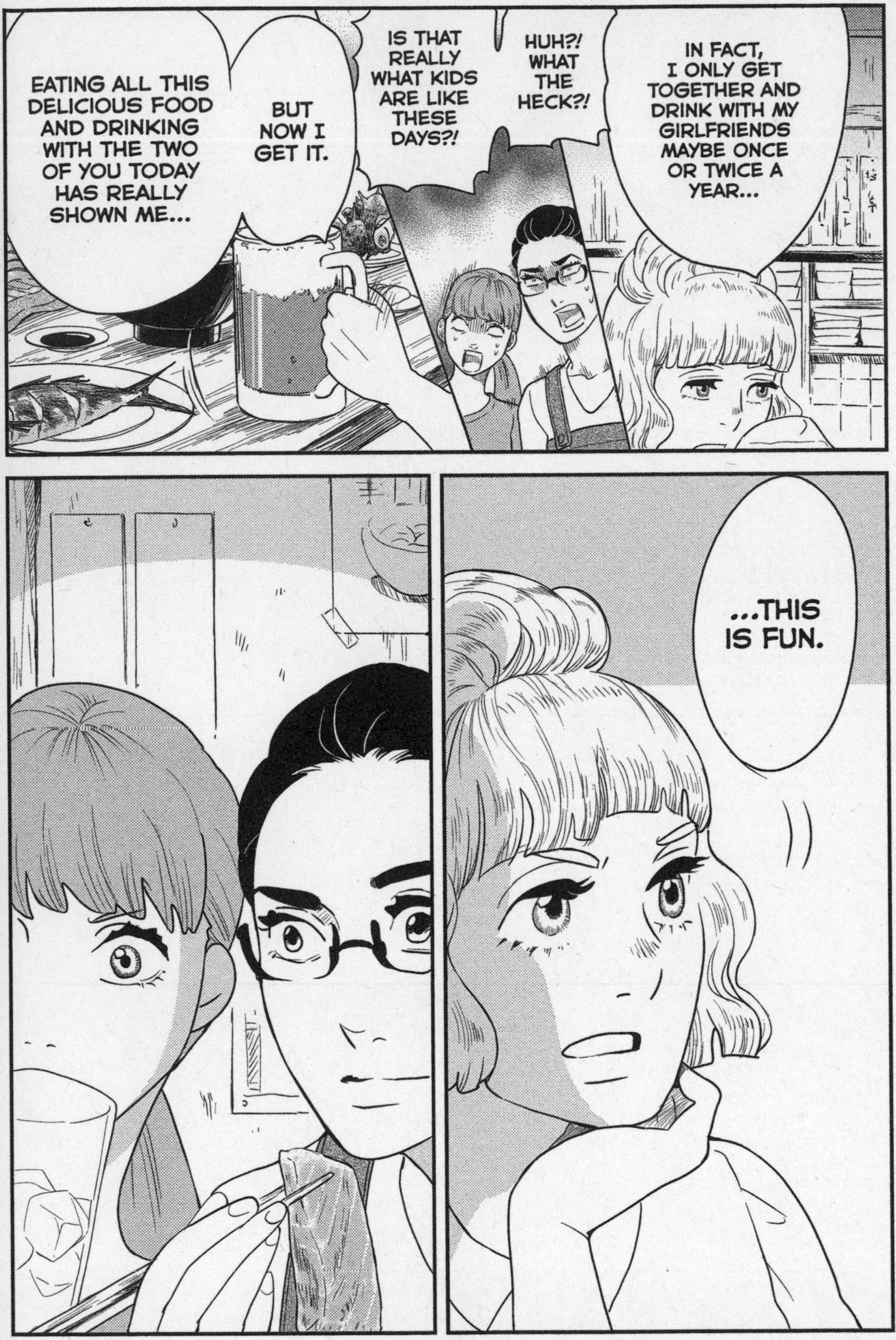
IN FACT, I ONLY GET TOGETHER AND DRINK WITH MY GIRLFRIENDS MAYBE ONCE OR TWICE A YEAR...
HUH?! WHAT THE HECK?!
IS THAT REALLY WHAT KIDS ARE LIKE THESE DAYS?!
BUT NOW I GET IT.
EATING ALL THIS DELICIOUS FOOD AND DRINKING WITH THE TWO OF YOU TODAY HAS REALLY SHOWN ME...
...THIS IS FUN.

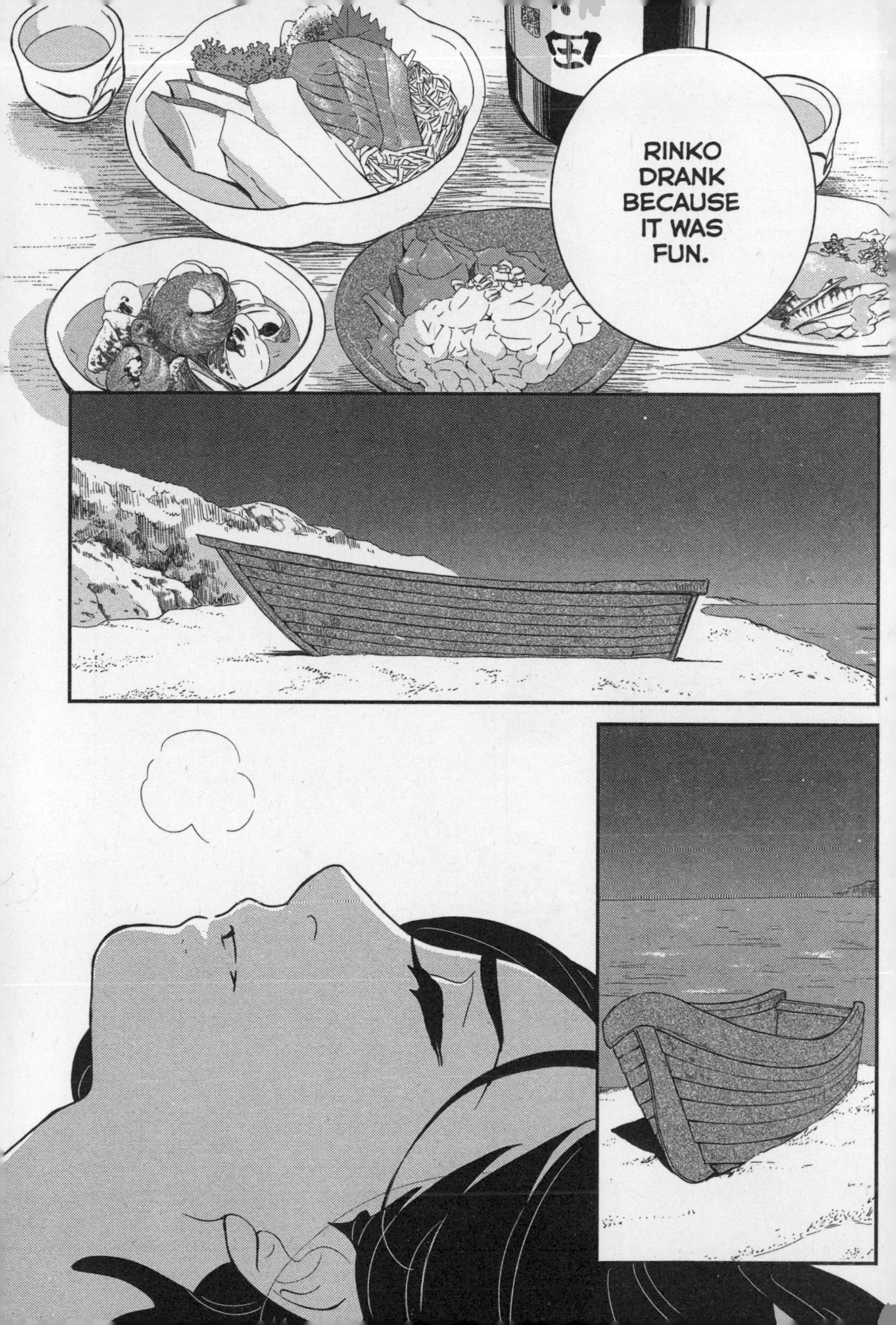
RINKO DRANK BECAUSE IT WAS FUN.

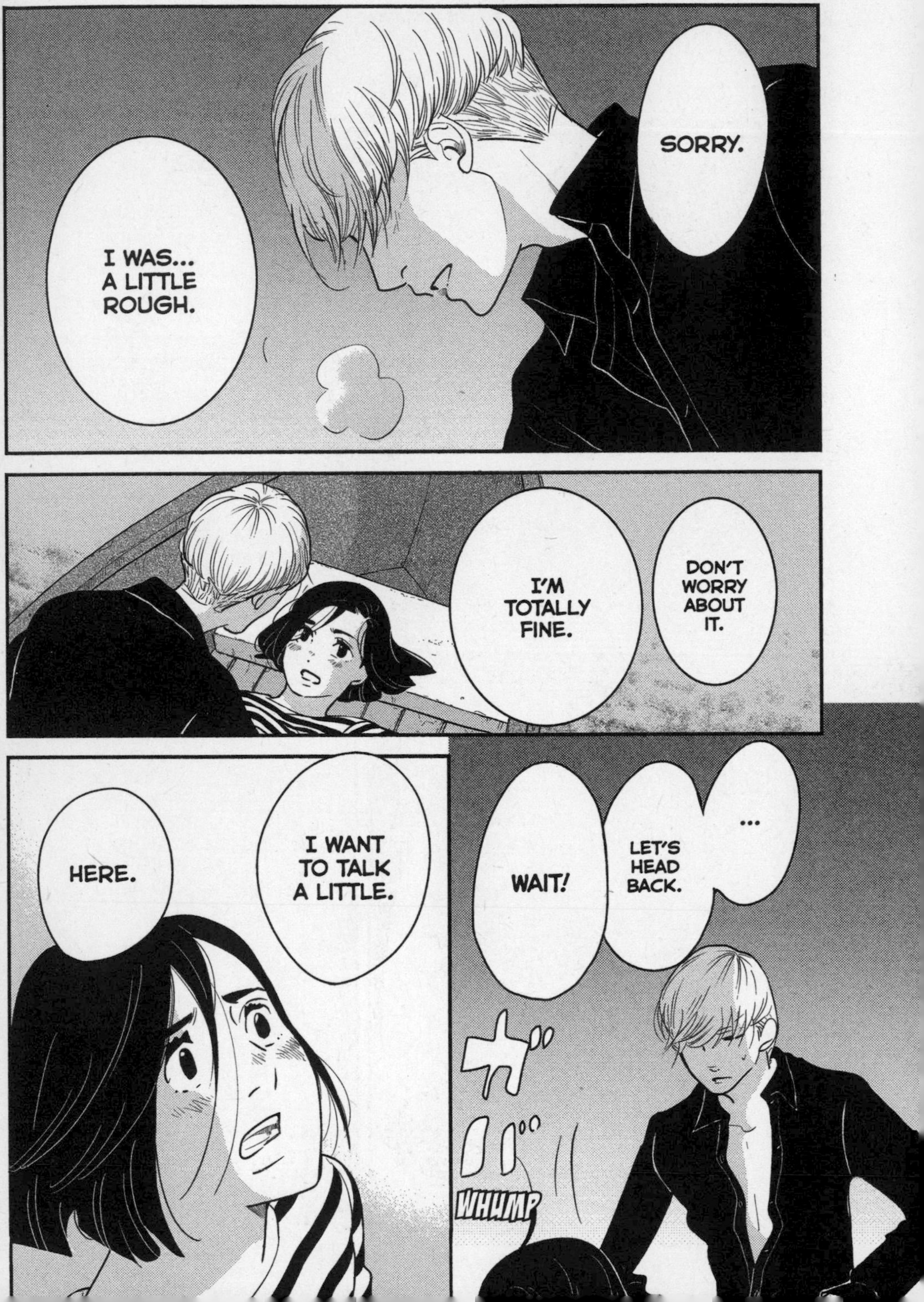
SORRY.
I WAS... A LITTLE ROUGH.
DON'T WORRY ABOUT IT.
I'M TOTALLY FINE.
...
LET'S HEAD BACK.
WAIT!
WHUMP
I WANT TO TALK A LITTLE.
HERE.

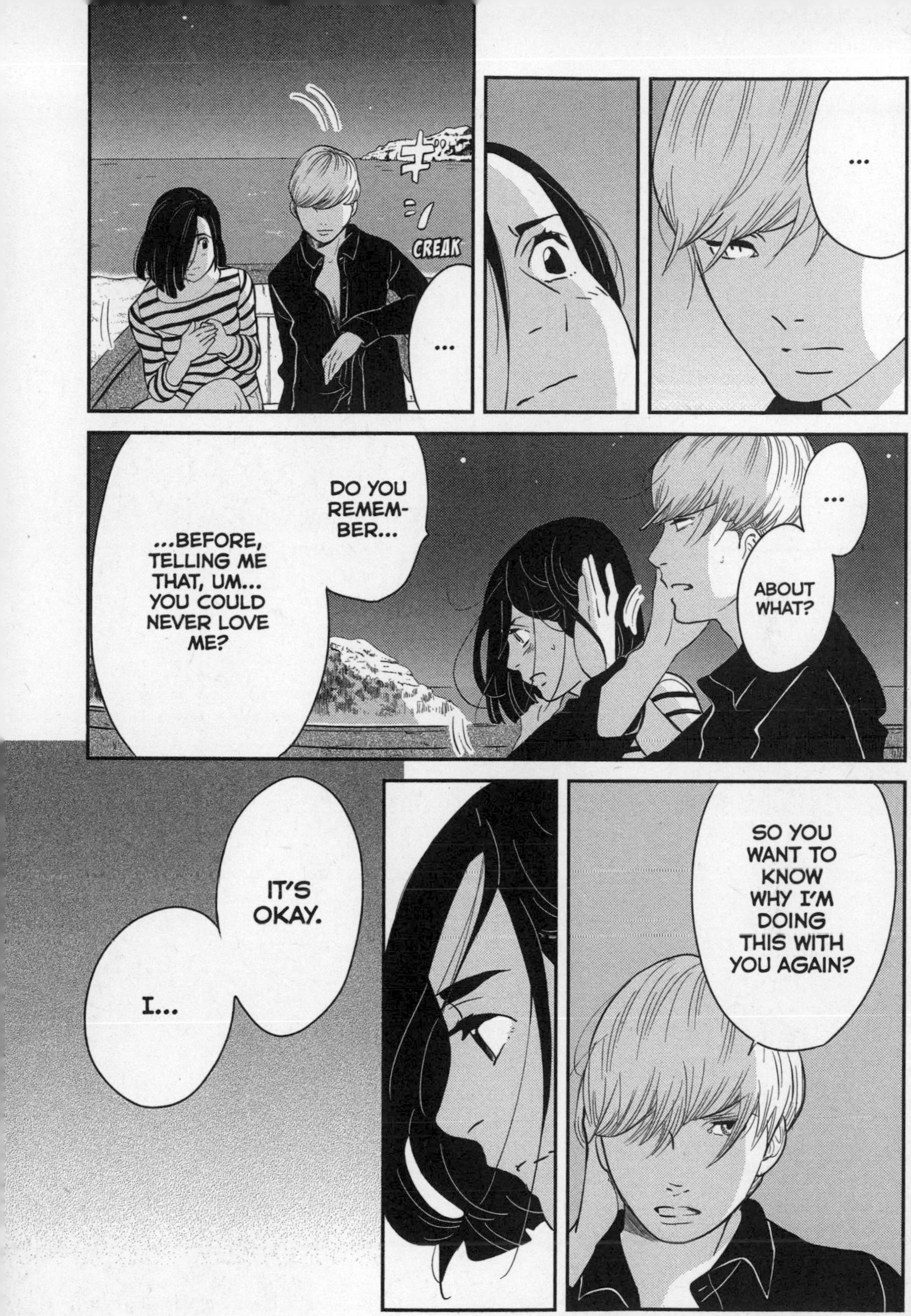
...
CREAK
...
...
ABOUT WHAT?
DO YOU REMEMBER...
...BEFORE, TELLING ME THAT, UM... YOU COULD NEVER LOVE ME?
SO YOU WANT TO KNOW WHY I'M DOING THIS WITH YOU AGAIN?
IT'S OKAY.
I...

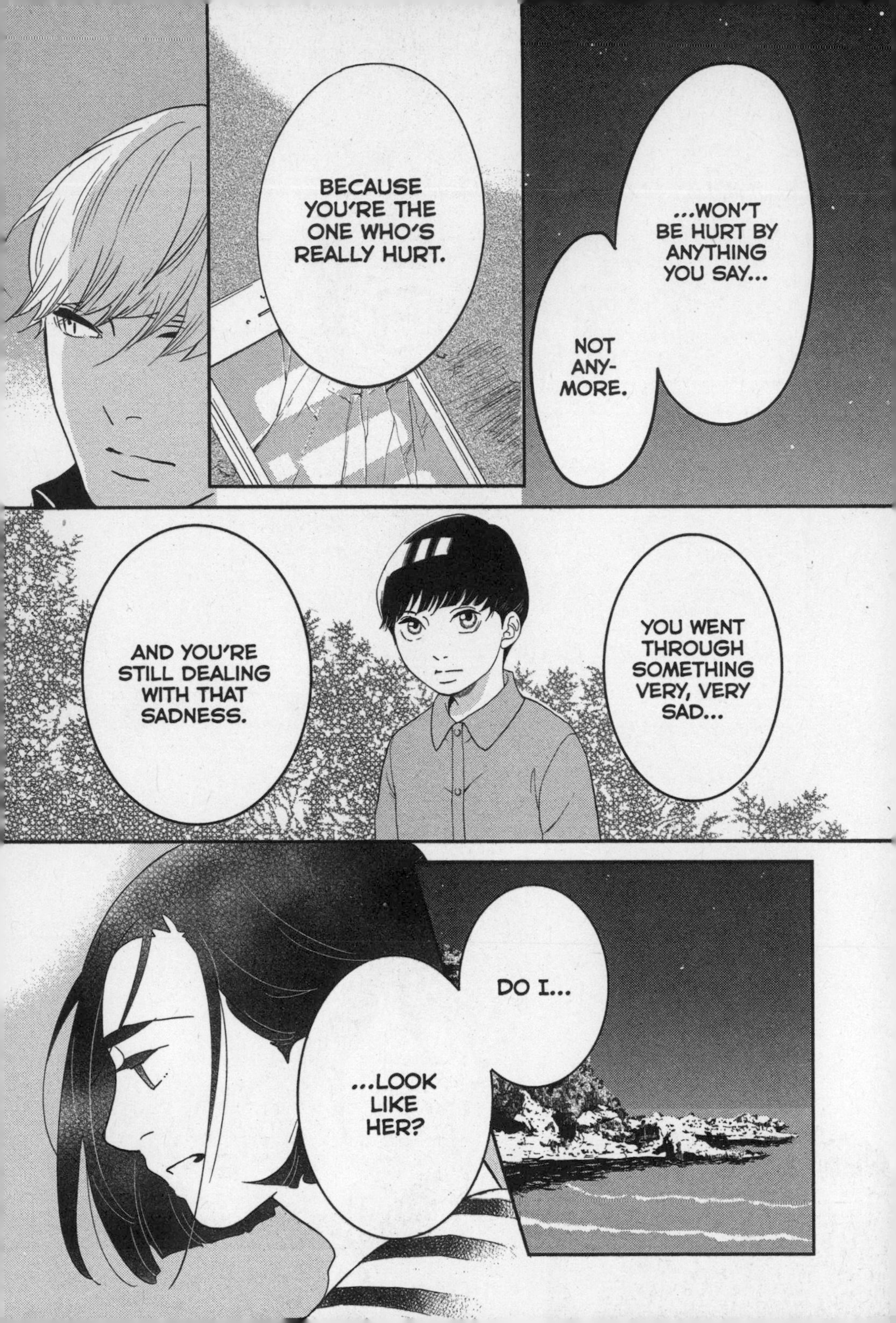
...WON'T BE HURT BY ANYTHING YOU SAY...
NOT ANY-MORE.
BECAUSE YOU'RE THE ONE WHO'S REALLY HURT.
YOU WENT THROUGH SOMETHING VERY, VERY SAD...
AND YOU'RE STILL DEALING WITH THAT SADNESS.
DO I...
...LOOK LIKE HER?

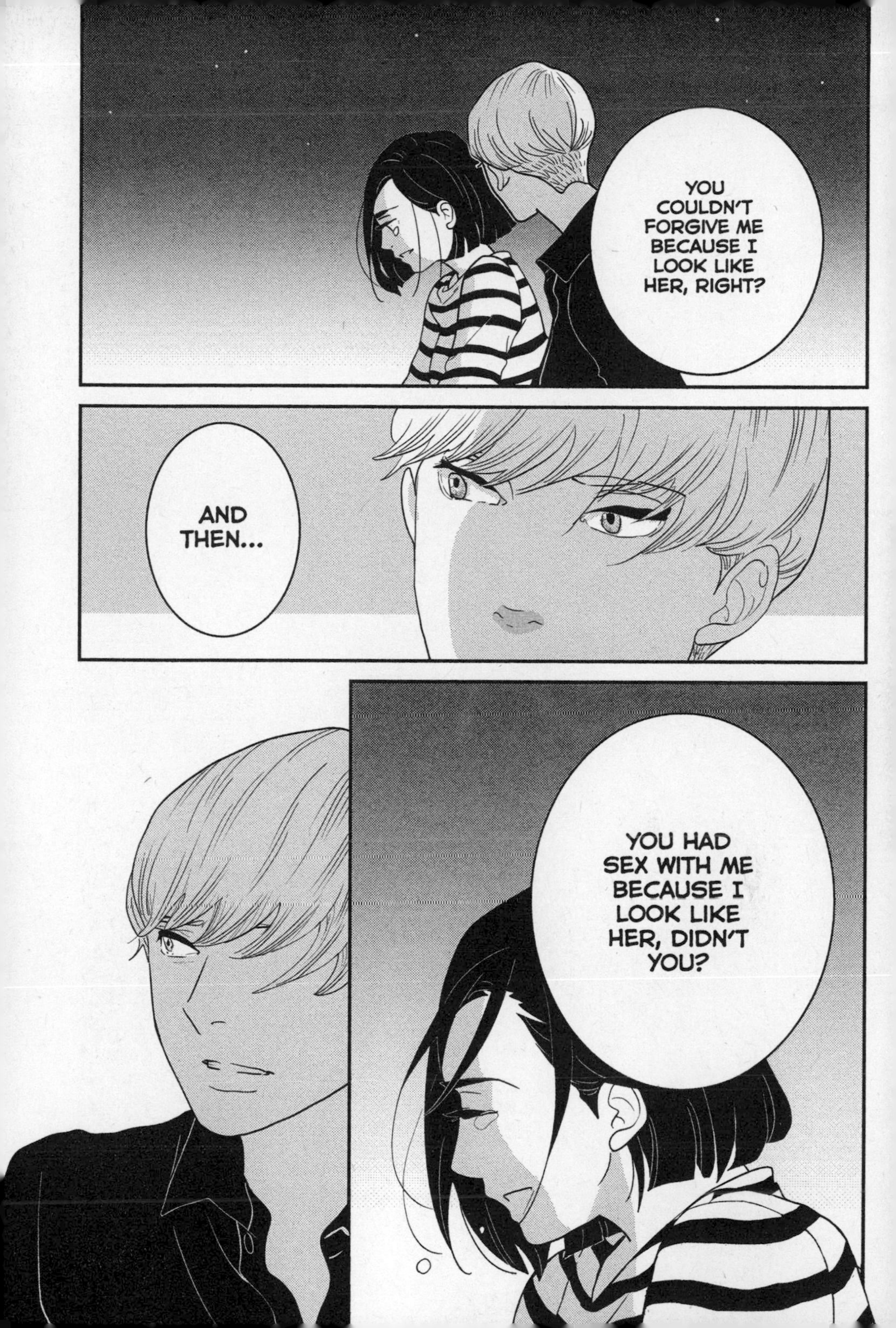
YOU COULDN'T FORGIVE ME BECAUSE I LOOK LIKE HER, RIGHT?
AND THEN...
YOU HAD SEX WITH ME BECAUSE I LOOK LIKE HER, DIDN'T YOU?

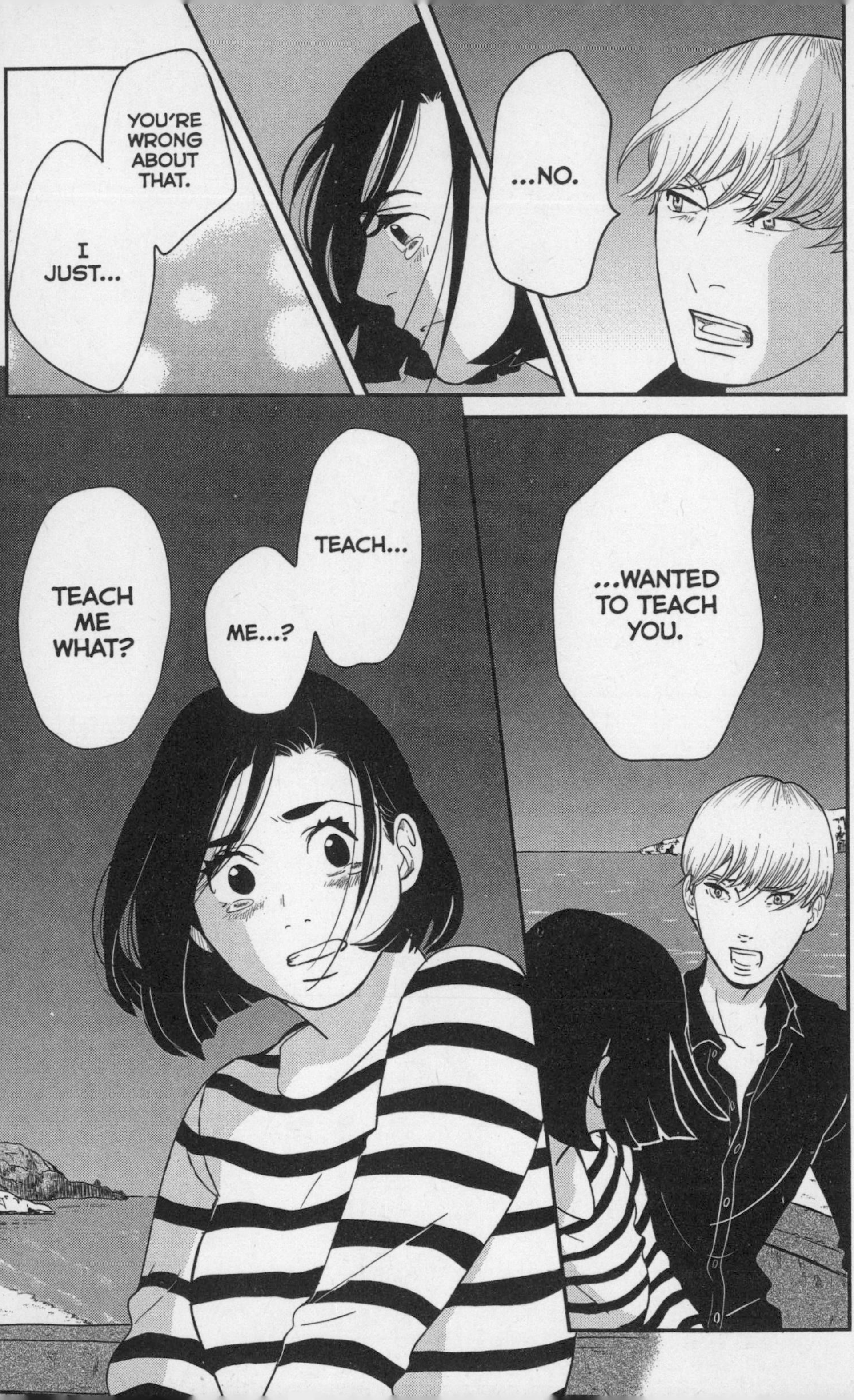
...NO.
YOU'RE WRONG ABOUT THAT.
I JUST...
...WANTED TO TEACH YOU.
TEACH...
ME...?
TEACH ME WHAT?

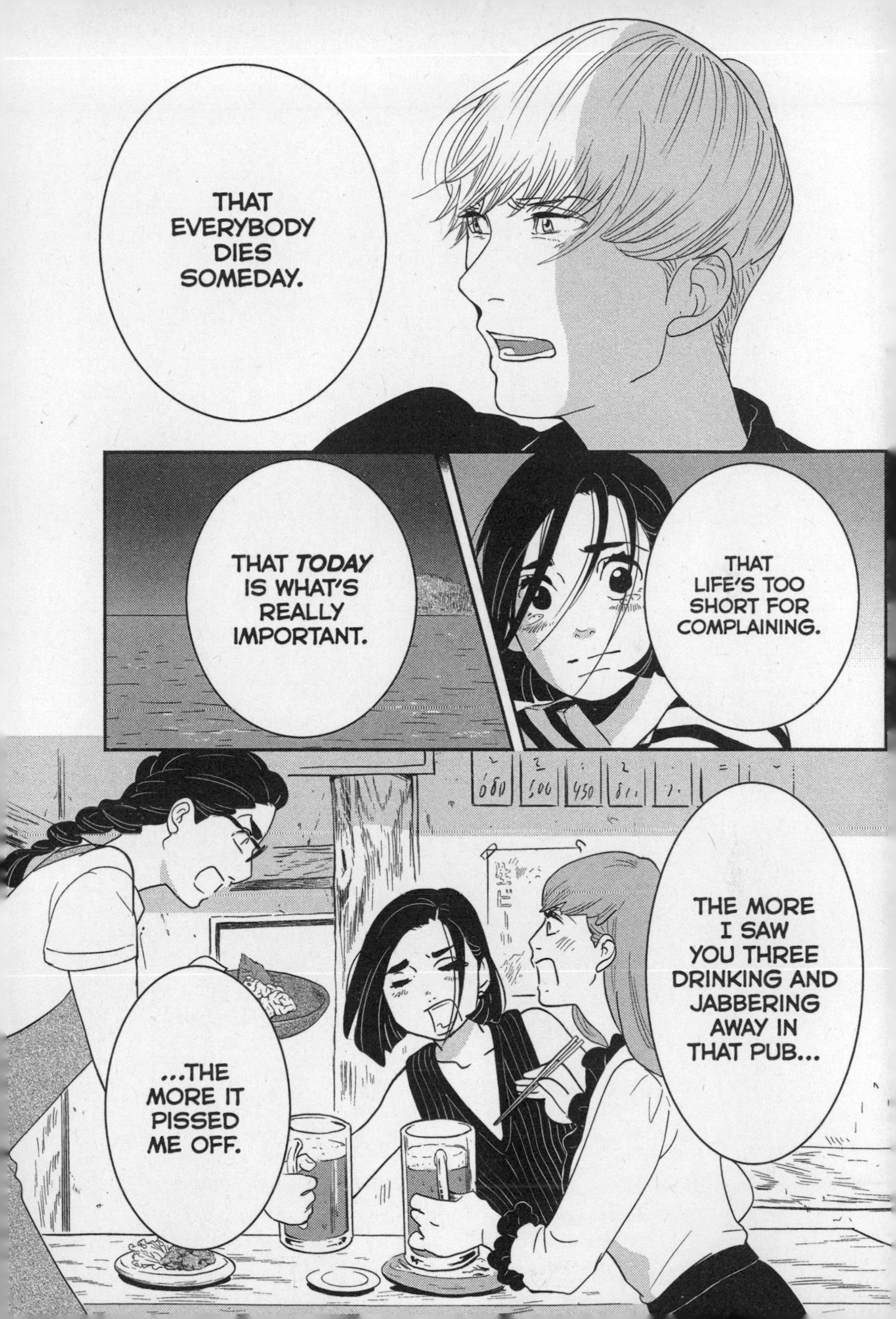
THAT EVERYBODY DIES SOMEDAY.
THAT LIFE'S TOO SHORT FOR COMPLAINING.
THAT *TODAY* IS WHAT'S REALLY IMPORTANT.
THE MORE I SAW YOU THREE DRINKING AND JABBERING AWAY IN THAT PUB...
...THE MORE IT PISSED ME OFF.

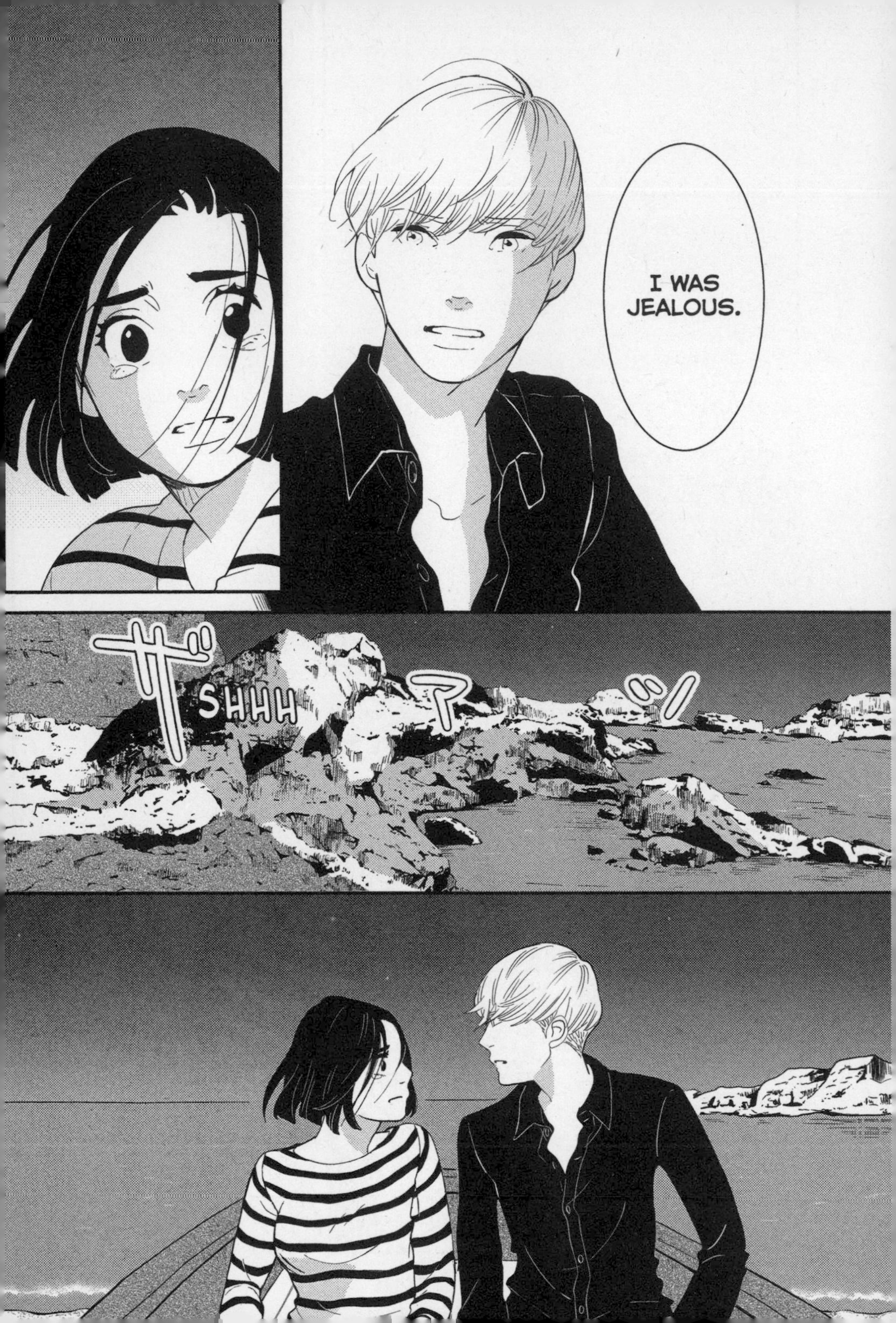
I WAS JEALOUS.
SHHH

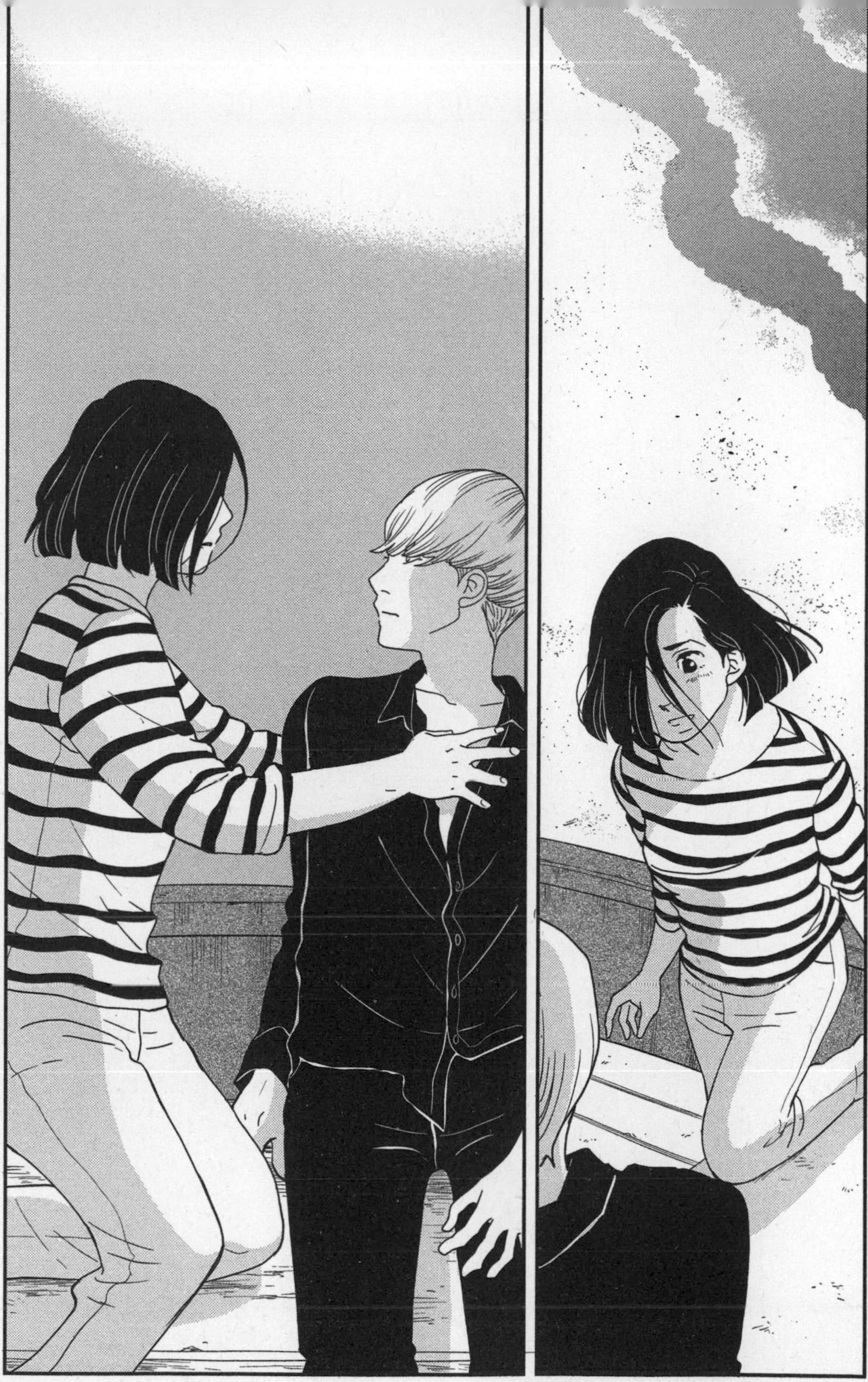

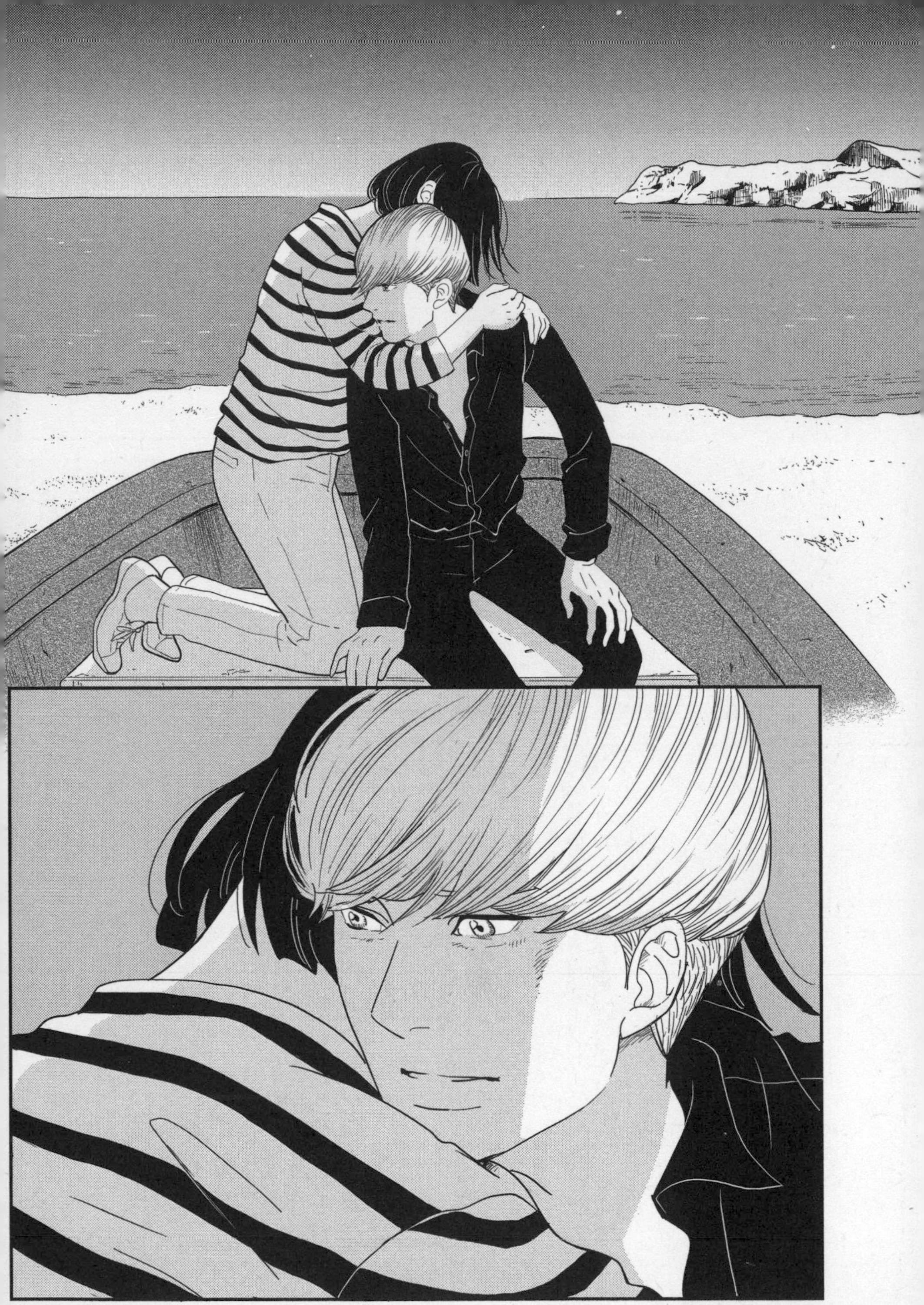

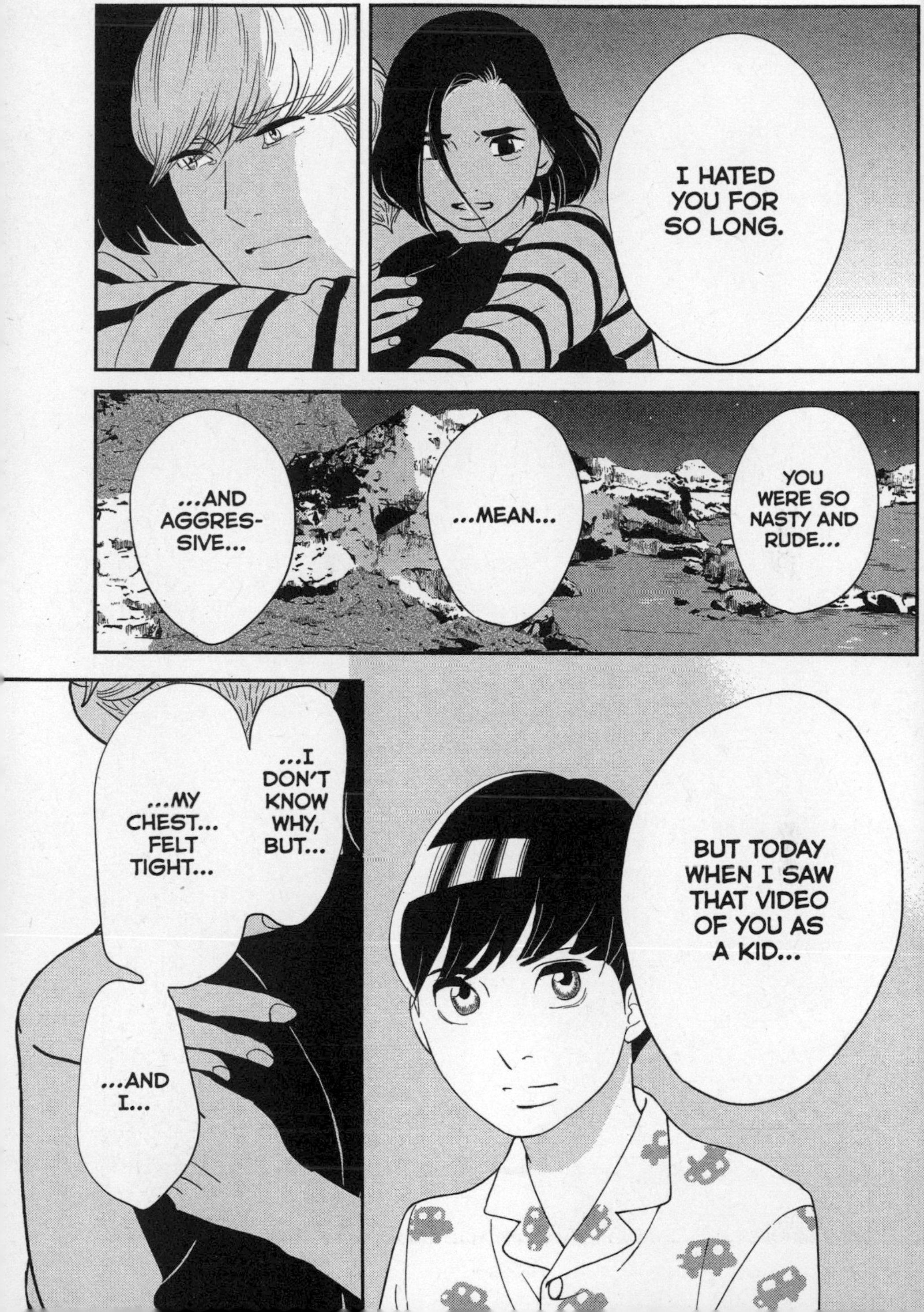
I HATED YOU FOR SO LONG.
YOU WERE SO NASTY AND RUDE...
...MEAN...
...AND AGGRES-SIVE...
BUT TODAY WHEN I SAW THAT VIDEO OF YOU AS A KID...
...I DON'T KNOW WHY, BUT...
...MY CHEST... FELT TIGHT...
...AND I...

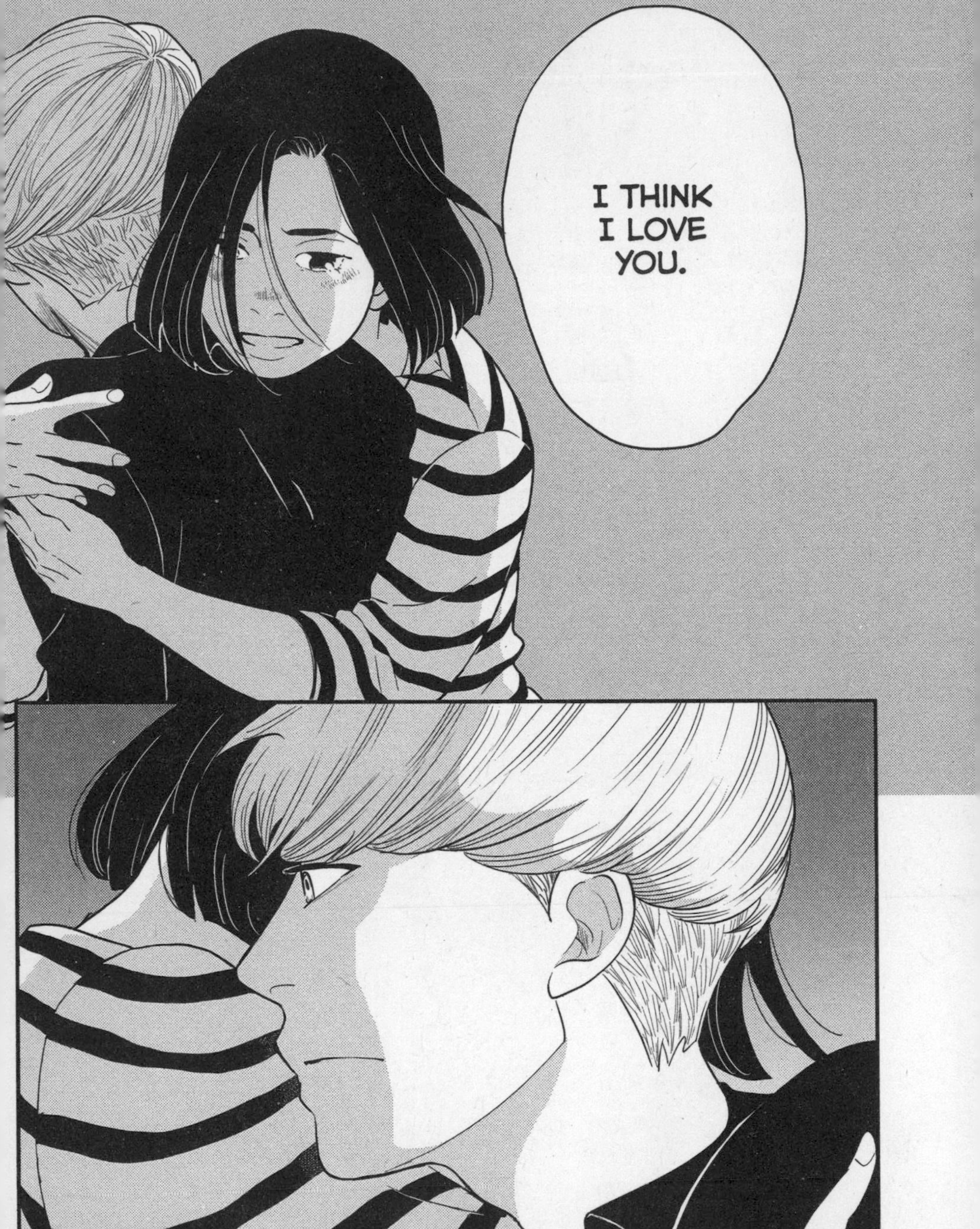
I THINK I LOVE YOU.

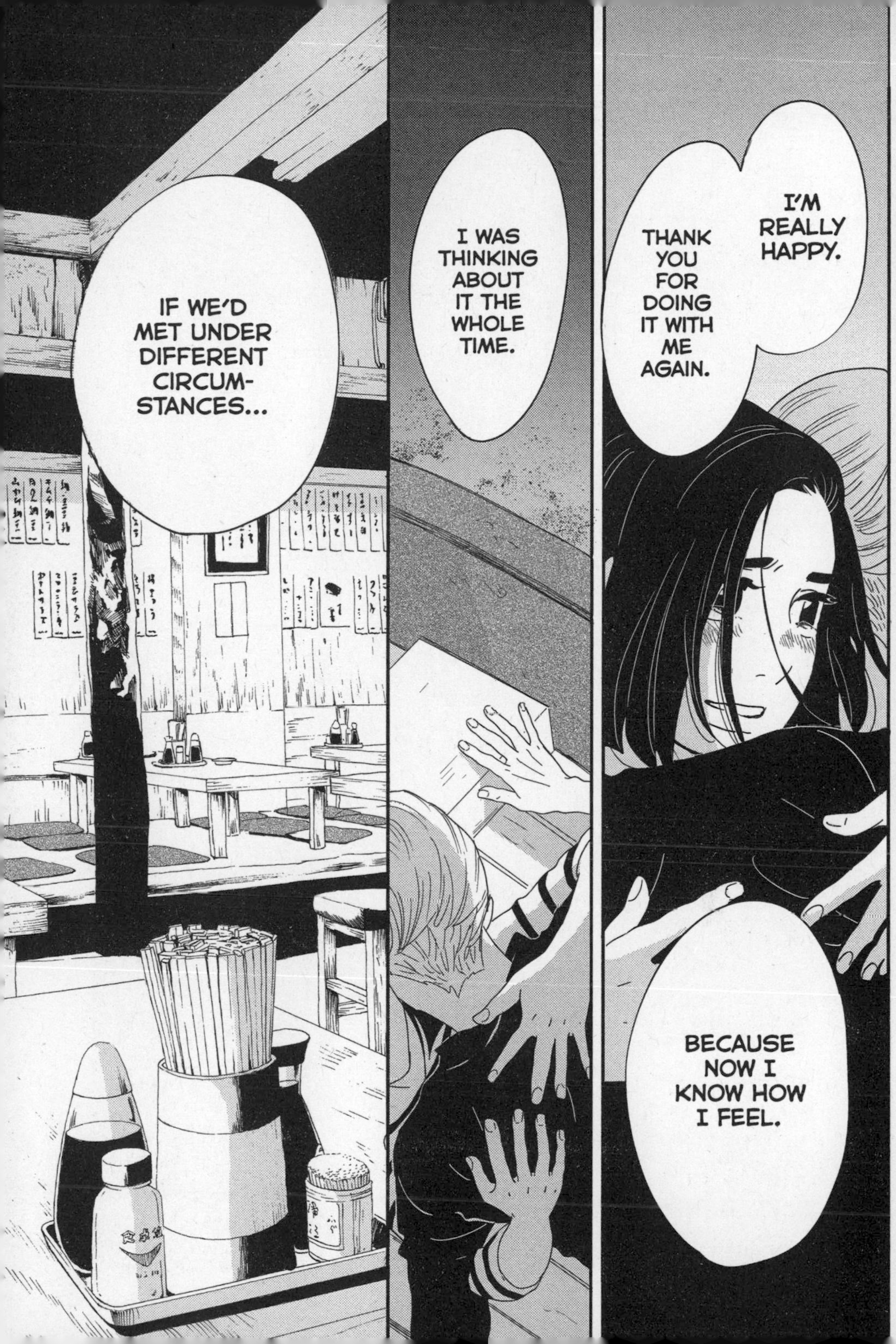
I'M REALLY HAPPY.
THANK YOU FOR DOING IT WITH ME AGAIN.
BECAUSE NOW I KNOW HOW I FEEL.
I WAS THINKING ABOUT IT THE WHOLE TIME.
IF WE'D MET UNDER DIFFERENT CIRCUMSTANCES...

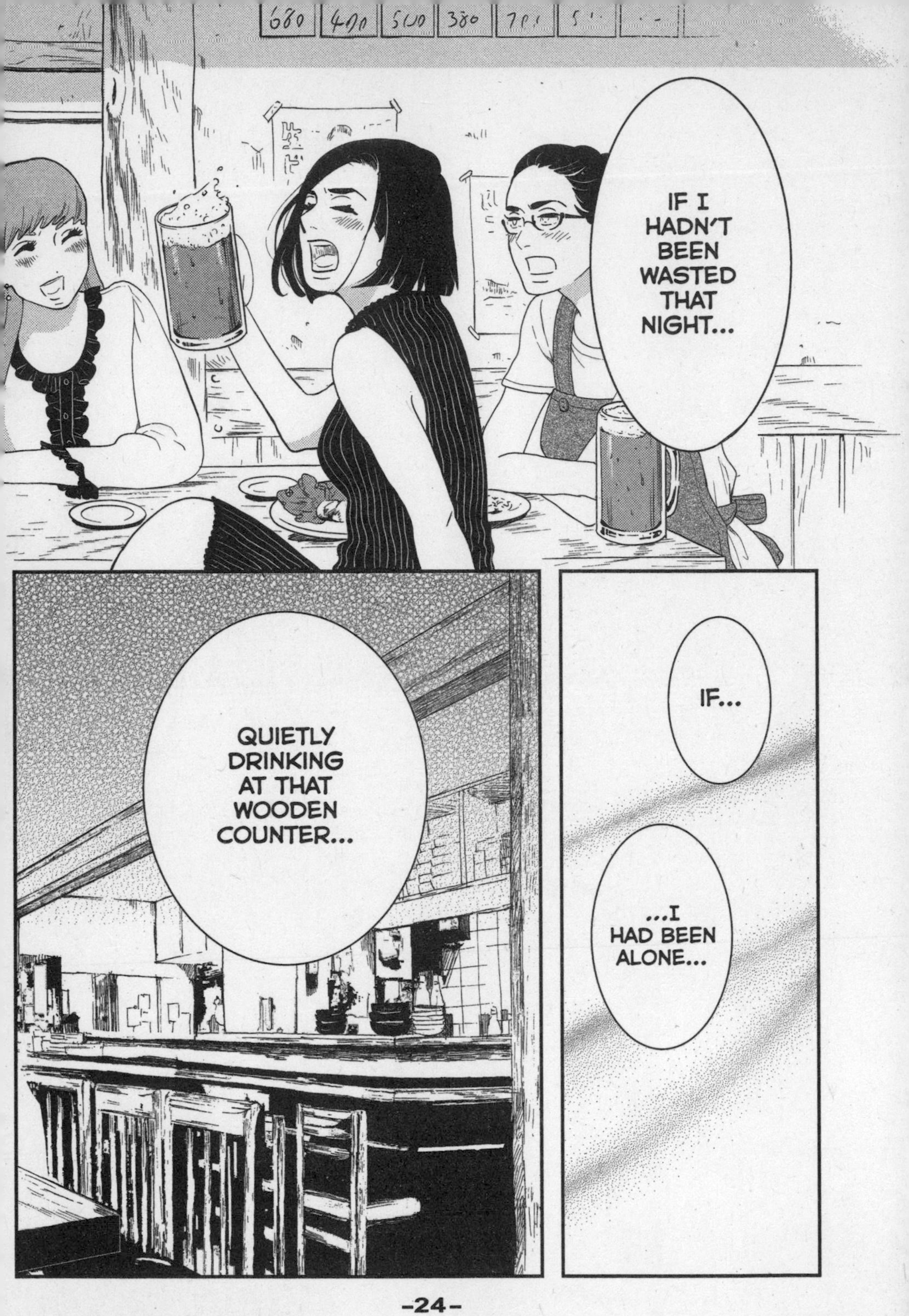
IF I HADN'T BEEN WASTED THAT NIGHT...
IF...
...I HAD BEEN ALONE...
QUIETLY DRINKING AT THAT WOODEN COUNTER...

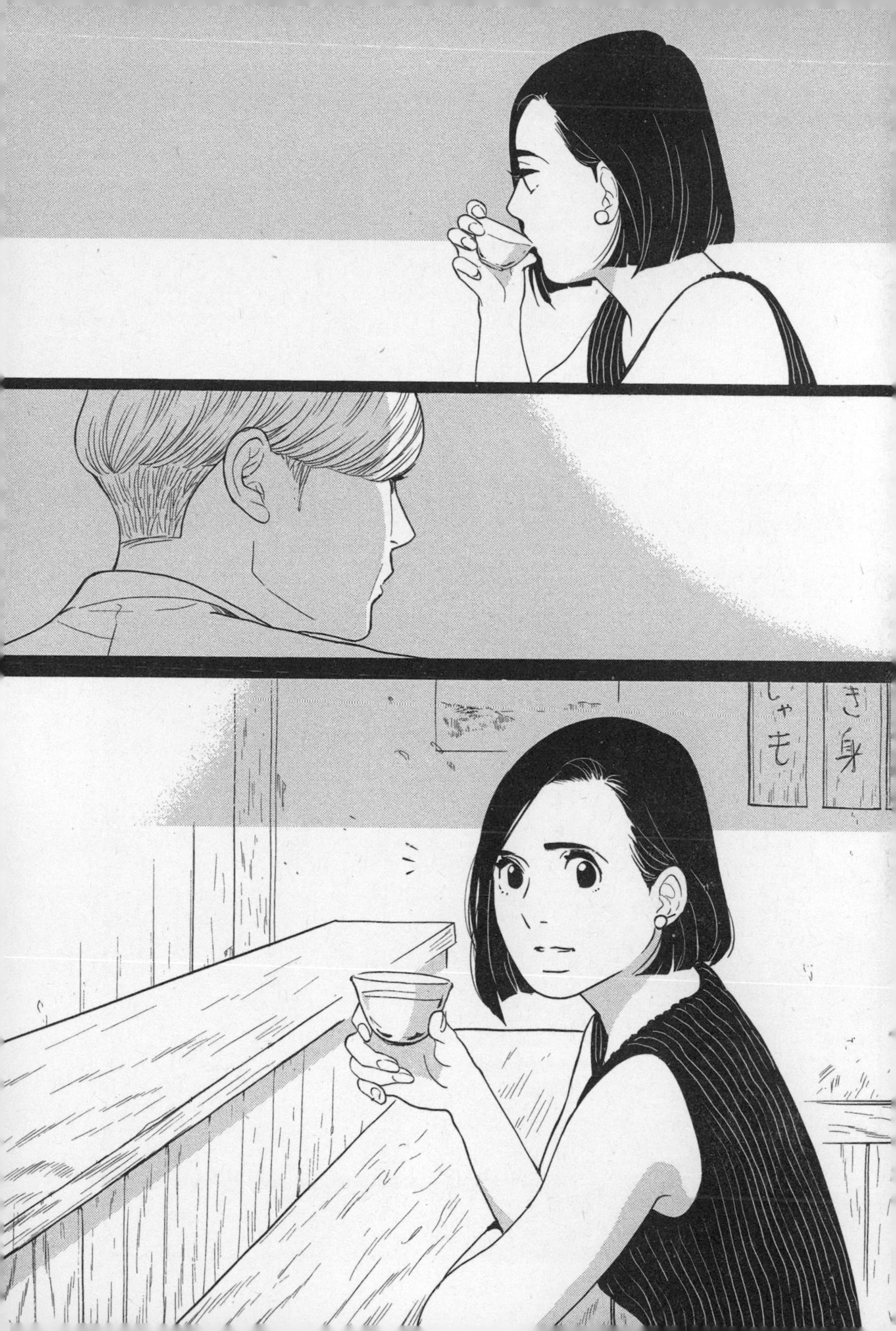
き身
しゃも

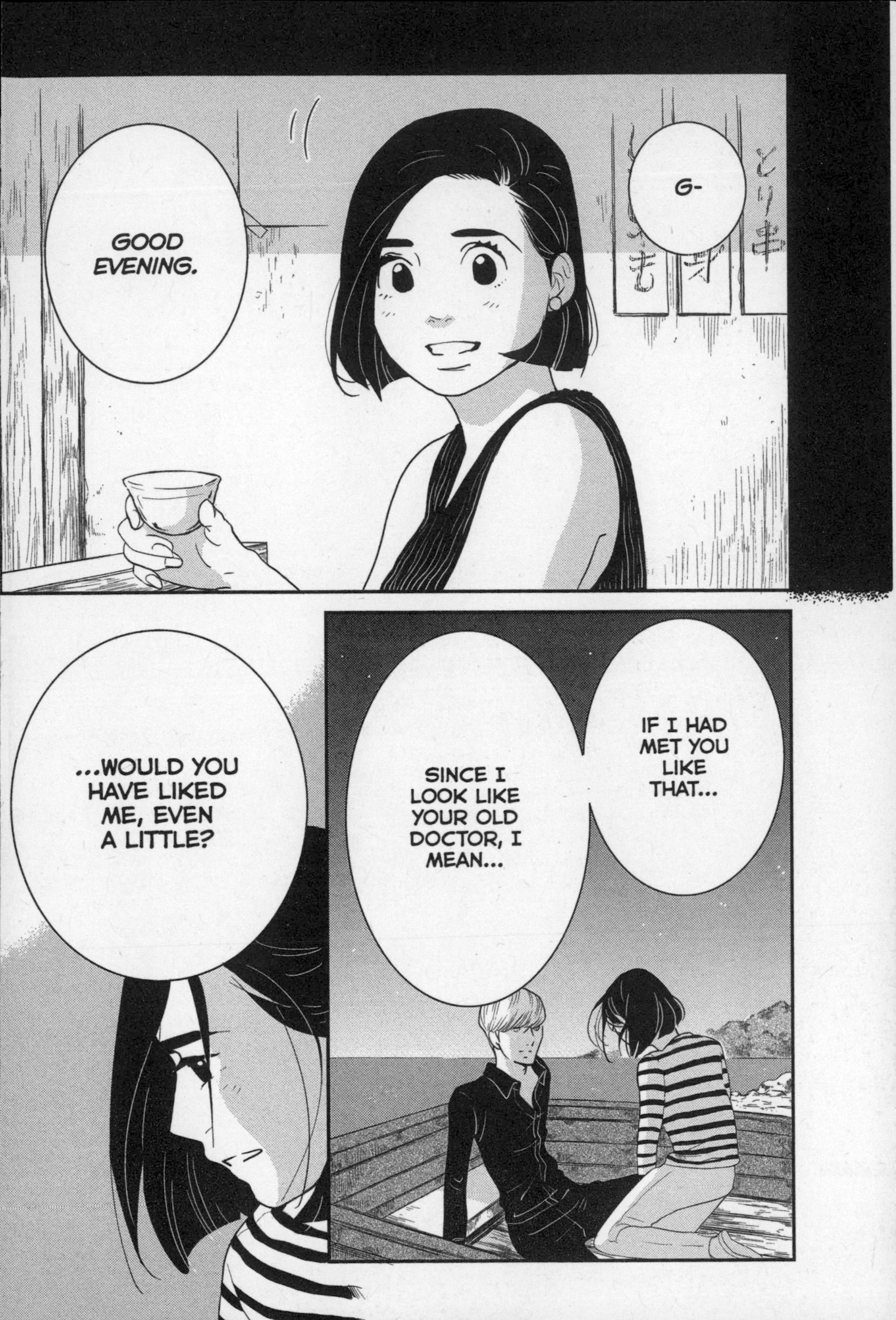
G-
GOOD EVENING.
IF I HAD MET YOU LIKE THAT...
SINCE I LOOK LIKE YOUR OLD DOCTOR, I MEAN...
...WOULD YOU HAVE LIKED ME, EVEN A LITTLE?

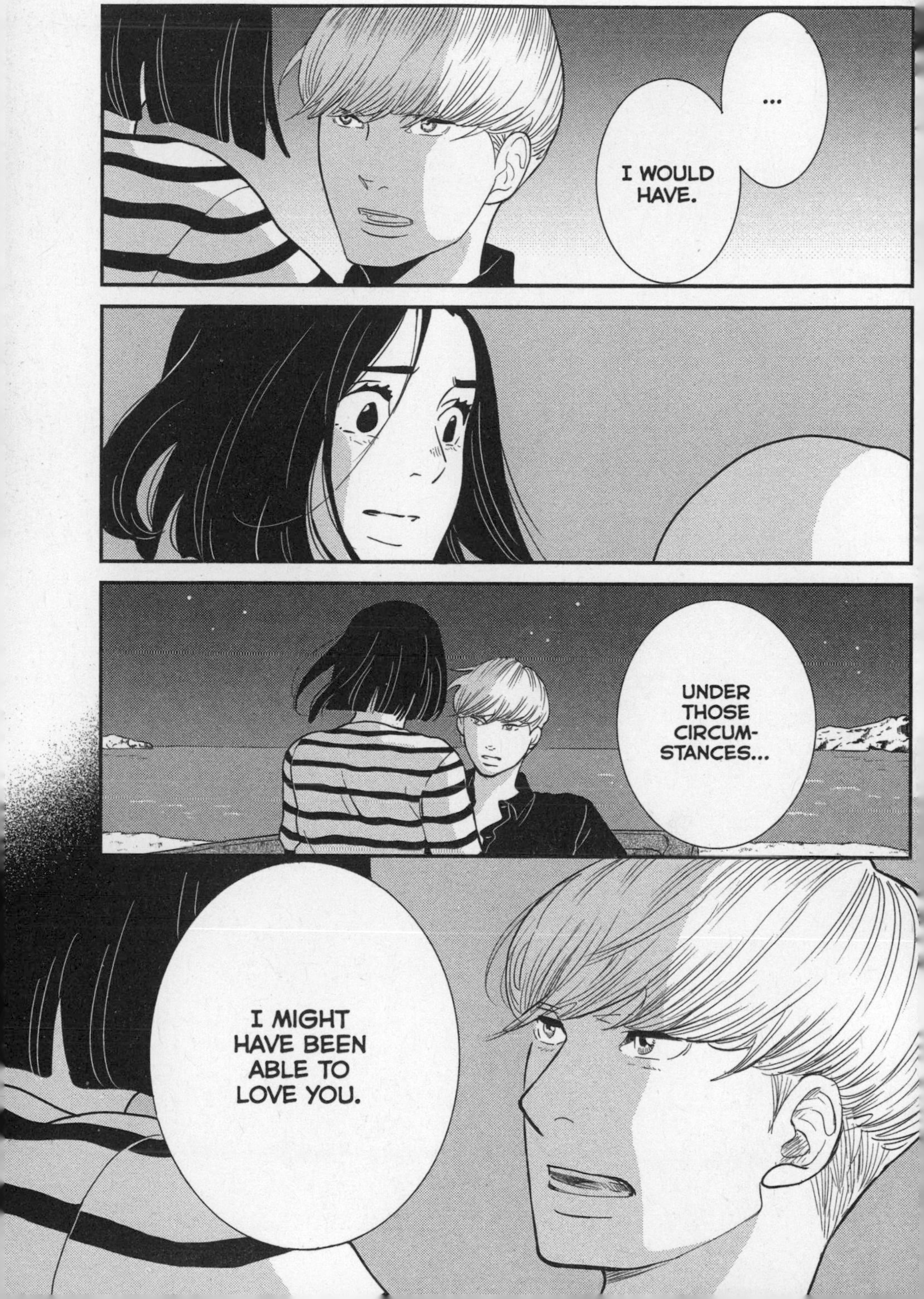
...
I WOULD HAVE.
UNDER THOSE CIRCUM- STANCES...
I MIGHT HAVE BEEN ABLE TO LOVE YOU.

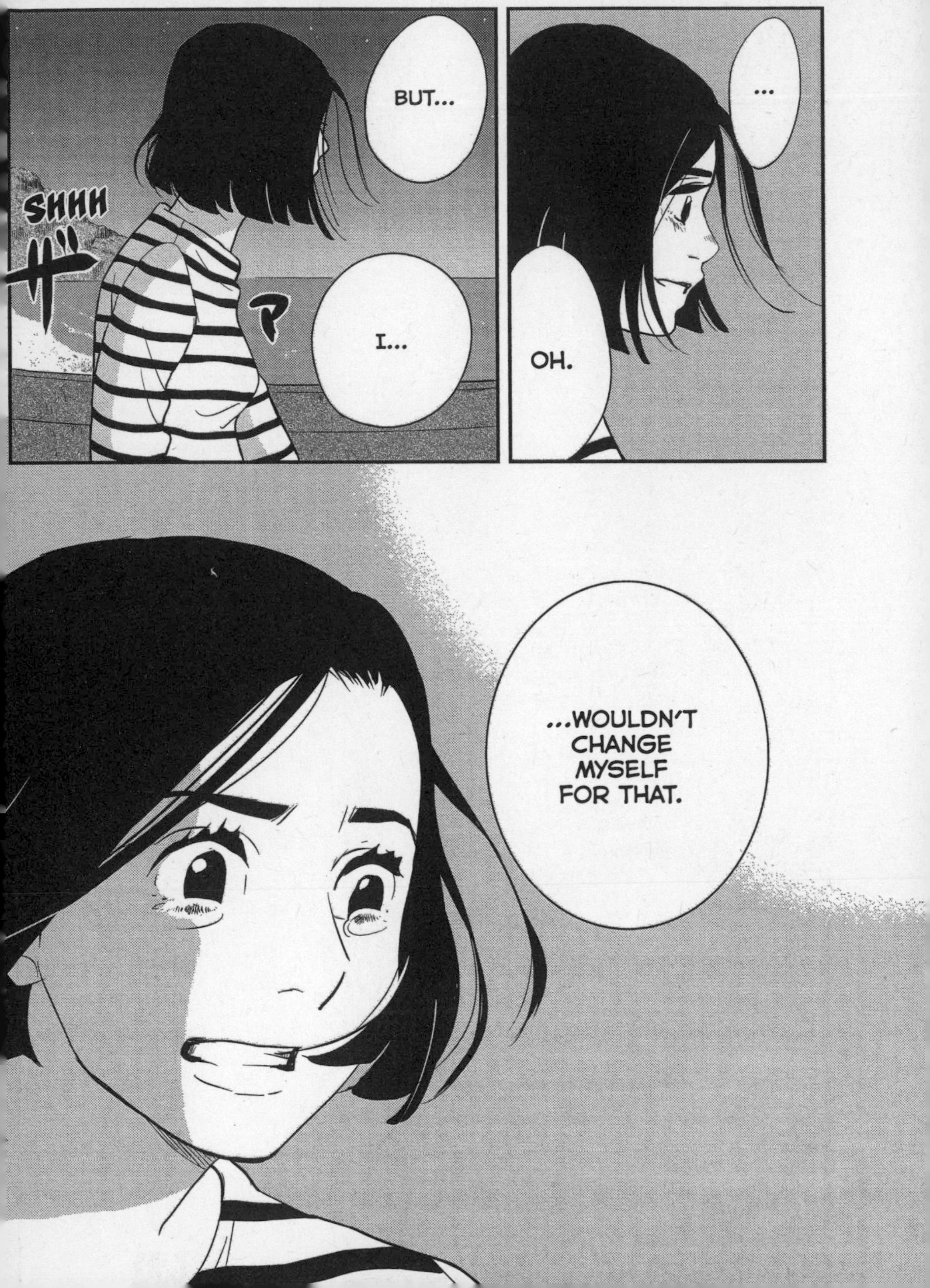
...
OH.
BUT...
I...
SHHH
ザァ
...WOULDN'T CHANGE MYSELF FOR THAT.

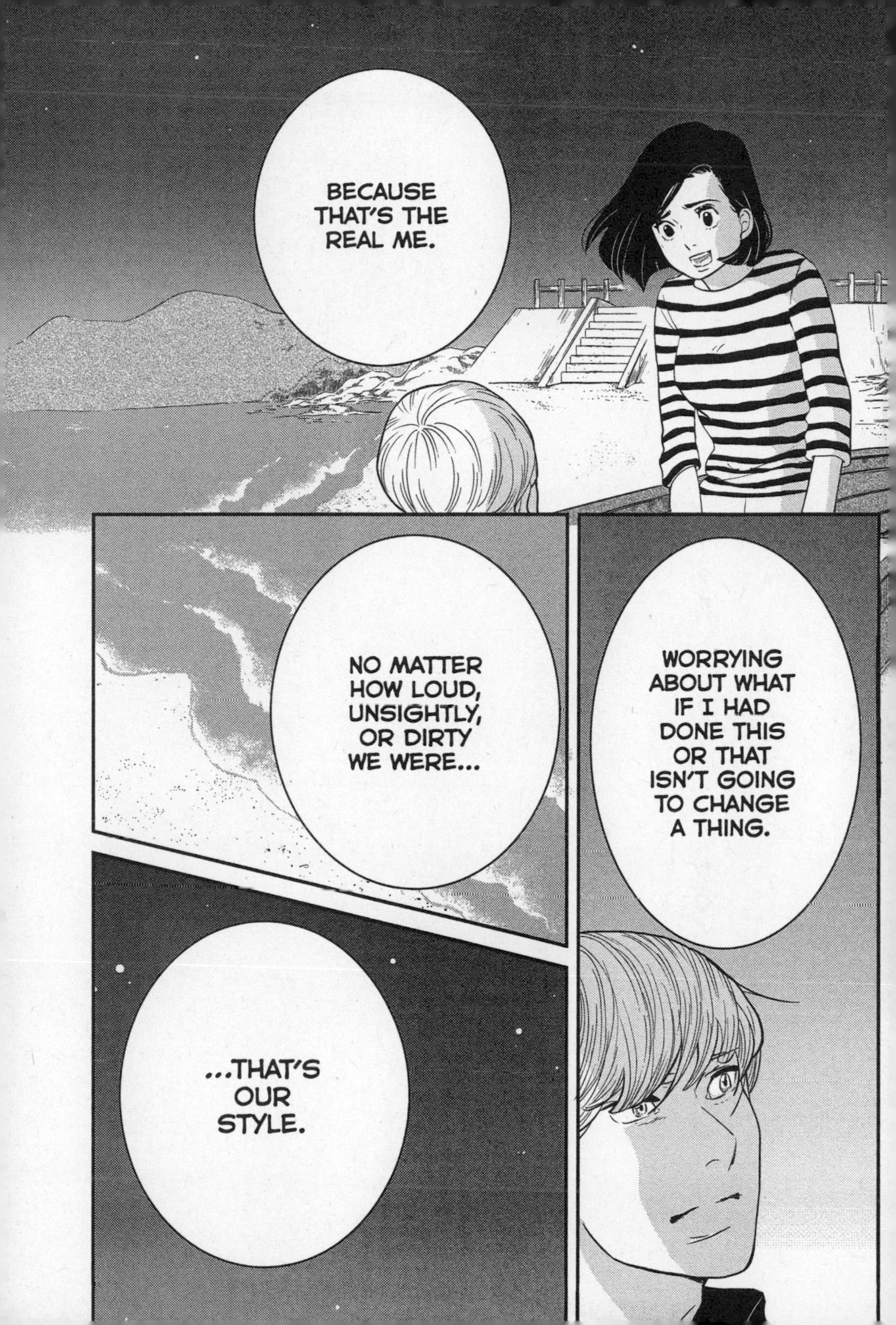
BECAUSE THAT'S THE REAL ME.
WORRYING ABOUT WHAT IF I HAD DONE THIS OR THAT ISN'T GOING TO CHANGE A THING.
NO MATTER HOW LOUD, UNSIGHTLY, OR DIRTY WE WERE...
...THAT'S OUR STYLE.

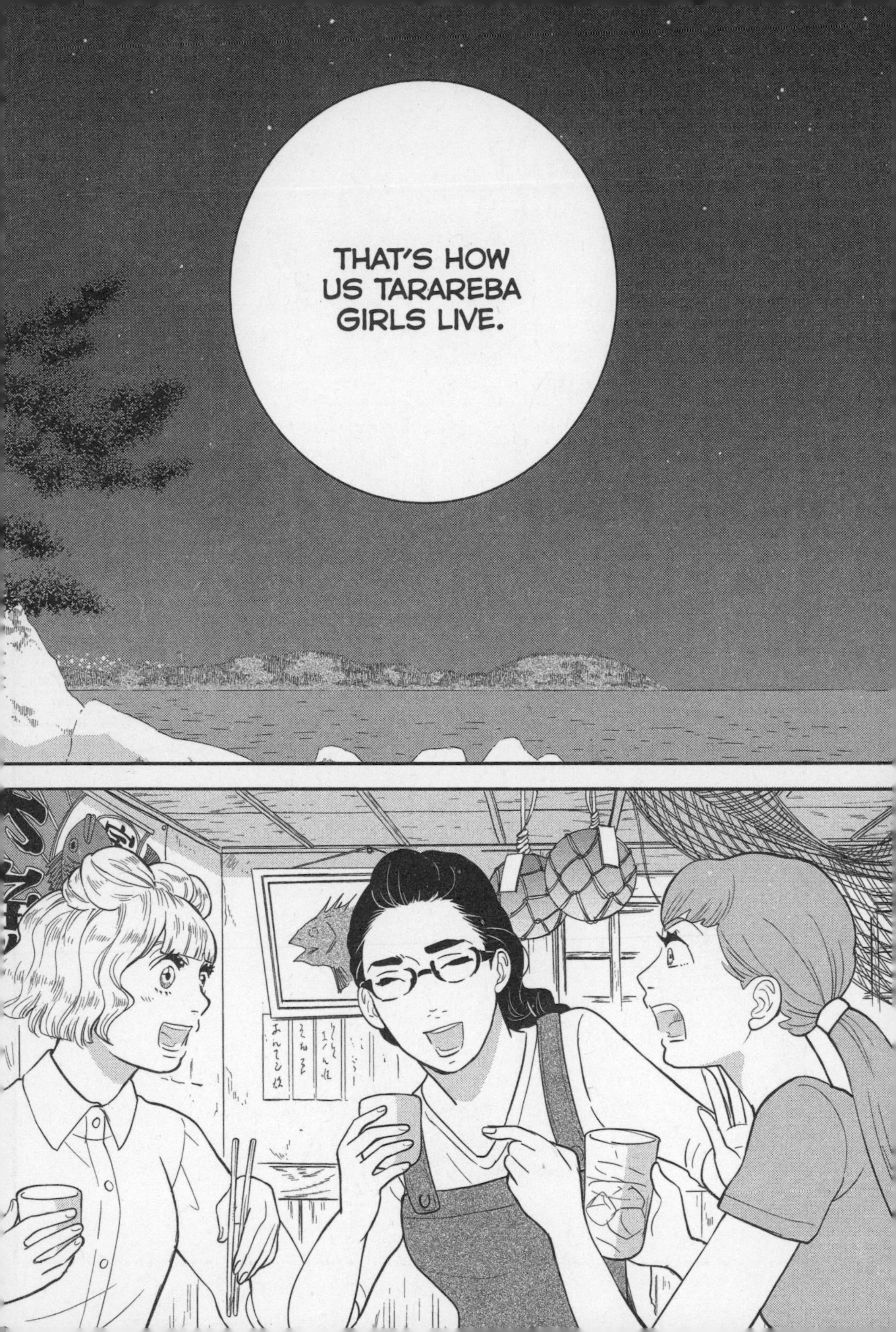
THAT'S HOW US TARARETBA GIRLS LIVE.

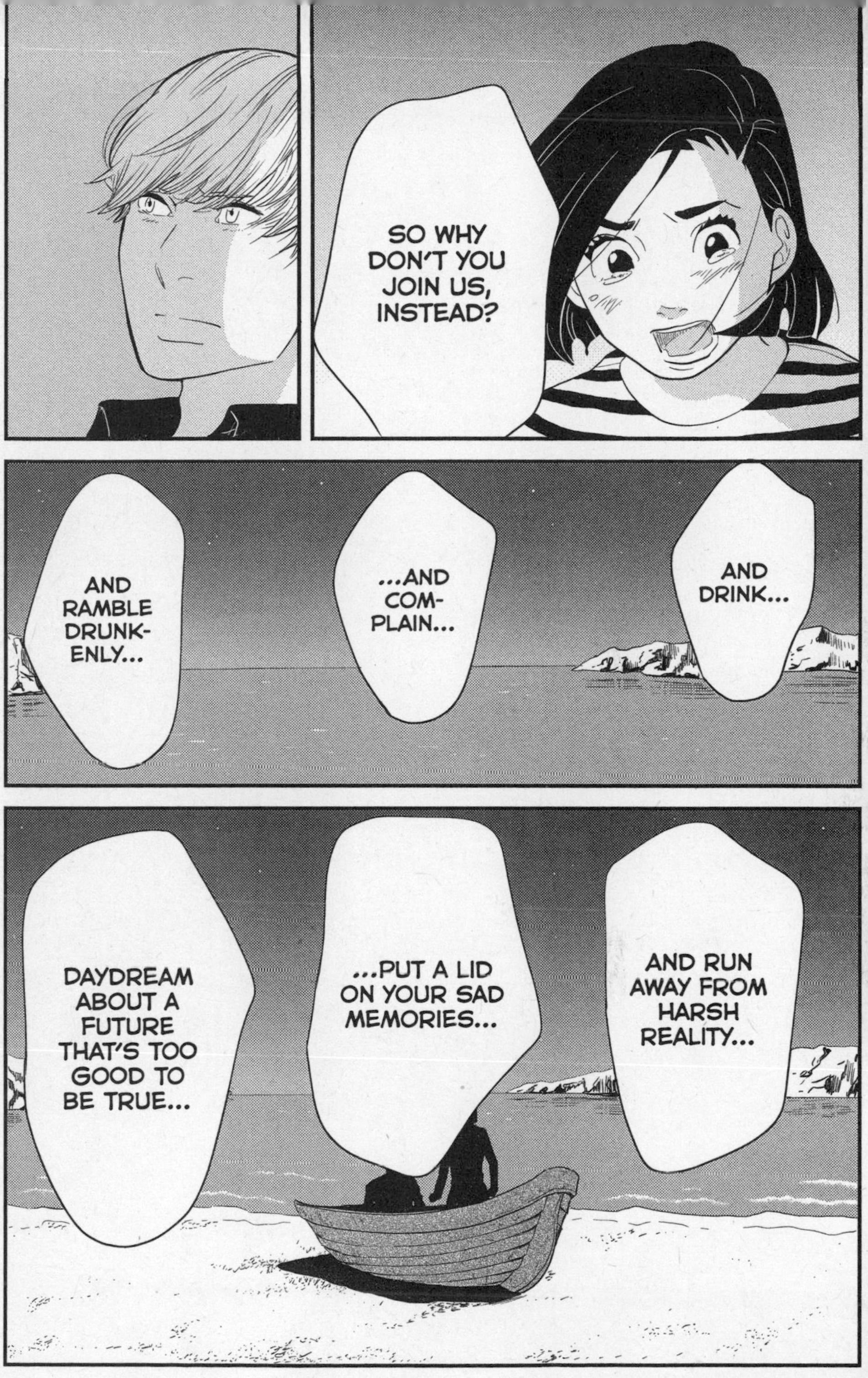
SO WHY DON'T YOU JOIN US, INSTEAD?
AND DRINK...
...AND COMPLAIN...
AND RAMBLE DRUNKENLY...
AND RUN AWAY FROM HARSH REALITY...
...PUT A LID ON YOUR SAD MEMORIES...
DAYDREAM ABOUT A FUTURE THAT'S TOO GOOD TO BE TRUE...

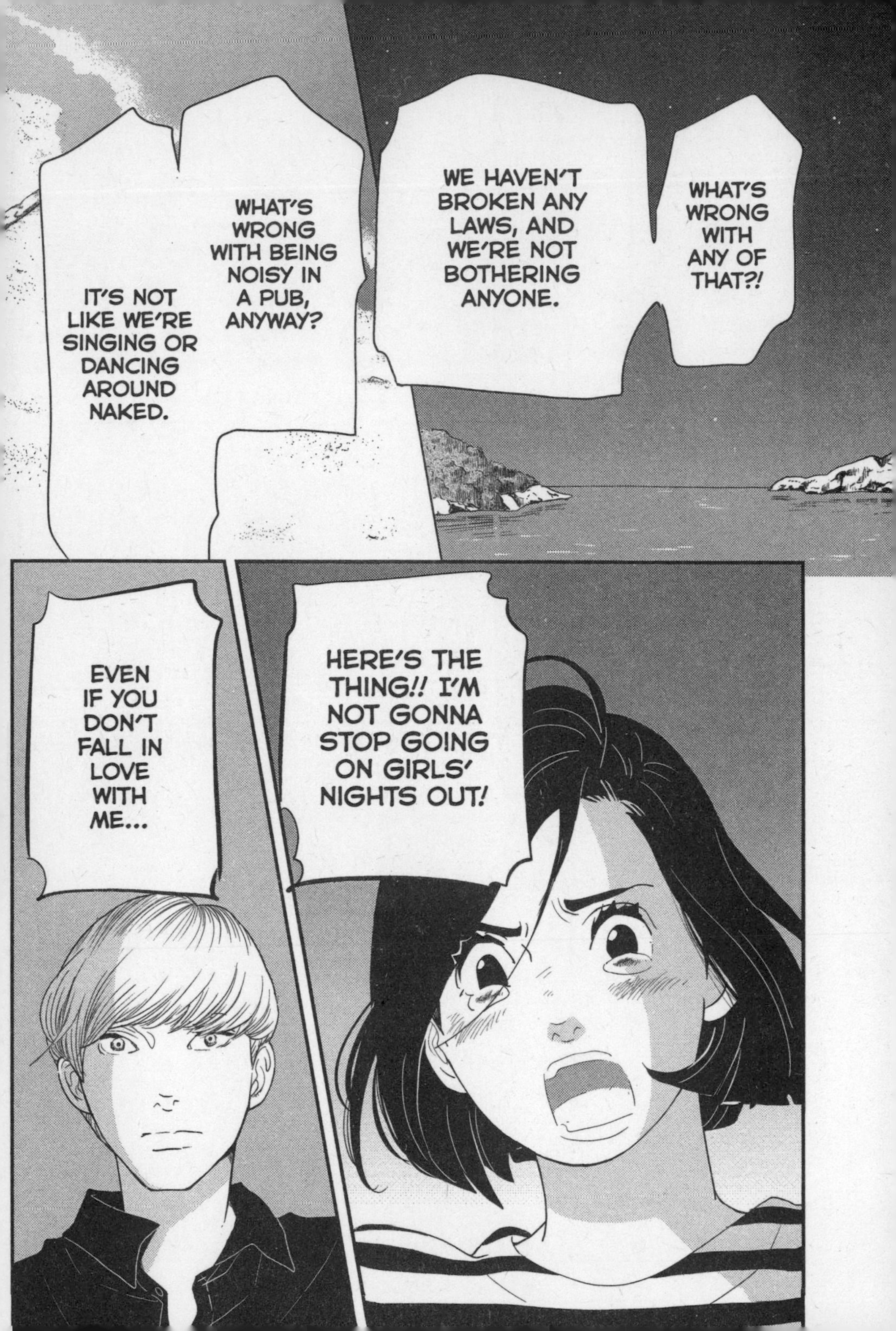
WHAT'S WRONG WITH ANY OF THAT?!
WE HAVEN'T BROKEN ANY LAWS, AND WE'RE NOT BOTHERING ANYONE.
WHAT'S WRONG WITH BEING NOISY IN A PUB, ANYWAY?
IT'S NOT LIKE WE'RE SINGING OR DANCING AROUND NAKED.
HERE'S THE THING!! I'M NOT GONNA STOP GOING ON GIRLS' NIGHTS OUT!
EVEN IF YOU DON'T FALL IN LOVE WITH ME...

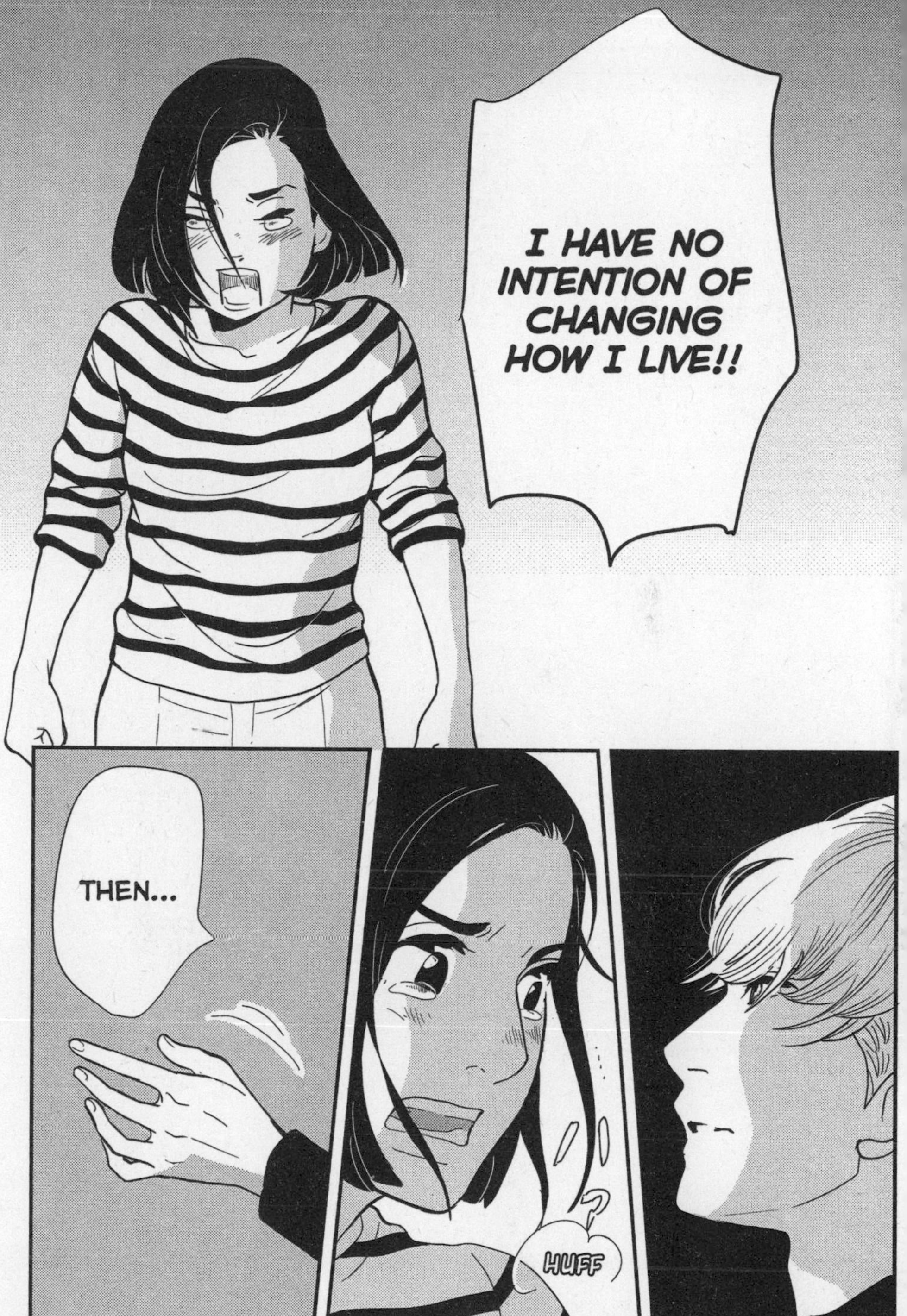

I HAVE NO INTENTION OF CHANGING HOW I LIVE!!
HUFF
THEN...

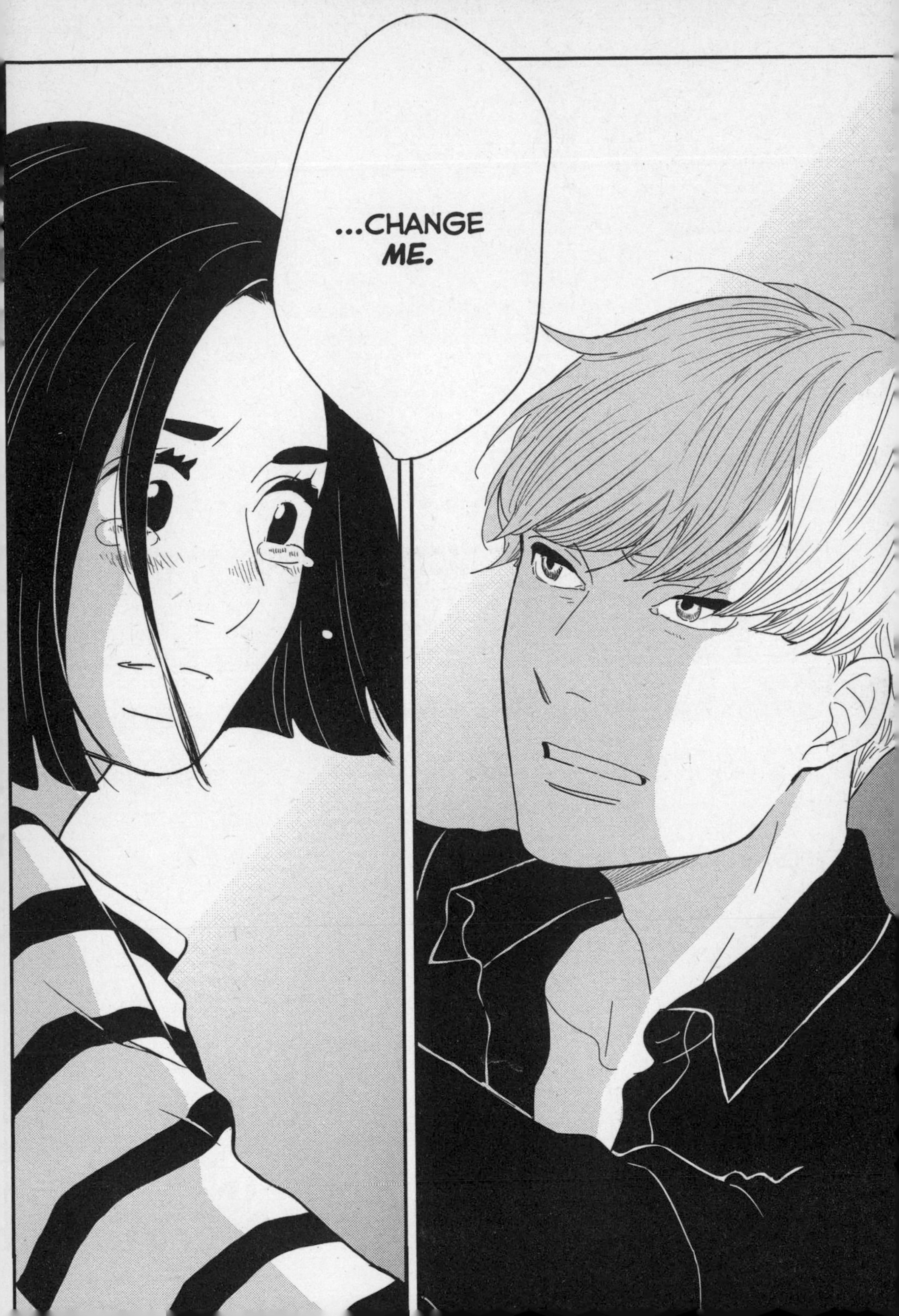
...CHANGE ME.

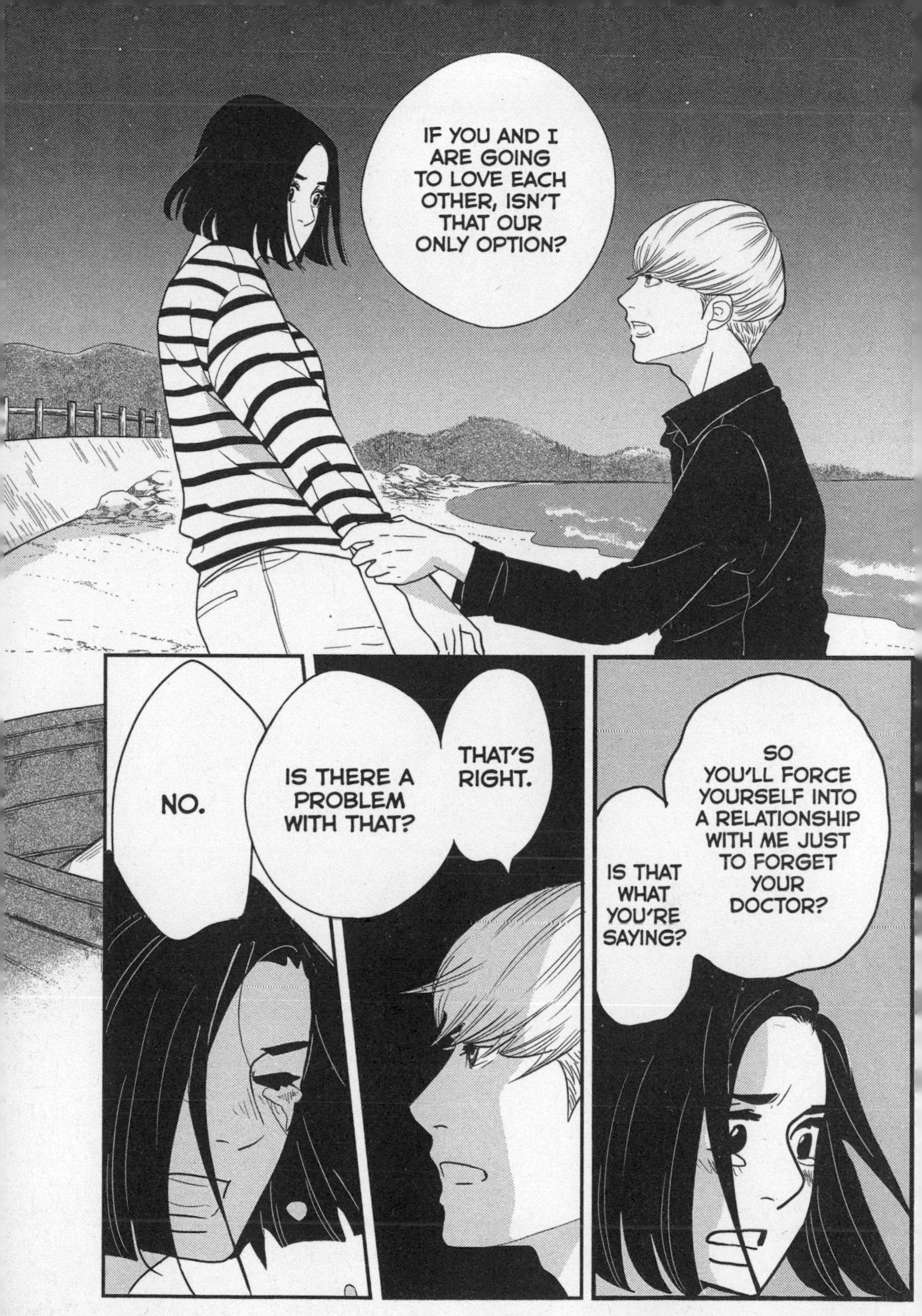
IF YOU AND I ARE GOING TO LOVE EACH OTHER, ISN'T THAT OUR ONLY OPTION?
SO YOU'LL FORCE YOURSELF INTO A RELATIONSHIP WITH ME JUST TO FORGET YOUR DOCTOR?
IS THAT WHAT YOU'RE SAYING?
THAT'S RIGHT.
IS THERE A PROBLEM WITH THAT?
NO.

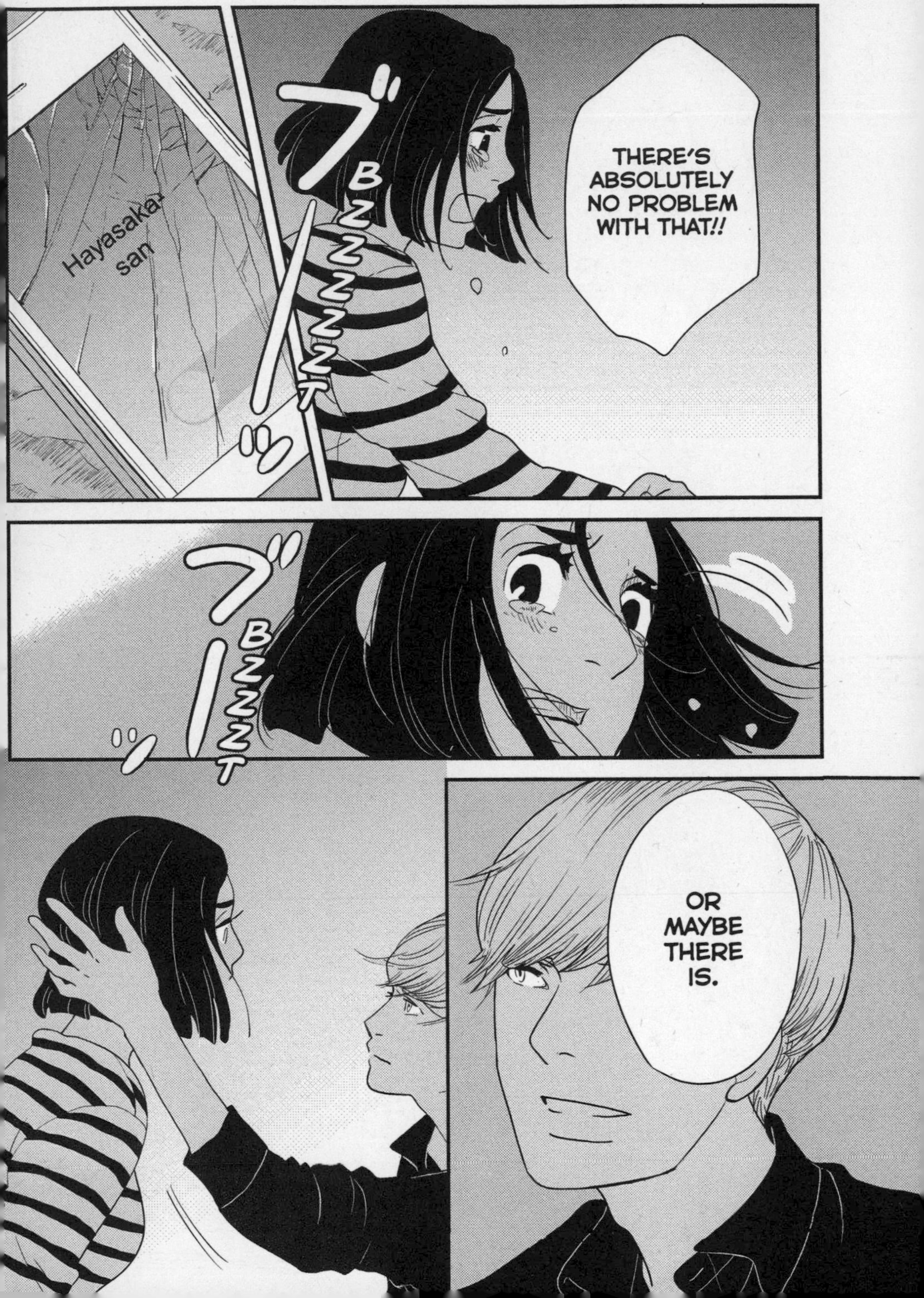
THERE'S ABSOLUTELY NO PROBLEM WITH THAT!!
ブ
BZZZZZT
ッ
Hayasaka-san
ブ
BZZZZT
ッ
OR MAYBE THERE IS.

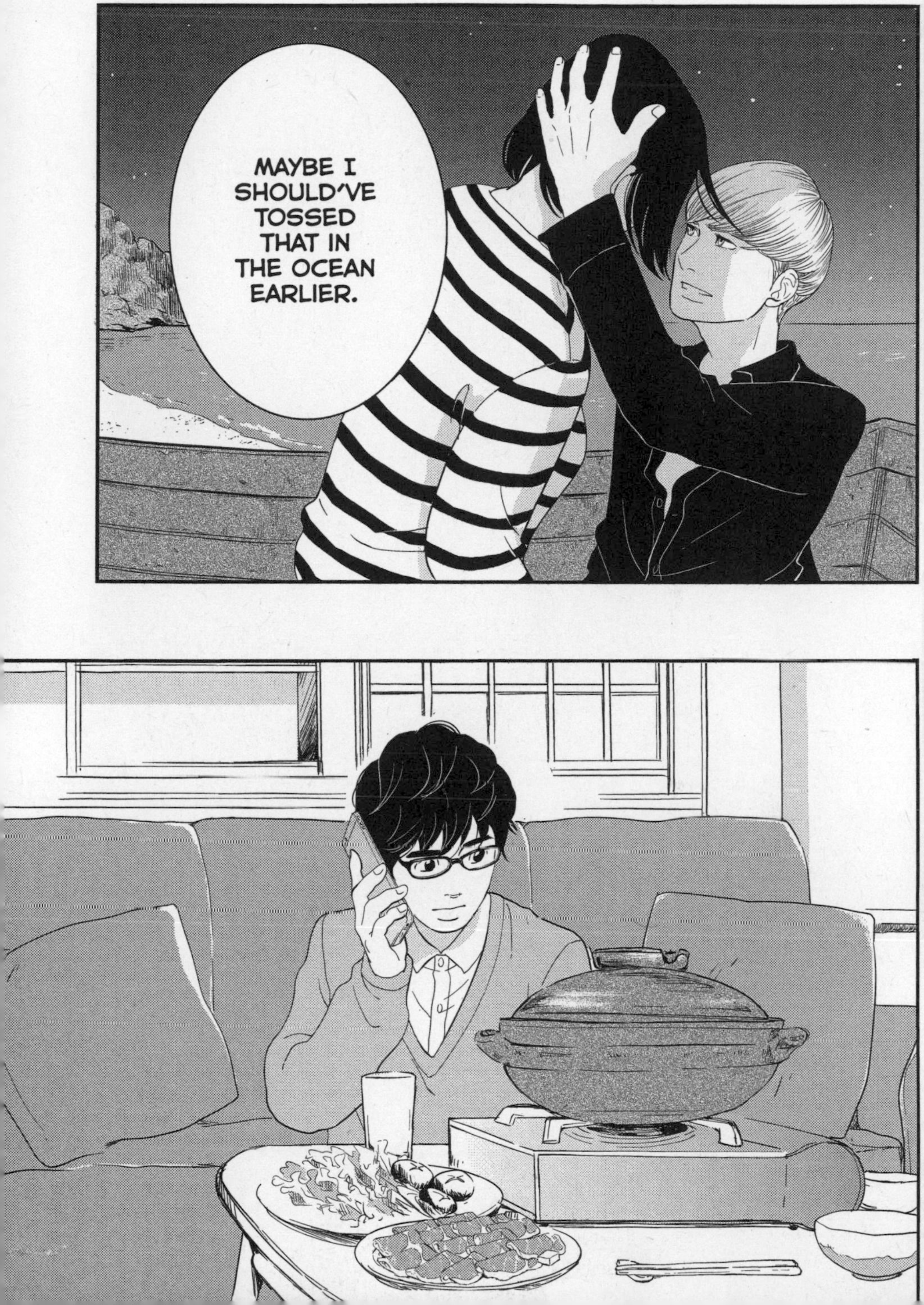
MAYBE I SHOULD'VE TOSSED THAT IN THE OCEAN EARLIER.

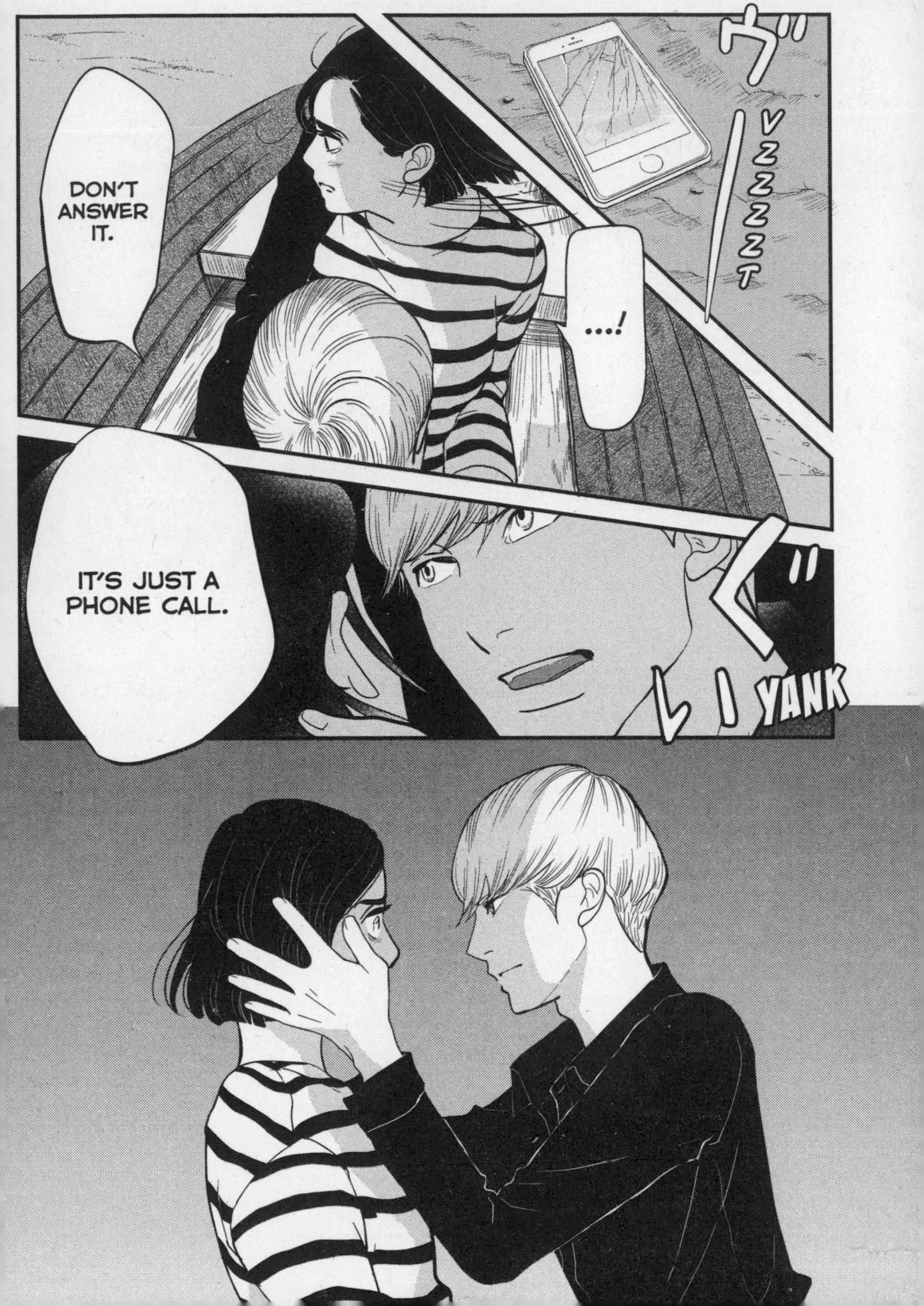
VZZZZZT
...!
DON'T ANSWER IT.
IT'S JUST A PHONE CALL.
YANK

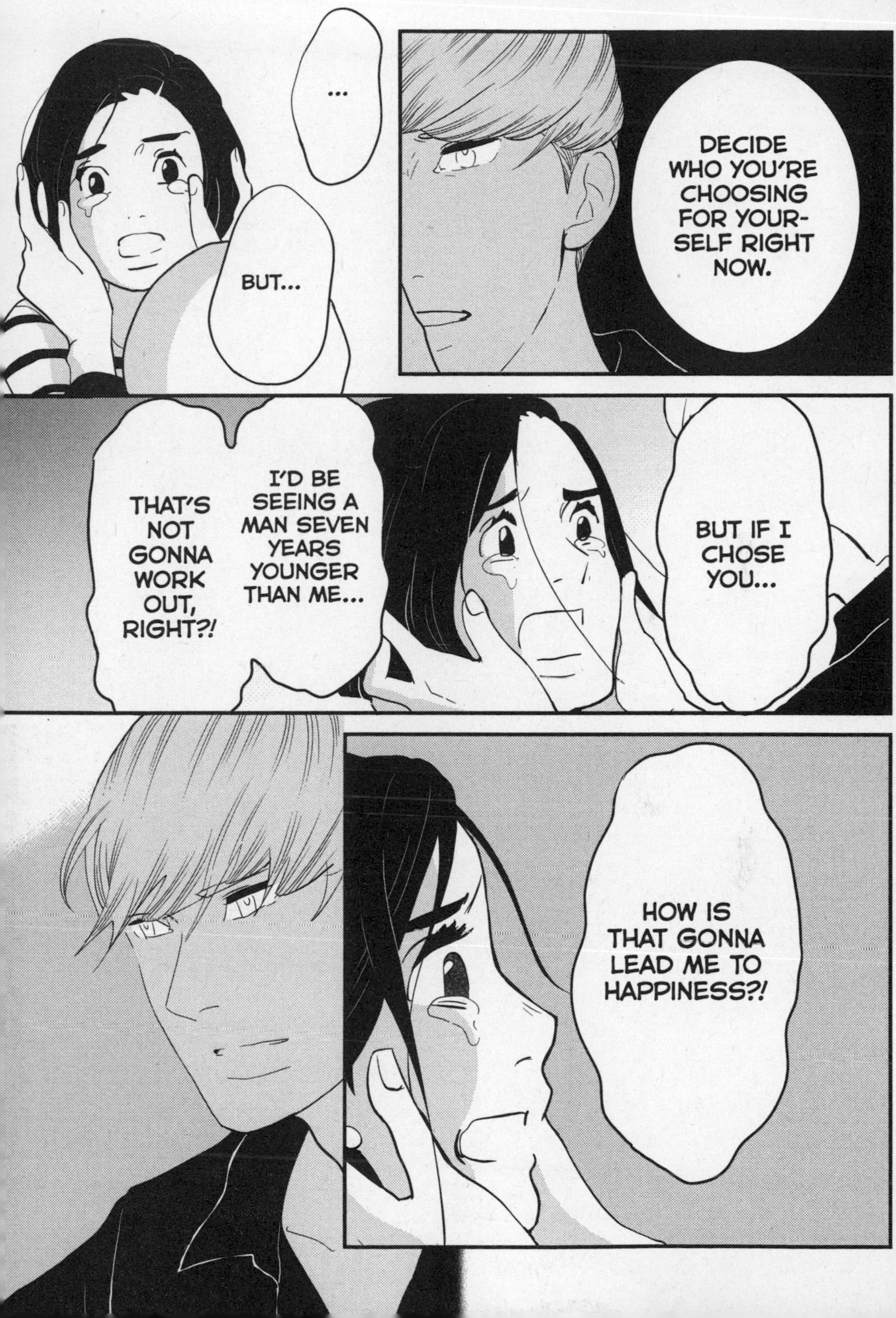
DECIDE WHO YOU'RE CHOOSING FOR YOUR-SELF RIGHT NOW.
...
BUT...
BUT IF I CHOSE YOU...
I'D BE SEEING A MAN SEVEN YEARS YOUNGER THAN ME...
THAT'S NOT GONNA WORK OUT, RIGHT?!
HOW IS THAT GONNA LEAD ME TO HAPPINESS?!

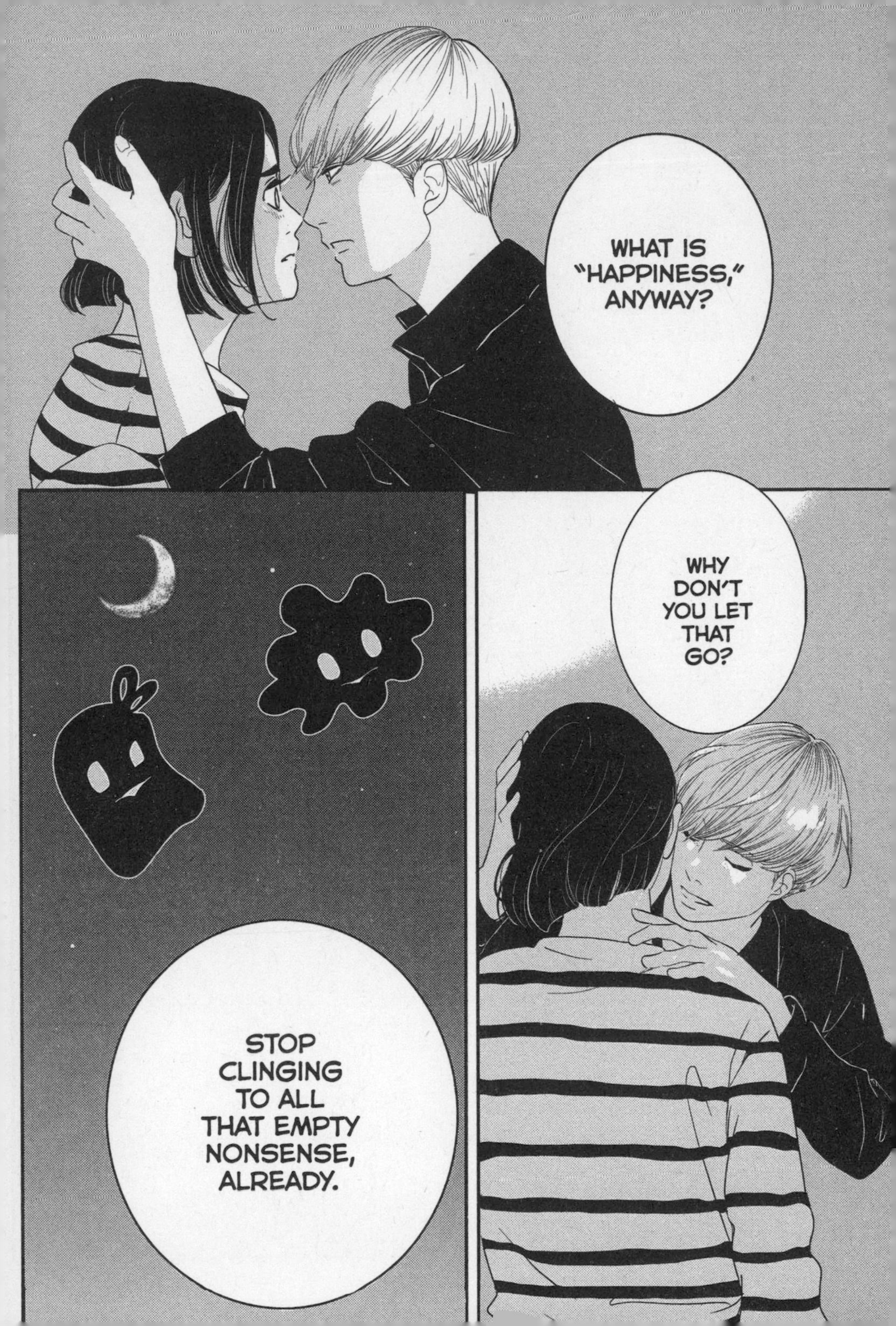
WHAT IS "HAPPINESS," ANYWAY?
WHY DON'T YOU LET THAT GO?
STOP CLINGING TO ALL THAT EMPTY NONSENSE, ALREADY.

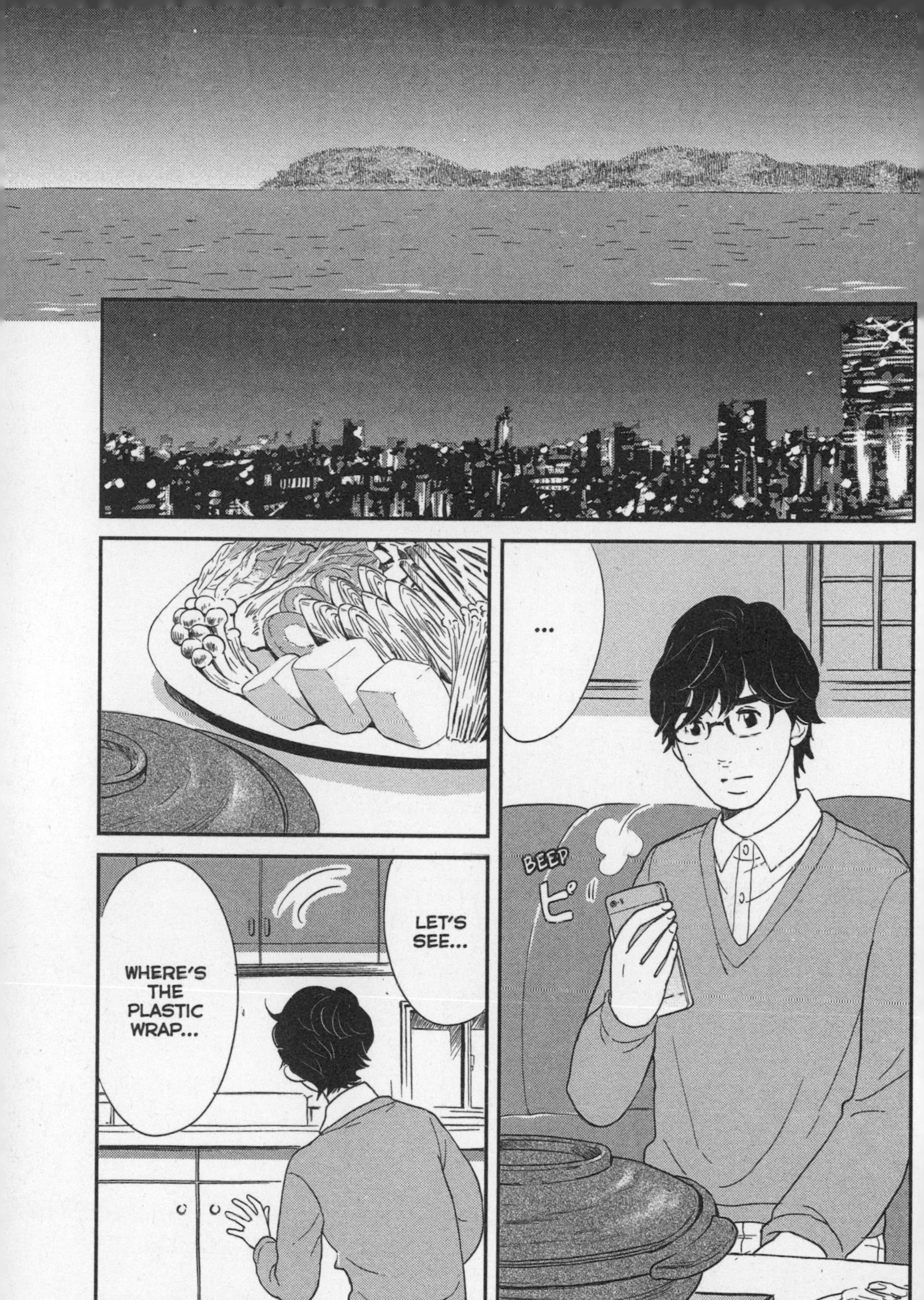
...
BEEP
ピ
LET'S SEE...
WHERE'S THE PLASTIC WRAP...

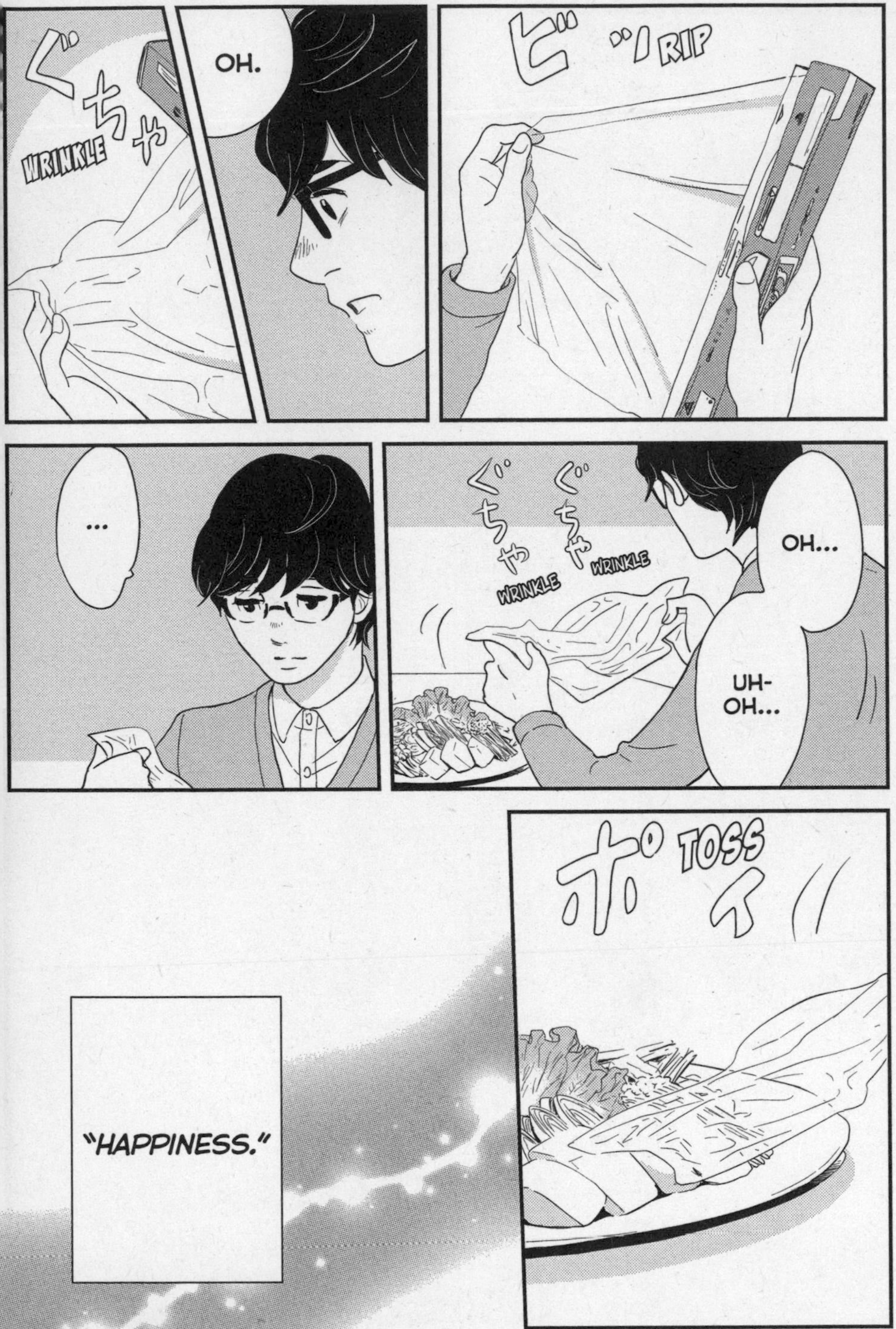
ビッ
RIP
OH.
ぐちゃ
WRINKLE
OH...
ぐちゃ
WRINKLE
ぐちゃ
WRINKLE
UH-OH...
...
ポイ
TOSS
"HAPPINESS."

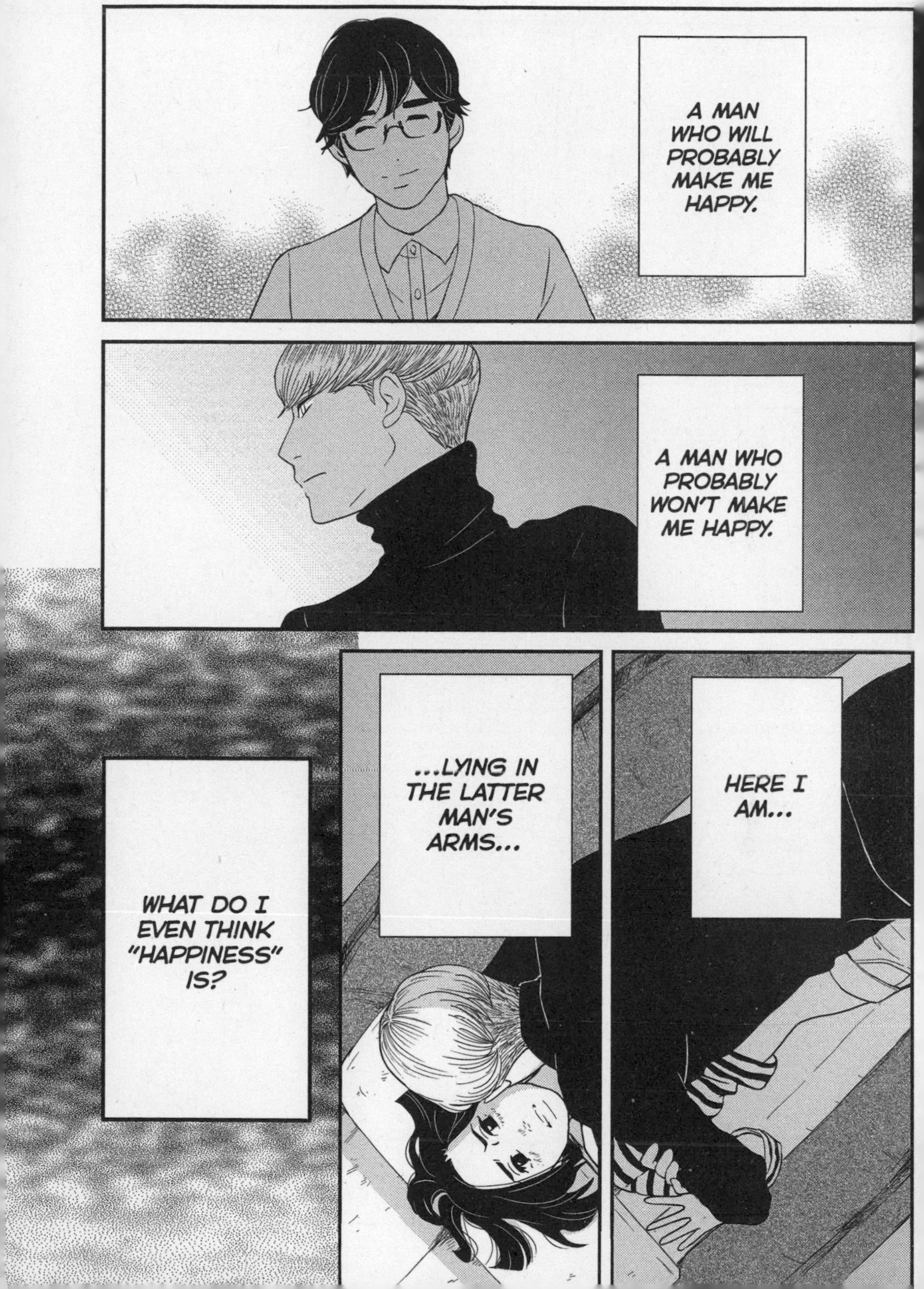
A MAN WHO WILL PROBABLY MAKE ME HAPPY.
A MAN WHO PROBABLY WON'T MAKE ME HAPPY.
HERE I AM...
...LYING IN THE LATTER MAN'S ARMS...
WHAT DO I EVEN THINK "HAPPINESS" IS?

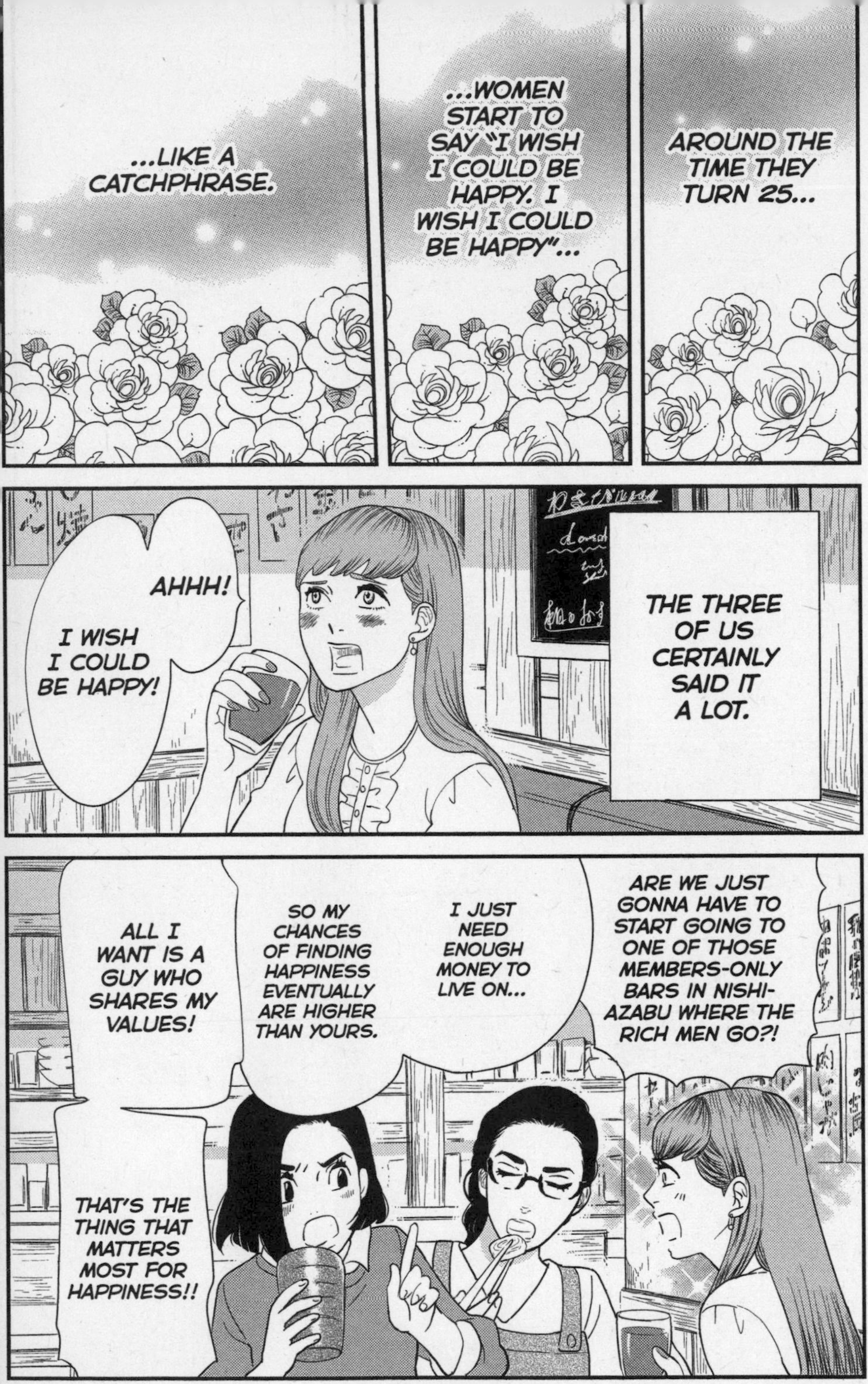

AROUND THE TIME THEY TURN 25...
...WOMEN START TO SAY "I WISH I COULD BE HAPPY. I WISH I COULD BE HAPPY"...
...LIKE A CATCHPHRASE.
THE THREE OF US CERTAINLY SAID IT A LOT.
AHHH! I WISH I COULD BE HAPPY!
ARE WE JUST GONNA HAVE TO START GOING TO ONE OF THOSE MEMBERS-ONLY BARS IN NISHI-AZABU WHERE THE RICH MEN GO?!
I JUST NEED ENOUGH MONEY TO LIVE ON...
SO MY CHANCES OF FINDING HAPPINESS EVENTUALLY ARE HIGHER THAN YOURS.
ALL I WANT IS A GUY WHO SHARES MY VALUES!
THAT'S THE THING THAT MATTERS MOST FOR HAPPINESS!!

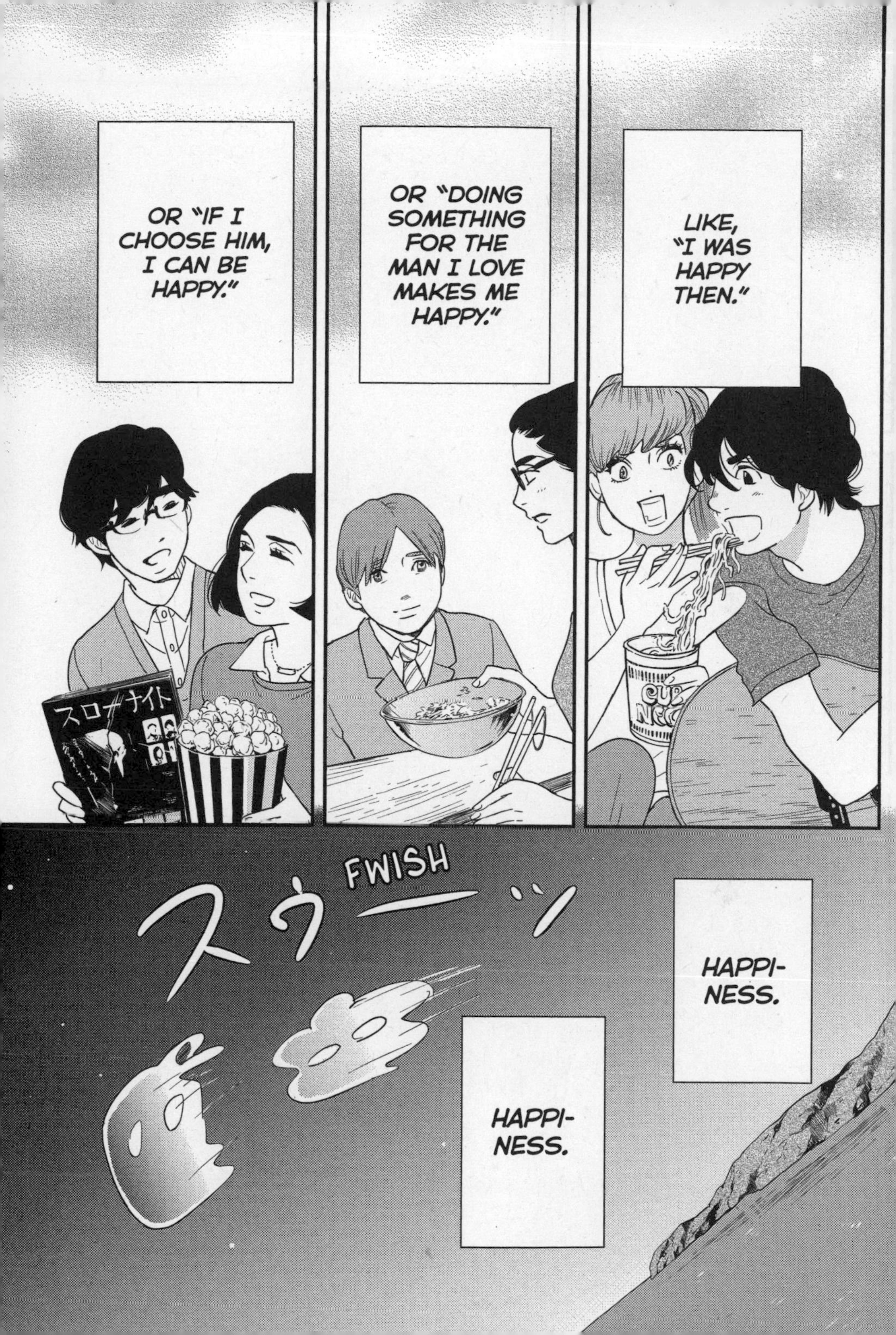
LIKE, "I WAS HAPPY THEN."
OR "DOING SOMETHING FOR THE MAN I LOVE MAKES ME HAPPY."
OR "IF I CHOOSE HIM, I CAN BE HAPPY."
FWISH
スウーッ
HAPPI-NESS.
HAPPI-NESS.

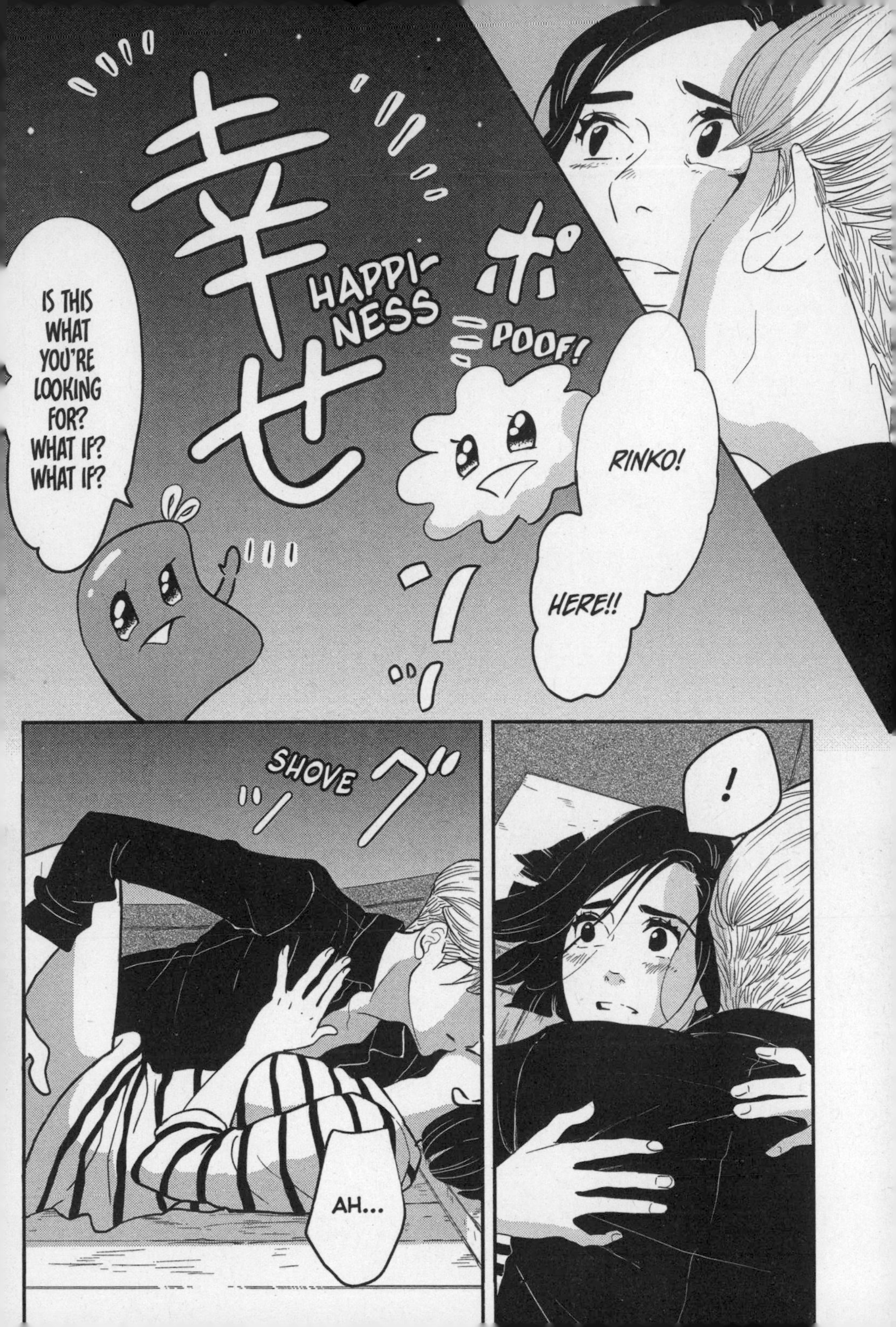
RINKO!
HERE!!
HAPPI-NESS
POOF!
IS THIS WHAT YOU'RE LOOKING FOR? WHAT IF? WHAT IF?
!
SHOVE
AH...

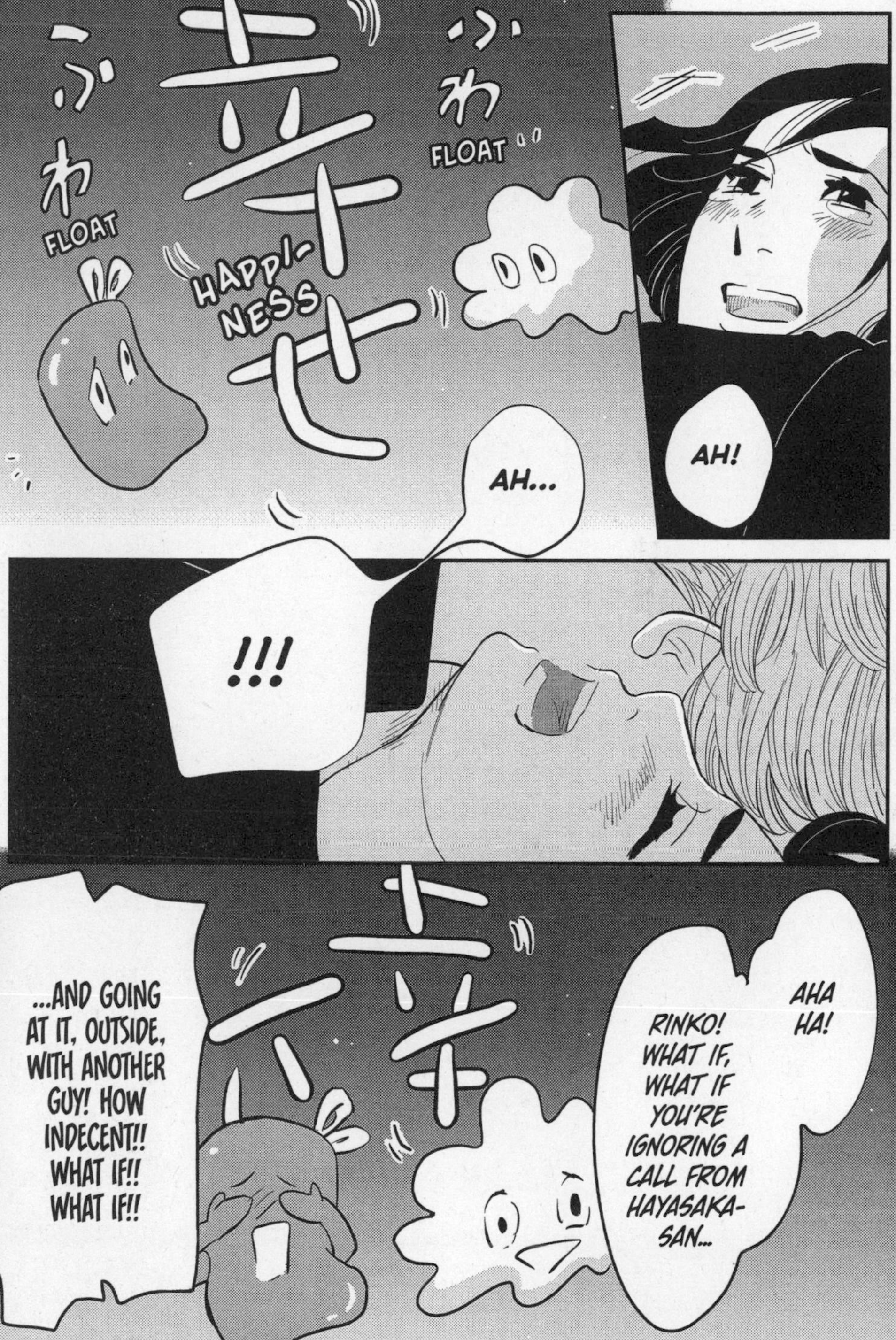
AH!
ふわ
FLOAT
幸せ
HAPPI-NESS
ふわ
FLOAT
AH...
!!!
AHA HA!
RINKO! WHAT IF, WHAT IF YOU'RE IGNORING A CALL FROM HAYASAKA-SAN...
...AND GOING AT IT, OUTSIDE, WITH ANOTHER GUY! HOW INDECENT!! WHAT IF!! WHAT IF!!

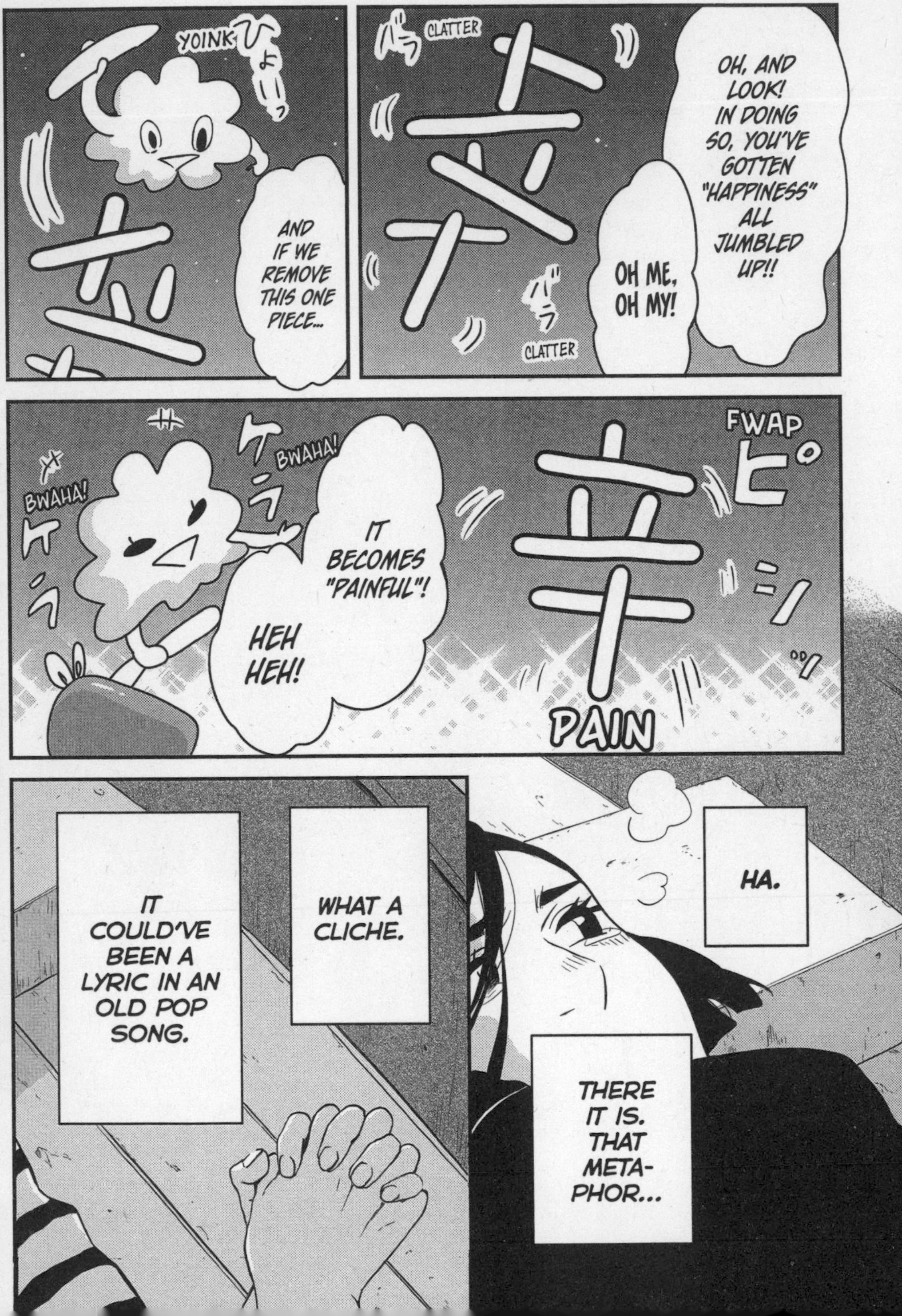
CLATTER
OH, AND LOOK! IN DOING SO, YOU'VE GOTTEN "HAPPINESS" ALL JUMBLED UP!!
OH ME, OH MY!
CLATTER
YOINK
AND IF WE REMOVE THIS ONE PIECE...
FWAP
PAIN
BWAHA!
IT BECOMES "PAINFUL"!
HEH HEH!
BWAHA!
HA.
THERE IT IS. THAT METAPHOR...
WHAT A CLICHE.
IT COULD'VE BEEN A LYRIC IN AN OLD POP SONG.

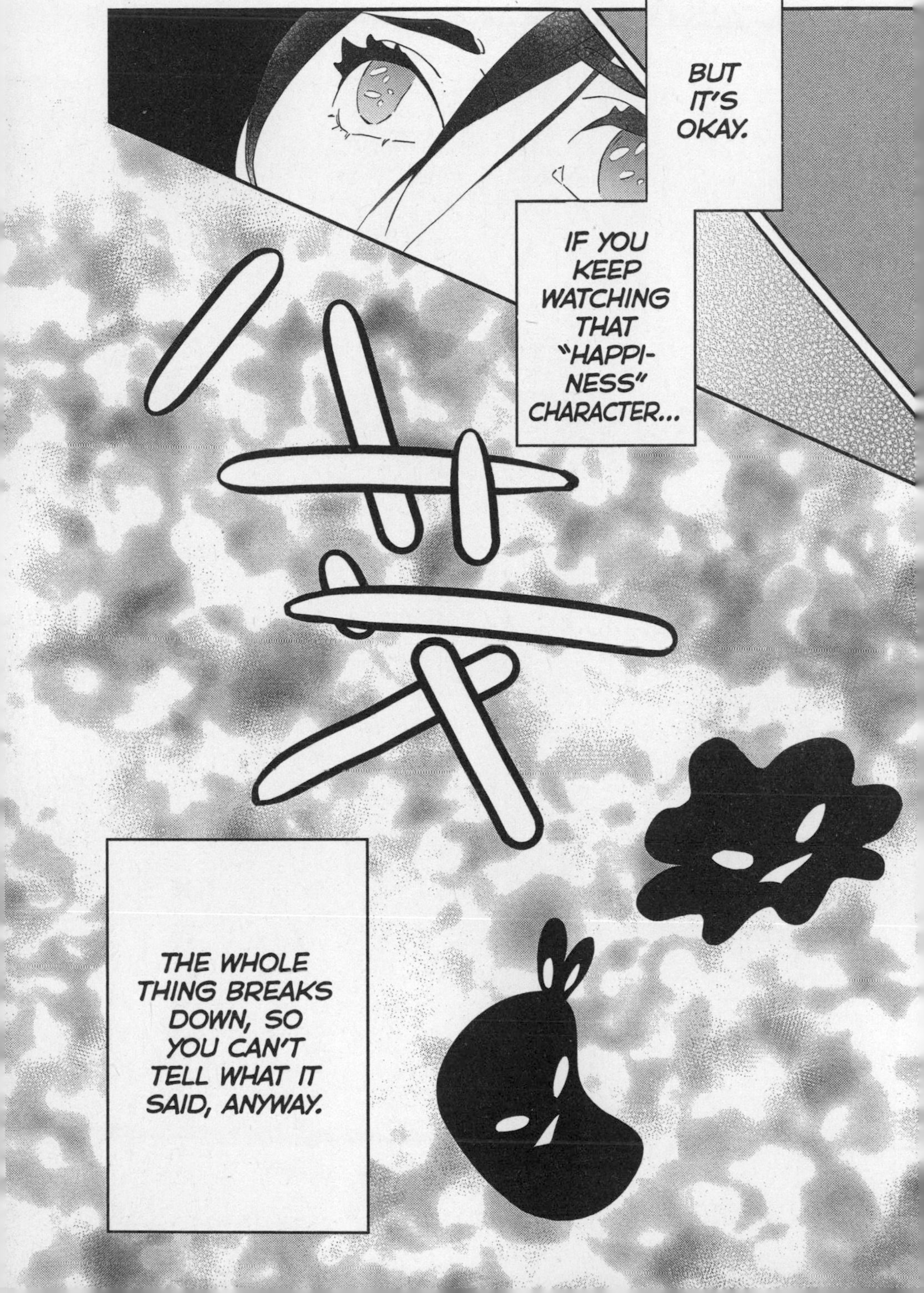
BUT IT'S OKAY.
IF YOU KEEP WATCHING THAT "HAPPINESS" CHARACTER...
THE WHOLE THING BREAKS DOWN, SO YOU CAN'T TELL WHAT IT SAID, ANYWAY.

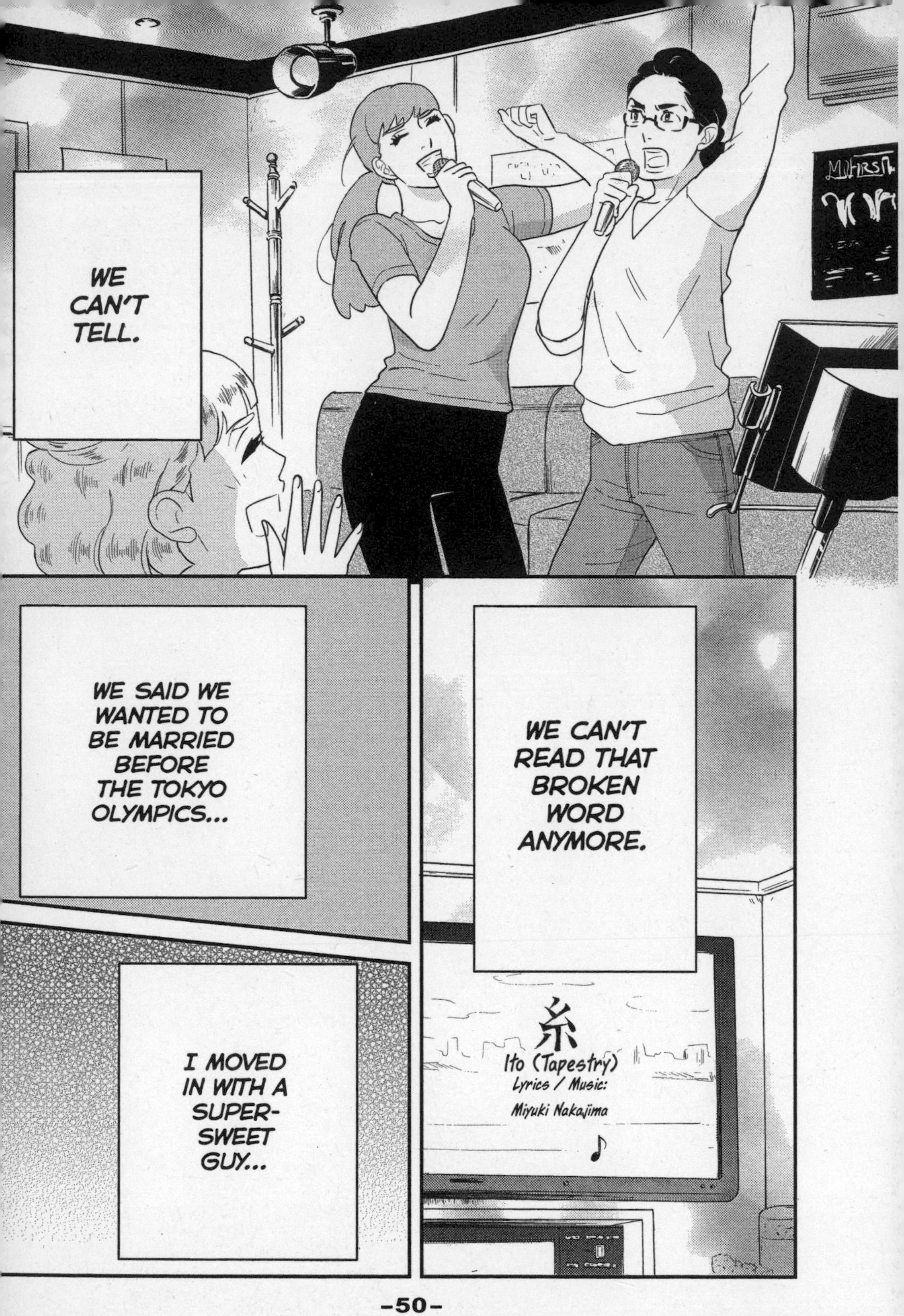
WE CAN'T TELL.
WE CAN'T READ THAT BROKEN WORD ANYMORE.
WE SAID WE WANTED TO BE MARRIED BEFORE THE TOKYO OLYMPICS...
糸
Ito (Tapestry)
Lyrics / Music:
Miyuki Nakajima
♪
I MOVED IN WITH A SUPER-SWEET GUY...

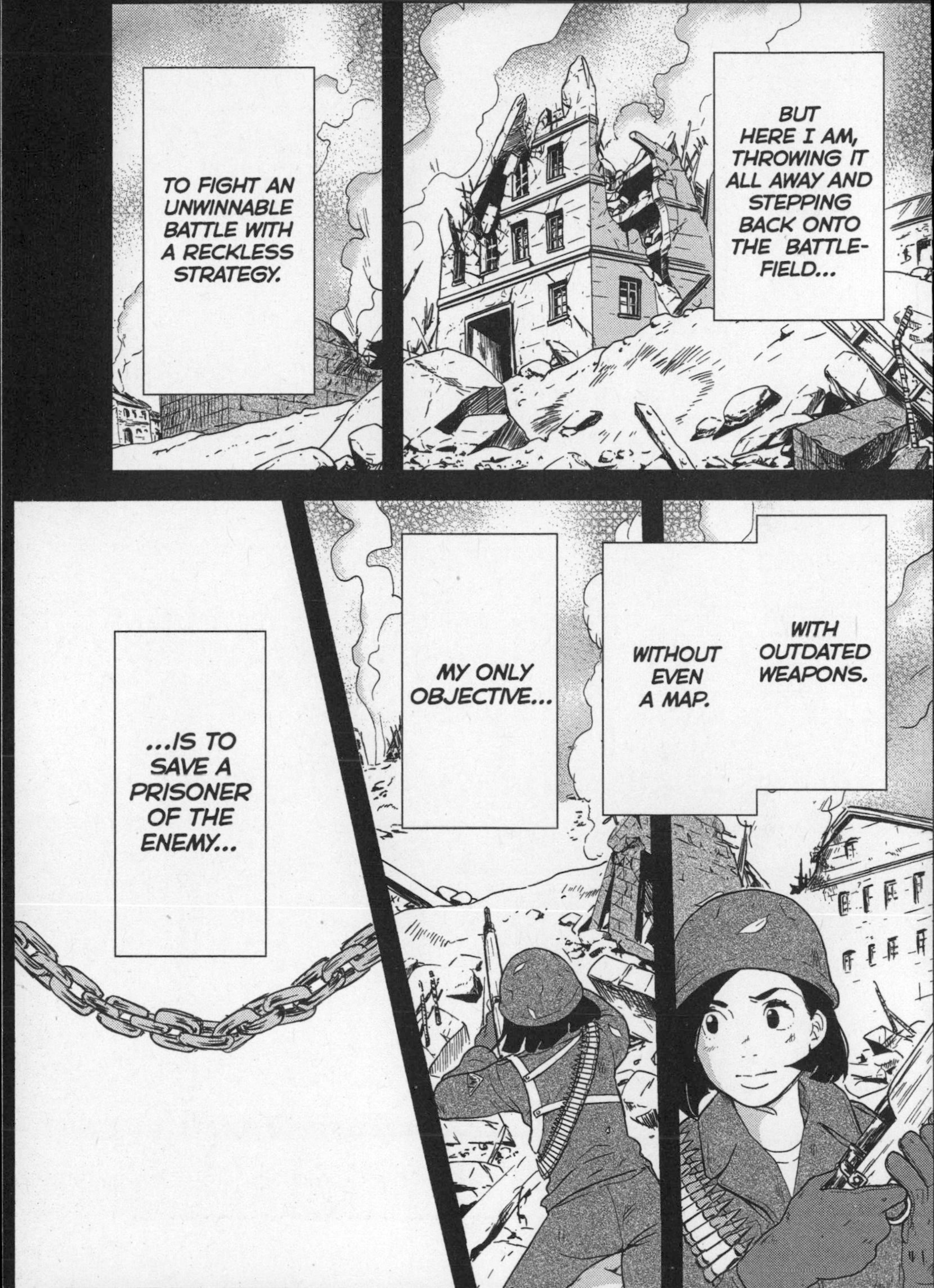
BUT HERE I AM, THROWING IT ALL AWAY AND STEPPING BACK ONTO THE BATTLE-FIELD...
TO FIGHT AN UNWINNABLE BATTLE WITH A RECKLESS STRATEGY.
WITH OUTDATED WEAPONS.
WITHOUT EVEN A MAP.
MY ONLY OBJECTIVE...
...IS TO SAVE A PRISONER OF THE ENEMY...

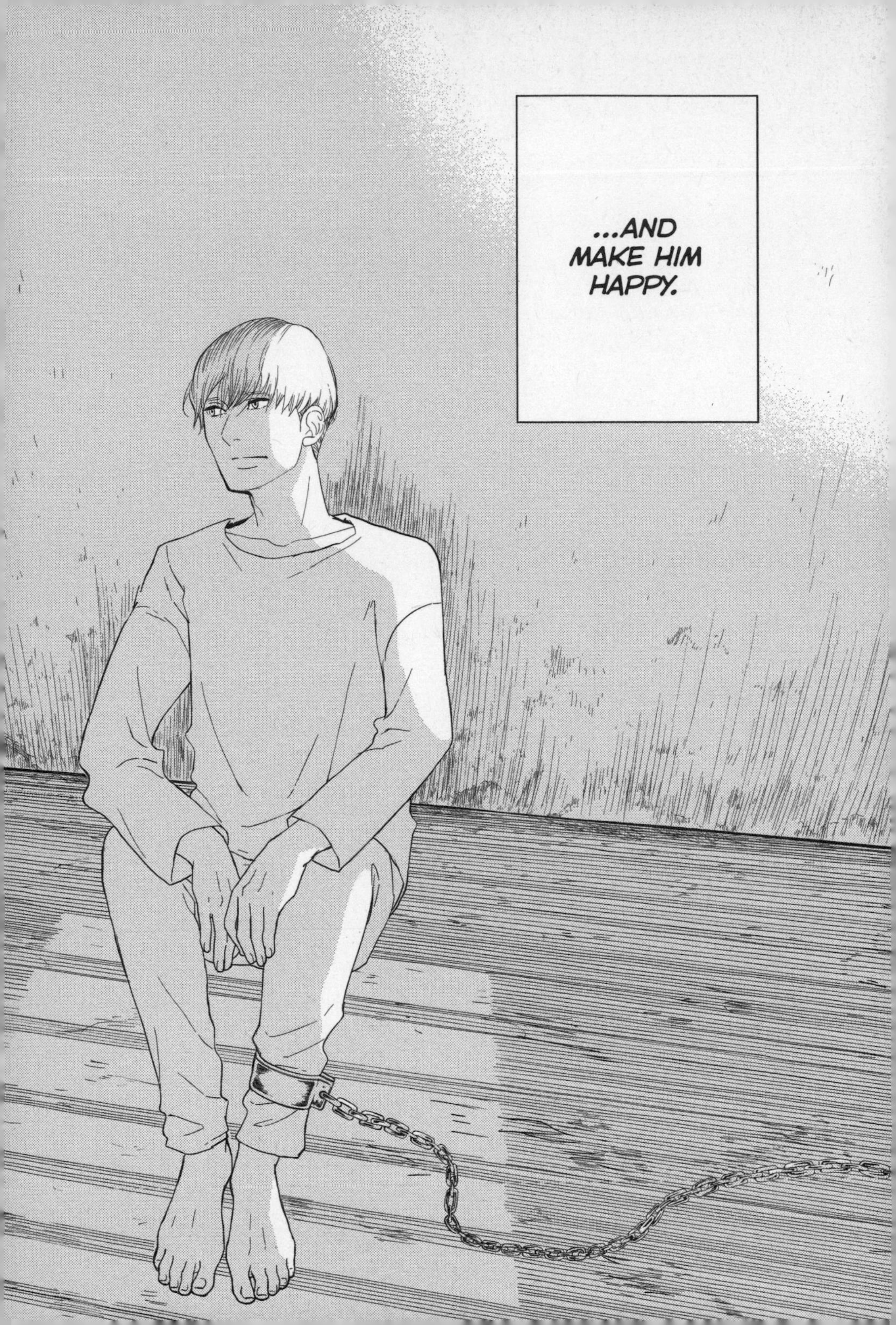
...AND MAKE HIM HAPPY.

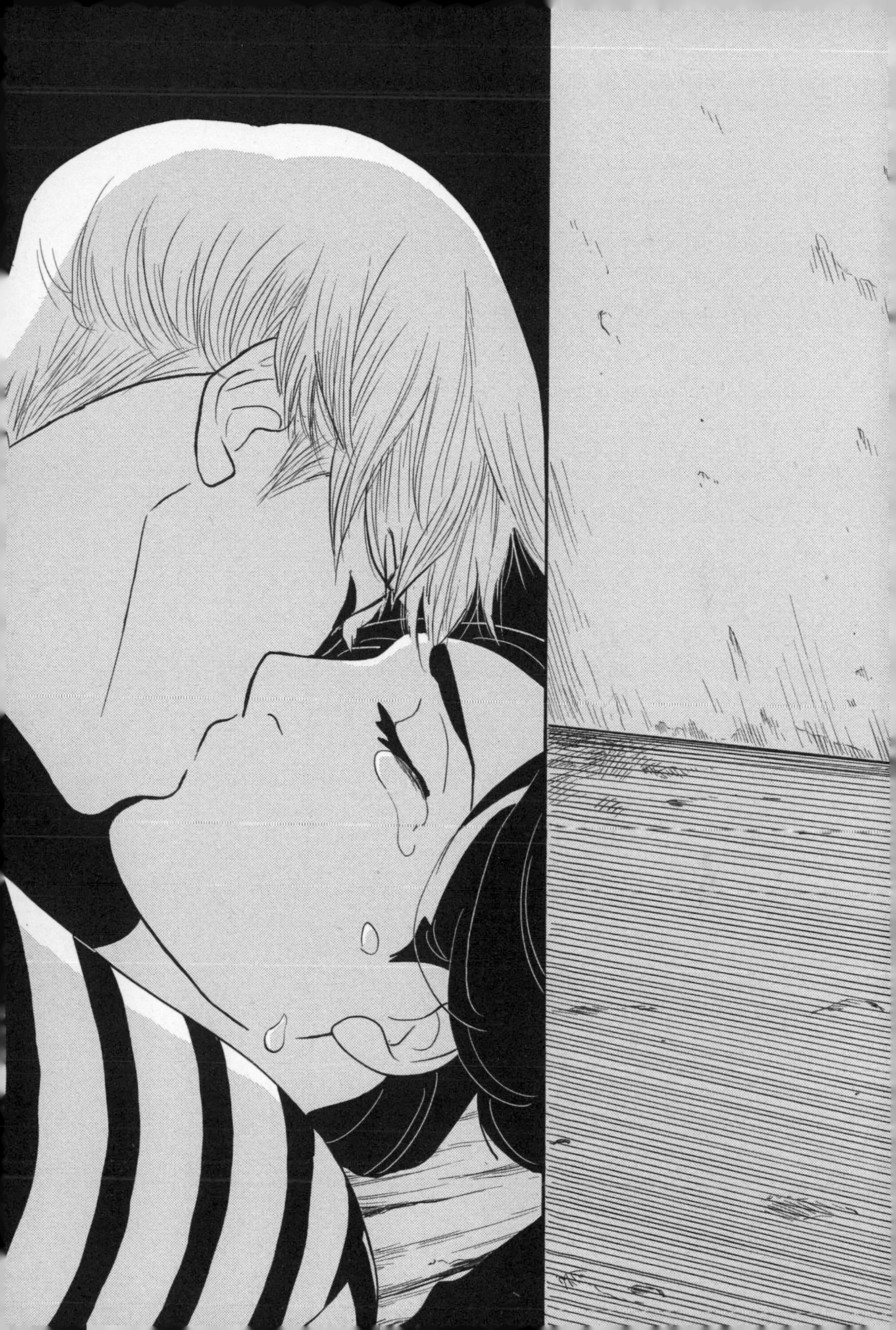

I WANT TO MAKE
YOU HAPPY.

I DON'T CARE
ABOUT MY OWN
HAPPINESS
ANYMORE.

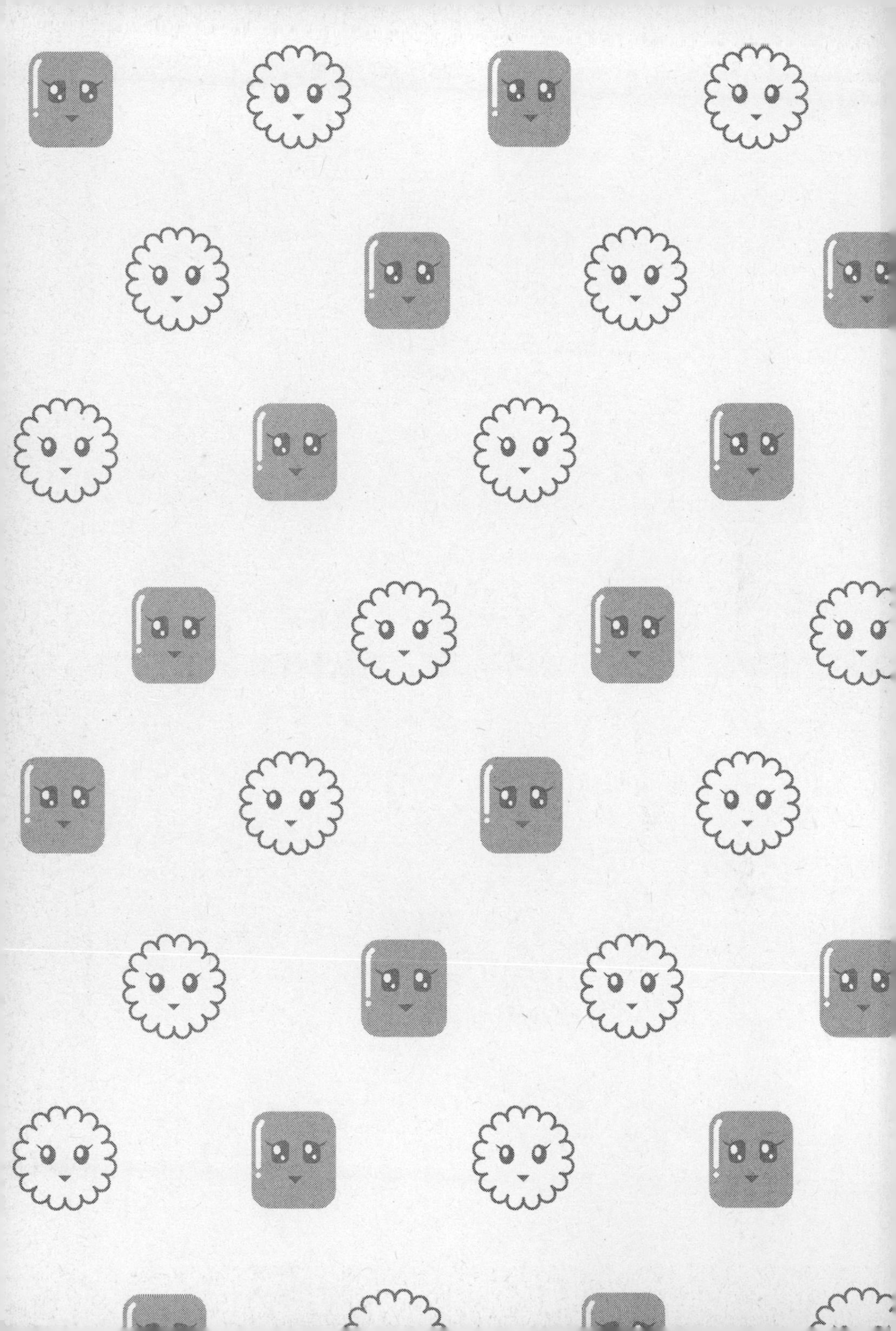

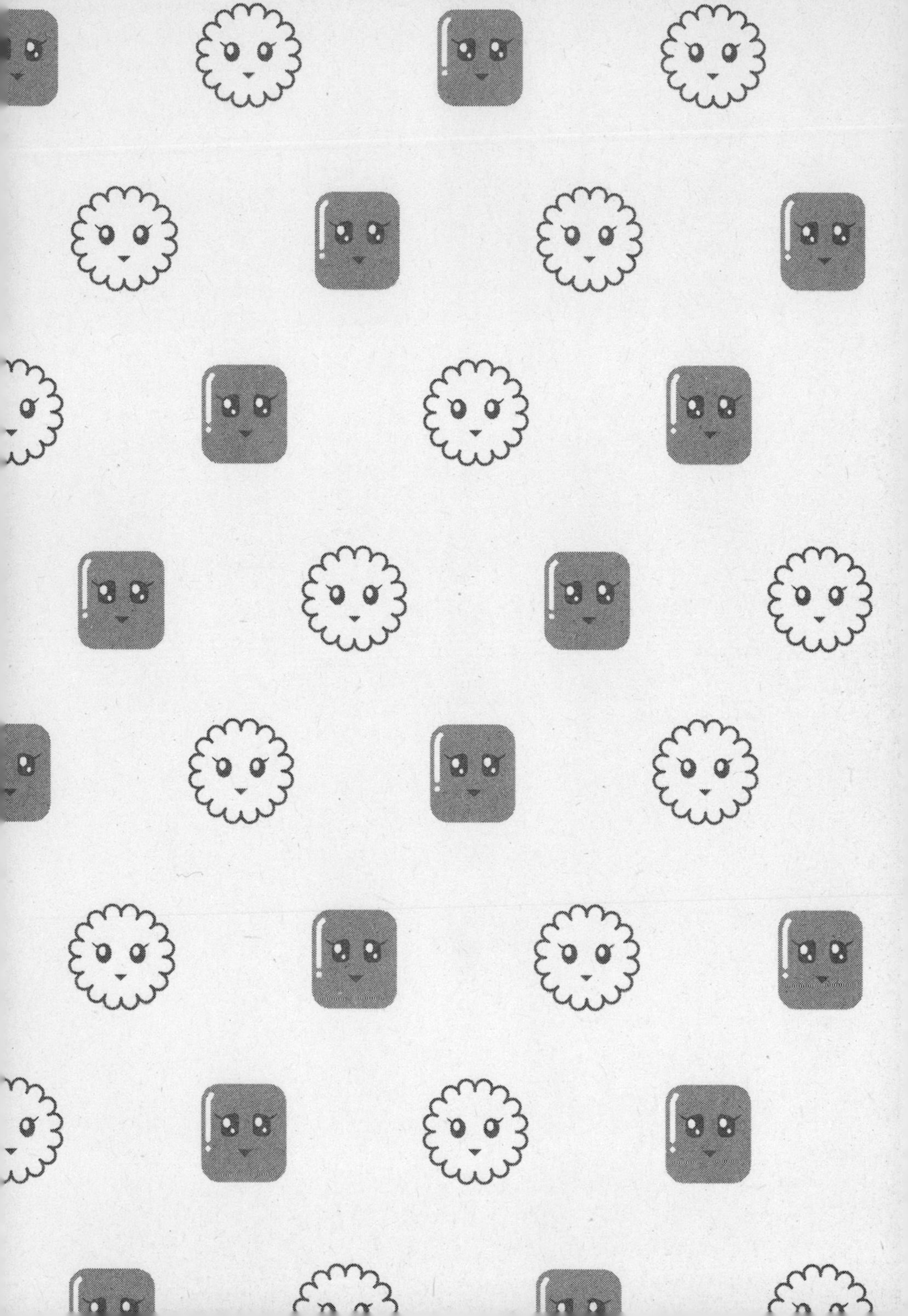

ACT 29 TOKYO TARAREBA GIRLS

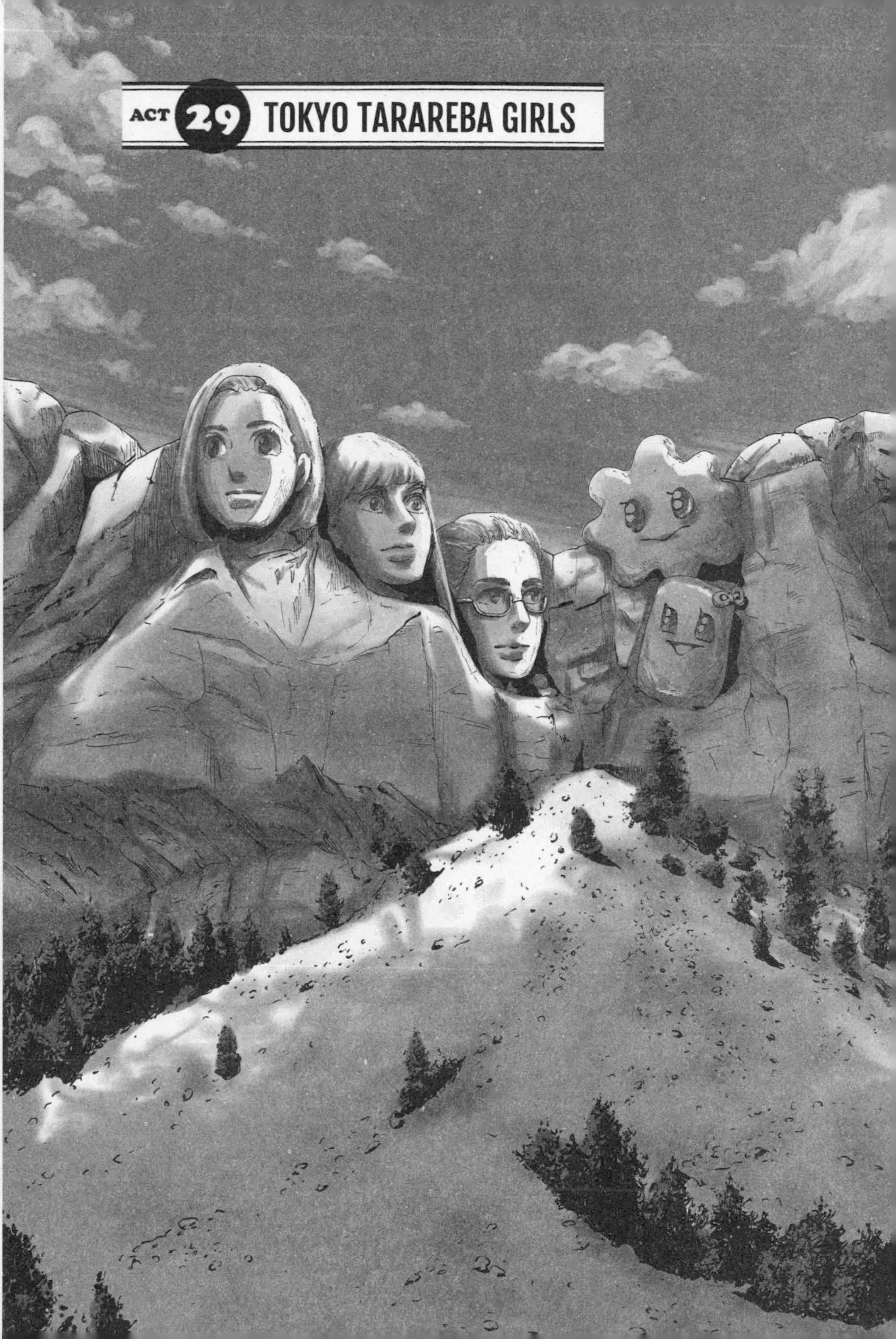

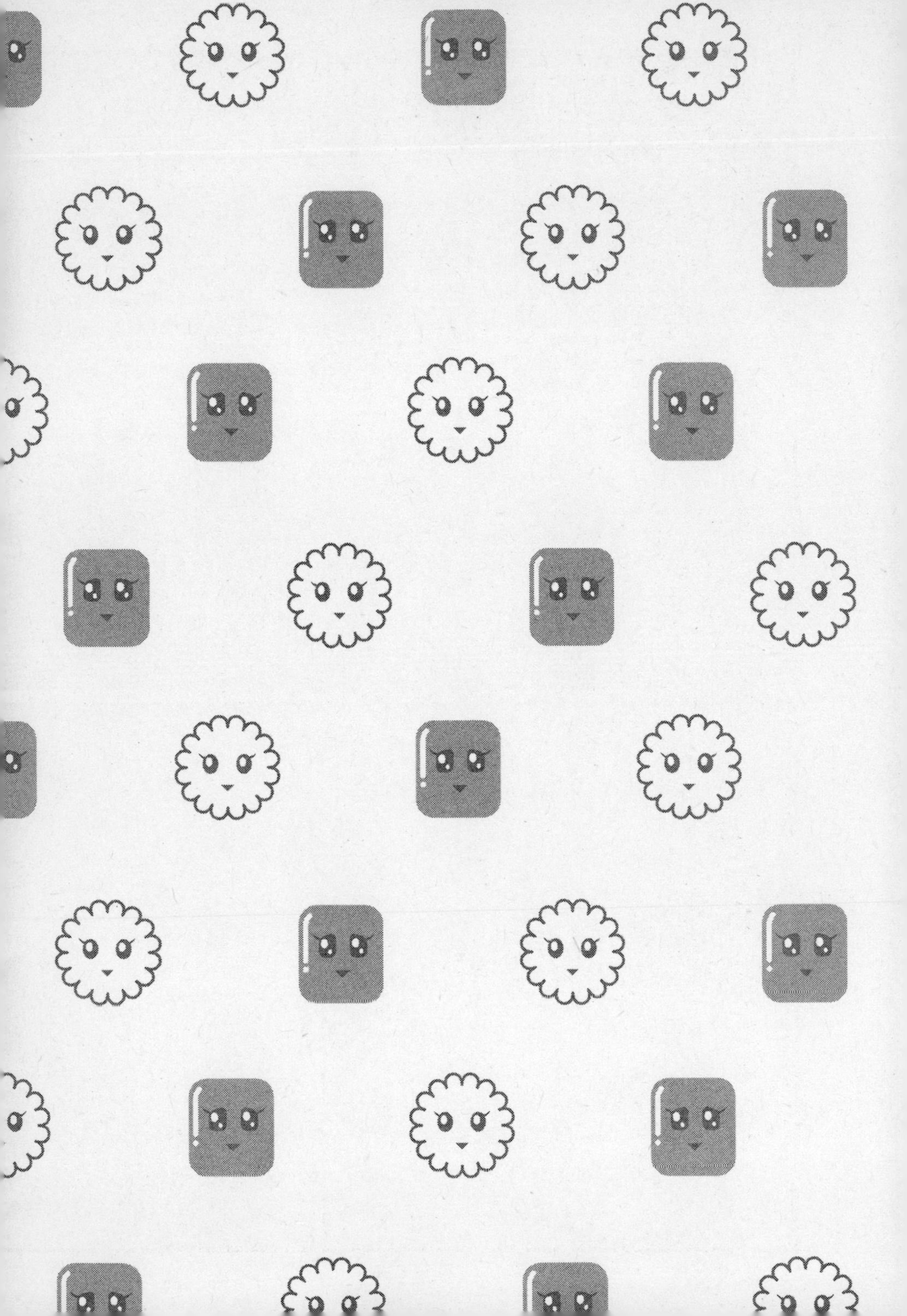

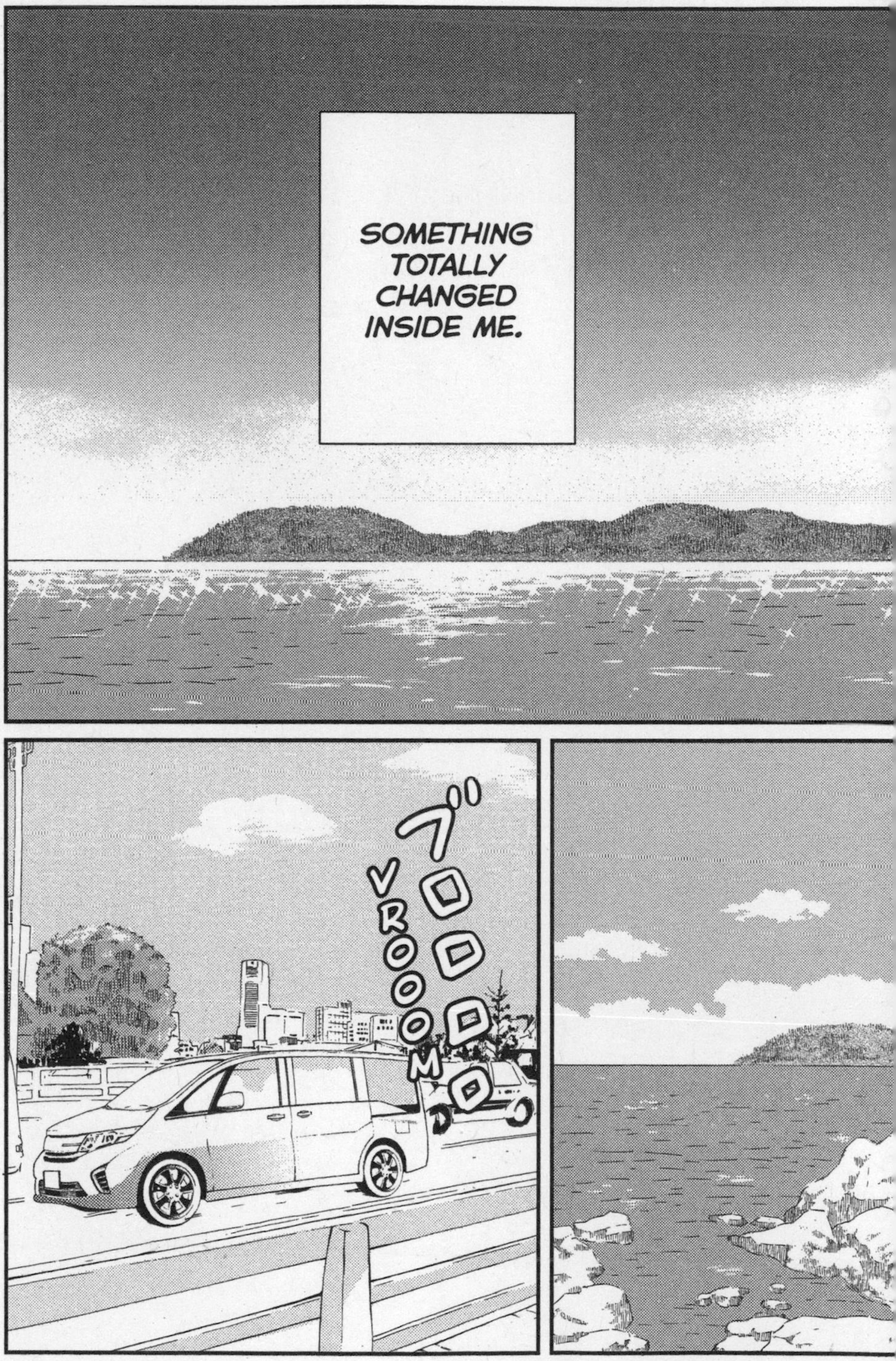
SOMETHING TOTALLY CHANGED INSIDE ME.
ブロロロロ
VROOOM

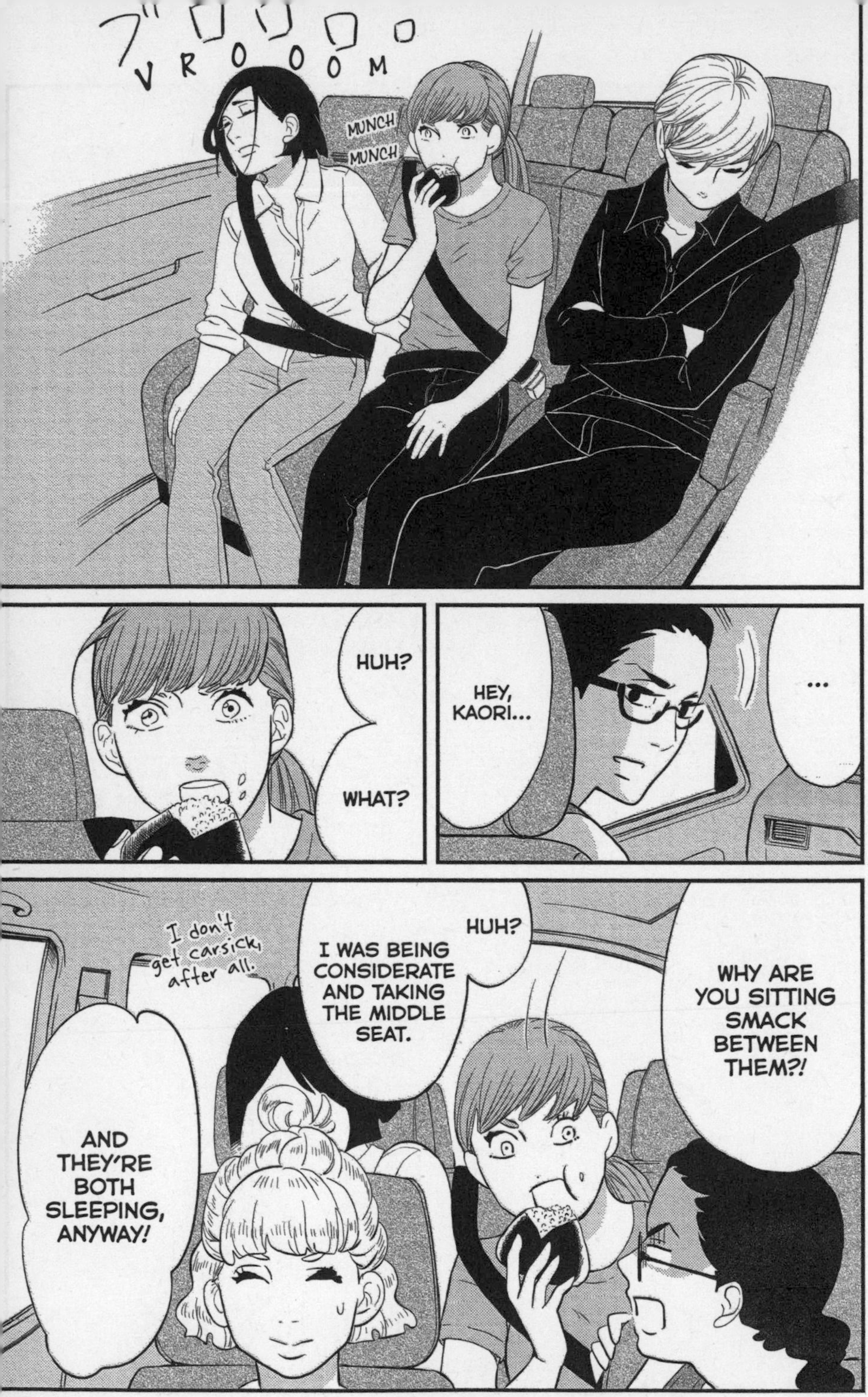
ブロロロロ
VROOOM
MUNCH
MUNCH
...
HEY, KAORI...
HUH?
WHAT?
WHY ARE YOU SITTING SMACK BETWEEN THEM?!
HUH?
I WAS BEING CONSIDERATE AND TAKING THE MIDDLE SEAT.
I don't get carsick, after all.
AND THEY'RE BOTH SLEEPING, ANYWAY!

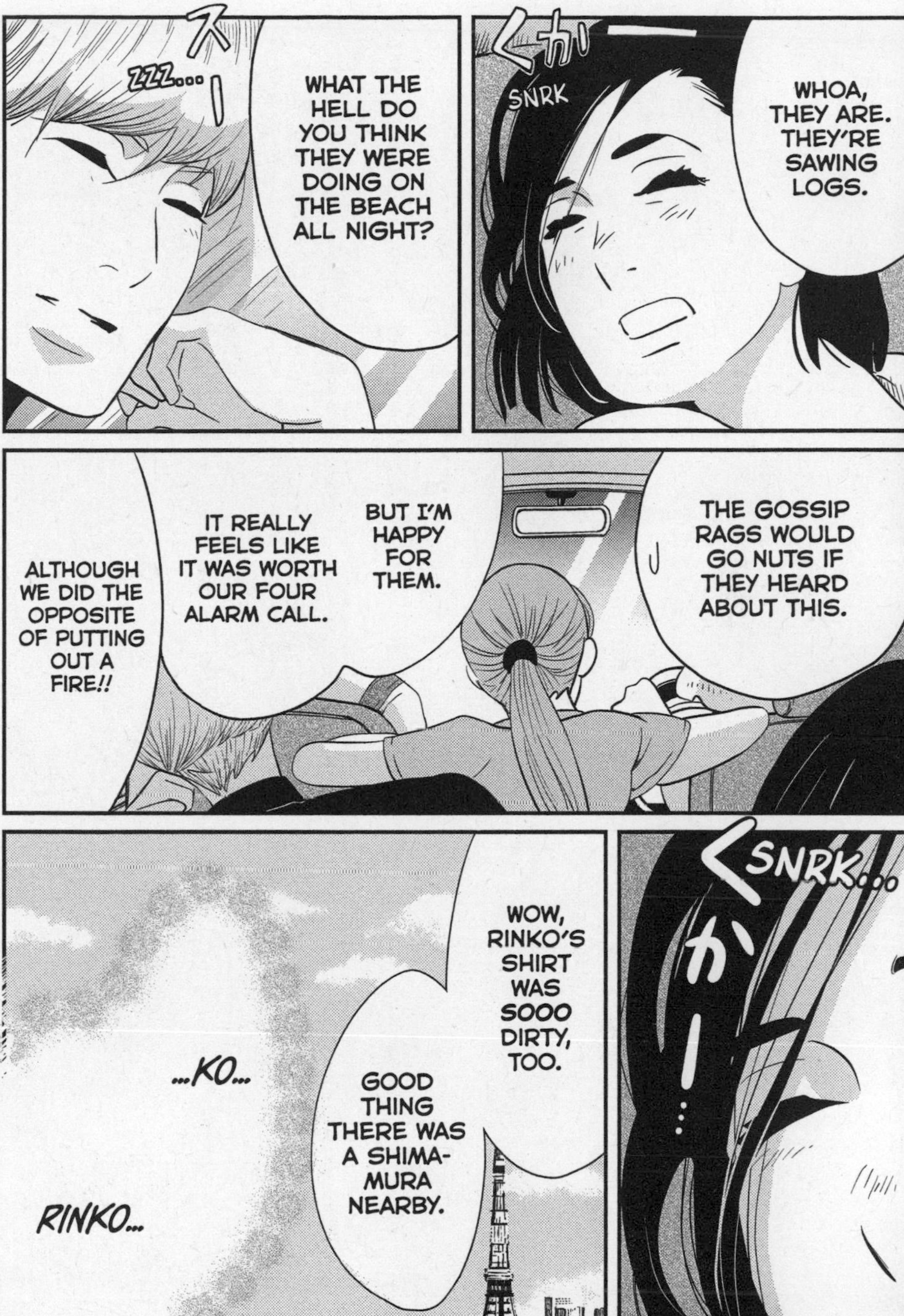
くかー
SNRK
WHOA, THEY ARE. THEY'RE SAWING LOGS.
スー
ZZZ...
WHAT THE HELL DO YOU THINK THEY WERE DOING ON THE BEACH ALL NIGHT?
THE GOSSIP RAGS WOULD GO NUTS IF THEY HEARD ABOUT THIS.
BUT I'M HAPPY FOR THEM.
IT REALLY FEELS LIKE IT WAS WORTH OUR FOUR ALARM CALL.
ALTHOUGH WE DID THE OPPOSITE OF PUTTING OUT A FIRE!!
くSNRK...
かー...
WOW, RINKO'S SHIRT WAS SOOO DIRTY, TOO.
GOOD THING THERE WAS A SHIMA-MURA NEARBY.
...KO...
RINKO...

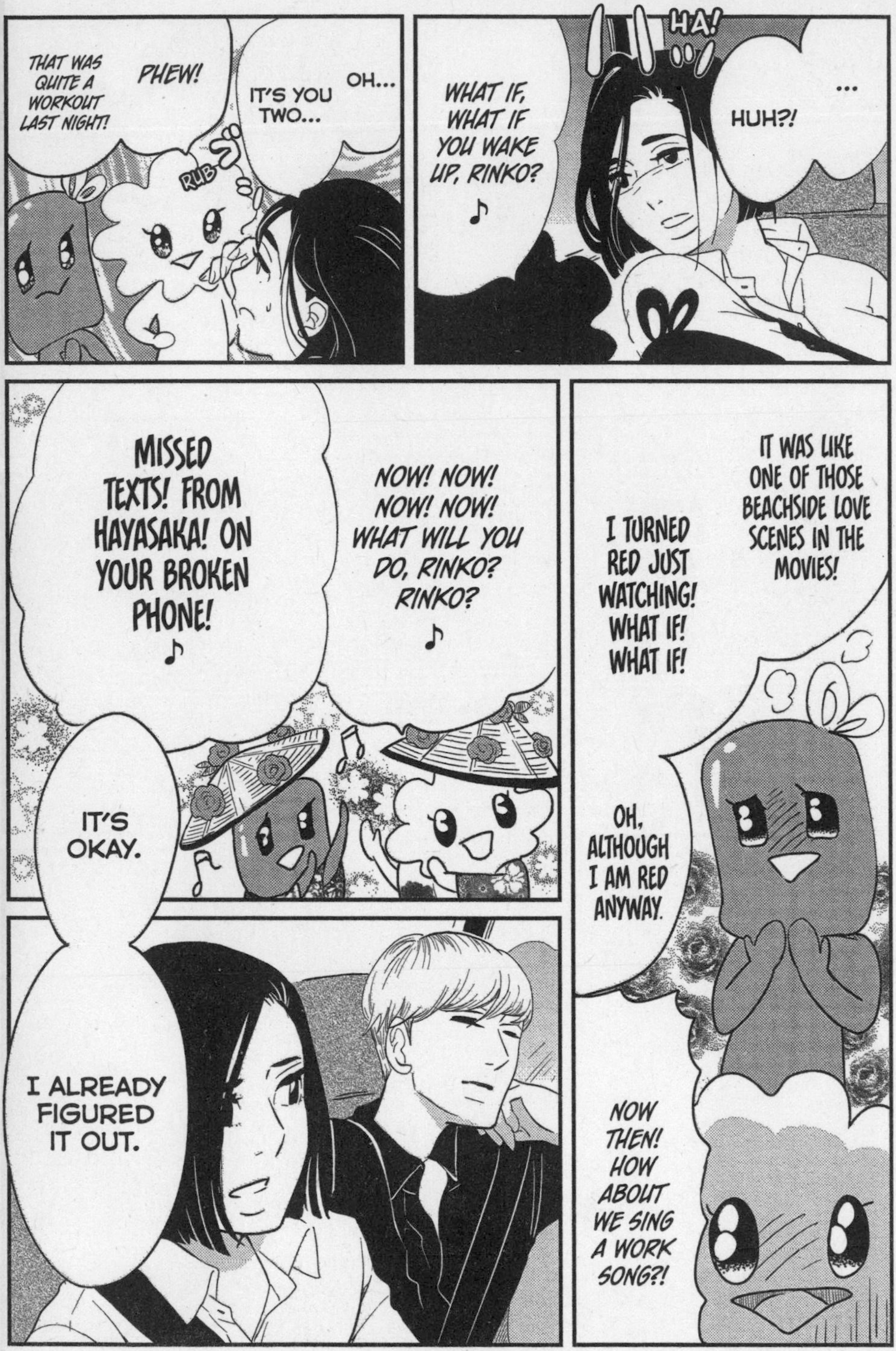
HA!
...
HUH?!
WHAT IF, WHAT IF YOU WAKE UP, RINKO? ♪
OH... IT'S YOU TWO...
RUB
PHEW!
THAT WAS QUITE A WORKOUT LAST NIGHT!
IT WAS LIKE ONE OF THOSE BEACHSIDE LOVE SCENES IN THE MOVIES!
I TURNED RED JUST WATCHING! WHAT IF! WHAT IF!
OH, ALTHOUGH I AM RED ANYWAY.
NOW THEN! HOW ABOUT WE SING A WORK SONG?!
NOW! NOW! NOW! NOW! WHAT WILL YOU DO, RINKO? RINKO? ♪
MISSED TEXTS! FROM HAYASAKA! ON YOUR BROKEN PHONE! ♪
IT'S OKAY.
I ALREADY FIGURED IT OUT.

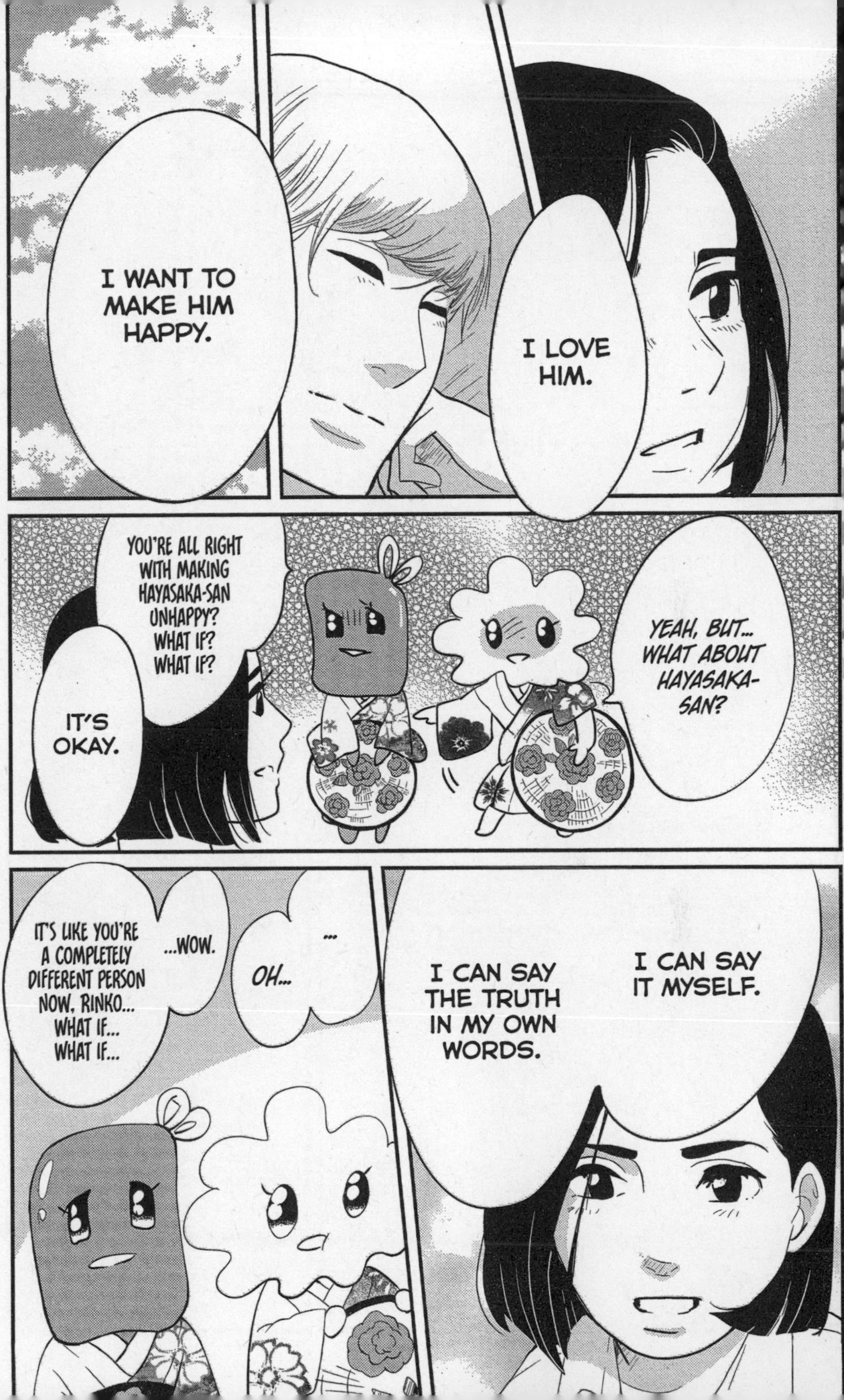
I LOVE HIM.
I WANT TO MAKE HIM HAPPY.
YEAH, BUT... WHAT ABOUT HAYASAKA-SAN?
YOU'RE ALL RIGHT WITH MAKING HAYASAKA-SAN UNHAPPY? WHAT IF? WHAT IF?
IT'S OKAY.
I CAN SAY IT MYSELF.
I CAN SAY THE TRUTH IN MY OWN WORDS.
...
OH...
...WOW.
IT'S LIKE YOU'RE A COMPLETELY DIFFERENT PERSON NOW, RINKO... WHAT IF... WHAT IF...

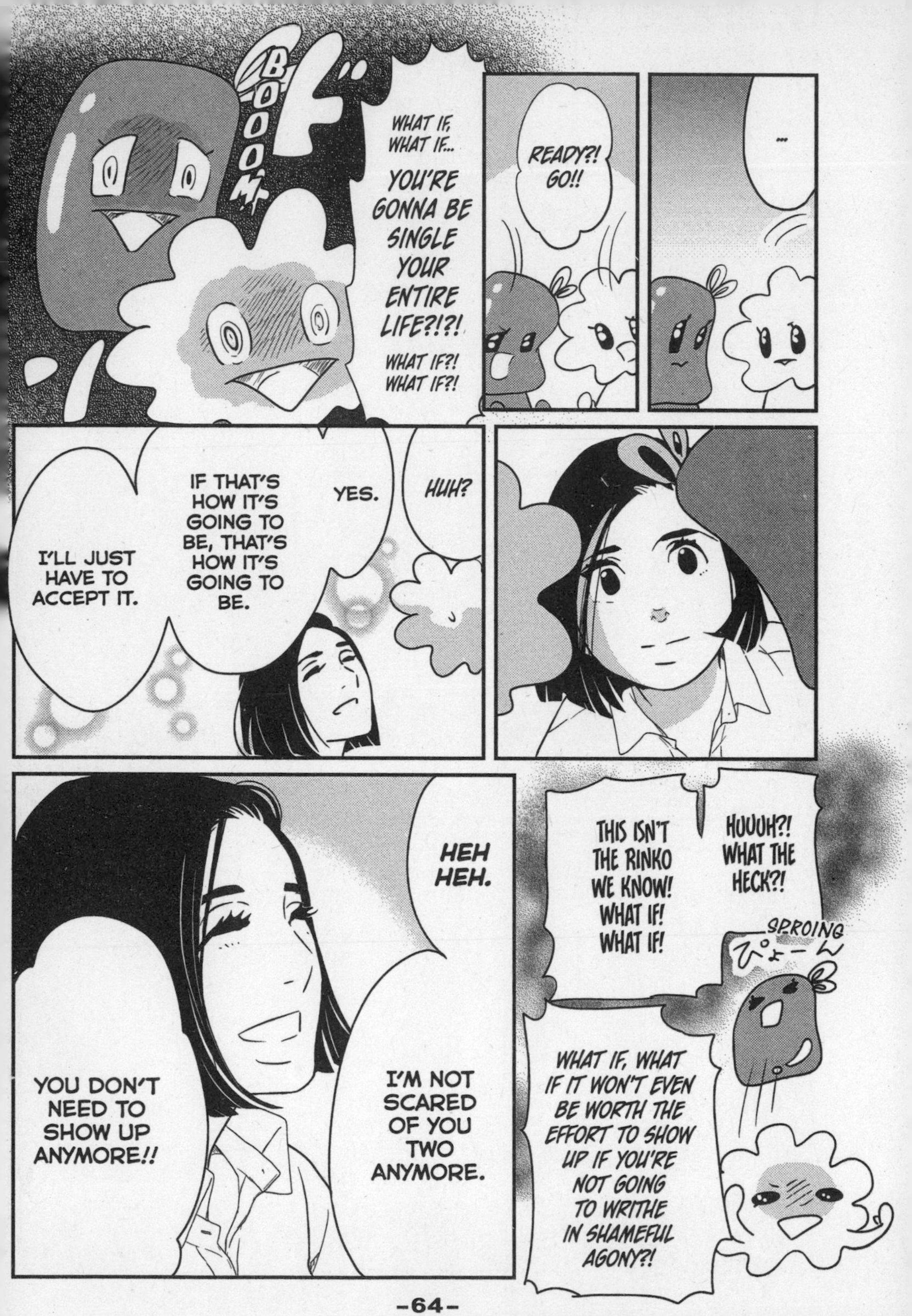
...
READY?! GO!!
BOOOOM
WHAT IF, WHAT IF...
YOU'RE GONNA BE SINGLE YOUR ENTIRE LIFE?!?!
WHAT IF?! WHAT IF?!
HUH?
YES.
IF THAT'S HOW IT'S GOING TO BE, THAT'S HOW IT'S GOING TO BE.
I'LL JUST HAVE TO ACCEPT IT.
HUUUH?! WHAT THE HECK?!
THIS ISN'T THE RINKO WE KNOW! WHAT IF! WHAT IF!
SPROING
ぴょーん
WHAT IF, WHAT IF IT WON'T EVEN BE WORTH THE EFFORT TO SHOW UP IF YOU'RE NOT GOING TO WRITHE IN SHAMEFUL AGONY?!
HEH HEH.
I'M NOT SCARED OF YOU TWO ANYMORE.
YOU DON'T NEED TO SHOW UP ANYMORE!!

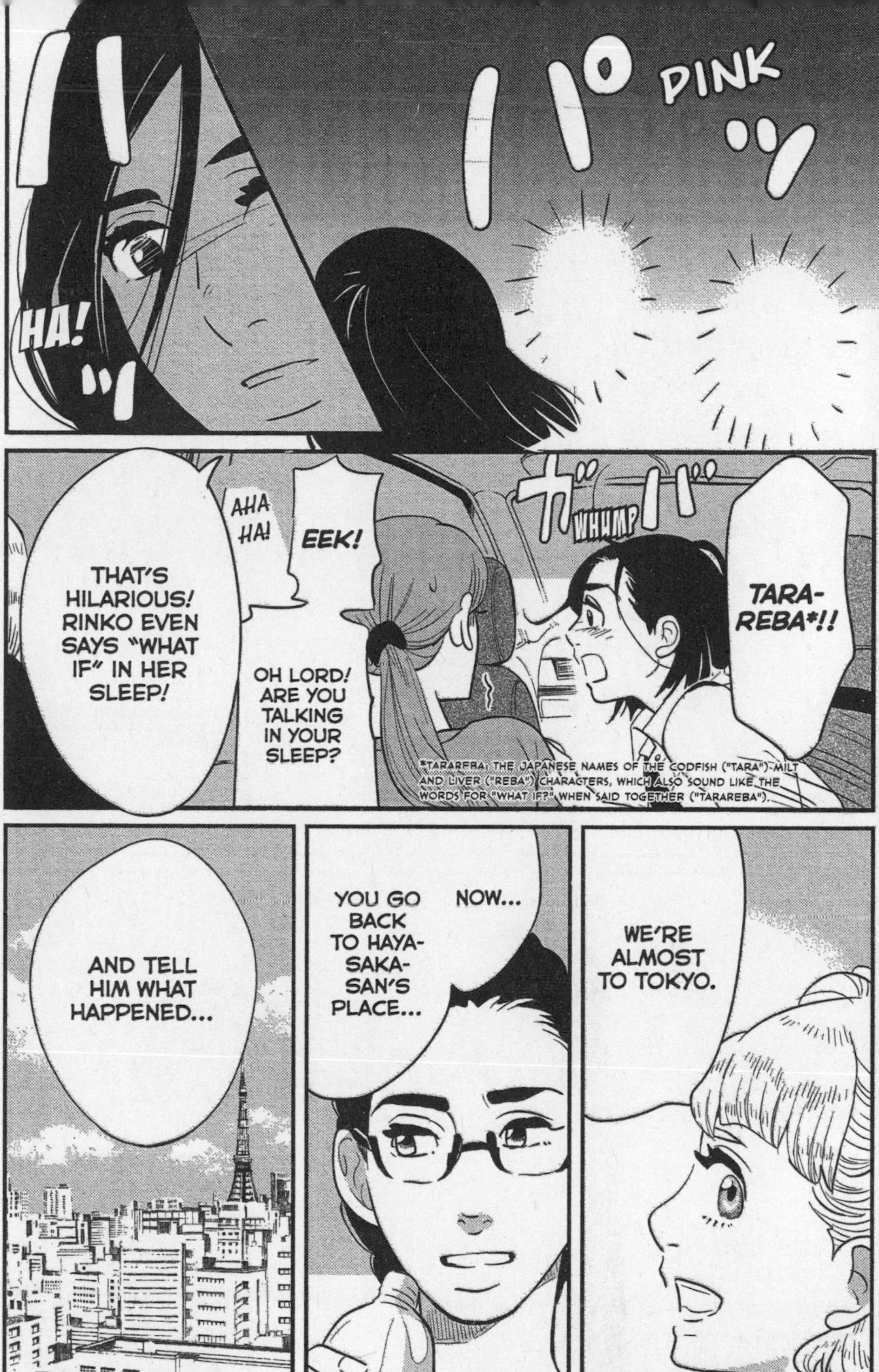
PINK
HA!
TARA-REBA*!!
WHHUMP
EEK!
OH LORD! ARE YOU TALKING IN YOUR SLEEP?
AHA HA!
THAT'S HILARIOUS! RINKO EVEN SAYS "WHAT IF" IN HER SLEEP!
*TARAREBA: THE JAPANESE NAMES OF THE CODFISH ("TARA")-MILT AND LIVER ("REBA") CHARACTERS, WHICH ALSO SOUND LIKE THE WORDS FOR "WHAT IF?" WHEN SAID TOGETHER ("TARAREBA").
WE'RE ALMOST TO TOKYO.
NOW...
YOU GO BACK TO HAYA-SAKA-SAN'S PLACE...
AND TELL HIM WHAT HAPPENED...

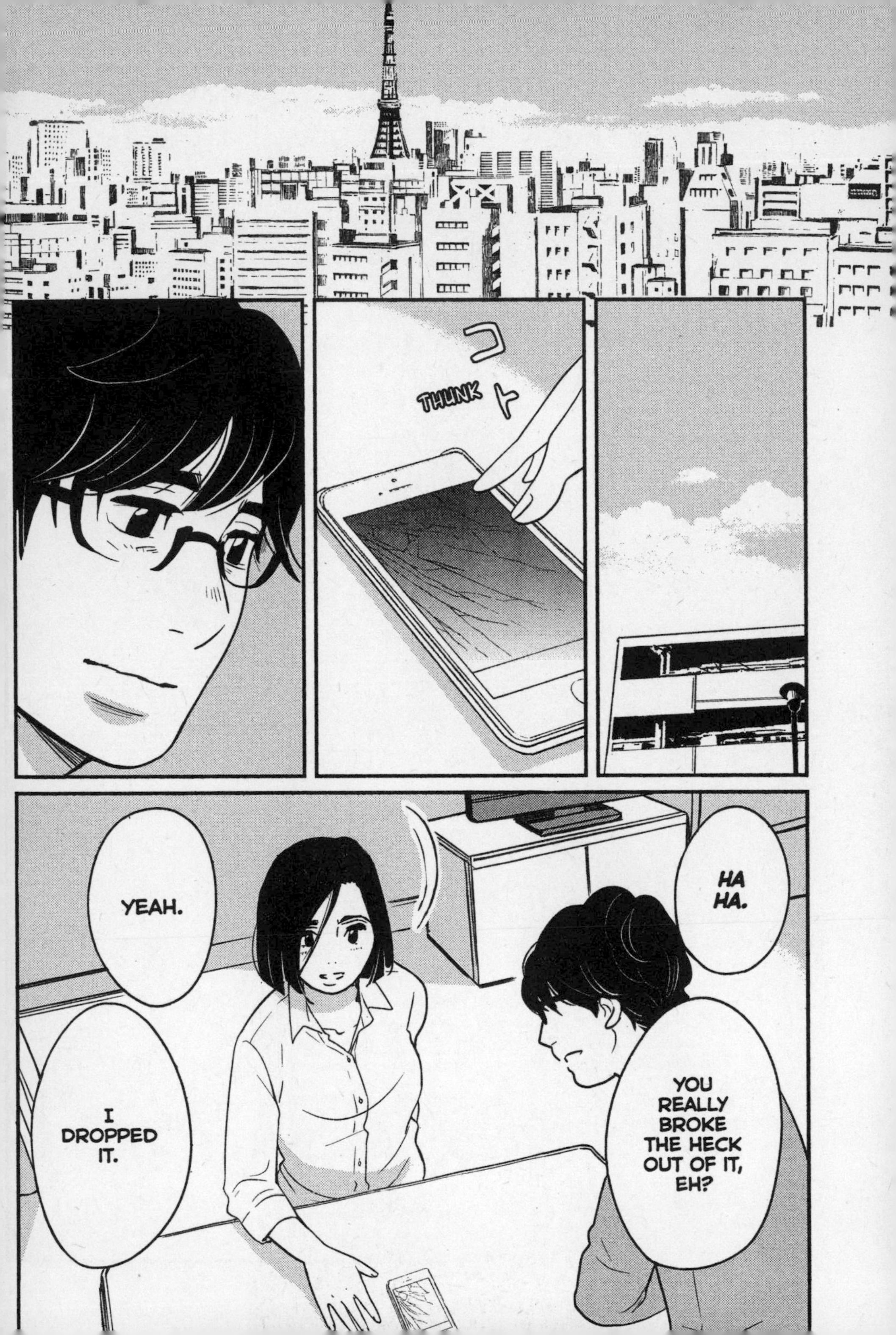
コト
THUNK
HA HA.
YOU REALLY BROKE THE HECK OUT OF IT, EH?
YEAH.
I DROPPED IT.

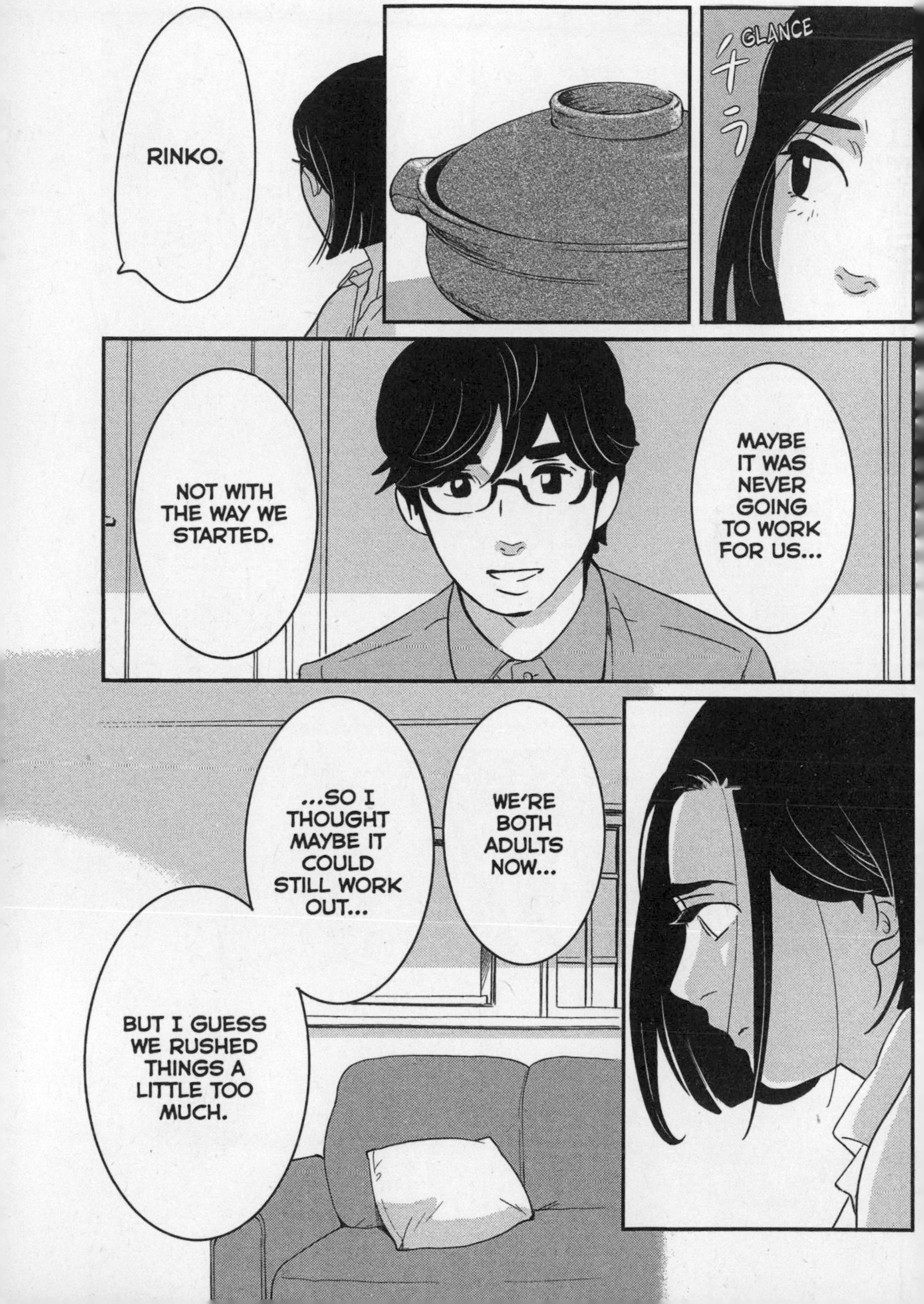
GLANCE
チラ
RINKO.
MAYBE IT WAS NEVER GOING TO WORK FOR US...
NOT WITH THE WAY WE STARTED.
WE'RE BOTH ADULTS NOW...
...SO I THOUGHT MAYBE IT COULD STILL WORK OUT...
BUT I GUESS WE RUSHED THINGS A LITTLE TOO MUCH.

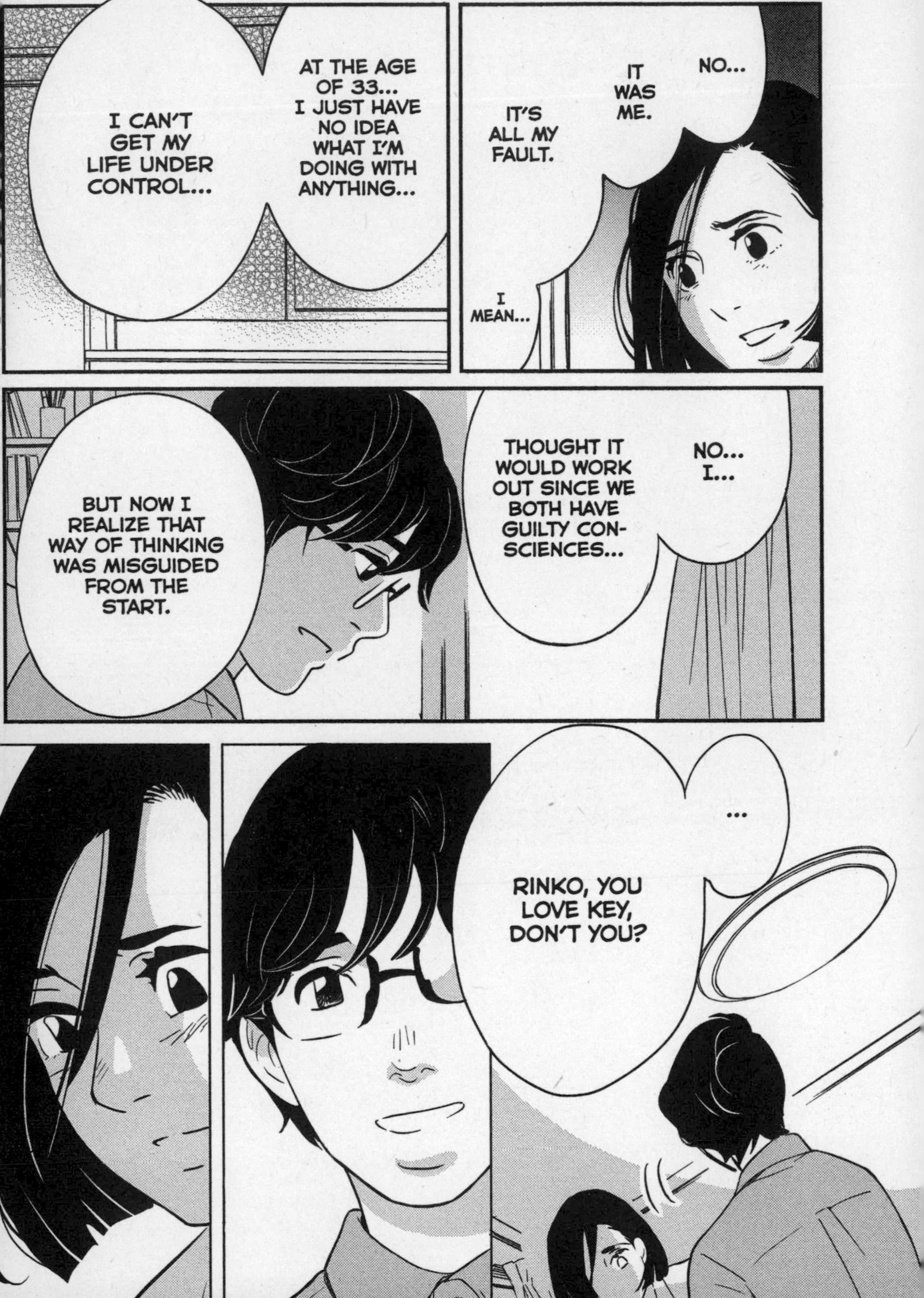
NO...
IT WAS ME.
IT'S ALL MY FAULT.
I MEAN...
AT THE AGE OF 33... I JUST HAVE NO IDEA WHAT I'M DOING WITH ANYTHING...
I CAN'T GET MY LIFE UNDER CONTROL...
NO... I...
THOUGHT IT WOULD WORK OUT SINCE WE BOTH HAVE GUILTY CON-SCIENCES...
BUT NOW I REALIZE THAT WAY OF THINKING WAS MISGUIDED FROM THE START.
...
RINKO, YOU LOVE KEY, DON'T YOU?

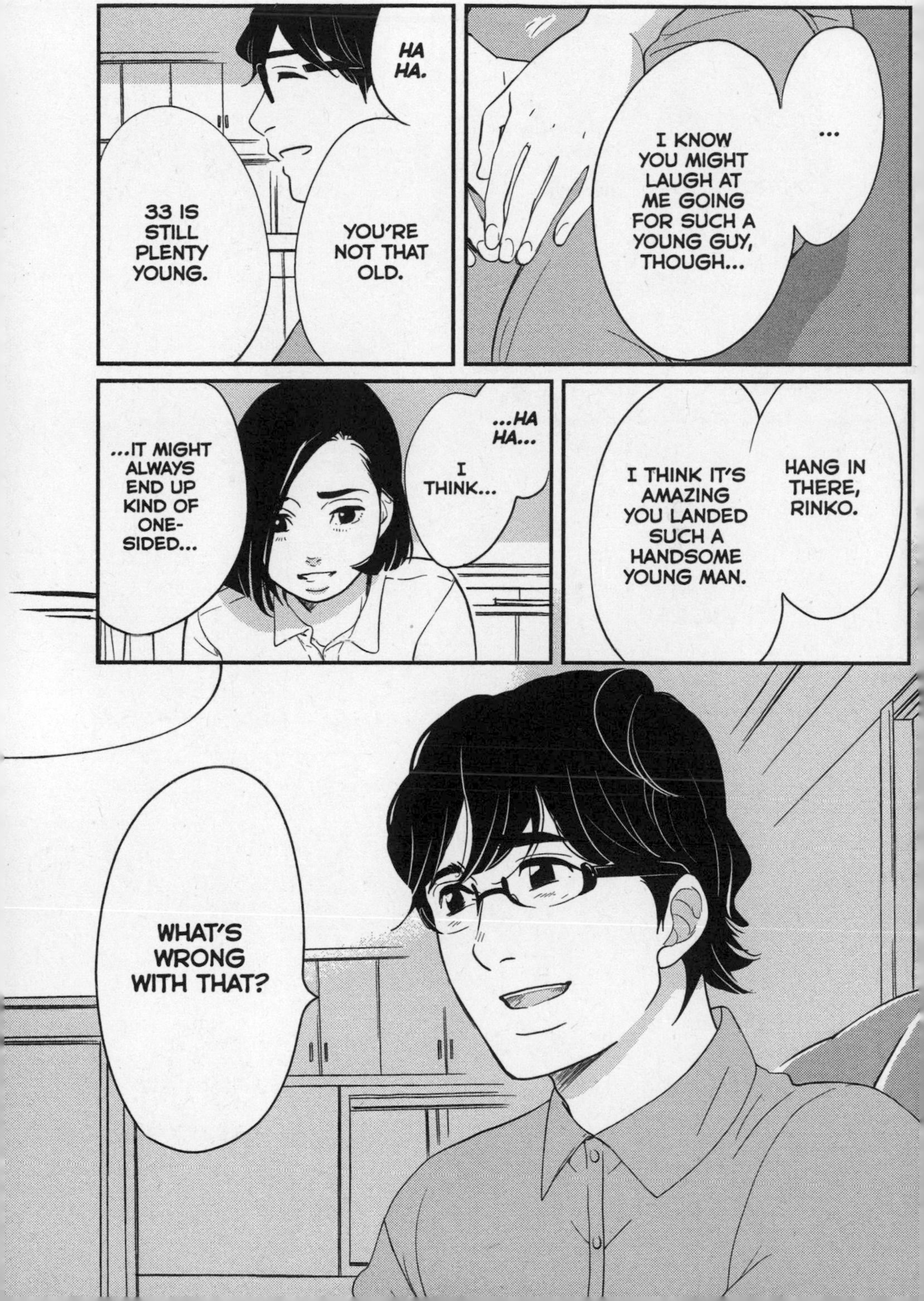
...
I KNOW YOU MIGHT LAUGH AT ME GOING FOR SUCH A YOUNG GUY, THOUGH...
HA HA.
YOU'RE NOT THAT OLD.
33 IS STILL PLENTY YOUNG.
HANG IN THERE, RINKO.
I THINK IT'S AMAZING YOU LANDED SUCH A HANDSOME YOUNG MAN.
...HA HA...
I THINK...
...IT MIGHT ALWAYS END UP KIND OF ONE-SIDED...
WHAT'S WRONG WITH THAT?

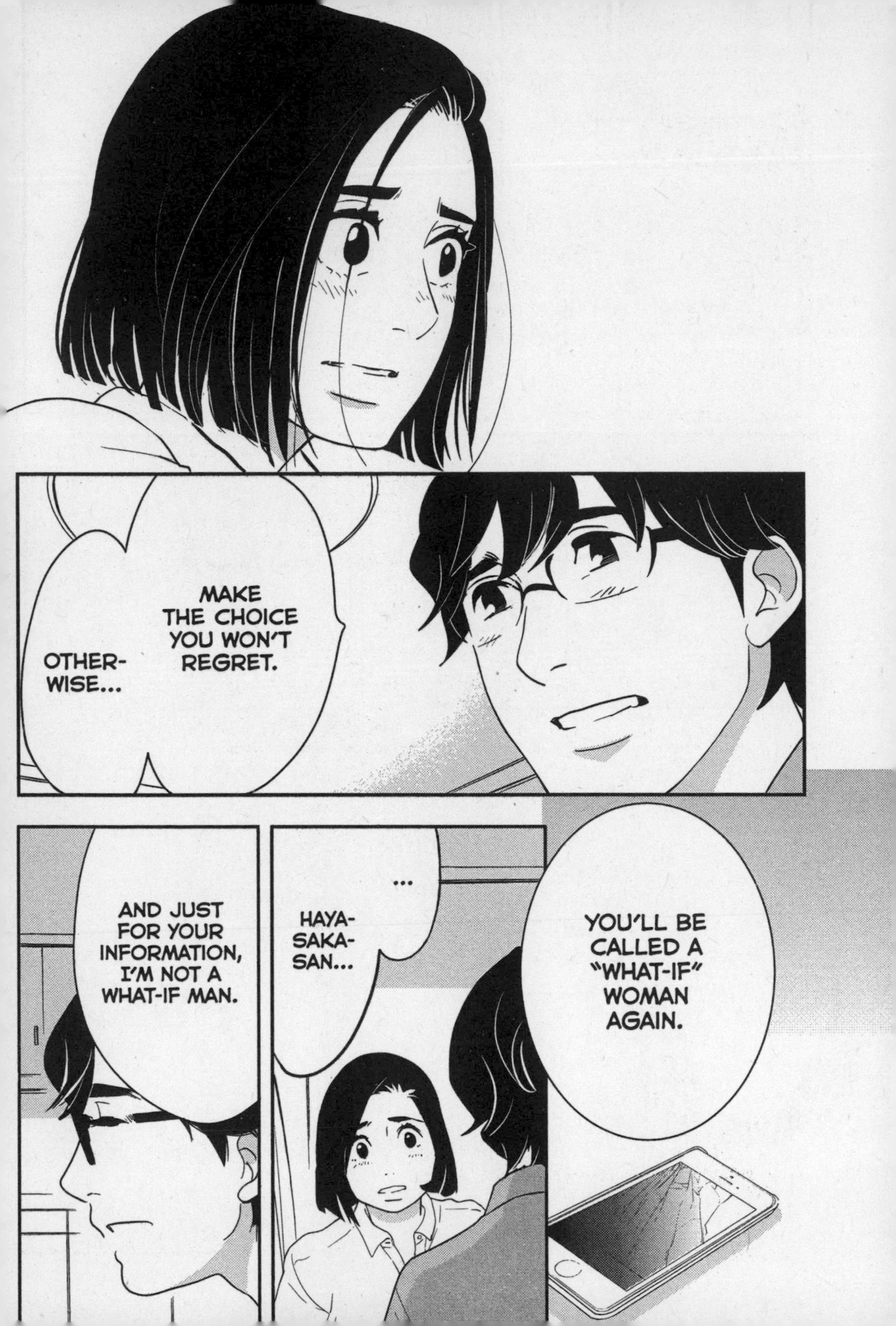
MAKE THE CHOICE YOU WON'T REGRET.
OTHER-WISE...
YOU'LL BE CALLED A "WHAT-IF" WOMAN AGAIN.
...
HAYA-SAKA-SAN...
AND JUST FOR YOUR INFORMATION, I'M NOT A WHAT-IF MAN.

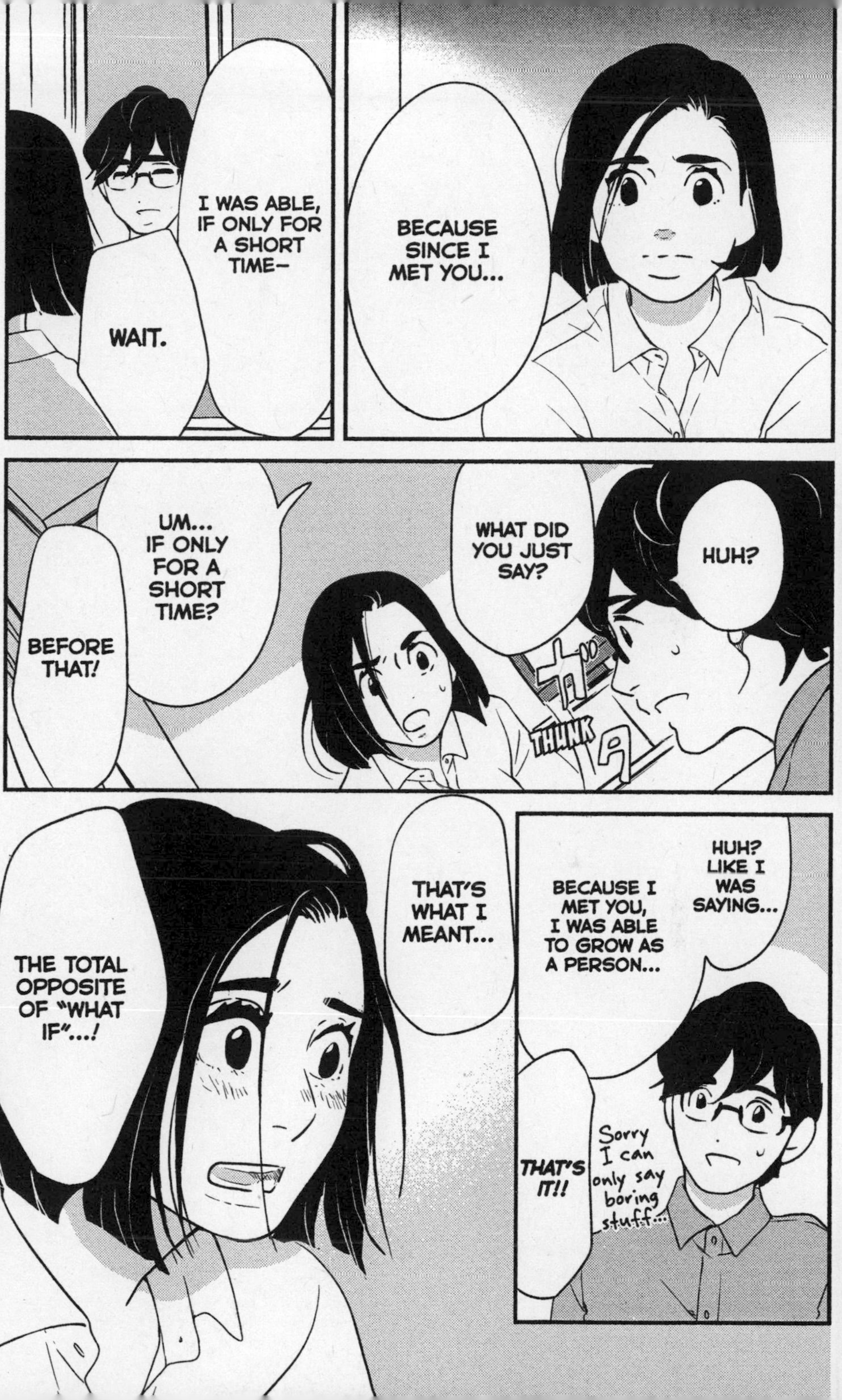
BECAUSE SINCE I MET YOU...
I WAS ABLE, IF ONLY FOR A SHORT TIME—
WAIT.
HUH?
WHAT DID YOU JUST SAY?
THUNK
UM... IF ONLY FOR A SHORT TIME?
BEFORE THAT!
HUH? LIKE I WAS SAYING...
BECAUSE I MET YOU, I WAS ABLE TO GROW AS A PERSON...
Sorry I can only say boring stuff...
THAT'S IT!!
THAT'S WHAT I MEANT...
THE TOTAL OPPOSITE OF "WHAT IF"...!

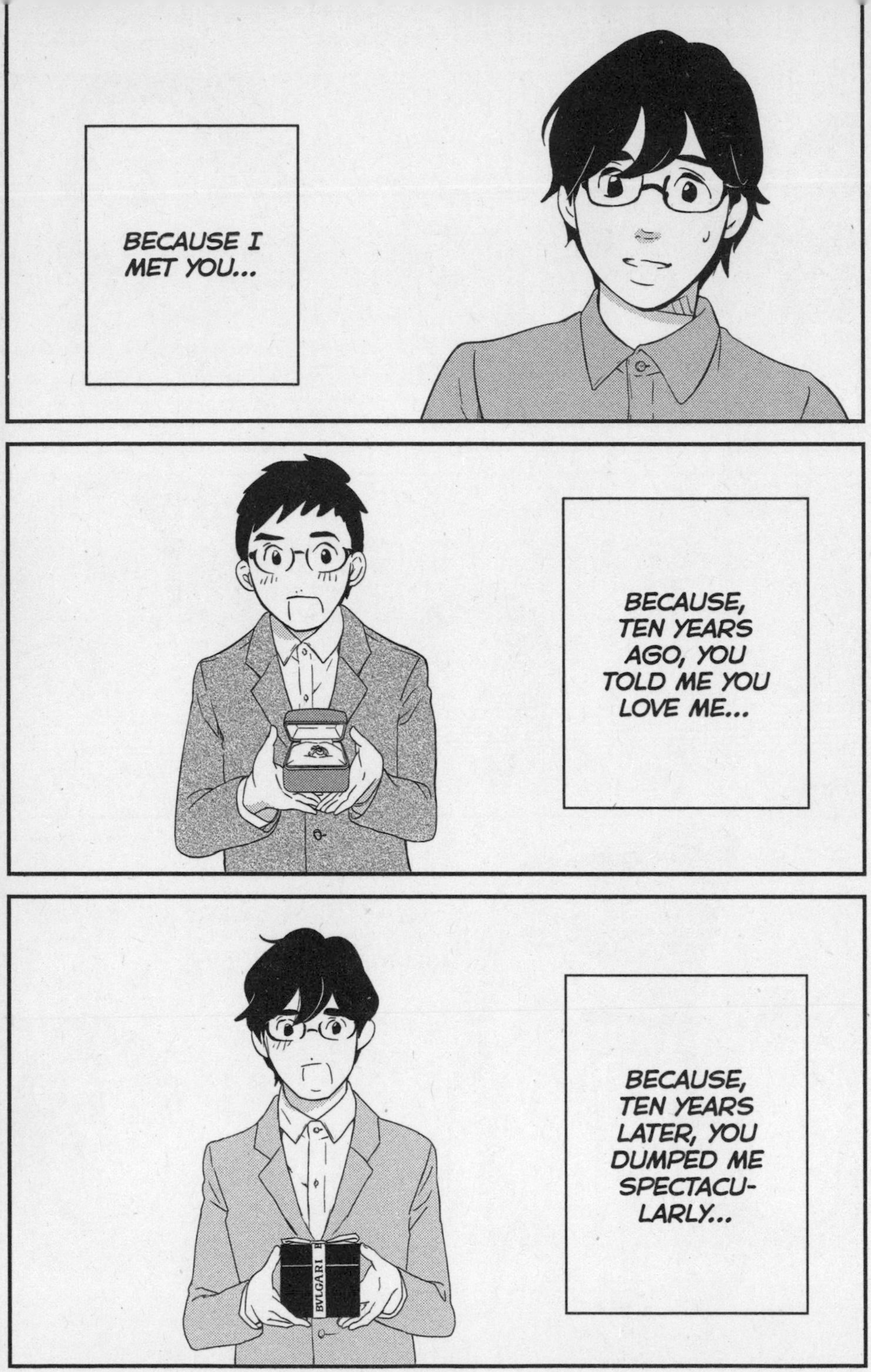
BECAUSE I MET YOU...
BECAUSE, TEN YEARS AGO, YOU TOLD ME YOU LOVE ME...
BECAUSE, TEN YEARS LATER, YOU DUMPED ME SPECTACU-LARLY...
BVLGARI

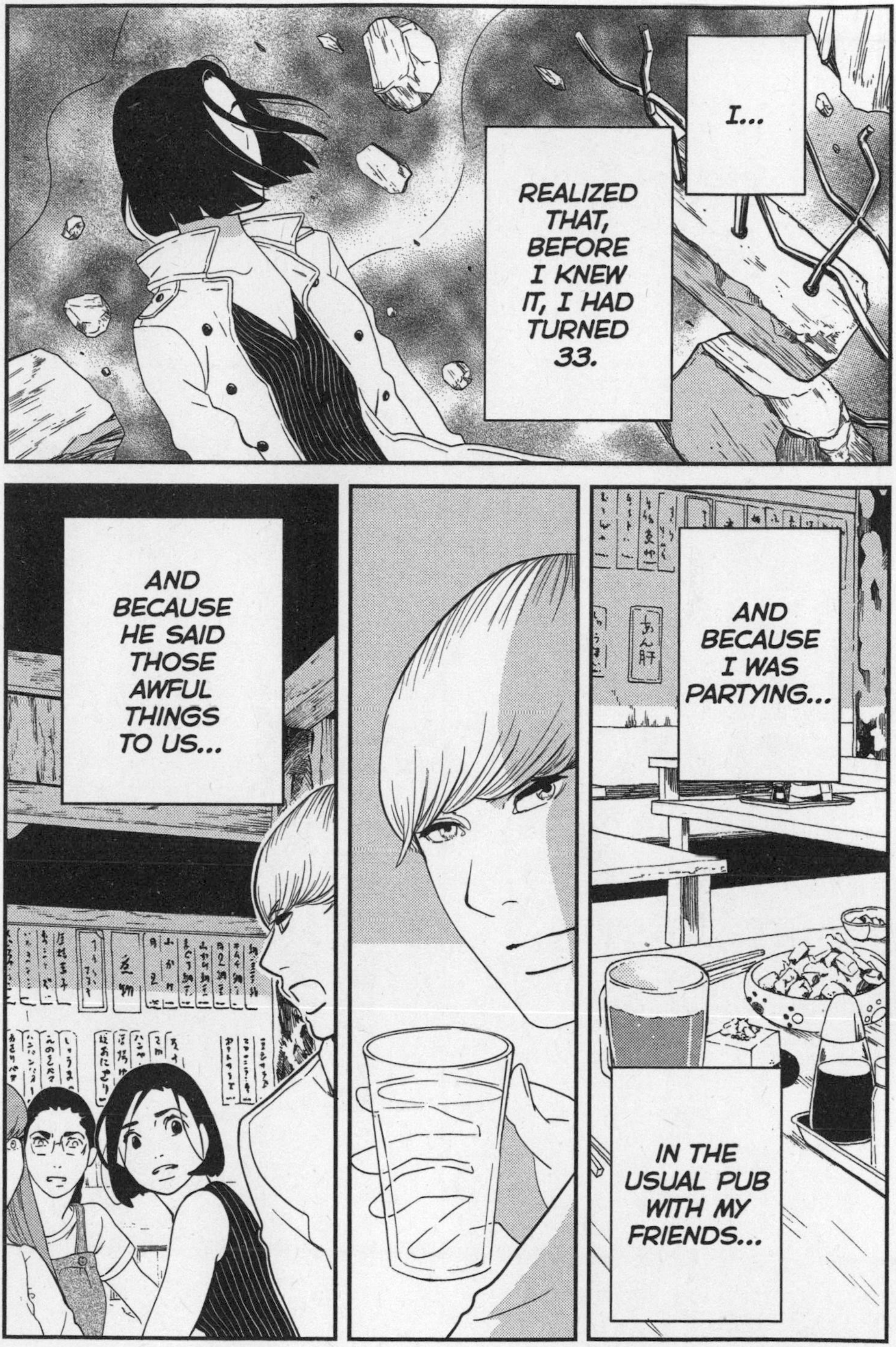
I...
REALIZED THAT, BEFORE I KNEW IT, I HAD TURNED 33.
AND BECAUSE I WAS PARTYING...
IN THE USUAL PUB WITH MY FRIENDS...
AND BECAUSE HE SAID THOSE AWFUL THINGS TO US...

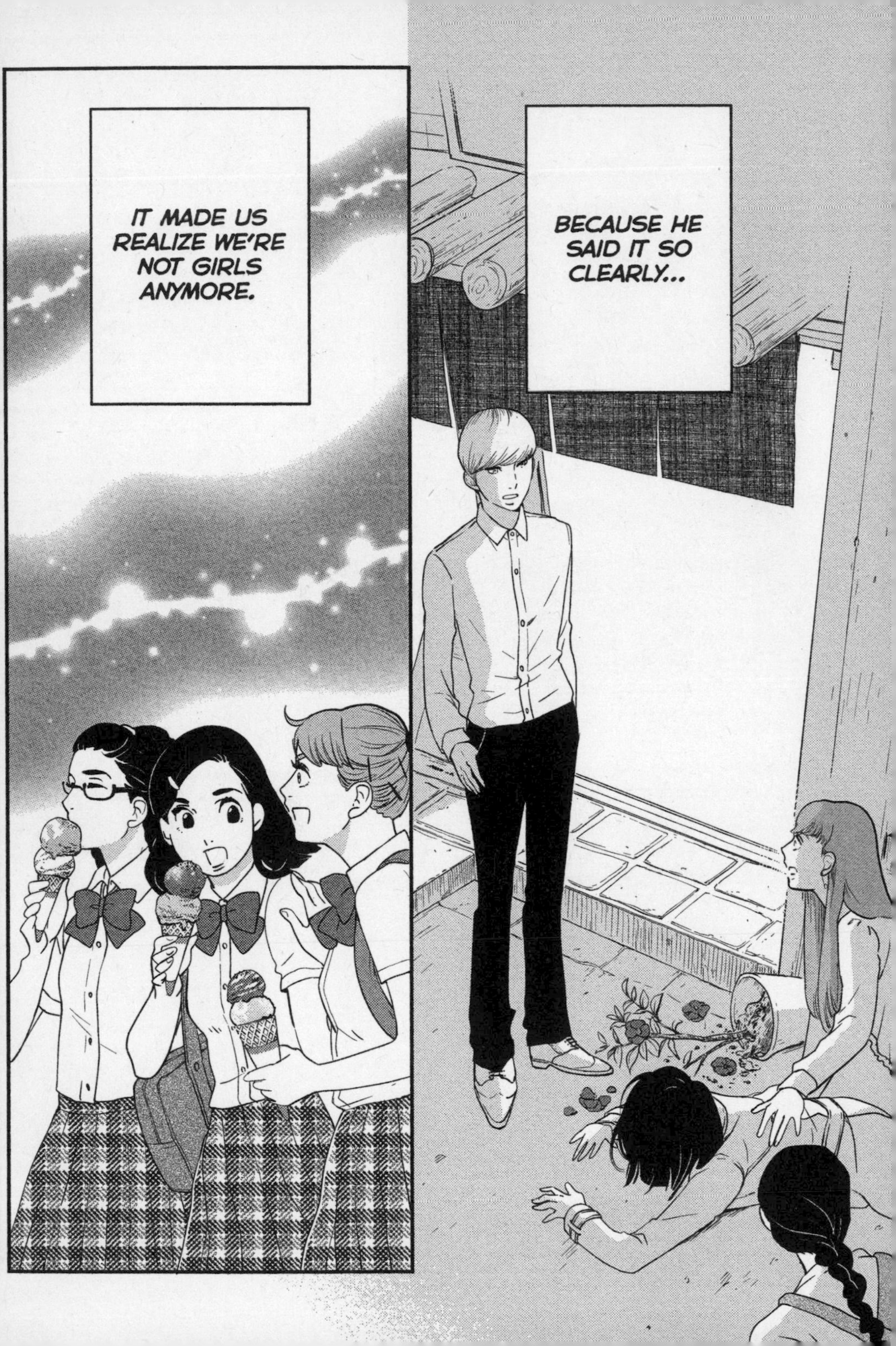
BECAUSE HE SAID IT SO CLEARLY...
IT MADE US REALIZE WE'RE NOT GIRLS ANYMORE.

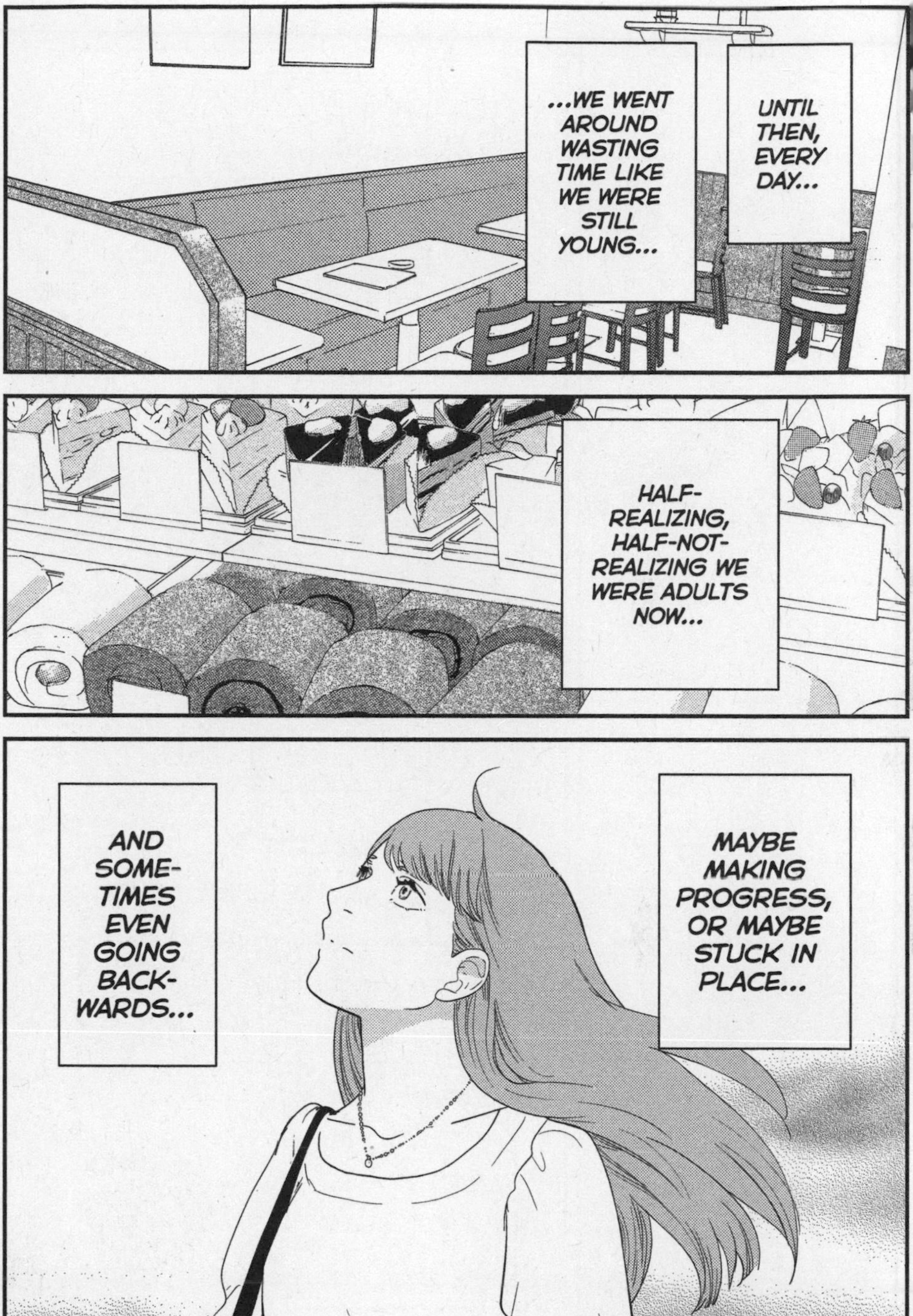
UNTIL THEN, EVERY DAY...
...WE WENT AROUND WASTING TIME LIKE WE WERE STILL YOUNG...
HALF-REALIZING, HALF-NOT-REALIZING WE WERE ADULTS NOW...
MAYBE MAKING PROGRESS, OR MAYBE STUCK IN PLACE...
AND SOMETIMES EVEN GOING BACKWARDS...

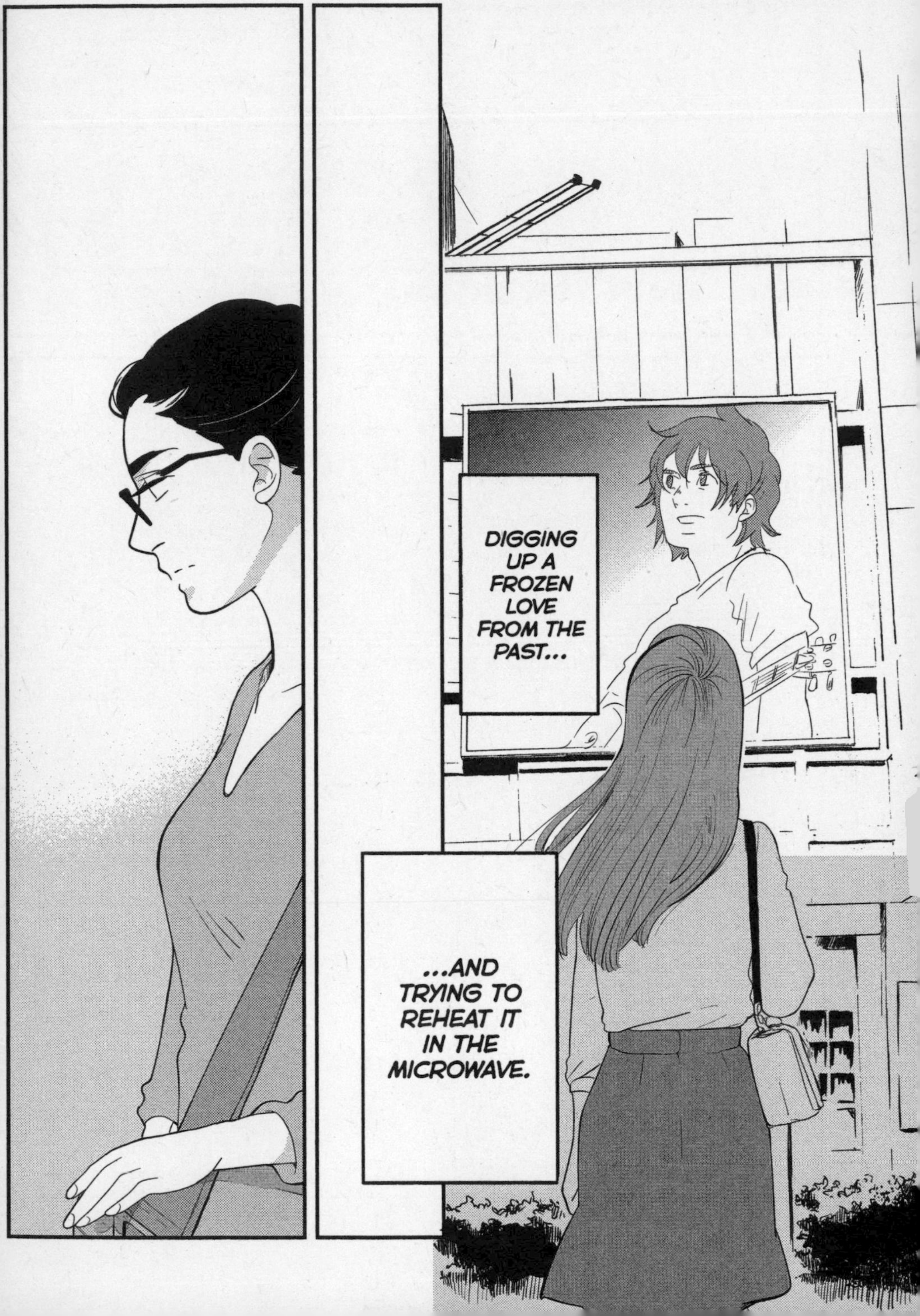
DIGGING UP A FROZEN LOVE FROM THE PAST...
...AND TRYING TO REHEAT IT IN THE MICROWAVE.

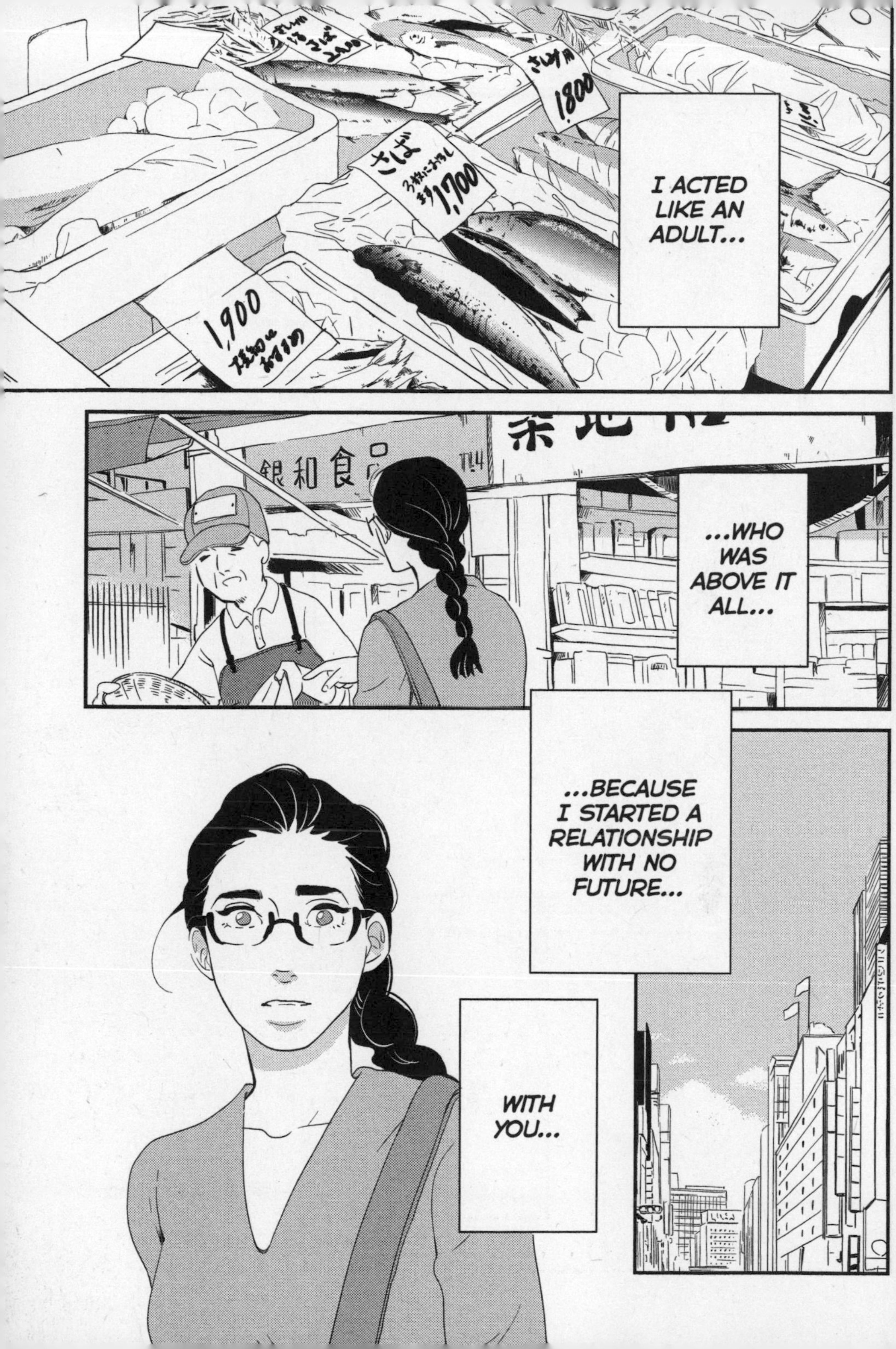
I ACTED LIKE AN ADULT...
...WHO WAS ABOVE IT ALL...
...BECAUSE I STARTED A RELATIONSHIP WITH NO FUTURE...
WITH YOU...

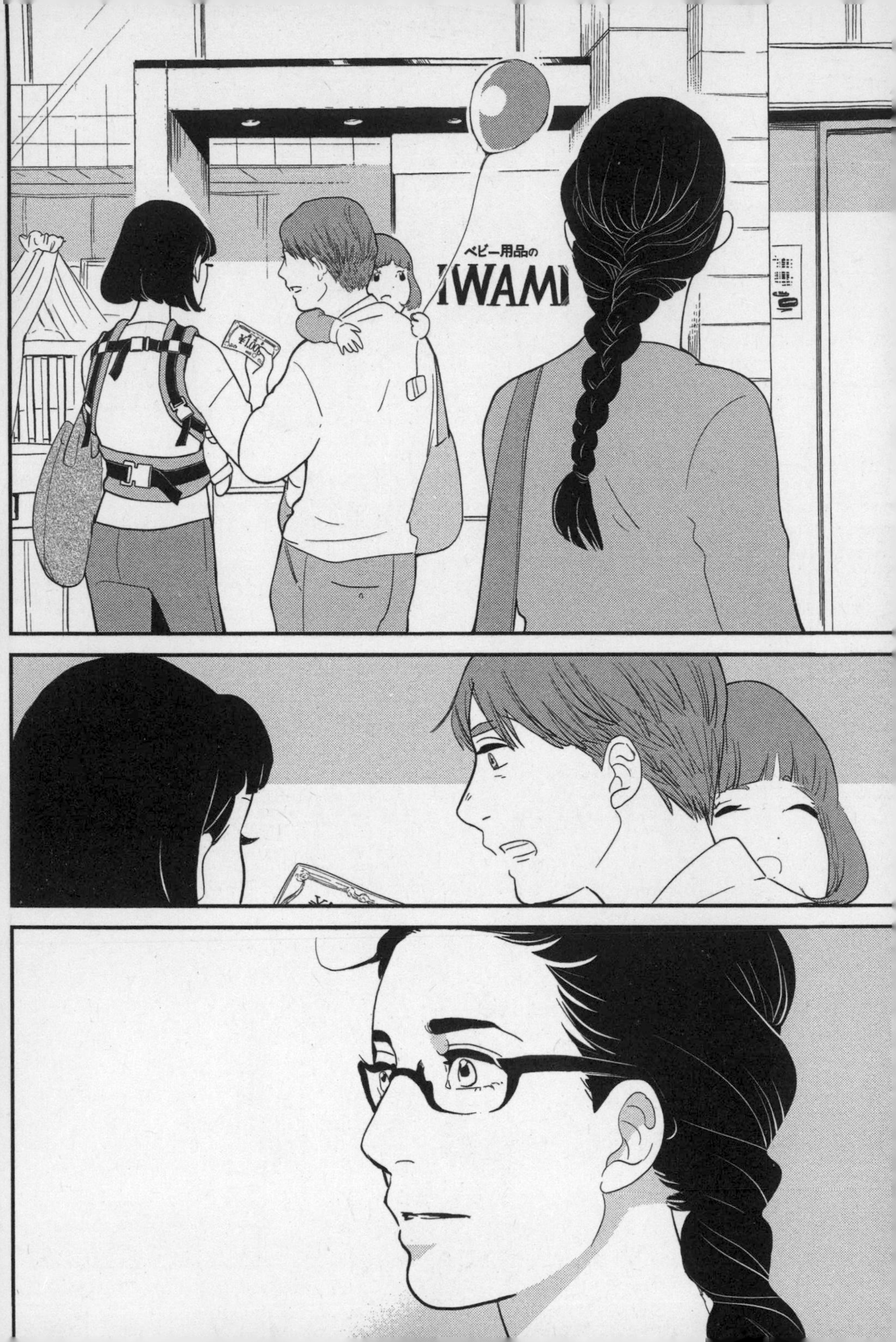
ベビー用品の
IWAMI

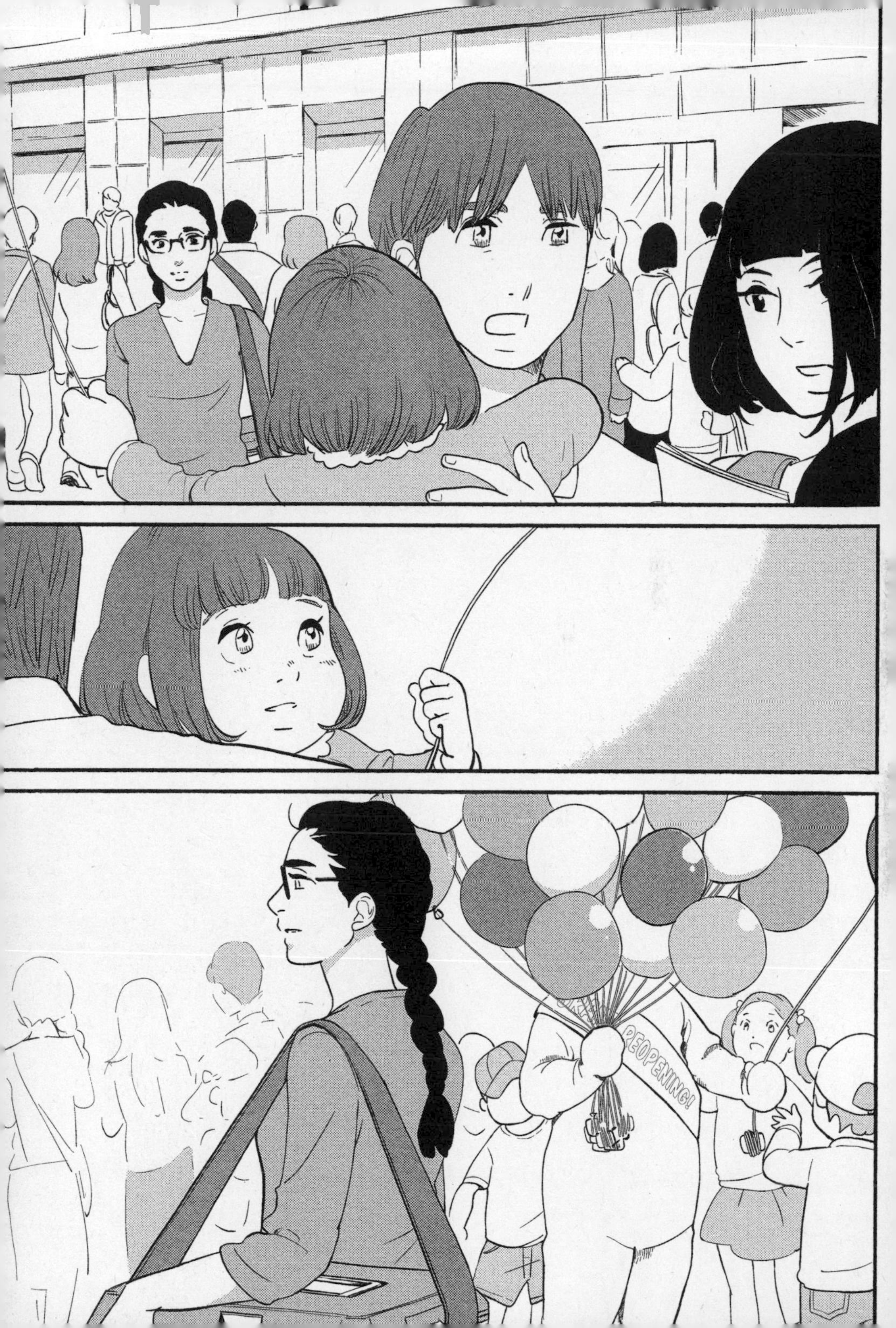
REOPENING!

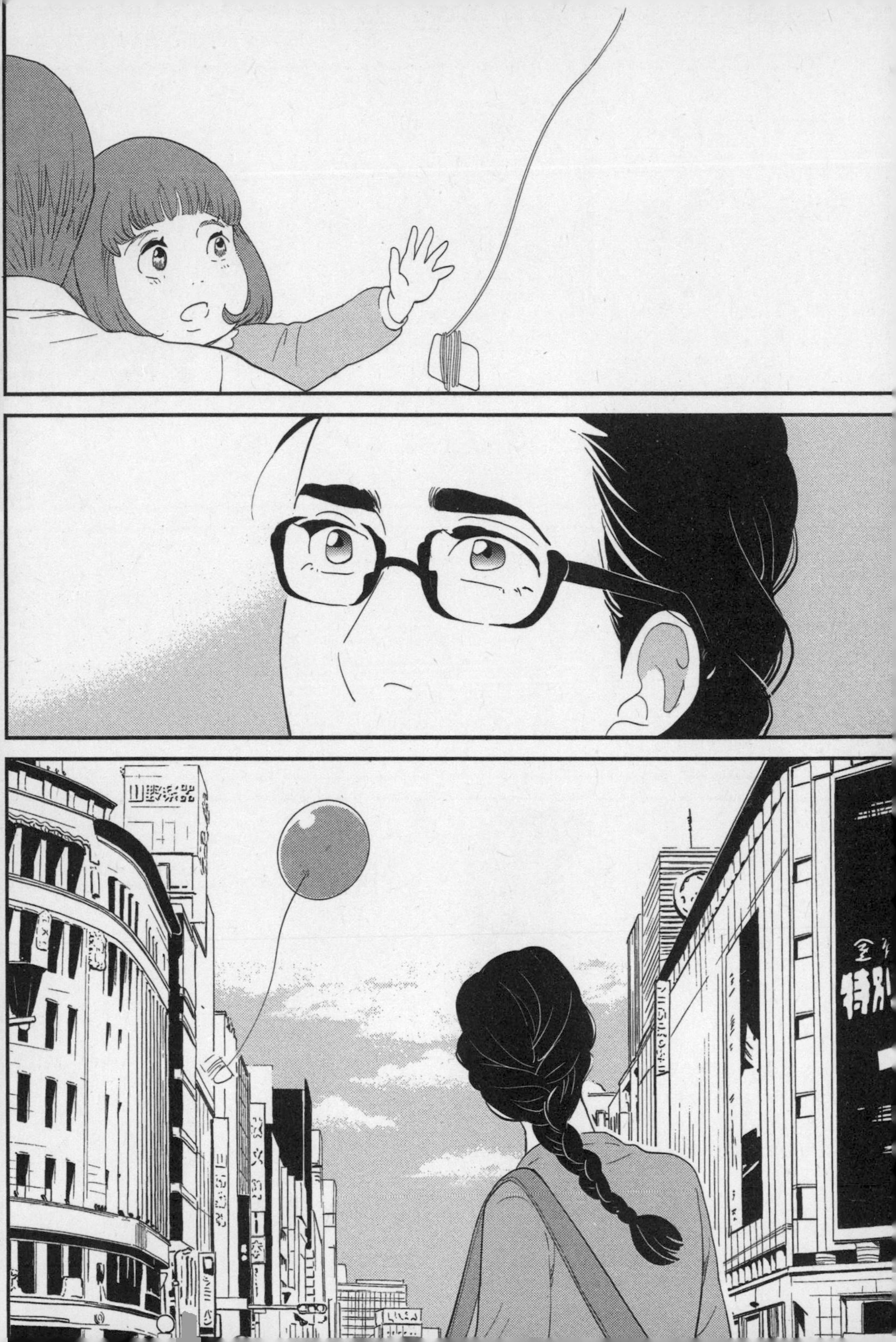
山野楽器
特別

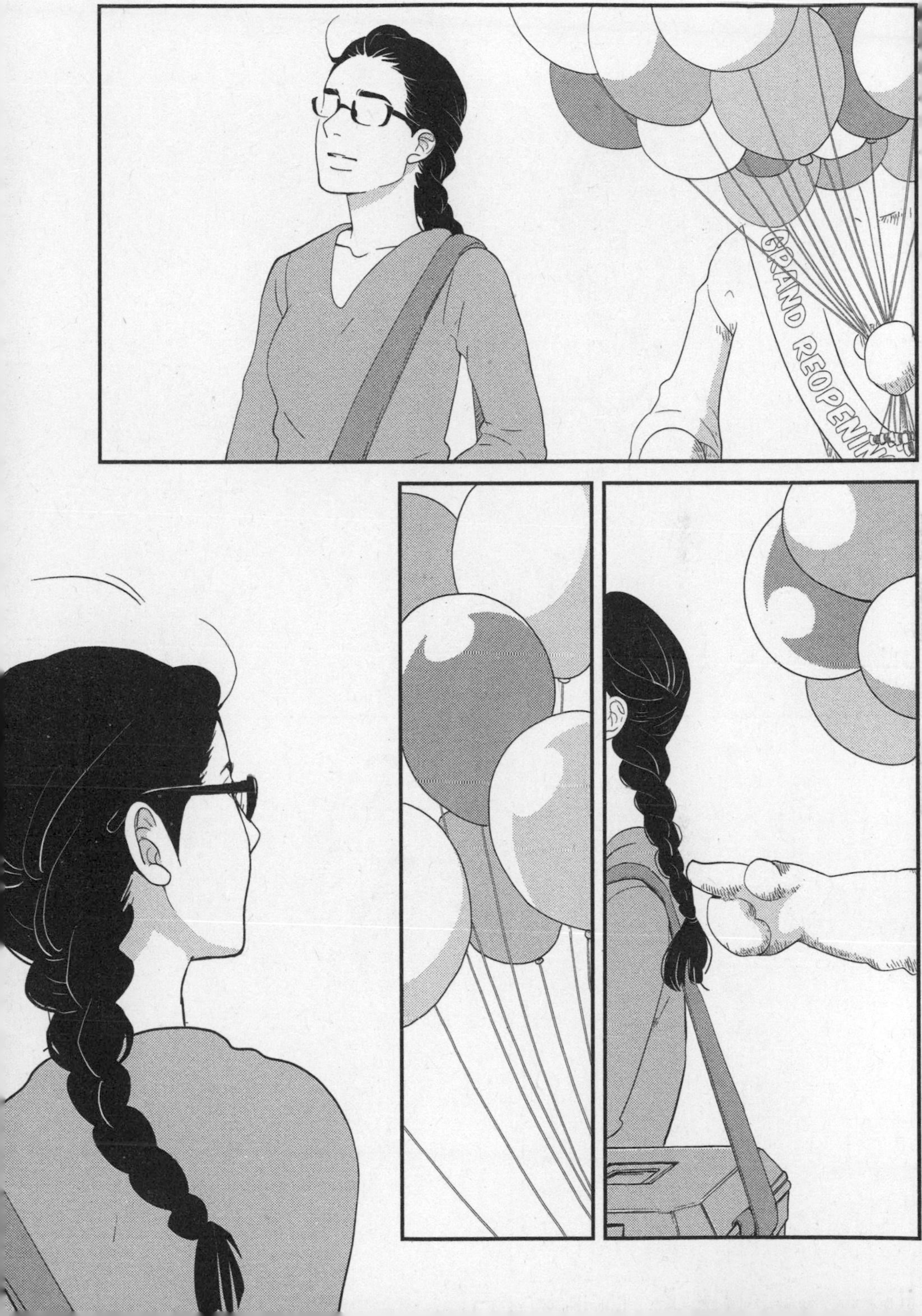
GRAND REOPENIN

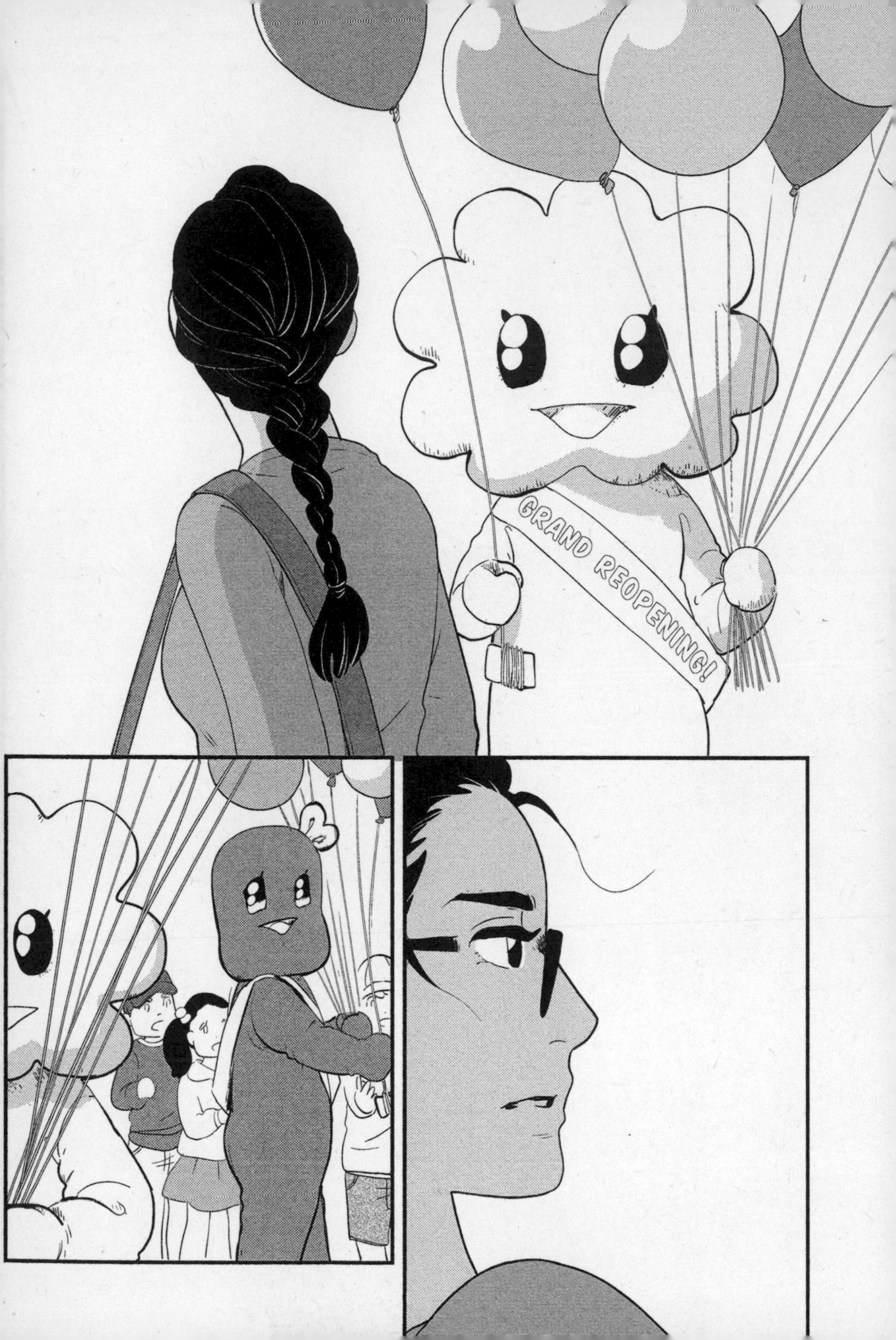
GRAND REOPENING!

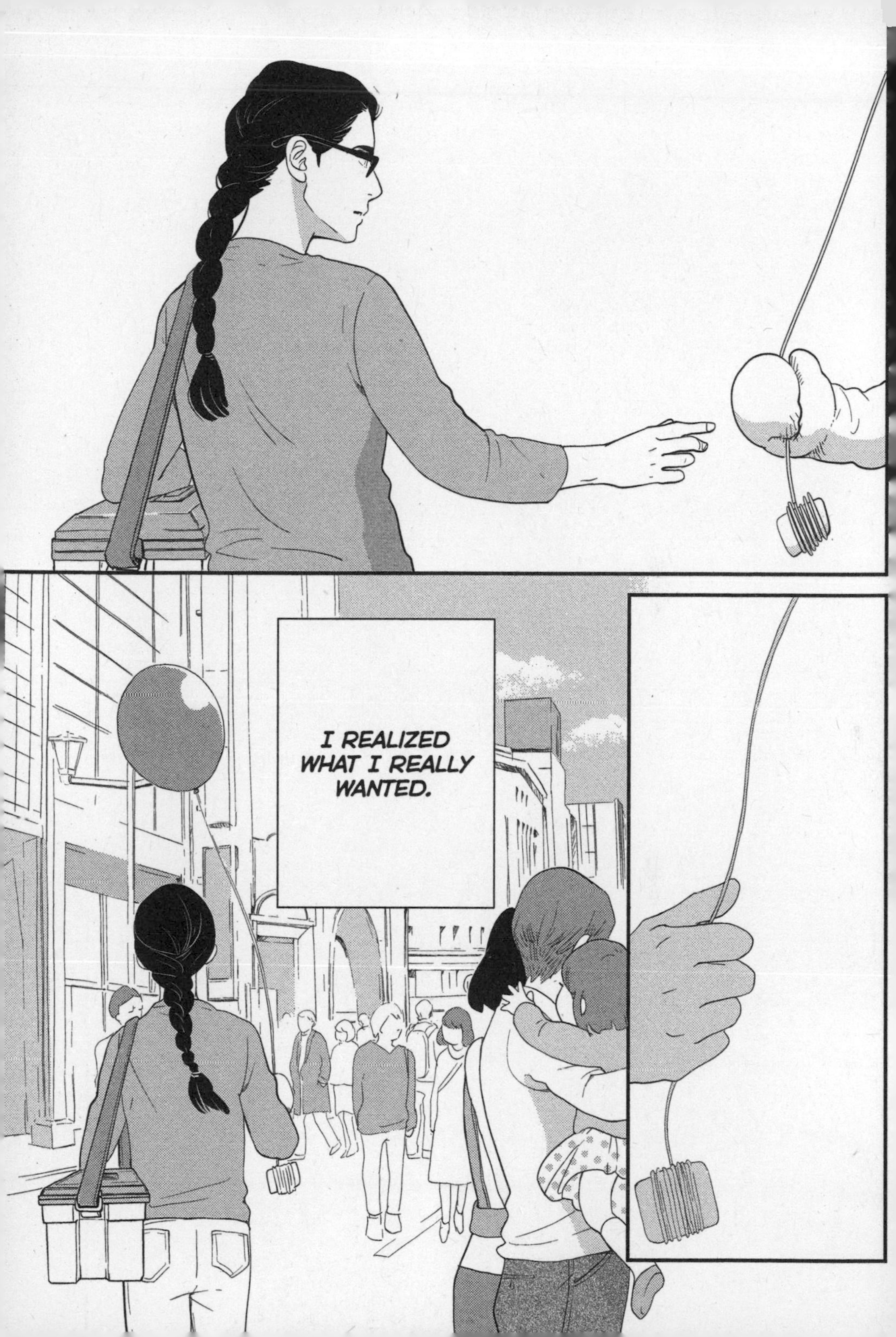
I REALIZED WHAT I REALLY WANTED.

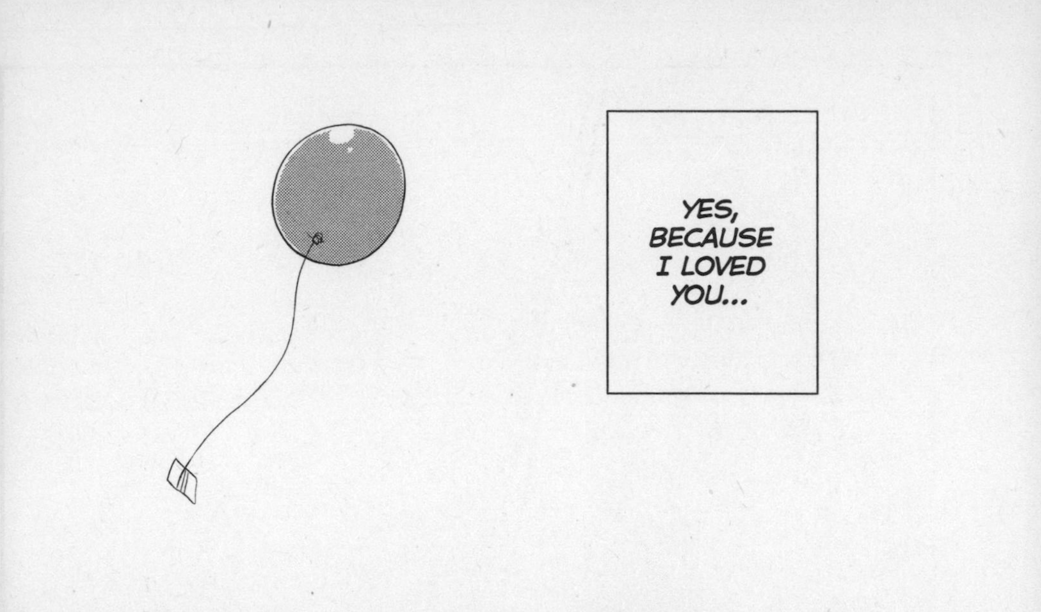
YES, BECAUSE I LOVED YOU...
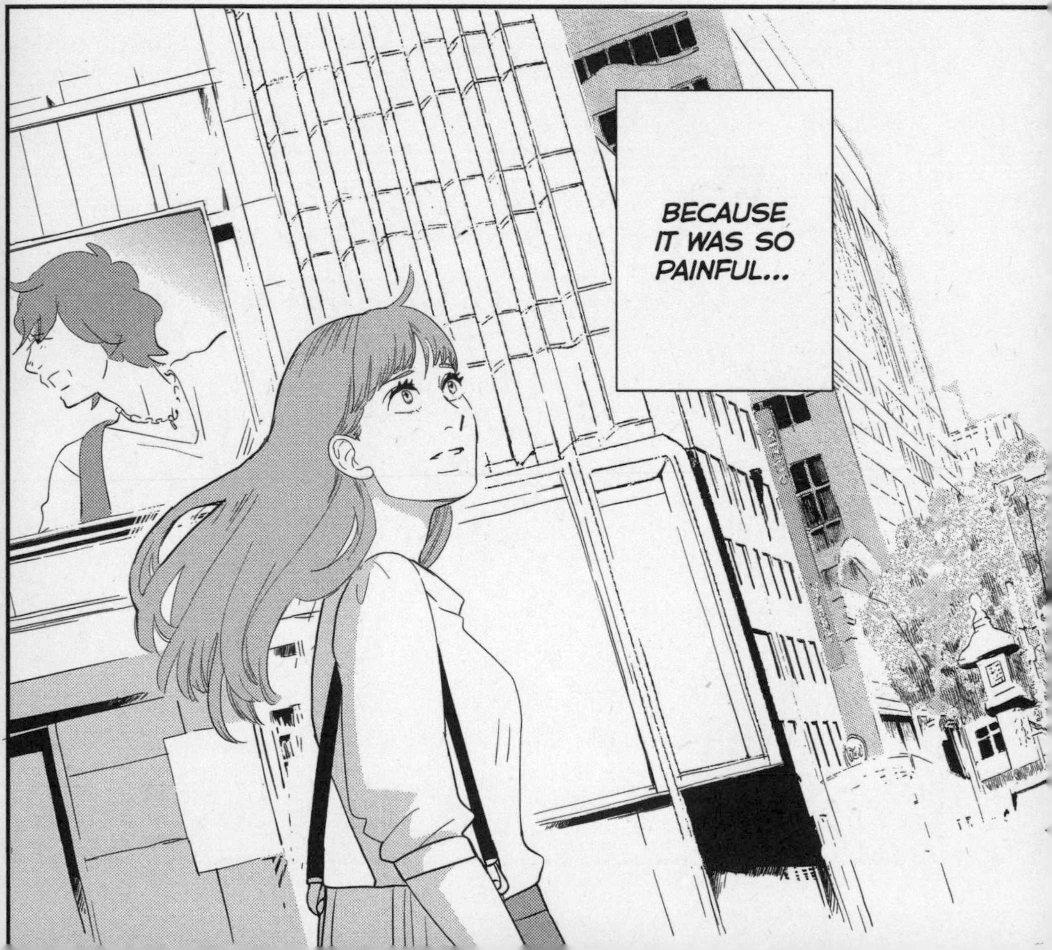
BECAUSE IT WAS SO PAINFUL...

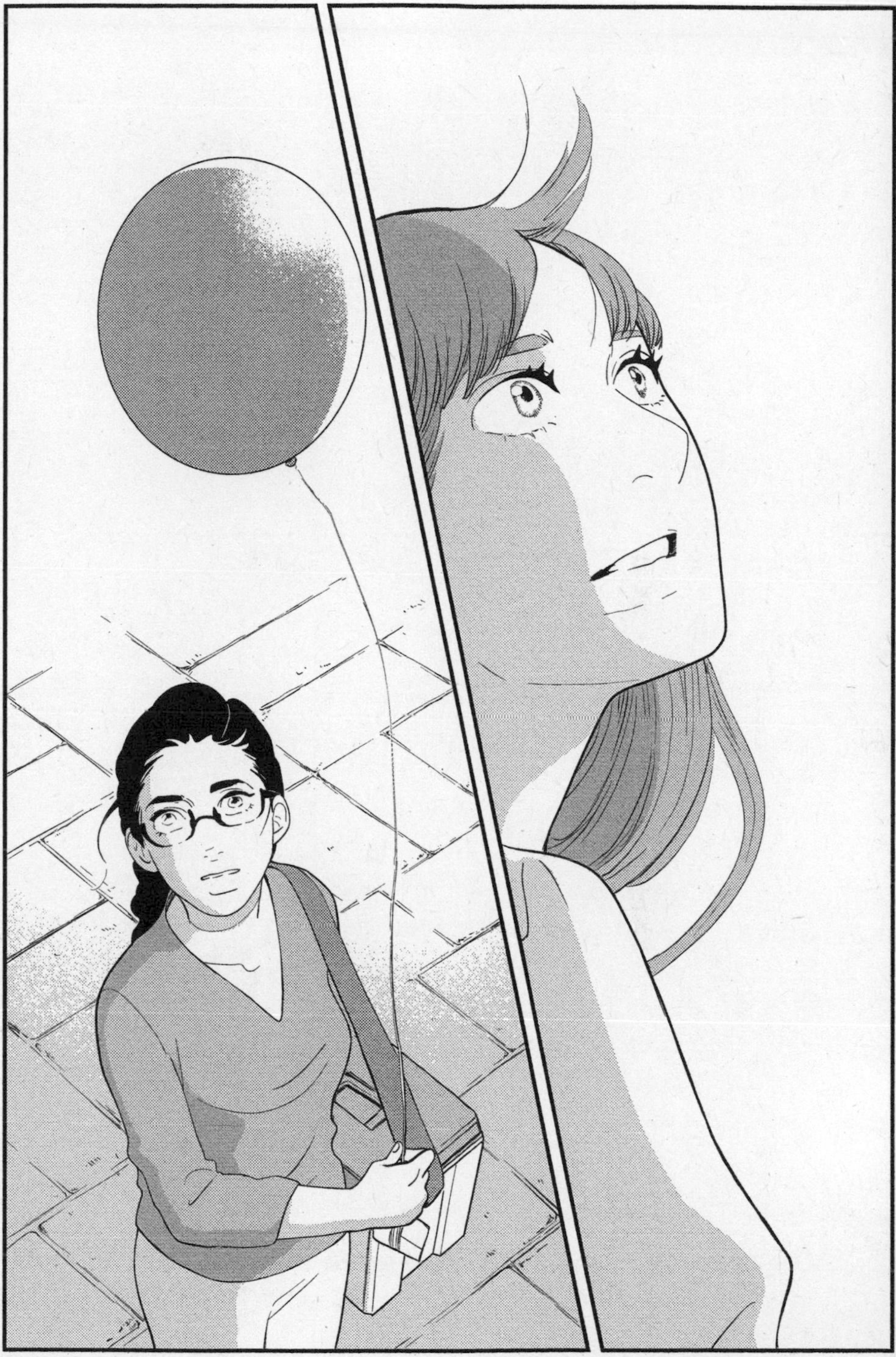

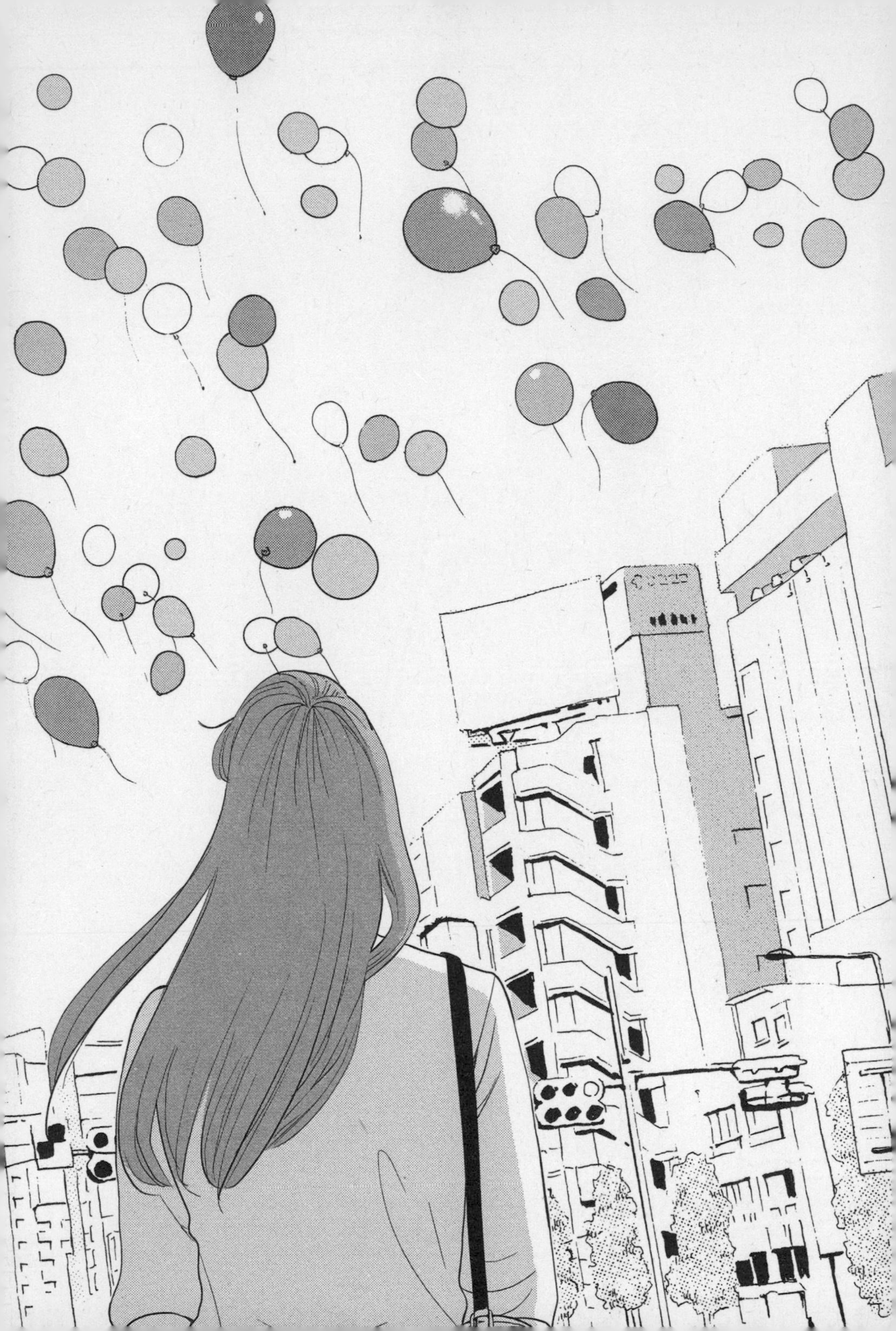

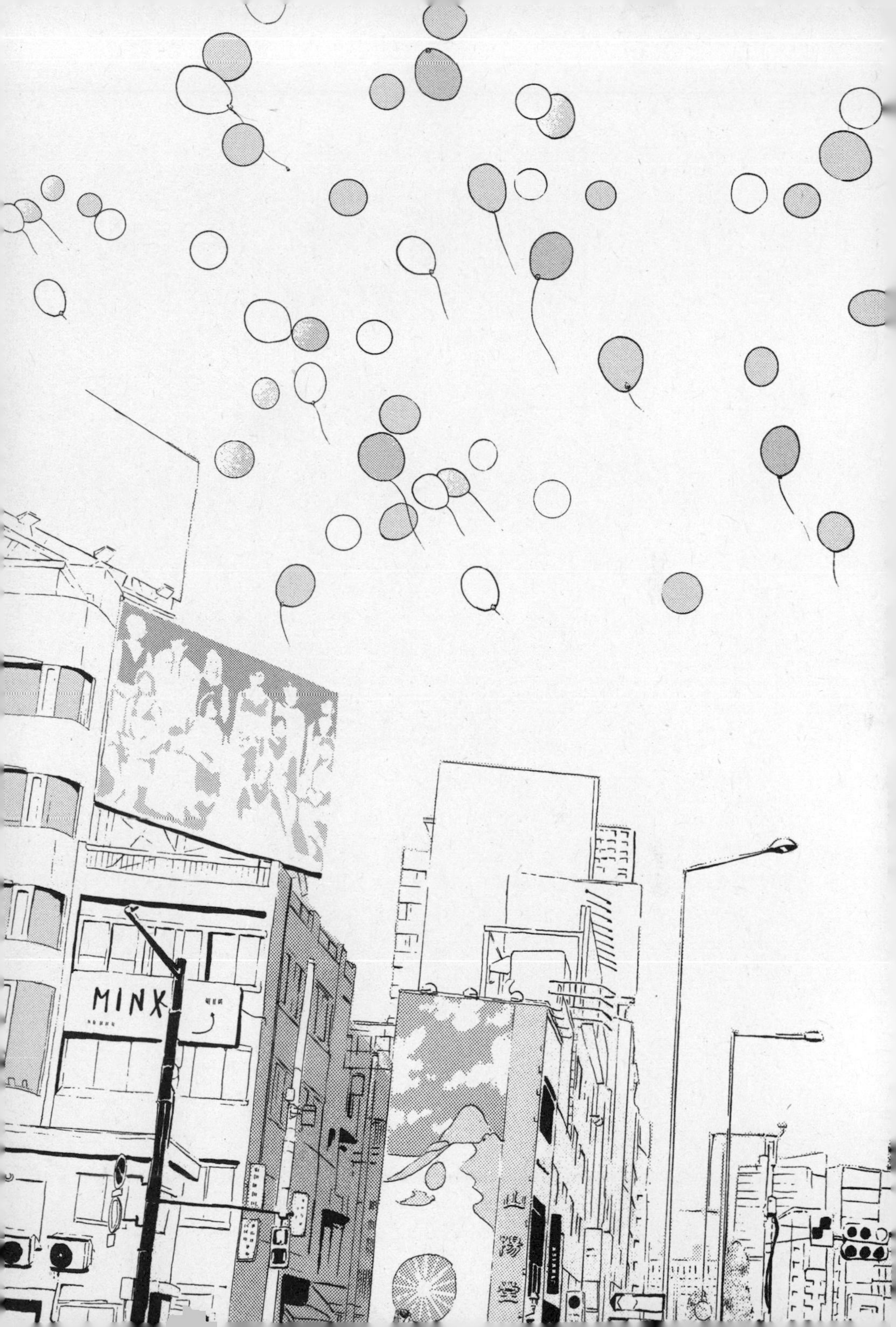
MINX

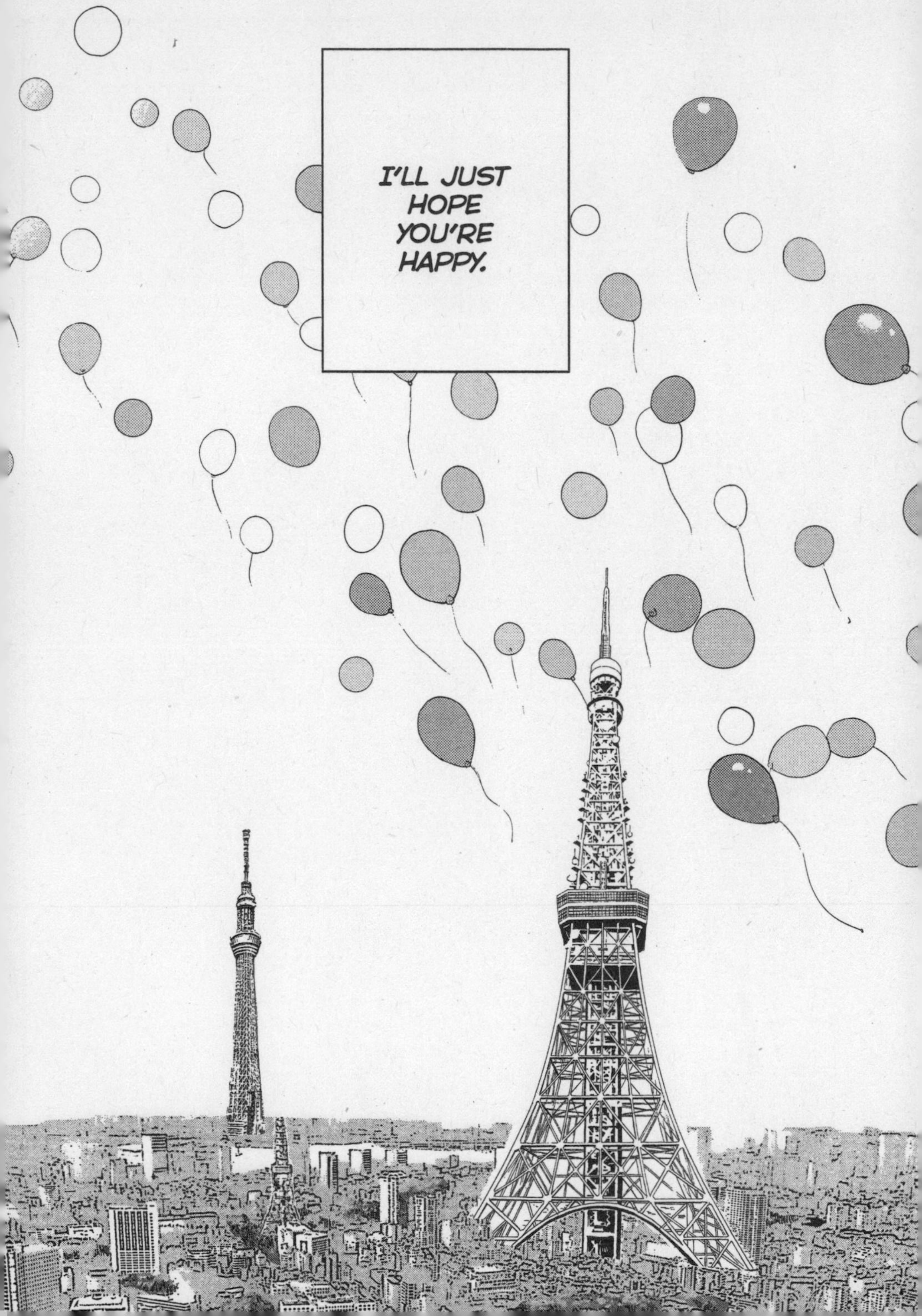
I'LL JUST HOPE YOU'RE HAPPY.

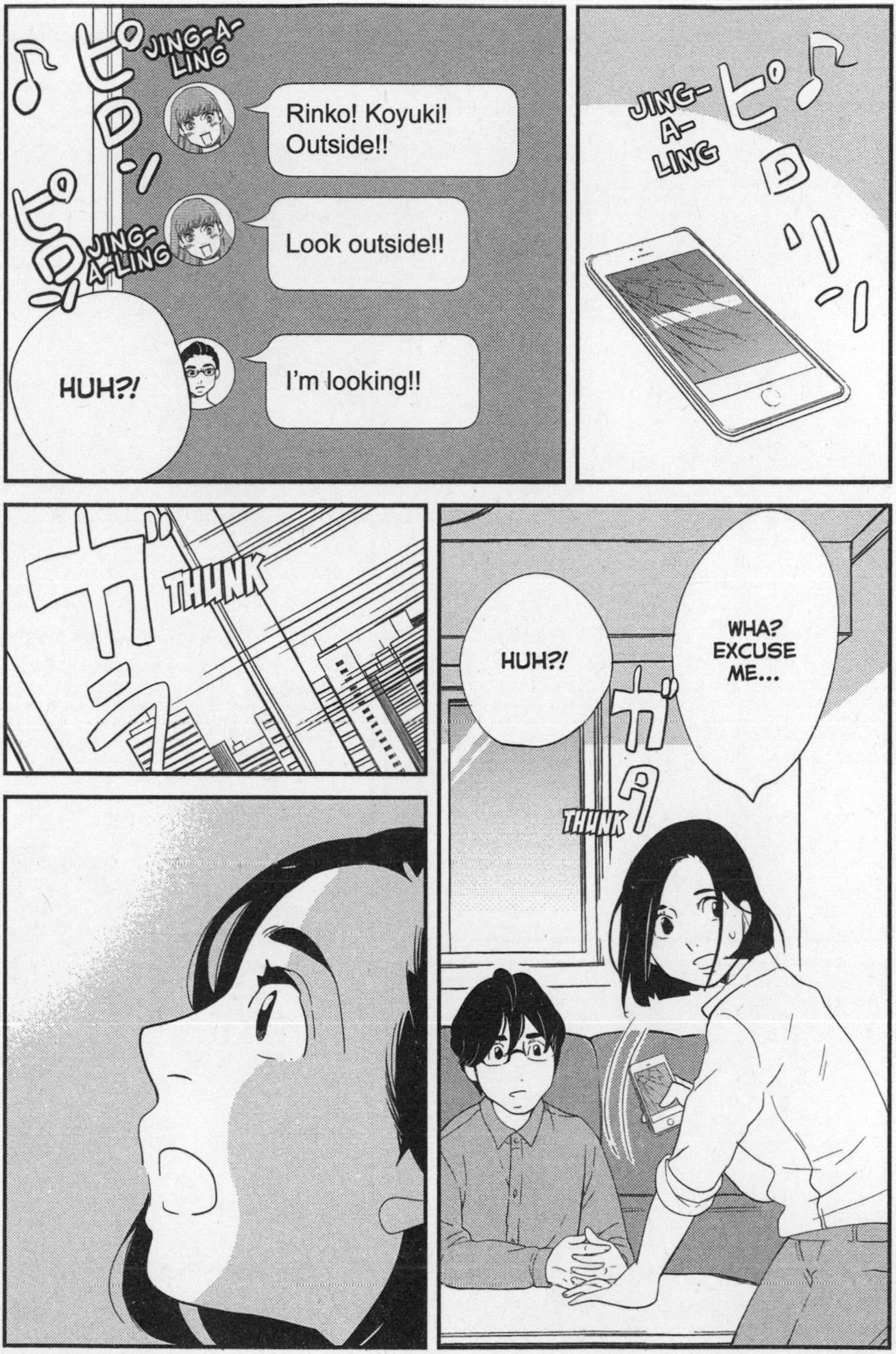
JING-A-LING
JING-A-LING
Rinko! Koyuki! Outside!!
JING-A-LING
Look outside!!
I'm looking!!
HUH?!
WHA? EXCUSE ME...
HUH?!
THUNK
THUNK

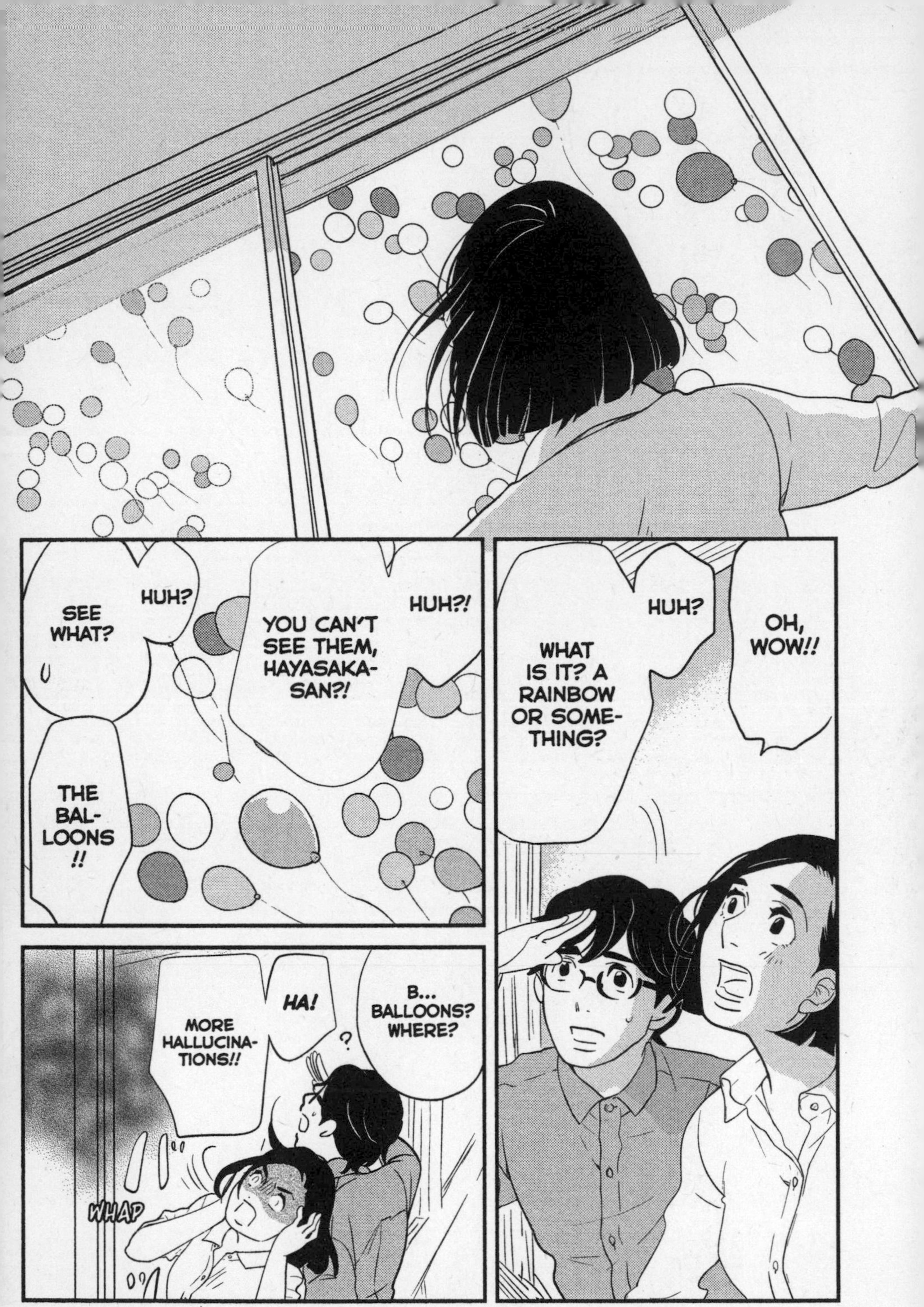
OH, WOW!!
HUH?
WHAT IS IT? A RAINBOW OR SOME-THING?
HUH?!
YOU CAN'T SEE THEM, HAYASAKA-SAN?!
HUH?
SEE WHAT?
THE BAL-LOONS!!
B... BALLOONS? WHERE?
HA!
MORE HALLUCINA-TIONS!!
WHAP

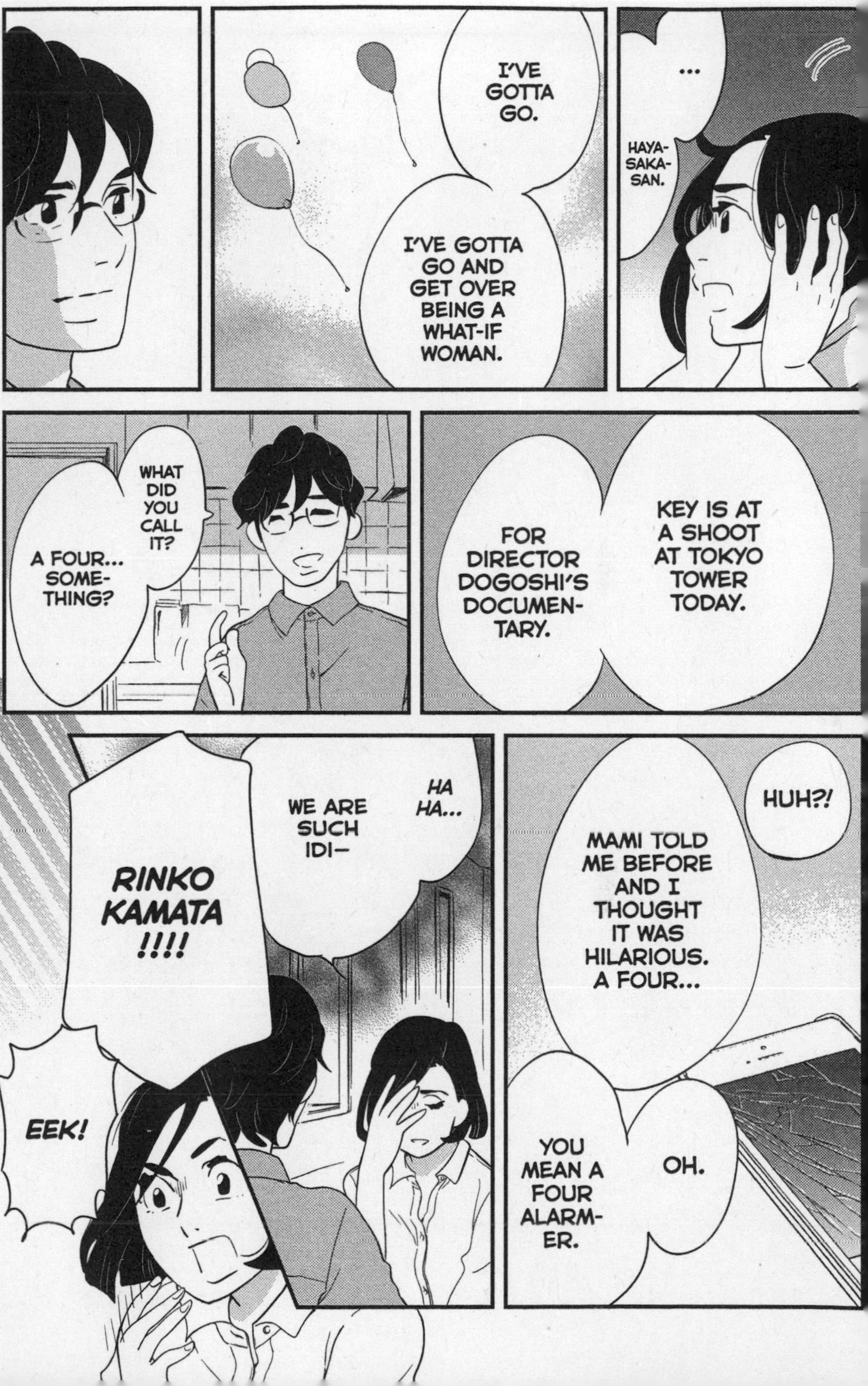
...
HAYA-SAKA-SAN.
I'VE GOTTA GO.
I'VE GOTTA GO AND GET OVER BEING A WHAT-IF WOMAN.
KEY IS AT A SHOOT AT TOKYO TOWER TODAY.
FOR DIRECTOR DOGOSHI'S DOCUMEN-TARY.
WHAT DID YOU CALL IT?
A FOUR... SOME-THING?
HUH?!
MAMI TOLD ME BEFORE AND I THOUGHT IT WAS HILARIOUS. A FOUR...
OH.
YOU MEAN A FOUR ALARM-ER.
HA HA...
WE ARE SUCH IDI—
RINKO KAMATA !!!!
EEK!

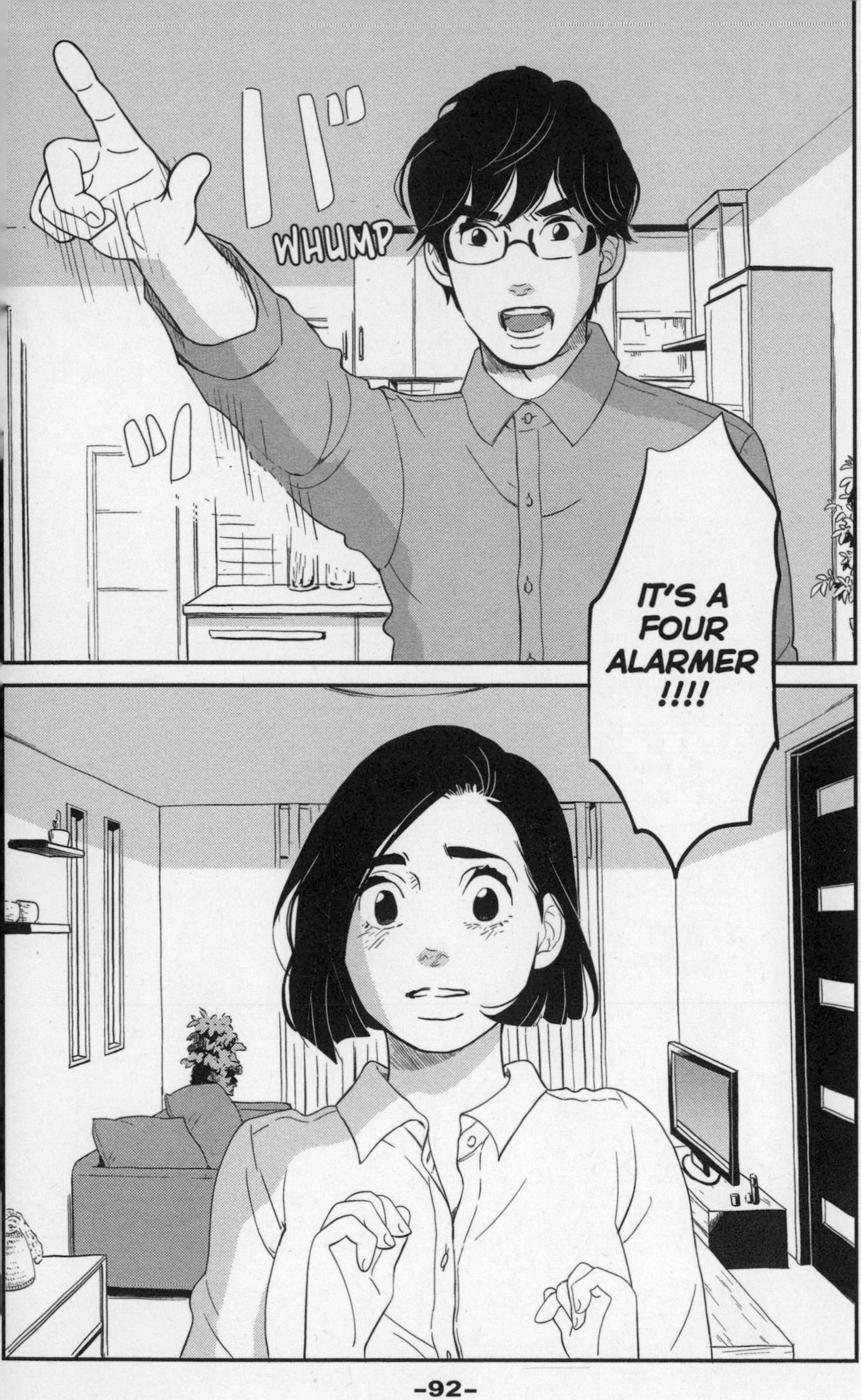
WHUMP
IT'S A FOUR ALARMER !!!!

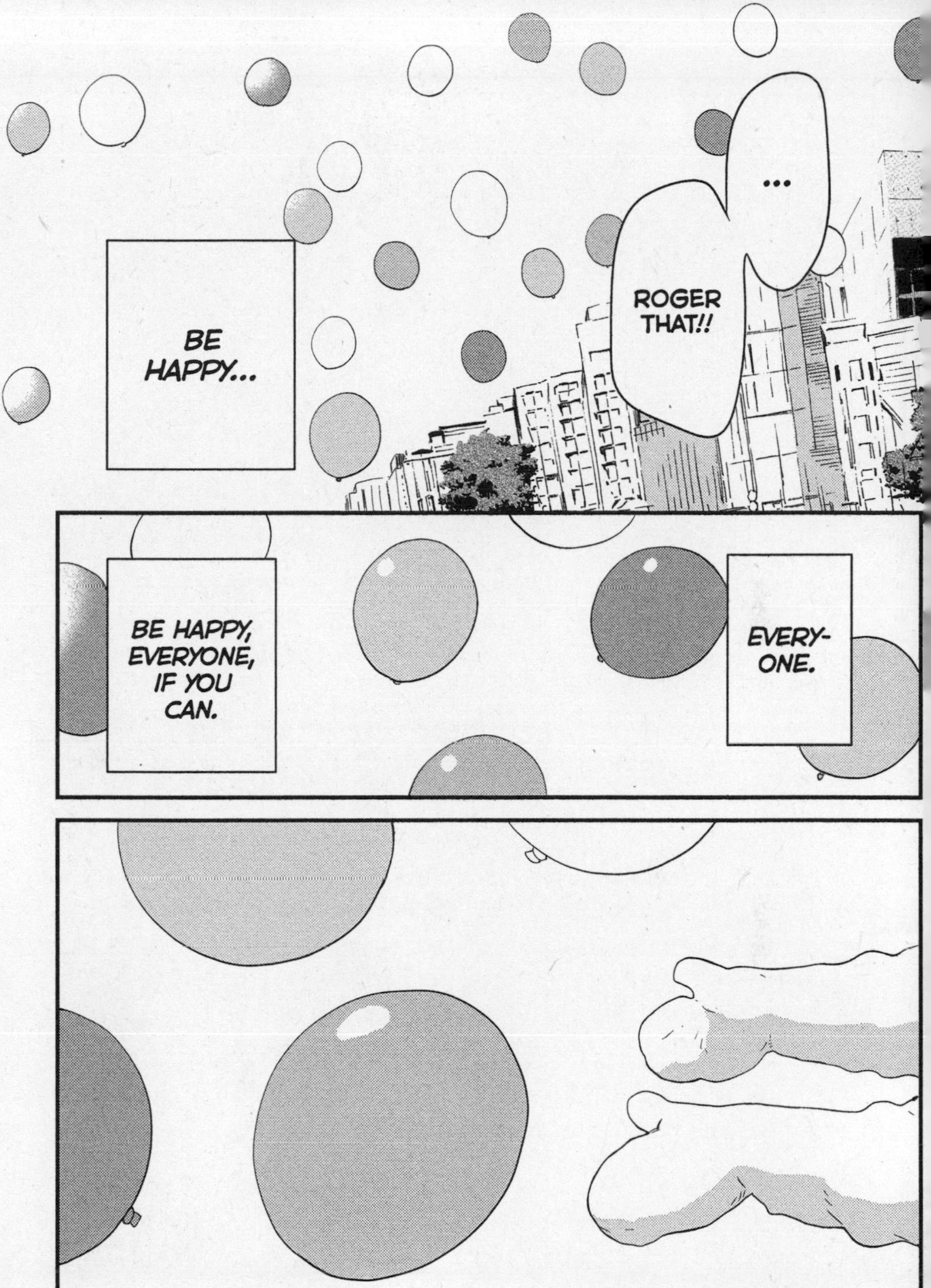
...
ROGER THAT!!
BE HAPPY...
EVERY-ONE.
BE HAPPY, EVERYONE, IF YOU CAN.

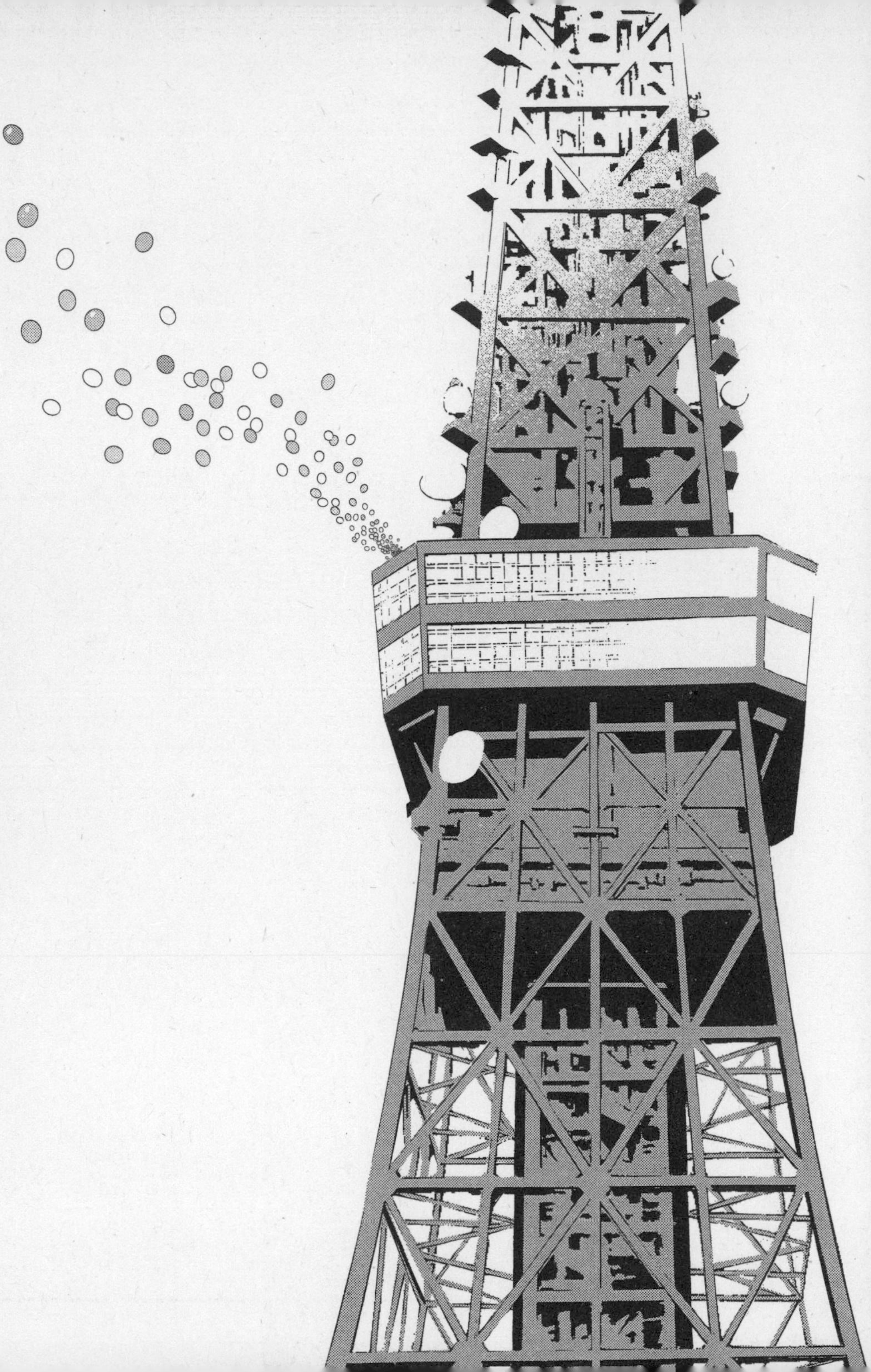

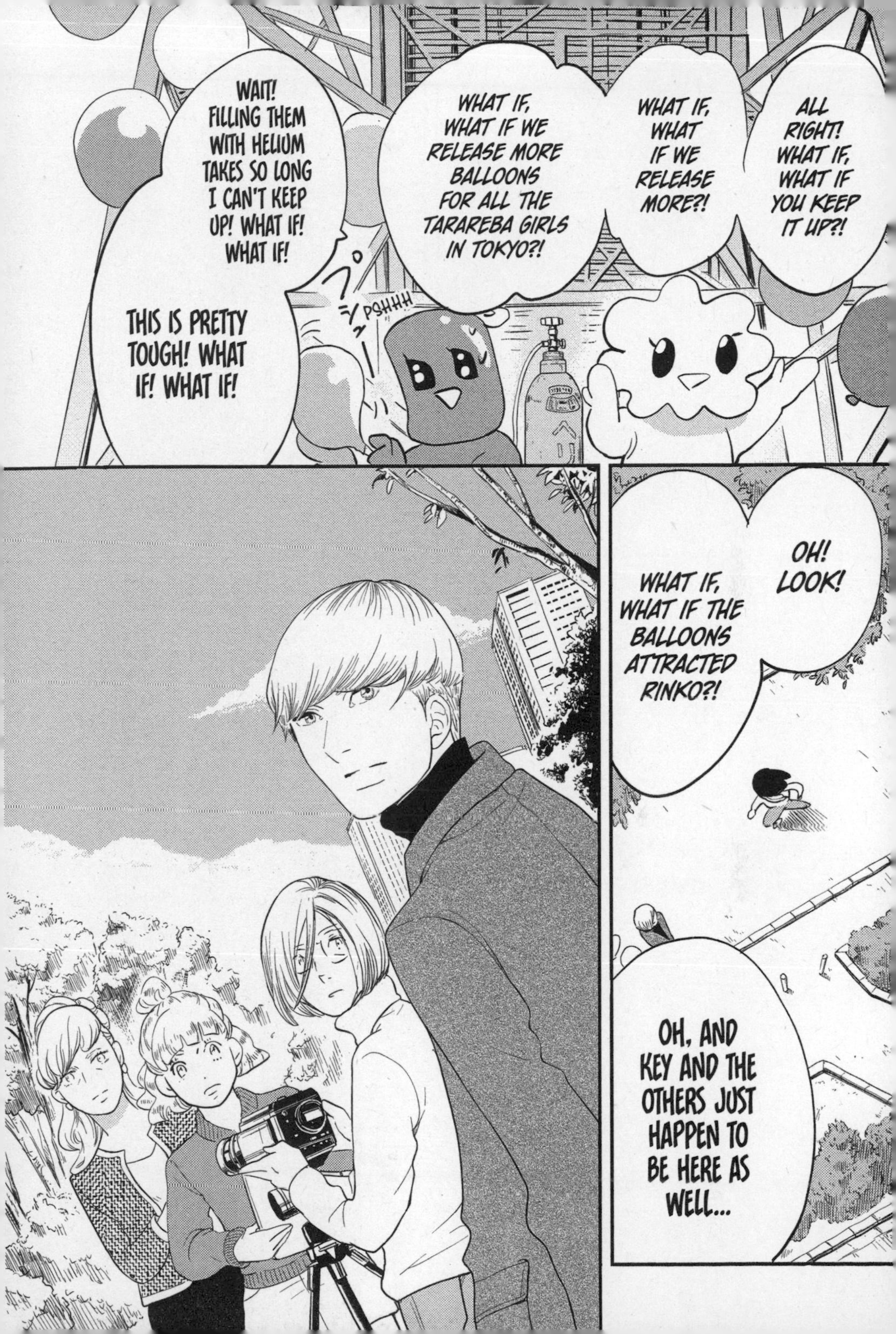
ALL RIGHT! WHAT IF, WHAT IF YOU KEEP IT UP?!
WHAT IF, WHAT IF WE RELEASE MORE?!
WHAT IF, WHAT IF WE RELEASE MORE BALLOONS FOR ALL THE TARAREBA GIRLS IN TOKYO?!
WAIT! FILLING THEM WITH HELIUM TAKES SO LONG I CAN'T KEEP UP! WHAT IF! WHAT IF!
PSHHH
THIS IS PRETTY TOUGH! WHAT IF! WHAT IF!
OH! LOOK!
WHAT IF, WHAT IF THE BALLOONS ATTRACTED RINKO?!
OH, AND KEY AND THE OTHERS JUST HAPPEN TO BE HERE AS WELL...

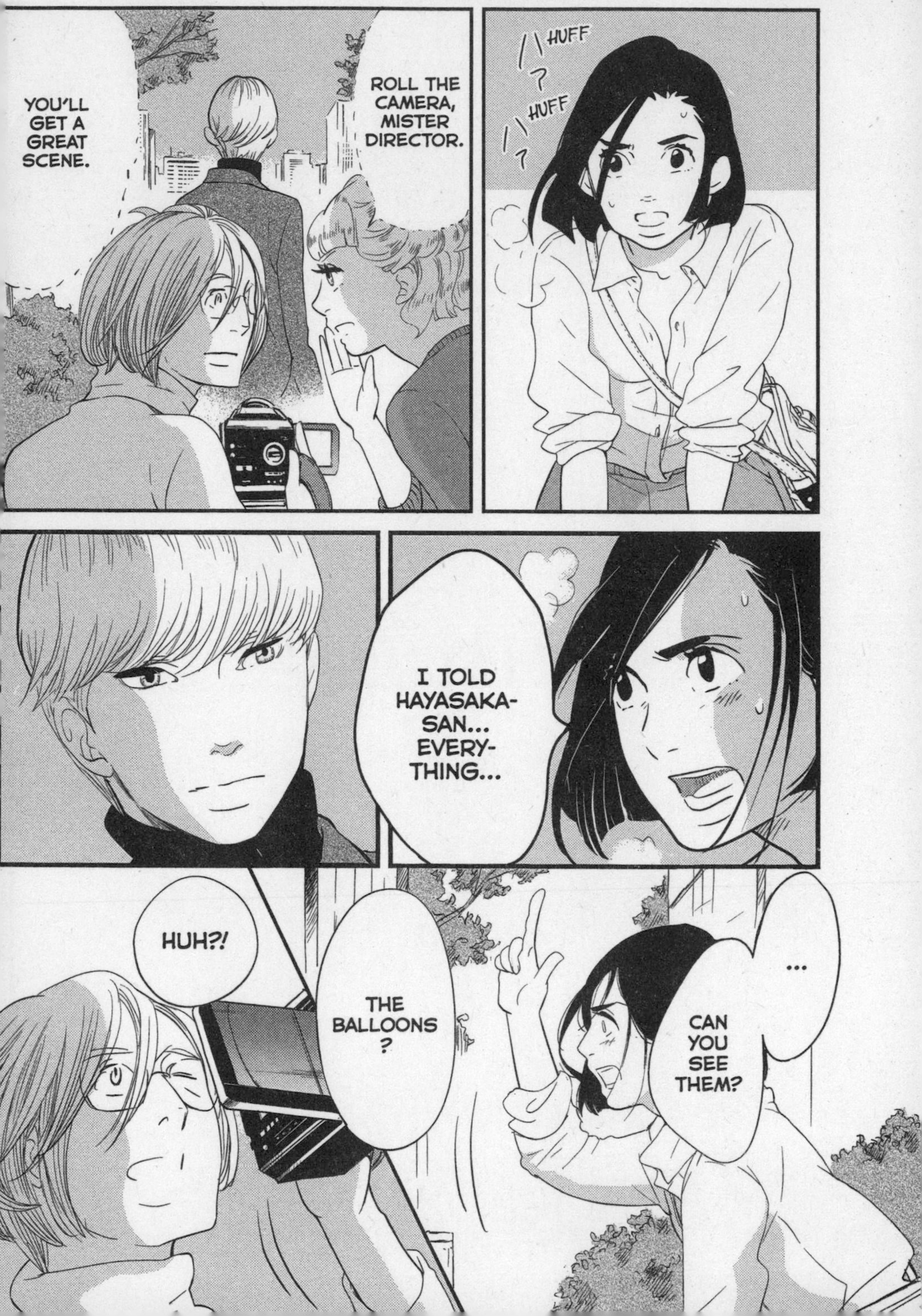
HUFF
HUFF
ROLL THE CAMERA, MISTER DIRECTOR.
YOU'LL GET A GREAT SCENE.
I TOLD HAYASAKA-SAN... EVERYTHING...
...
CAN YOU SEE THEM?
THE BALLOONS?
HUH?!

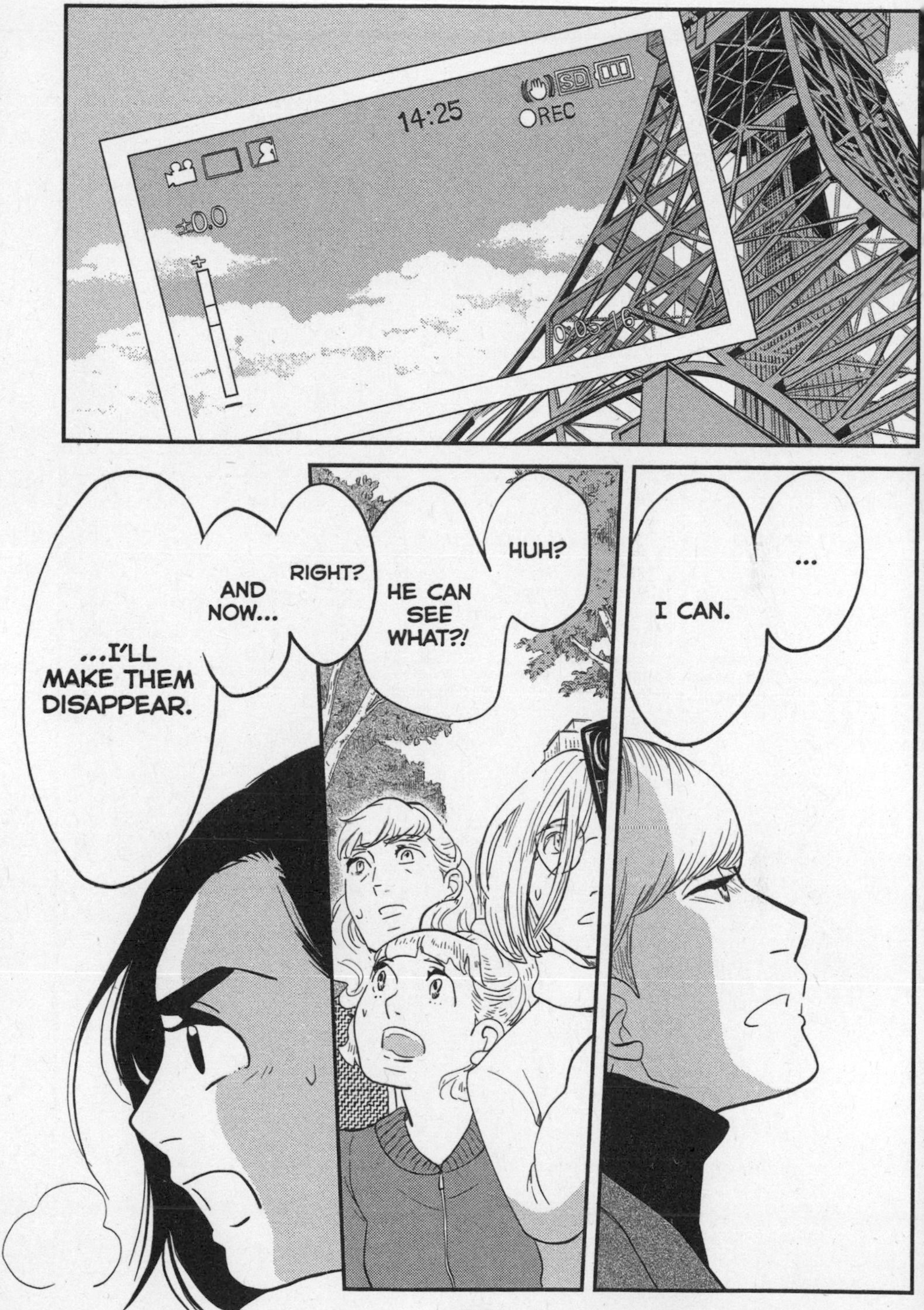
14:25
SD
REC
±0.0
0:05:16
...
I CAN.
HUH?
HE CAN SEE WHAT?!
RIGHT?
AND NOW...
...I'LL MAKE THEM DISAPPEAR.

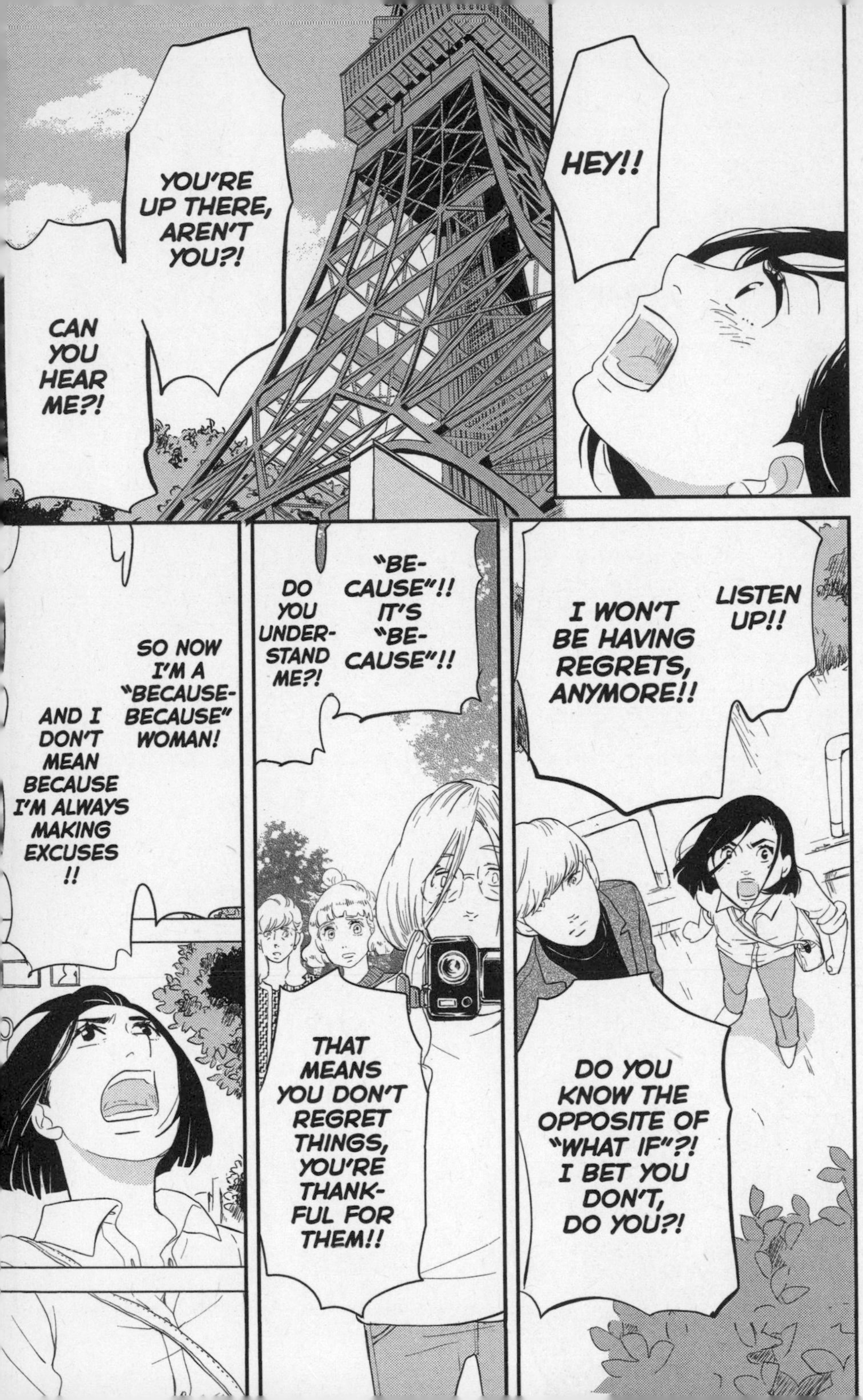
HEY!!
YOU'RE UP THERE, AREN'T YOU?!
CAN YOU HEAR ME?!
LISTEN UP!!
I WON'T BE HAVING REGRETS, ANYMORE!!
DO YOU KNOW THE OPPOSITE OF "WHAT IF"?! I BET YOU DON'T, DO YOU?!
"BE-CAUSE"!! IT'S "BE-CAUSE"!!
DO YOU UNDER-STAND ME?!
THAT MEANS YOU DON'T REGRET THINGS, YOU'RE THANK-FUL FOR THEM!!
SO NOW I'M A "BECAUSE-BECAUSE" WOMAN!
AND I DON'T MEAN BECAUSE I'M ALWAYS MAKING EXCUSES !!

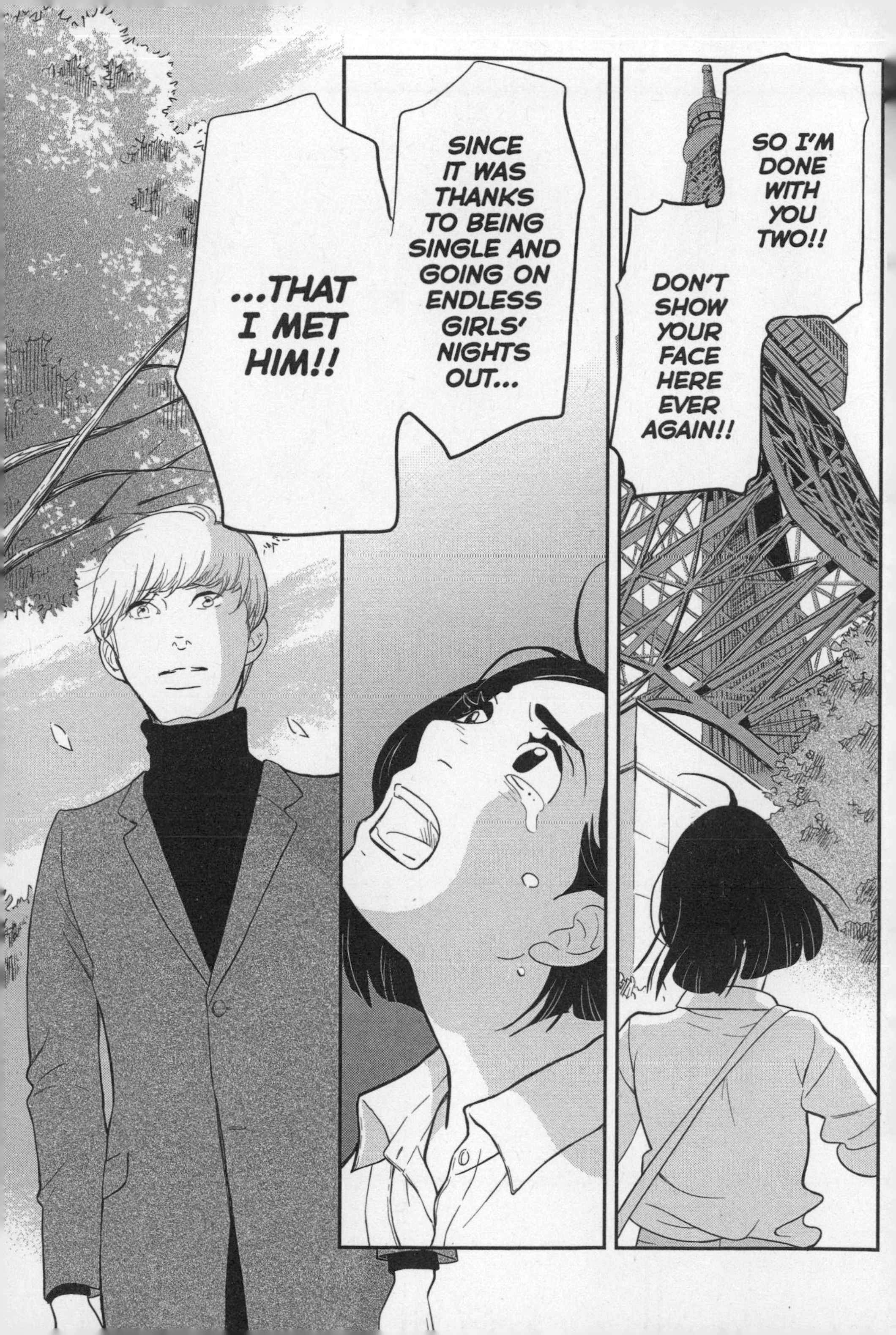
SO I'M DONE WITH YOU TWO!!
DON'T SHOW YOUR FACE HERE EVER AGAIN!!
SINCE IT WAS THANKS TO BEING SINGLE AND GOING ON ENDLESS GIRLS' NIGHTS OUT...
...THAT I MET HIM!!

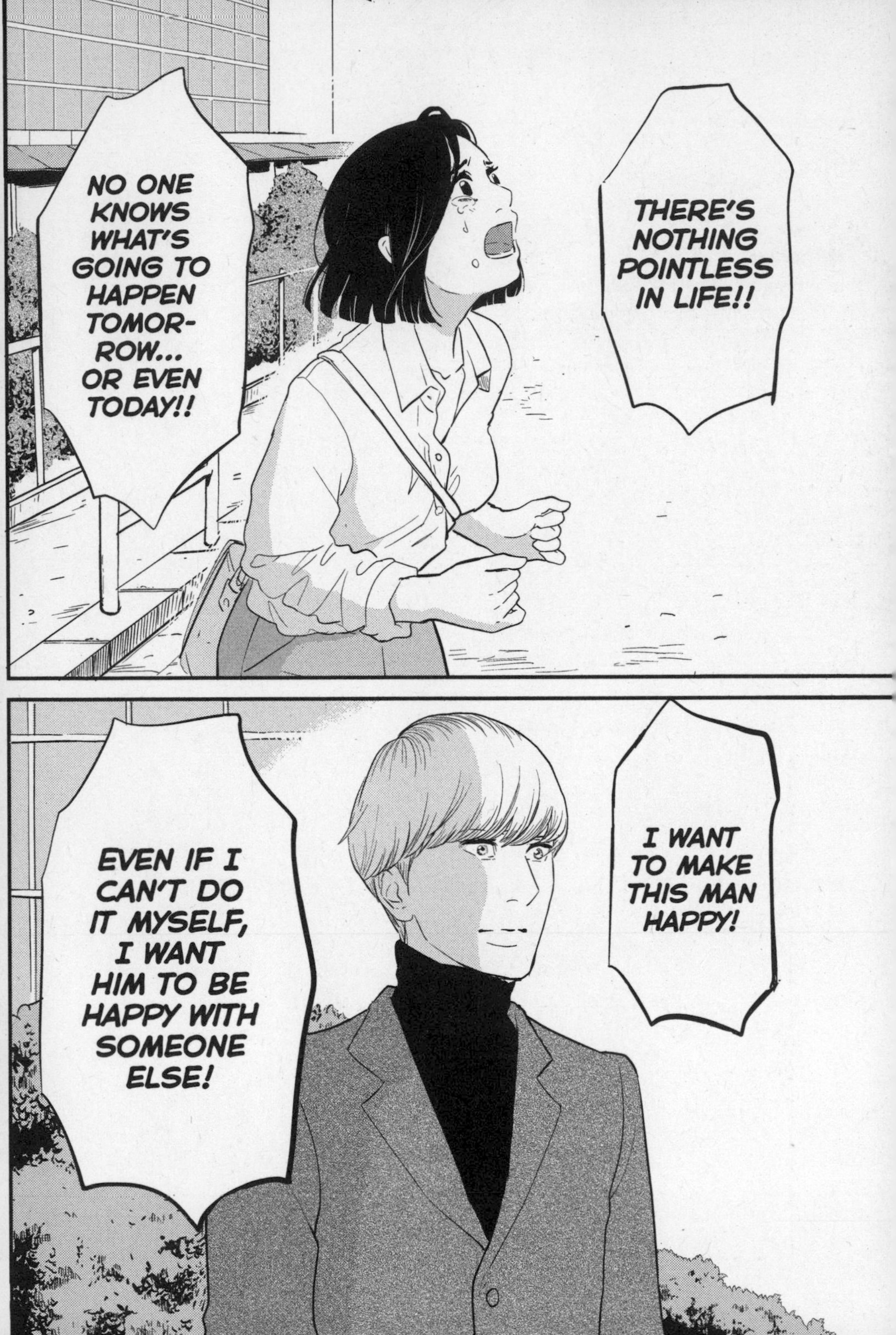
THERE'S NOTHING POINTLESS IN LIFE!!
NO ONE KNOWS WHAT'S GOING TO HAPPEN TOMORROW... OR EVEN TODAY!!
I WANT TO MAKE THIS MAN HAPPY!
EVEN IF I CAN'T DO IT MYSELF, I WANT HIM TO BE HAPPY WITH SOMEONE ELSE!

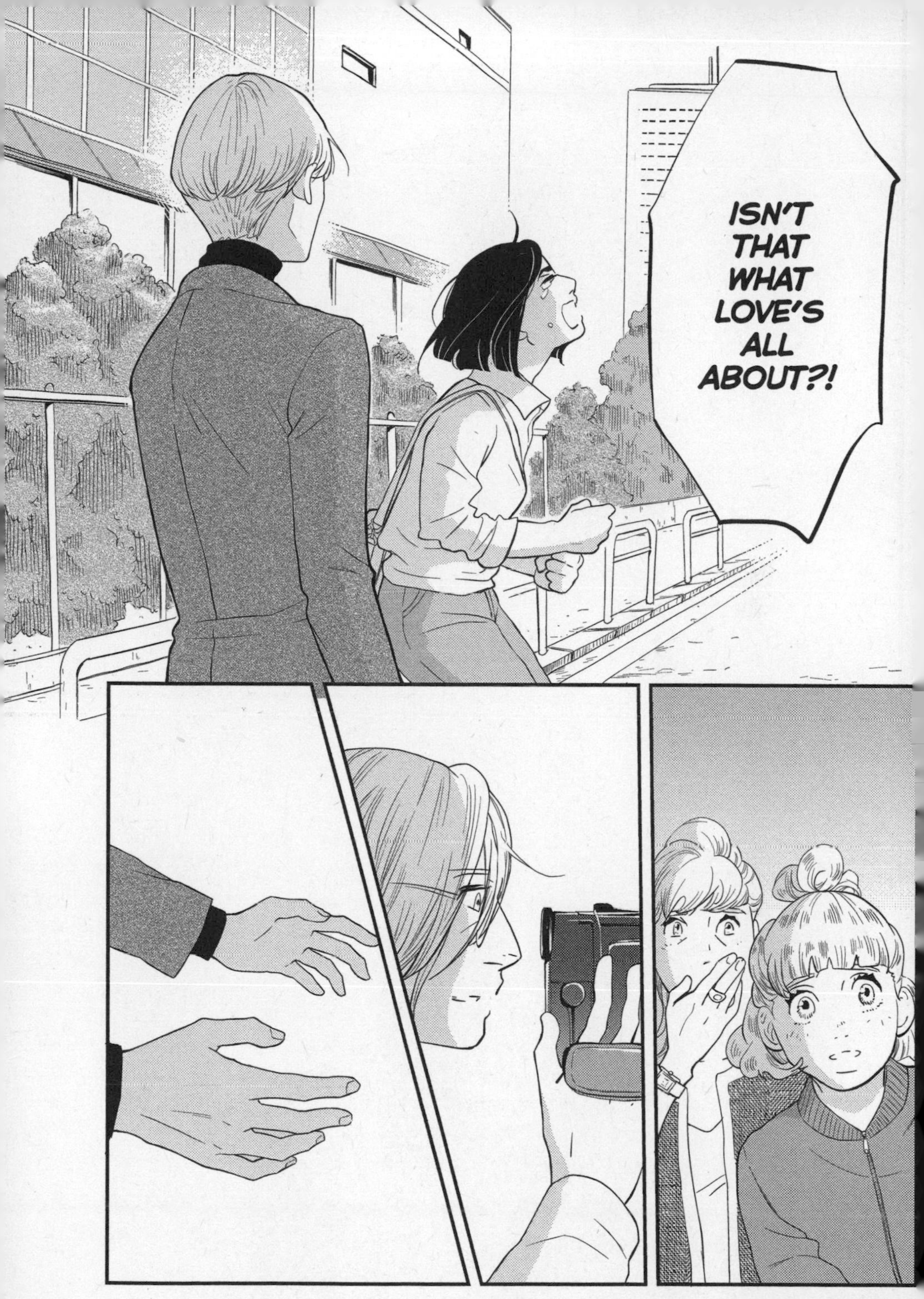
ISN'T THAT WHAT LOVE'S ALL ABOUT?!

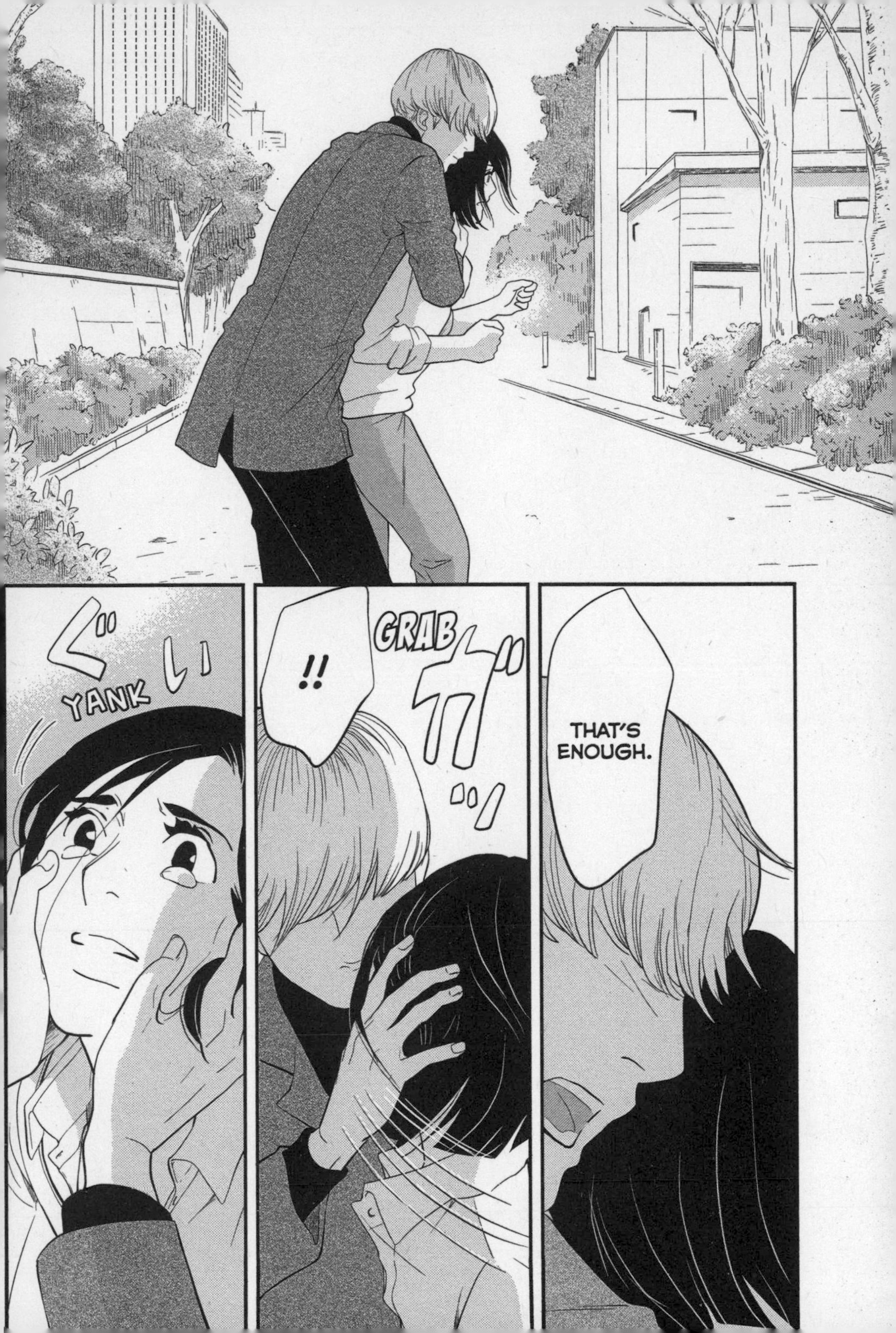
THAT'S ENOUGH.
!!
GRAB
ガッ
ぐい
YANK

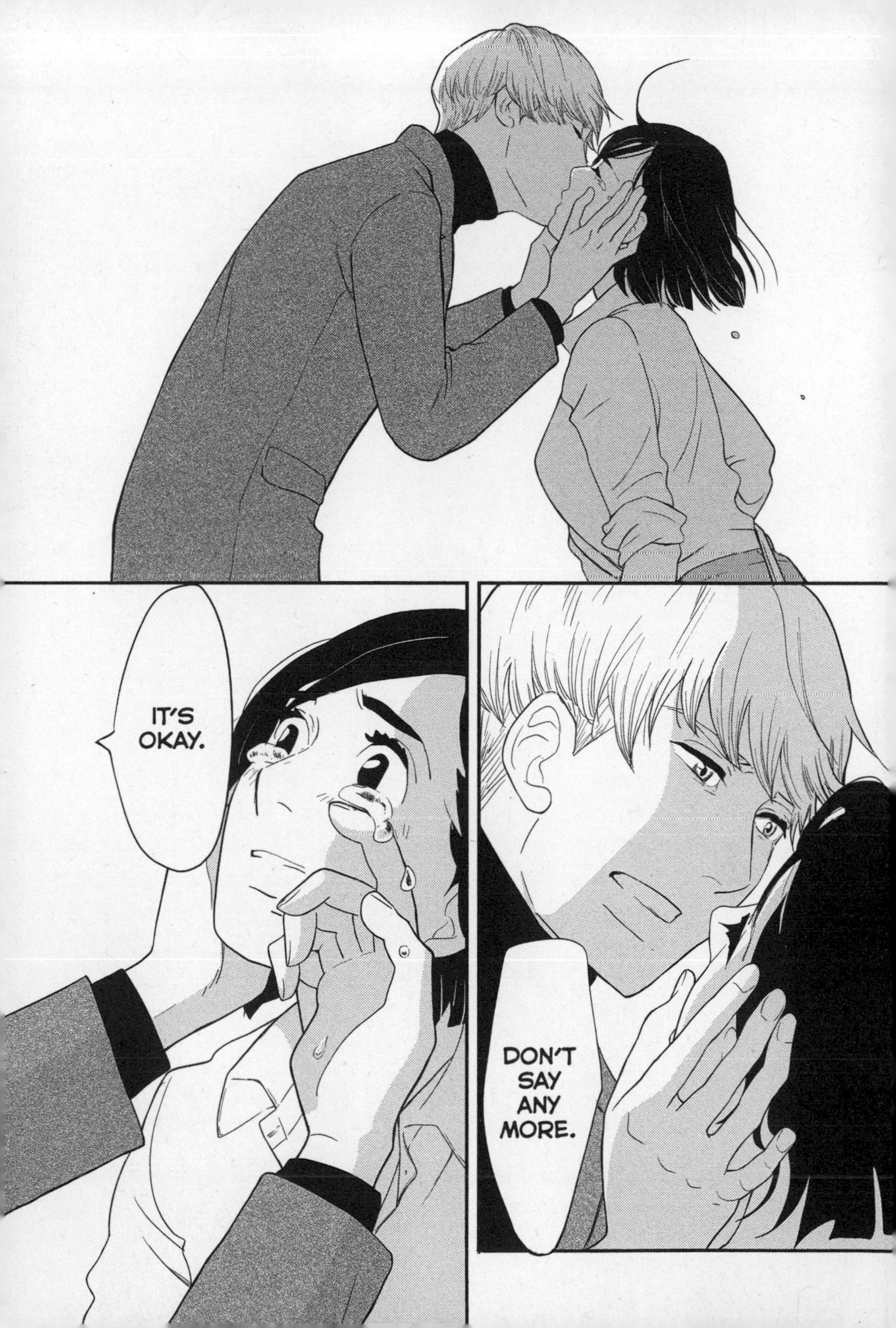
DON'T SAY ANY MORE.
IT'S OKAY.

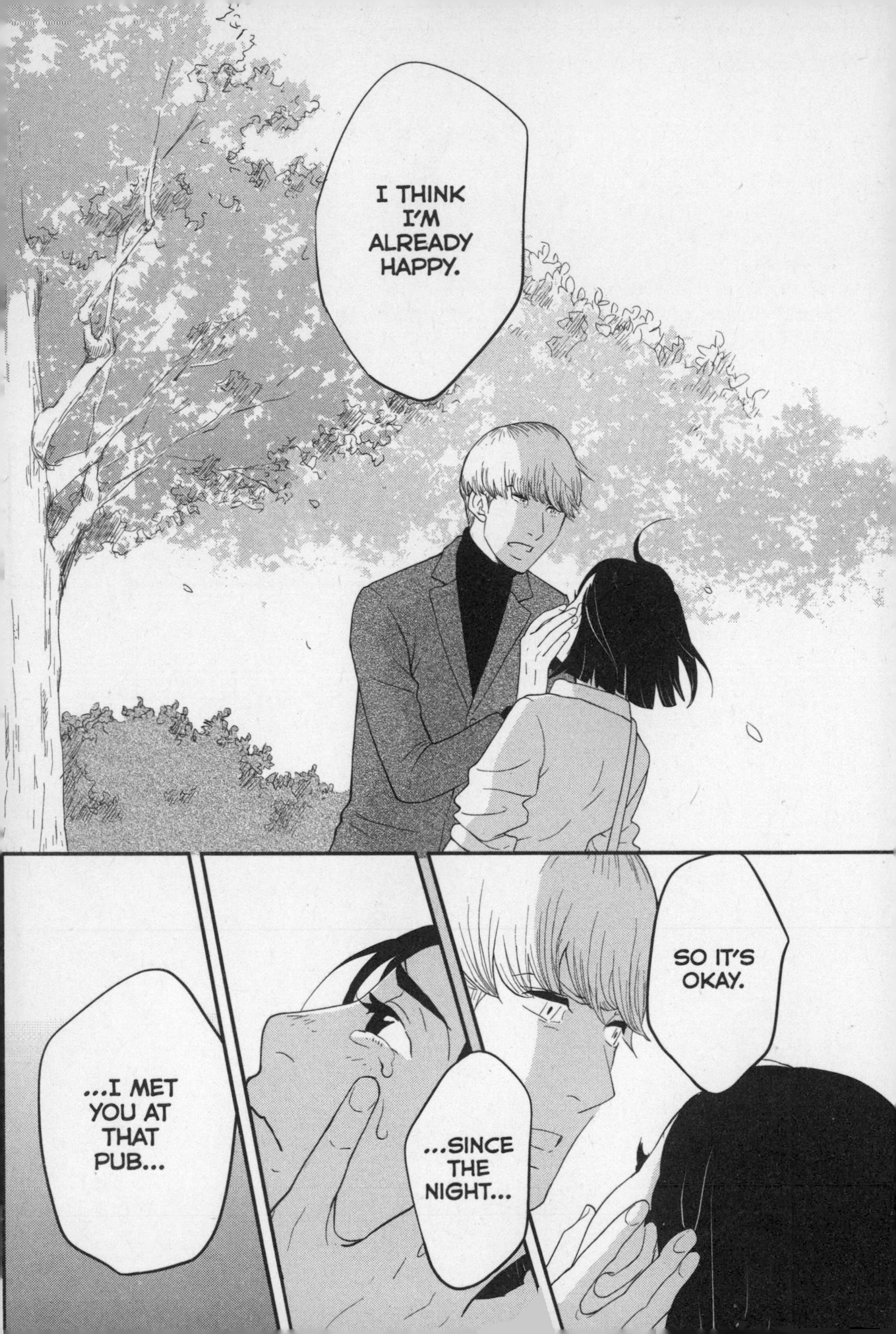
I THINK I'M ALREADY HAPPY.
SO IT'S OKAY.
...SINCE THE NIGHT...
...I MET YOU AT THAT PUB...

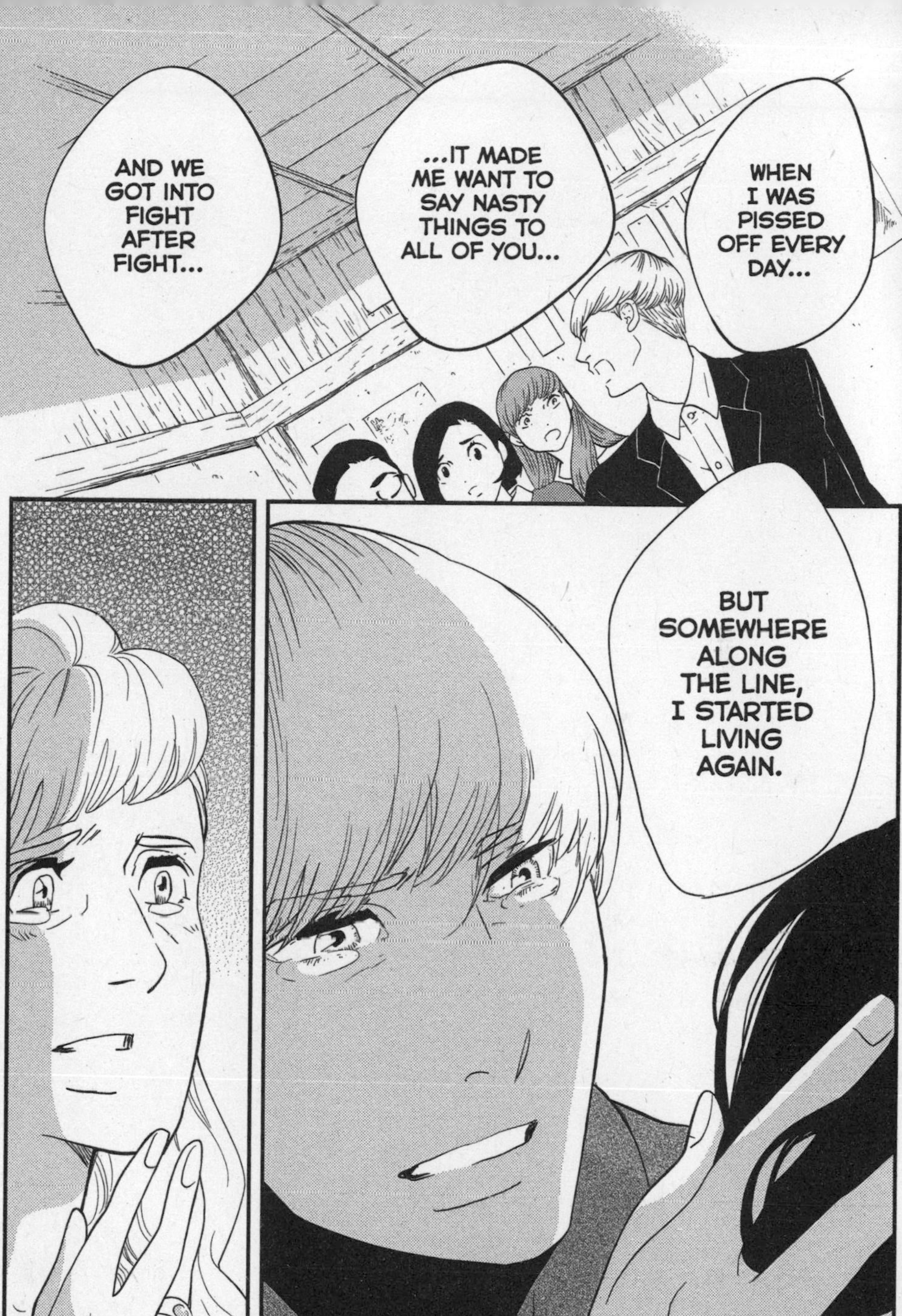
WHEN I WAS PISSED OFF EVERY DAY...
...IT MADE ME WANT TO SAY NASTY THINGS TO ALL OF YOU...
AND WE GOT INTO FIGHT AFTER FIGHT...
BUT SOMEWHERE ALONG THE LINE, I STARTED LIVING AGAIN.

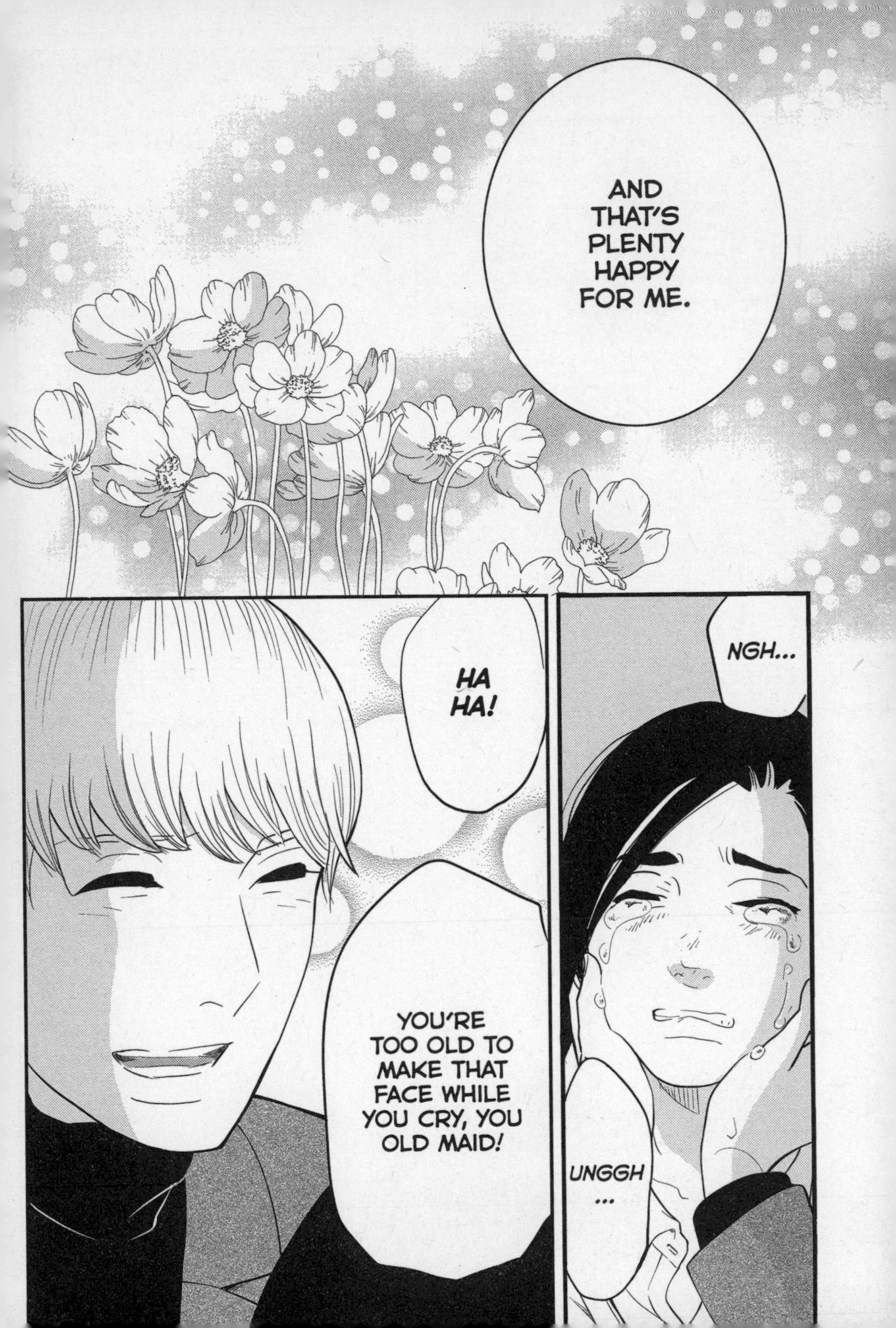
AND THAT'S PLENTY HAPPY FOR ME.
NGH...
UNGGH ...
HA HA!
YOU'RE TOO OLD TO MAKE THAT FACE WHILE YOU CRY, YOU OLD MAID!

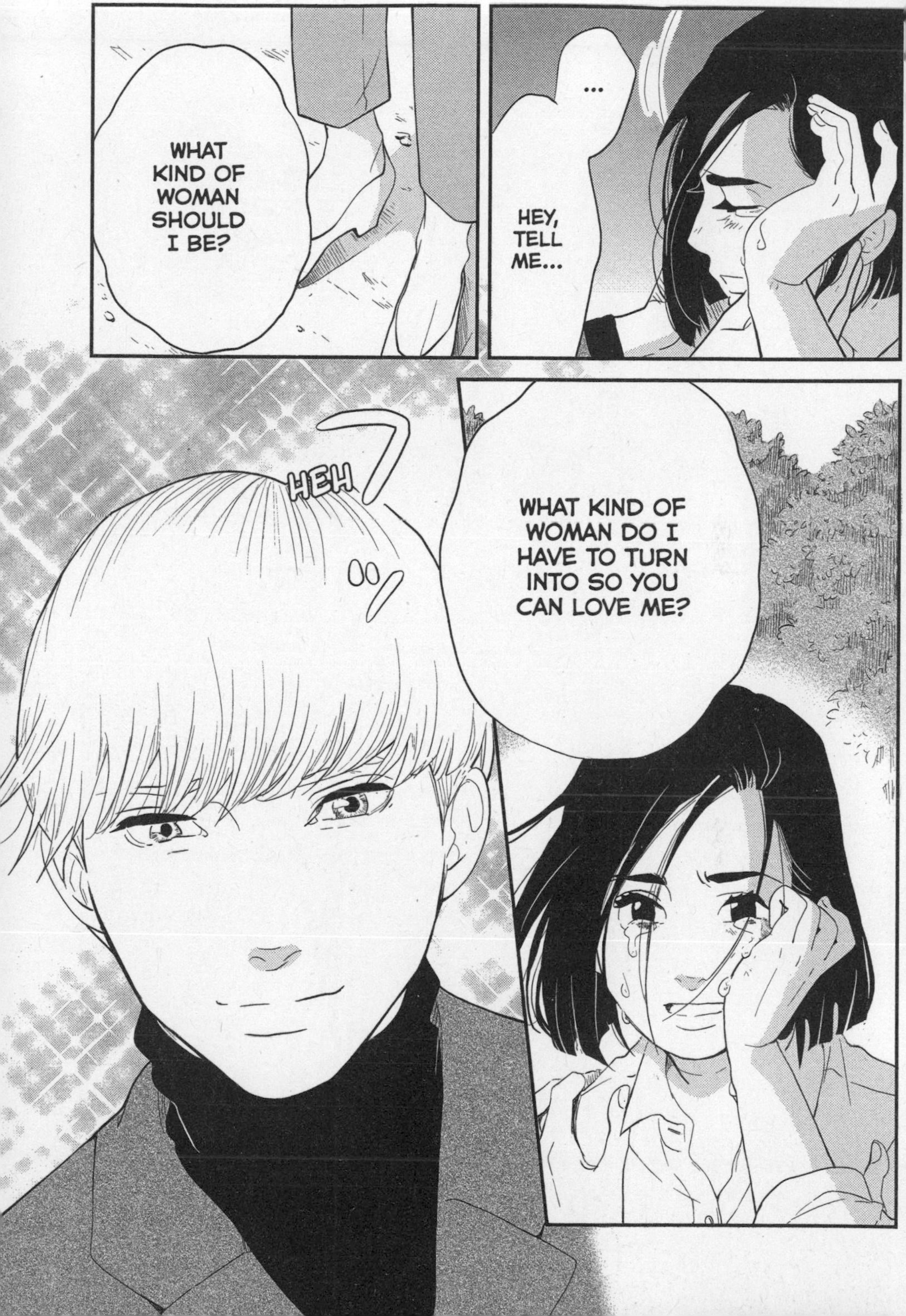
...
HEY, TELL ME...
WHAT KIND OF WOMAN SHOULD I BE?
WHAT KIND OF WOMAN DO I HAVE TO TURN INTO SO YOU CAN LOVE ME?
HEH

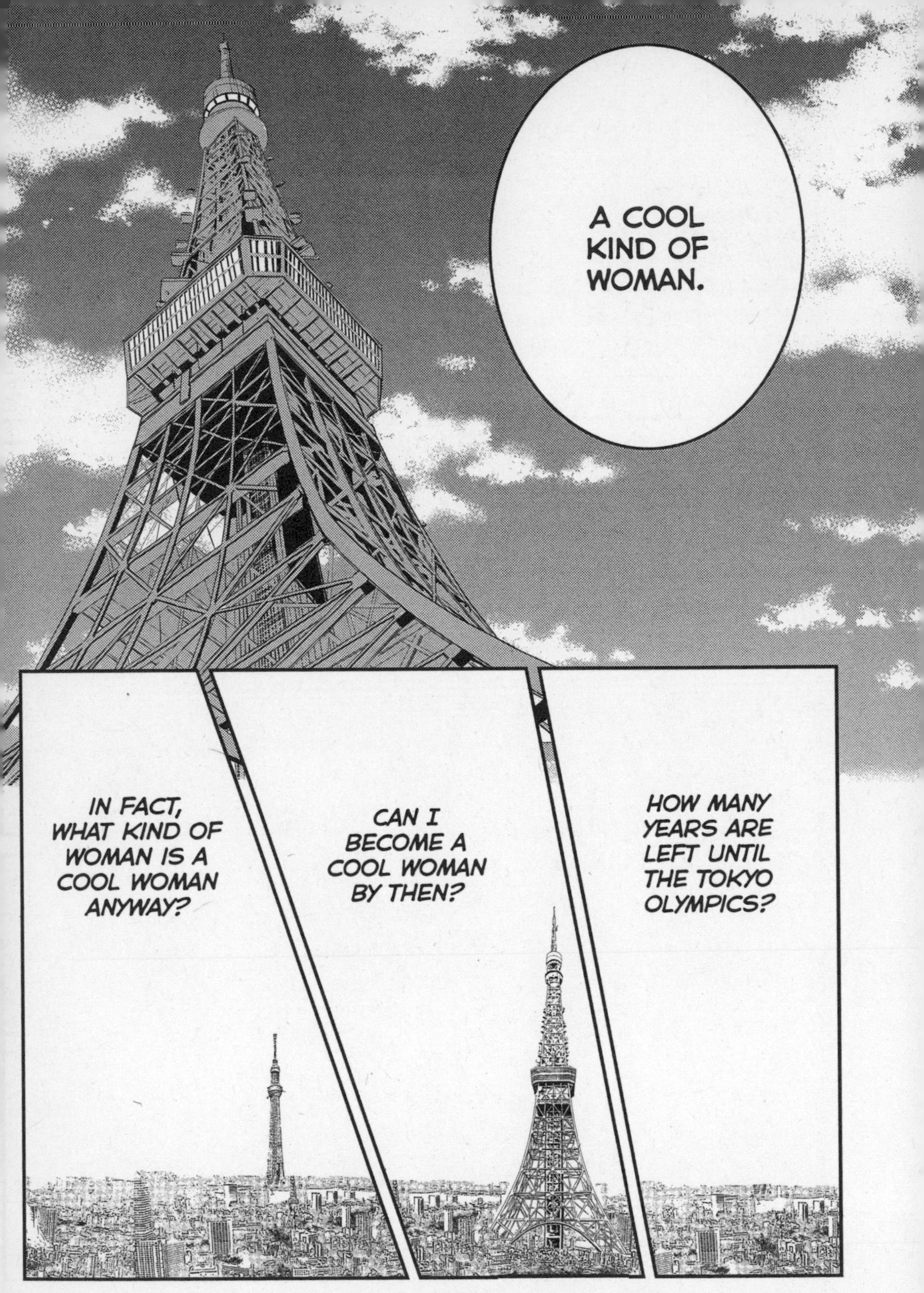
A COOL KIND OF WOMAN.
HOW MANY YEARS ARE LEFT UNTIL THE TOKYO OLYMPICS?
CAN I BECOME A COOL WOMAN BY THEN?
IN FACT, WHAT KIND OF WOMAN IS A COOL WOMAN ANYWAY?

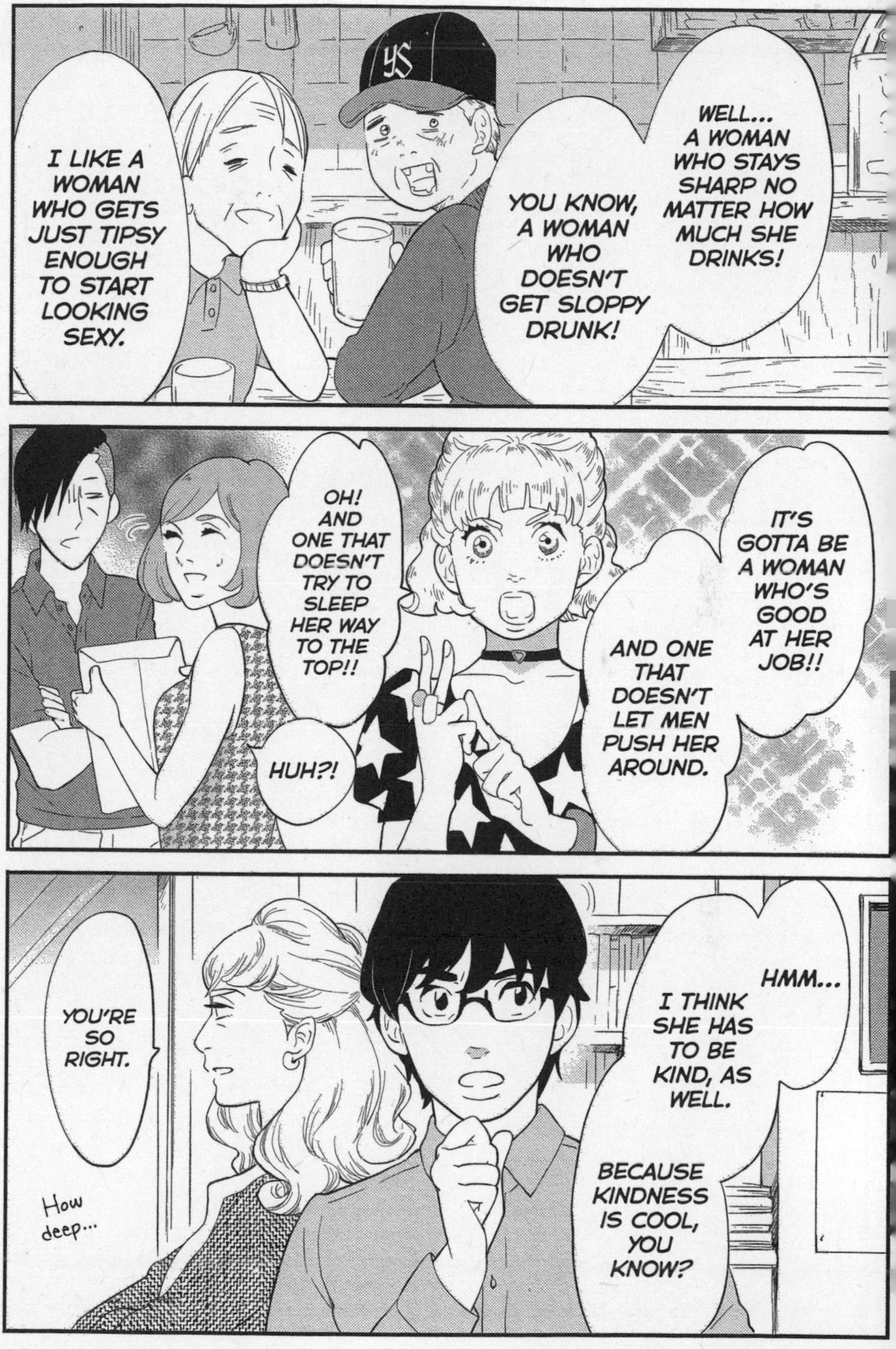
WELL... A WOMAN WHO STAYS SHARP NO MATTER HOW MUCH SHE DRINKS!
YOU KNOW, A WOMAN WHO DOESN'T GET SLOPPY DRUNK!
I LIKE A WOMAN WHO GETS JUST TIPSY ENOUGH TO START LOOKING SEXY.
IT'S GOTTA BE A WOMAN WHO'S GOOD AT HER JOB!!
AND ONE THAT DOESN'T LET MEN PUSH HER AROUND.
OH! AND ONE THAT DOESN'T TRY TO SLEEP HER WAY TO THE TOP!!
HUH?!
HMM...
I THINK SHE HAS TO BE KIND, AS WELL.
BECAUSE KINDNESS IS COOL, YOU KNOW?
YOU'RE SO RIGHT.
How deep...

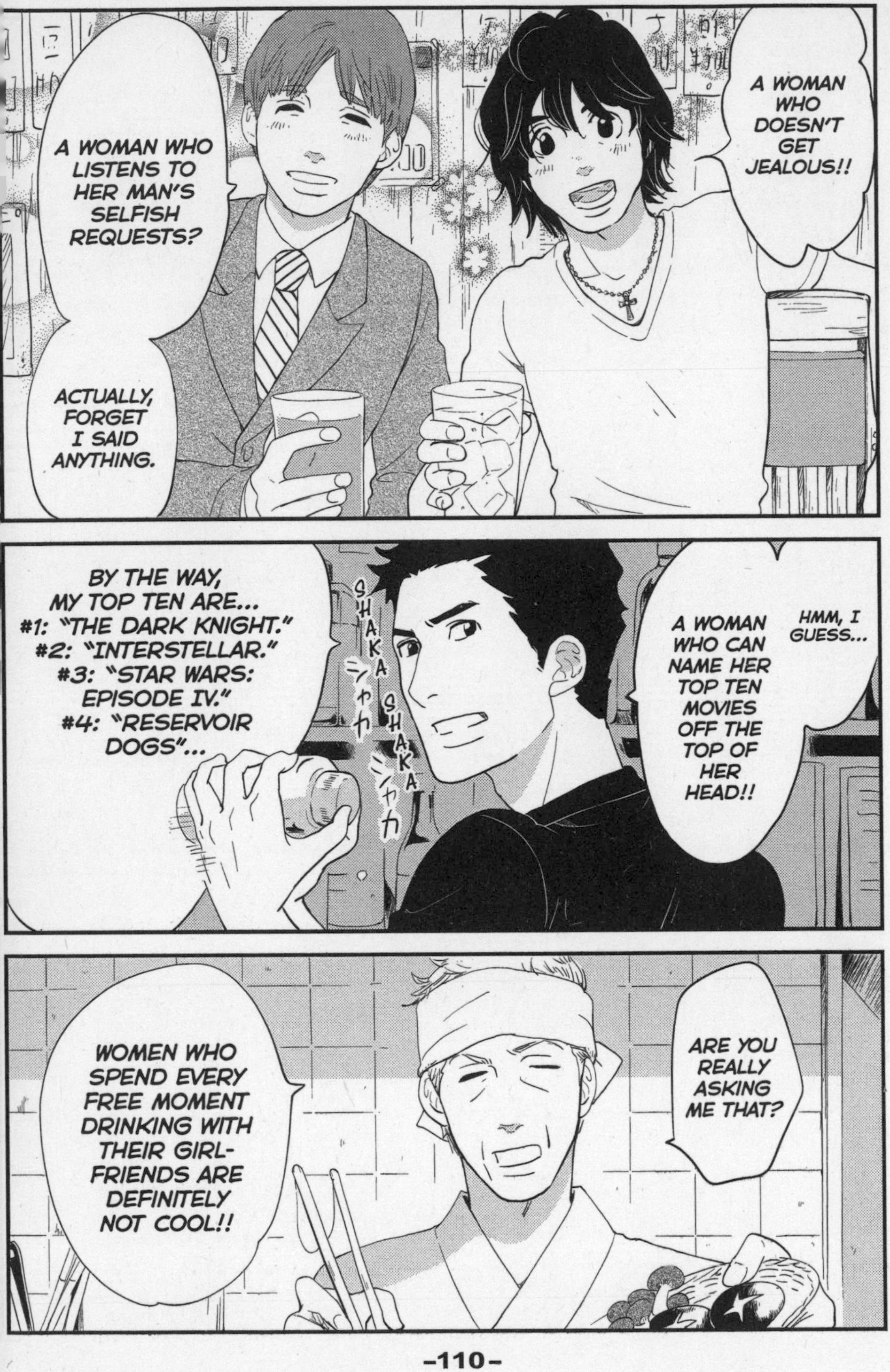
A WOMAN WHO DOESN'T GET JEALOUS!!
A WOMAN WHO LISTENS TO HER MAN'S SELFISH REQUESTS?
ACTUALLY, FORGET I SAID ANYTHING.
HMM, I GUESS...
A WOMAN WHO CAN NAME HER TOP TEN MOVIES OFF THE TOP OF HER HEAD!!
SHAKA シャカ SHAKA シャカ
BY THE WAY, MY TOP TEN ARE... #1: "THE DARK KNIGHT." #2: "INTERSTELLAR." #3: "STAR WARS: EPISODE IV." #4: "RESERVOIR DOGS"...
ARE YOU REALLY ASKING ME THAT?
WOMEN WHO SPEND EVERY FREE MOMENT DRINKING WITH THEIR GIRL-FRIENDS ARE DEFINITELY NOT COOL!!

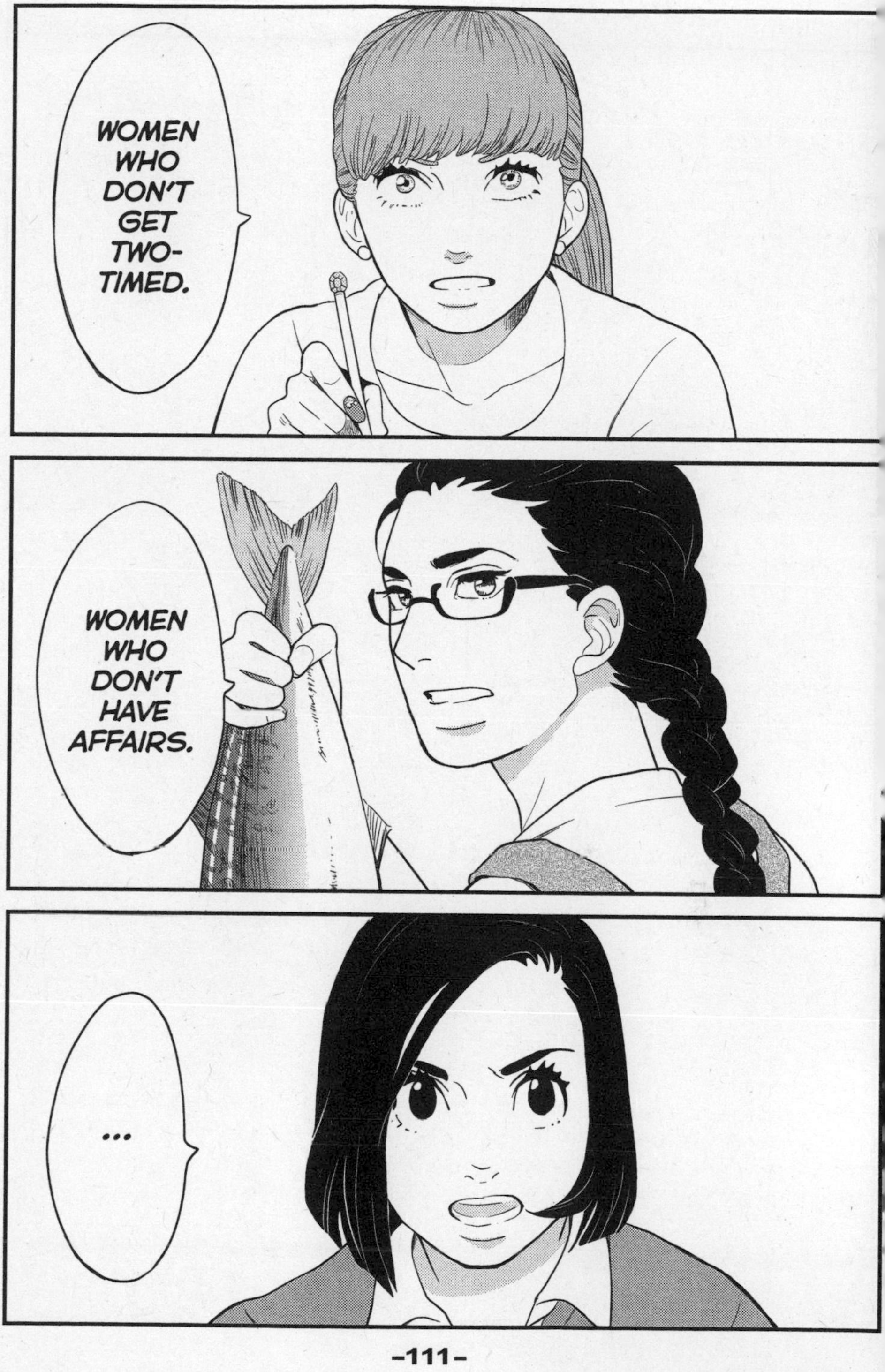
WOMEN WHO DON'T GET TWO-TIMED.
WOMEN WHO DON'T HAVE AFFAIRS.
...

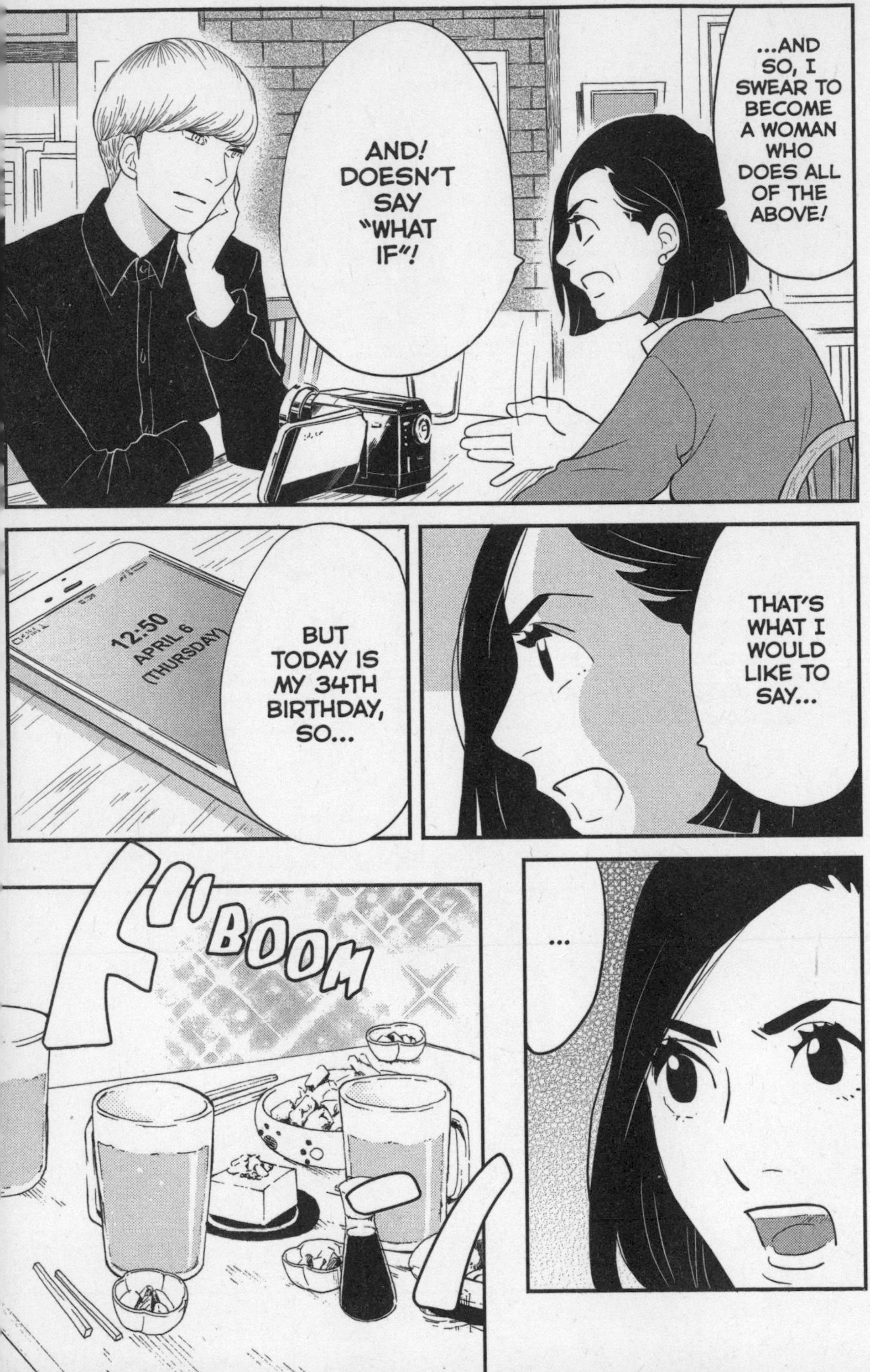
...AND SO, I SWEAR TO BECOME A WOMAN WHO DOES ALL OF THE ABOVE!
AND! DOESN'T SAY "WHAT IF"!
THAT'S WHAT I WOULD LIKE TO SAY...
12:50
APRIL 6
(THURSDAY)
BUT TODAY IS MY 34TH BIRTHDAY, SO...
...
BOOM

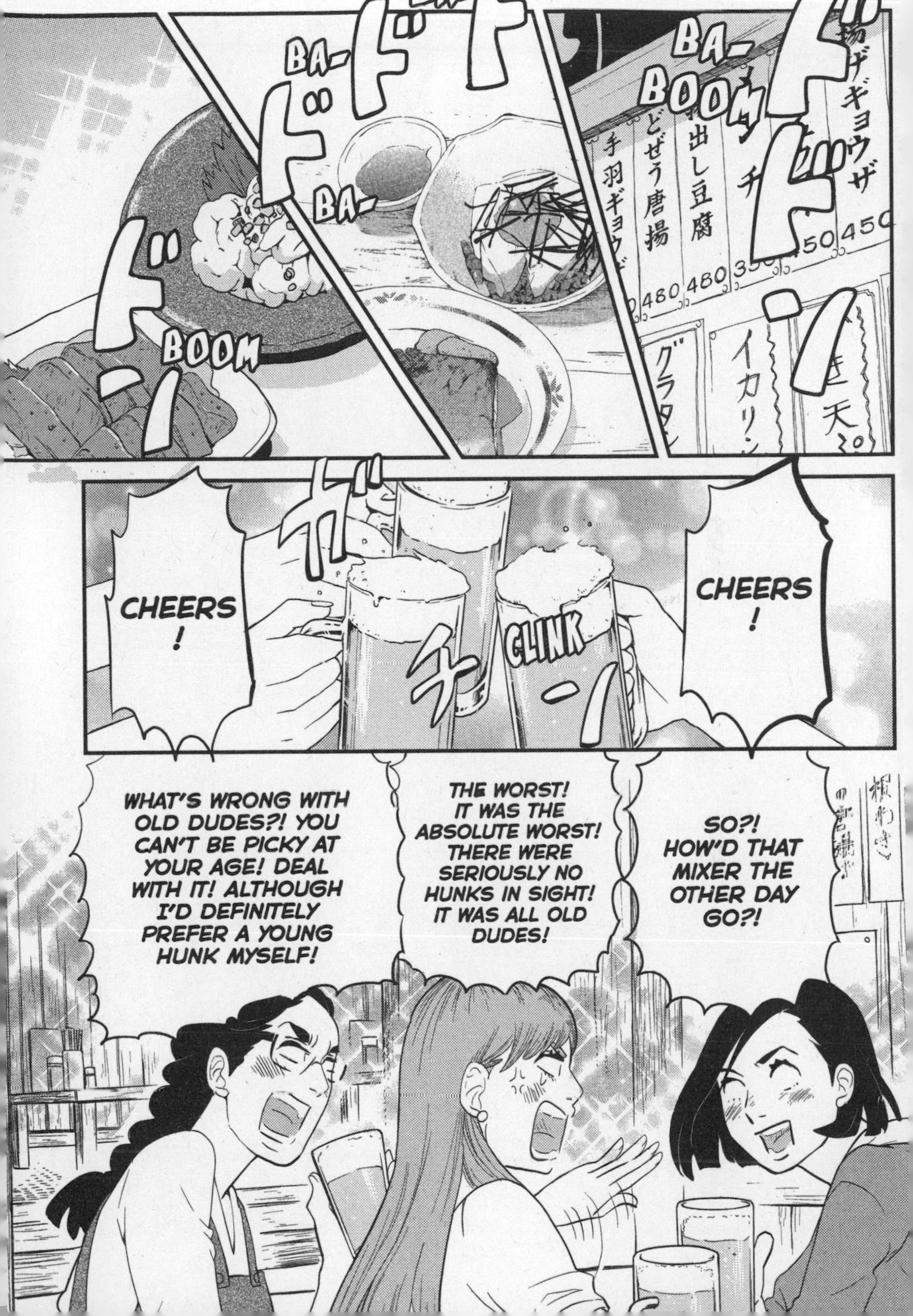
BA-BOOM
BA-BA-BA-
BOOM
CHEERS!
CLINK
CHEERS!
SO?! HOW'D THAT MIXER THE OTHER DAY GO?!
THE WORST! IT WAS THE ABSOLUTE WORST! THERE WERE SERIOUSLY NO HUNKS IN SIGHT! IT WAS ALL OLD DUDES!
WHAT'S WRONG WITH OLD DUDES?! YOU CAN'T BE PICKY AT YOUR AGE! DEAL WITH IT! ALTHOUGH I'D DEFINITELY PREFER A YOUNG HUNK MYSELF!

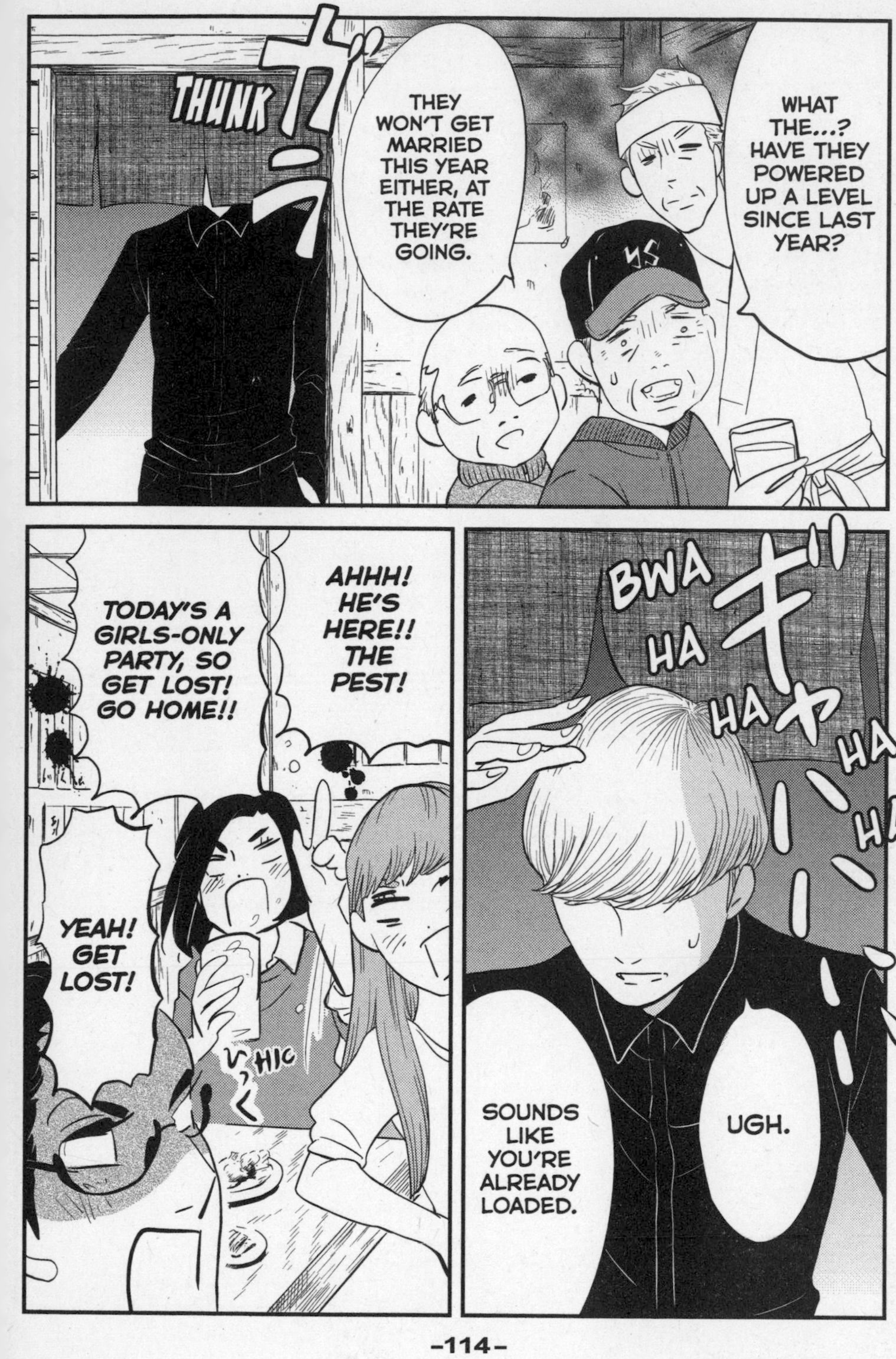
WHAT THE...? HAVE THEY POWERED UP A LEVEL SINCE LAST YEAR?
THEY WON'T GET MARRIED THIS YEAR EITHER, AT THE RATE THEY'RE GOING.
THUNK
ガッ
BWA HA HA HA HA HA!
ギャハハ
UGH.
SOUNDS LIKE YOU'RE ALREADY LOADED.
AHHH! HE'S HERE!! THE PEST!
TODAY'S A GIRLS-ONLY PARTY, SO GET LOST! GO HOME!!
YEAH! GET LOST!
HIC
ひっく

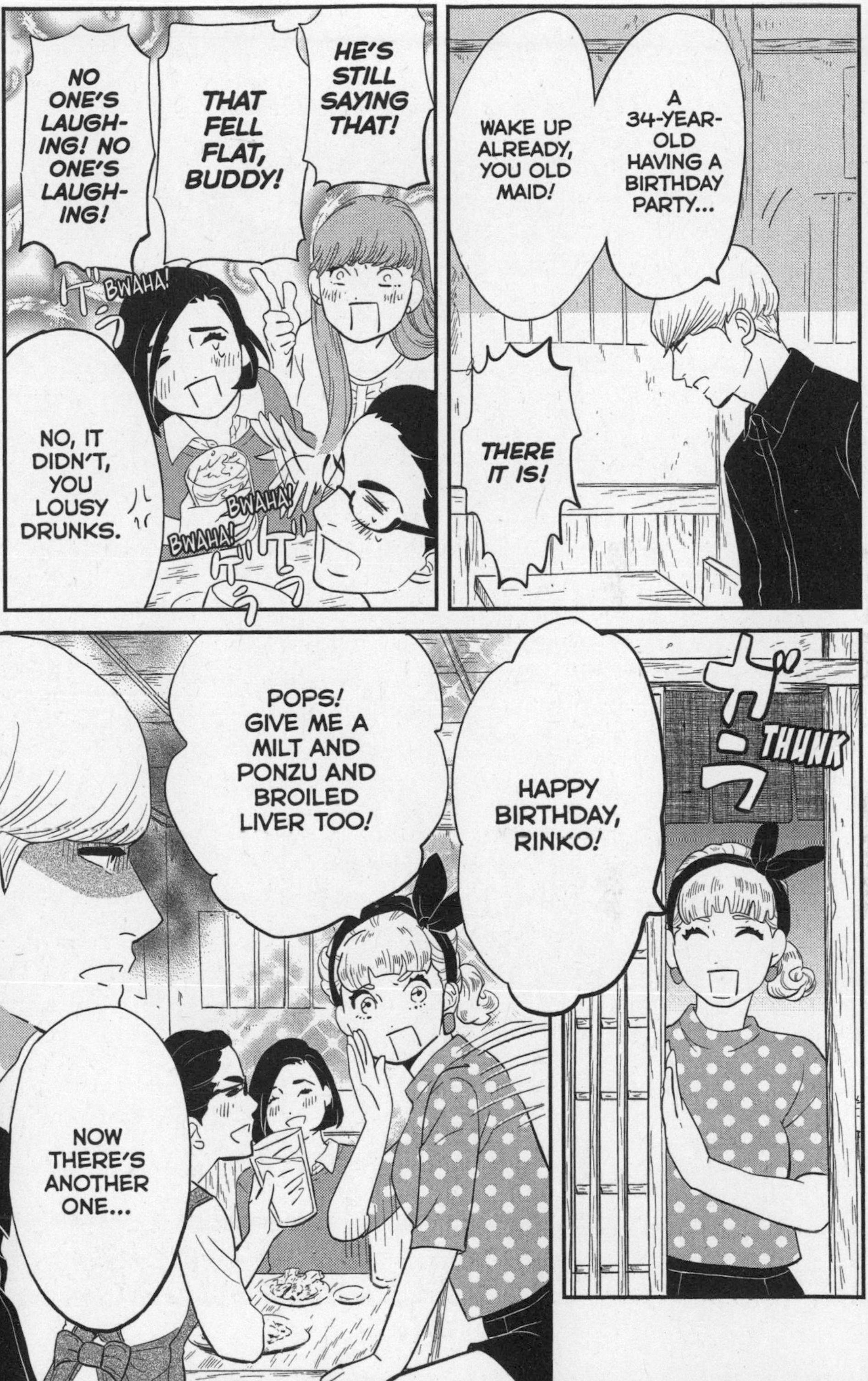
A 34-YEAR-OLD HAVING A BIRTHDAY PARTY...
WAKE UP ALREADY, YOU OLD MAID!
THERE IT IS!
HE'S STILL SAYING THAT!
THAT FELL FLAT, BUDDY!
NO ONE'S LAUGHING! NO ONE'S LAUGHING!
BWAHA!
BWAHA!
BWAHA!
NO, IT DIDN'T, YOU LOUSY DRUNKS.
THUNK
HAPPY BIRTHDAY, RINKO!
POPS! GIVE ME A MILT AND PONZU AND BROILED LIVER TOO!
NOW THERE'S ANOTHER ONE...

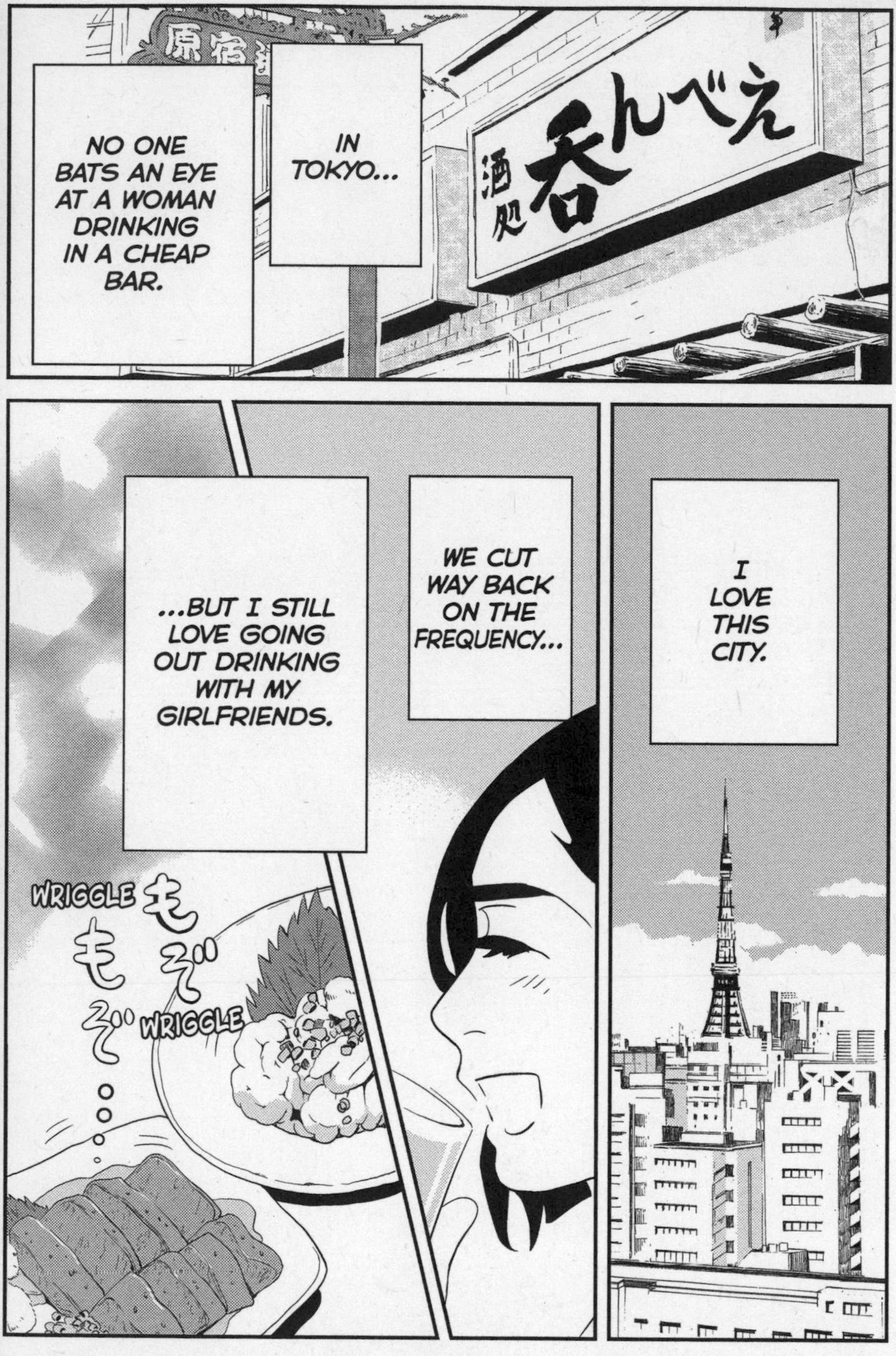
酒処 呑んべえ
IN TOKYO...
NO ONE BATS AN EYE AT A WOMAN DRINKING IN A CHEAP BAR.
I LOVE THIS CITY.
WE CUT WAY BACK ON THE FREQUENCY...
...BUT I STILL LOVE GOING OUT DRINKING WITH MY GIRLFRIENDS.
もぞもぞ
WRIGGLE
WRIGGLE

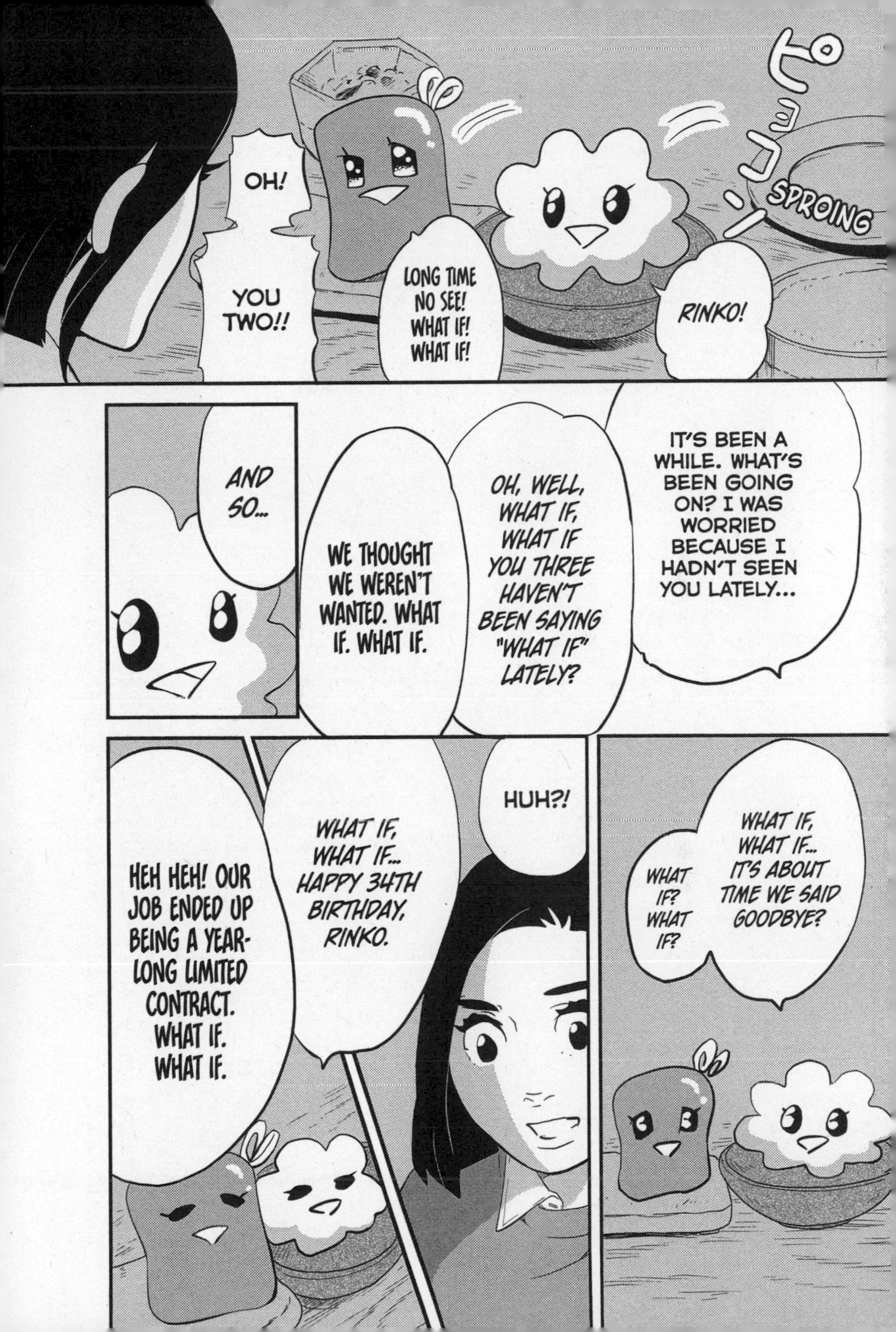
SPROING
RINKO!
LONG TIME NO SEE! WHAT IF! WHAT IF!
OH! YOU TWO!!
IT'S BEEN A WHILE. WHAT'S BEEN GOING ON? I WAS WORRIED BECAUSE I HADN'T SEEN YOU LATELY...
OH, WELL, WHAT IF, WHAT IF YOU THREE HAVEN'T BEEN SAYING "WHAT IF" LATELY?
WE THOUGHT WE WEREN'T WANTED. WHAT IF. WHAT IF.
AND SO...
WHAT IF, WHAT IF... IT'S ABOUT TIME WE SAID GOODBYE?
WHAT IF? WHAT IF?
HUH?!
WHAT IF, WHAT IF... HAPPY 34TH BIRTHDAY, RINKO.
HEH HEH! OUR JOB ENDED UP BEING A YEAR-LONG LIMITED CONTRACT. WHAT IF. WHAT IF.

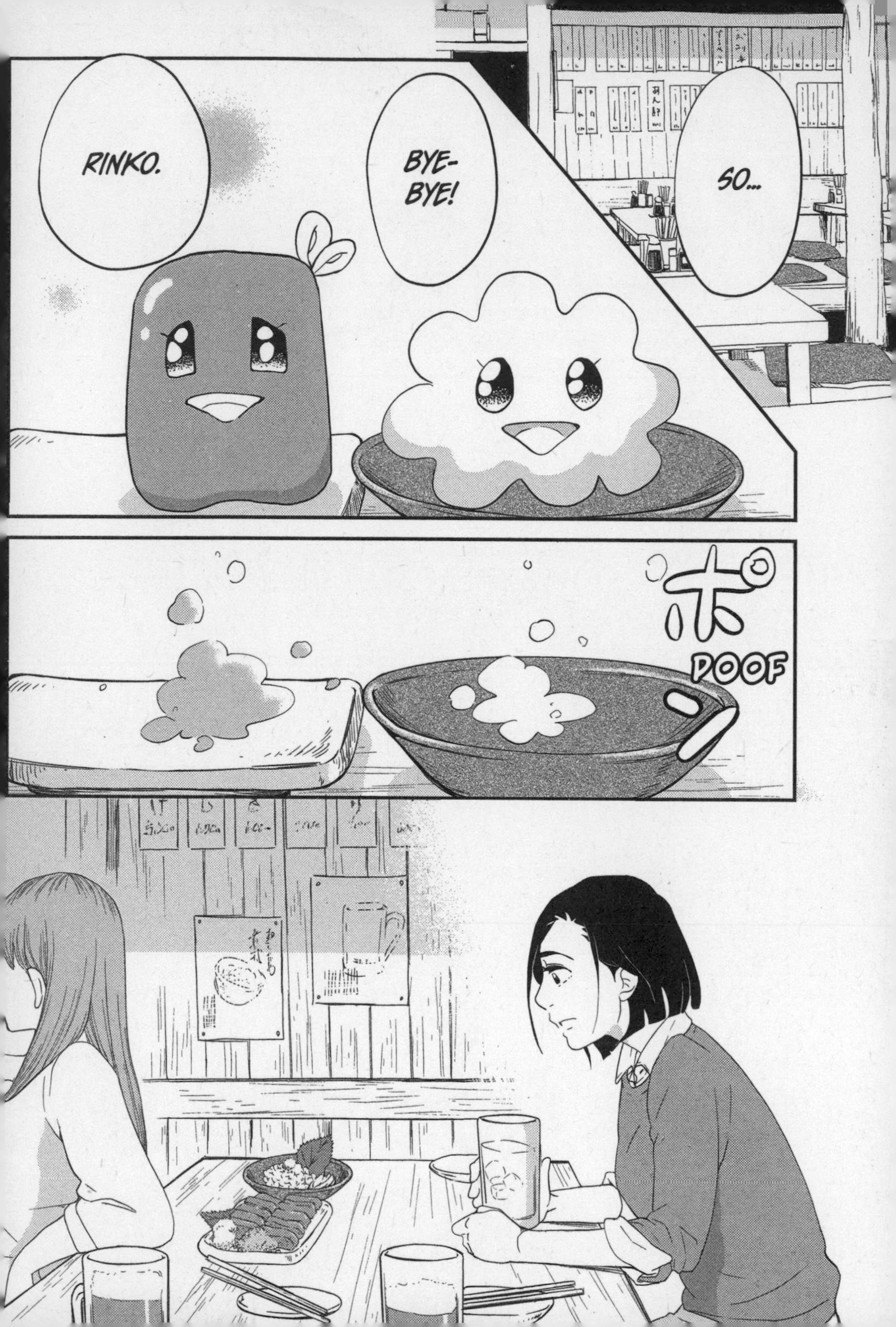
SO...
BYE-BYE!
RINKO.
ポ
POOF

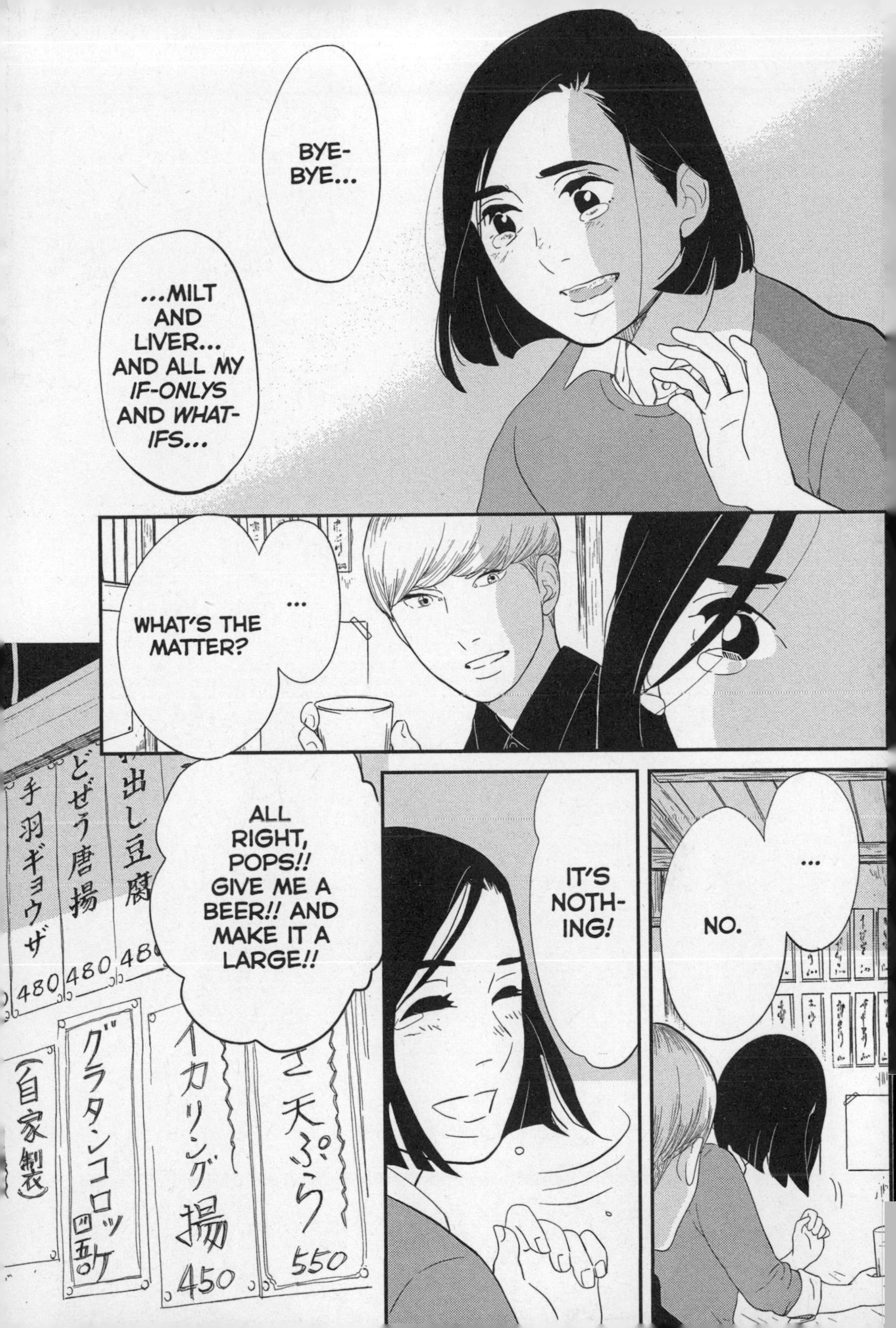
BYE-BYE...
...MILT AND LIVER... AND ALL MY IF-ONLYS AND WHAT-IFS...
... WHAT'S THE MATTER?
... NO.
IT'S NOTHING!
ALL RIGHT, POPS!! GIVE ME A BEER!! AND MAKE IT A LARGE!!
手羽ギョウザ 480
どぜう唐揚 480
イカリング揚 450
グラタンコロッ
(自家製)

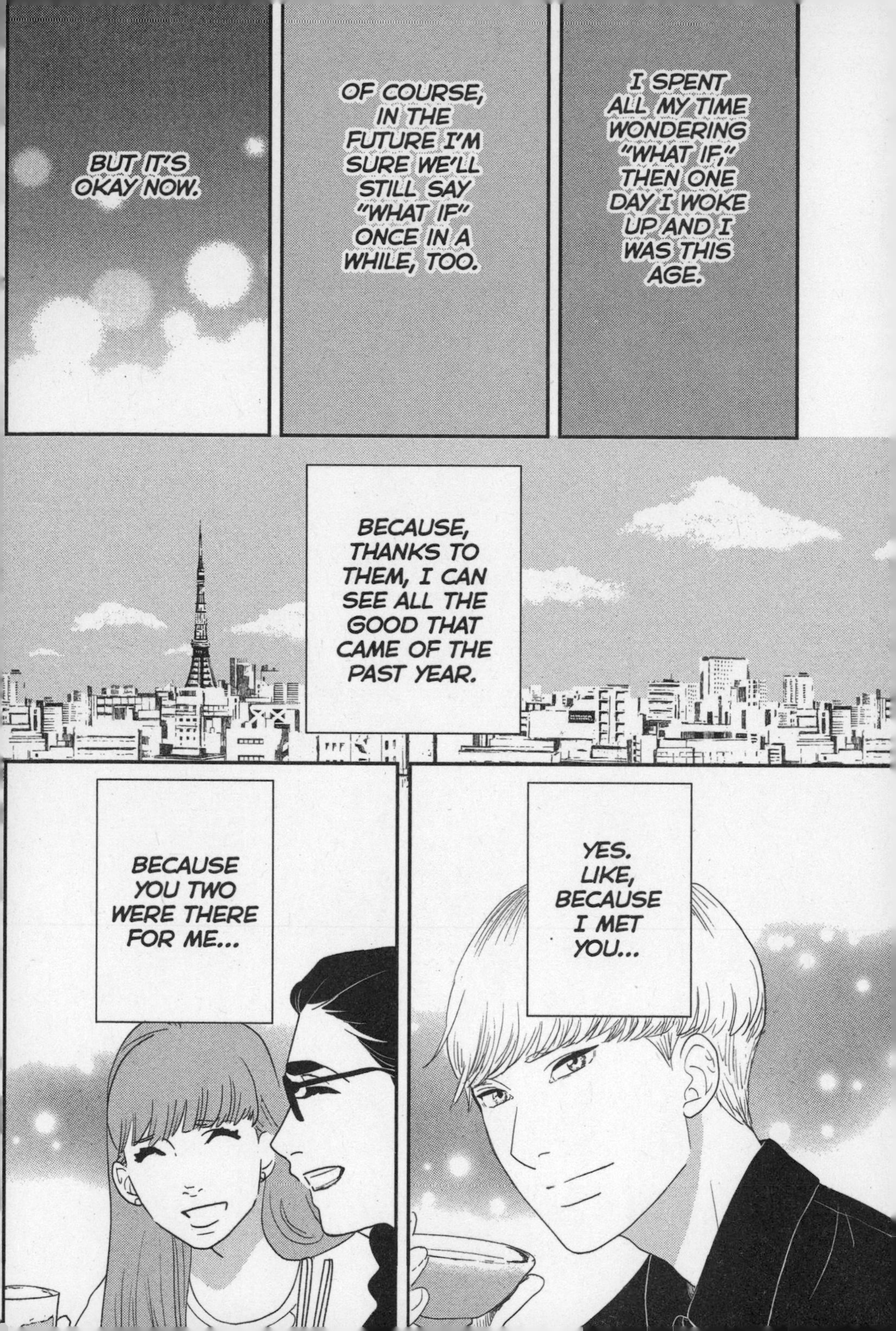
I SPENT ALL MY TIME WONDERING "WHAT IF," THEN ONE DAY I WOKE UP AND I WAS THIS AGE.
OF COURSE, IN THE FUTURE I'M SURE WE'LL STILL SAY "WHAT IF" ONCE IN A WHILE, TOO.
BUT IT'S OKAY NOW.
BECAUSE, THANKS TO THEM, I CAN SEE ALL THE GOOD THAT CAME OF THE PAST YEAR.
YES. LIKE, BECAUSE I MET YOU...
BECAUSE YOU TWO WERE THERE FOR ME...

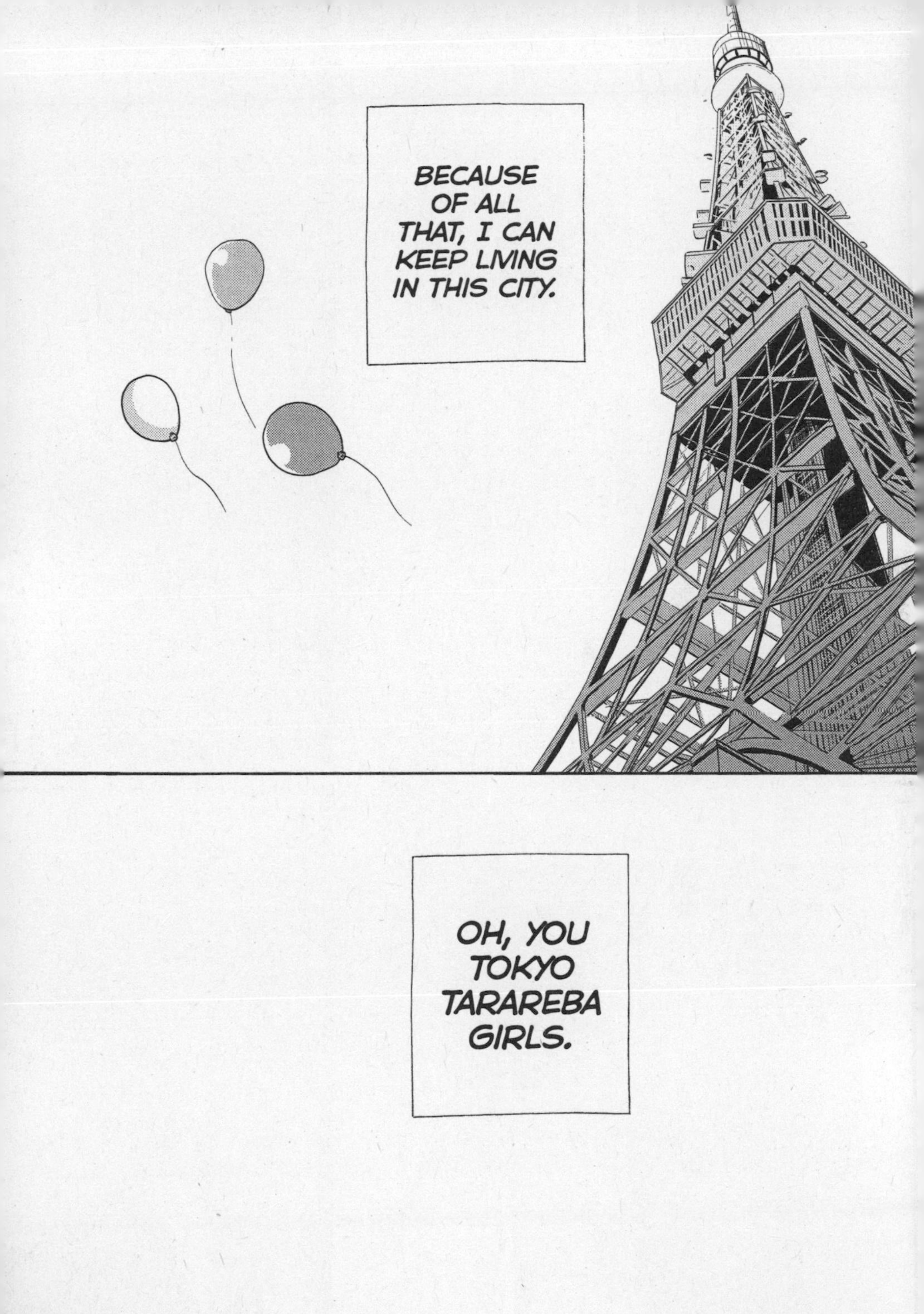
BECAUSE OF ALL THAT, I CAN KEEP LIVING IN THIS CITY.
OH, YOU TOKYO TARAREBA GIRLS.

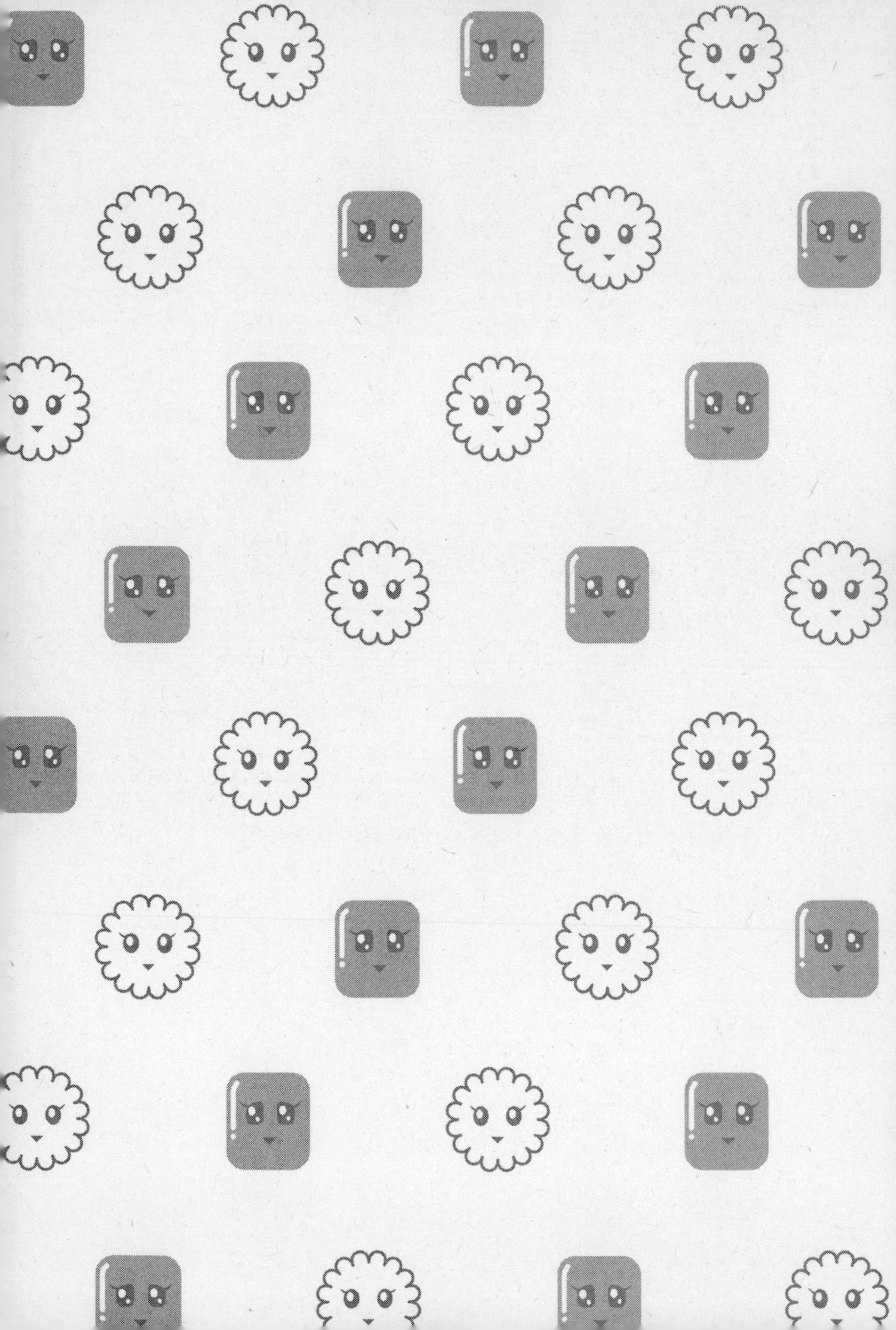

★ NIGHT 17 ★

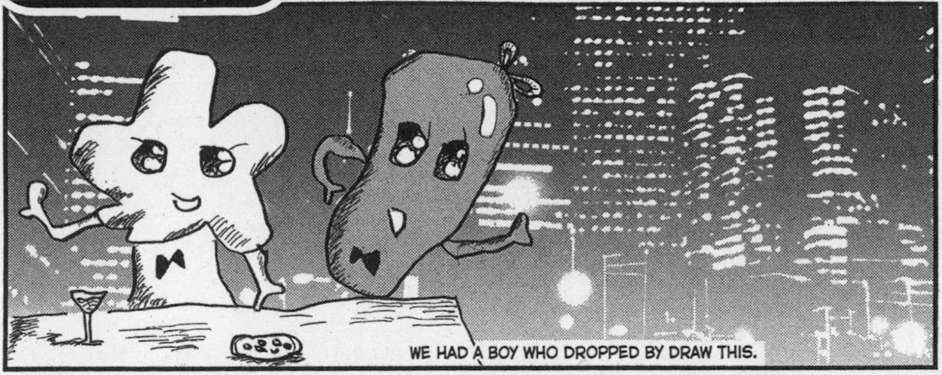
WE HAD A BOY WHO DROPPED BY DRAW THIS.

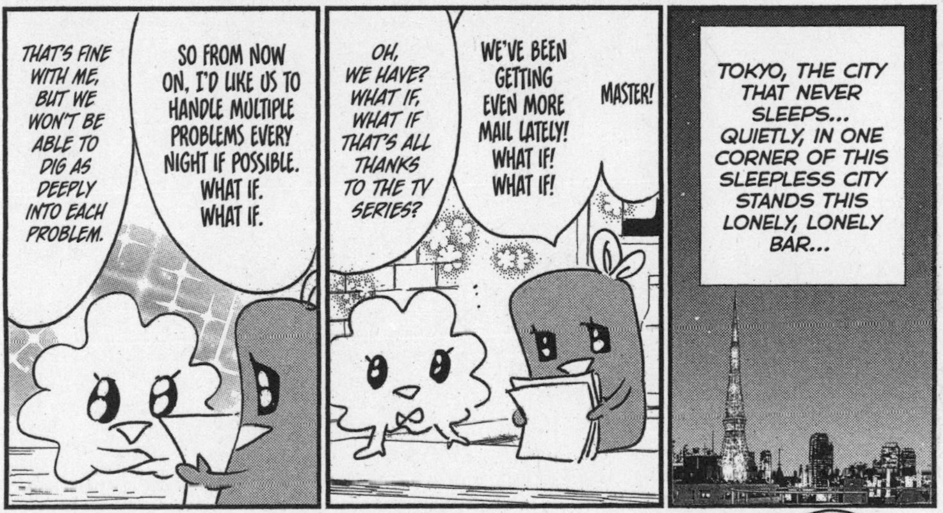
TOKYO, THE CITY THAT NEVER SLEEPS... QUIETLY, IN ONE CORNER OF THIS SLEEPLESS CITY STANDS THIS LONELY, LONELY BAR...
MASTER!
WE'VE BEEN GETTING EVEN MORE MAIL LATELY! WHAT IF! WHAT IF!
OH, WE HAVE? WHAT IF, WHAT IF THAT'S ALL THANKS TO THE TV SERIES?
SO FROM NOW ON, I'D LIKE US TO HANDLE MULTIPLE PROBLEMS EVERY NIGHT IF POSSIBLE. WHAT IF. WHAT IF.
THAT'S FINE WITH ME, BUT WE WON'T BE ABLE TO DIG AS DEEPLY INTO EACH PROBLEM.

I'M A 40-YEAR-OLD HOUSEWIFE.
I HAVE A SISTER TWO YEARS OLDER THAN ME.
MY SISTER LIVED HER TWENTIES AND THIRTIES LIKE THE THREE TARAREBA GIRLS, AND IS STILL SINGLE NOW. AFTER PASSING AGE 40, SHE MUST'VE STARTED PANICKING, BECAUSE SHE JOINED A BUNCH OF MATCHMAKING SITES AND STARTED GOING TO A BUNCH OF MATCHMAKING PARTIES, MEETING ALL KINDS OF MEN. BUT AFTER HER DATES, SHE COMES TO ME AND BADMOUTHS EVERY GUY. STUFF LIKE:
"THAT'S NO WAY TO RESPOND TO A TEXT!!"
"WHY DON'T YOU INVITE ME, HUH?!"
"LOOK IT UP YOURSELF, IDIOT!!"
WHAT SHOULD I TELL HER?

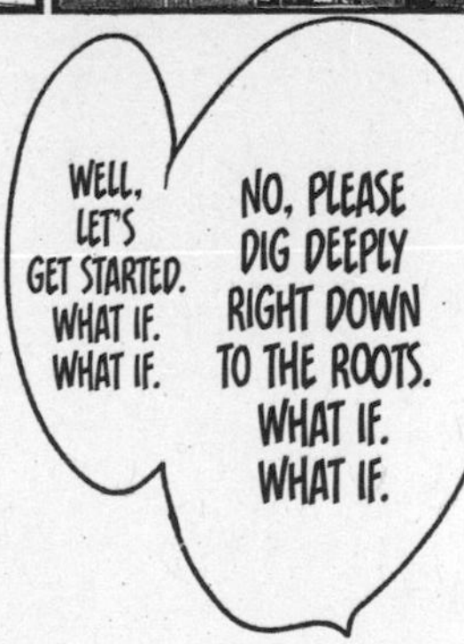
NO, PLEASE DIG DEEPLY RIGHT DOWN TO THE ROOTS. WHAT IF. WHAT IF.
WELL, LET'S GET STARTED. WHAT IF. WHAT IF.

PN: A WHAT-IF SISTER (40)

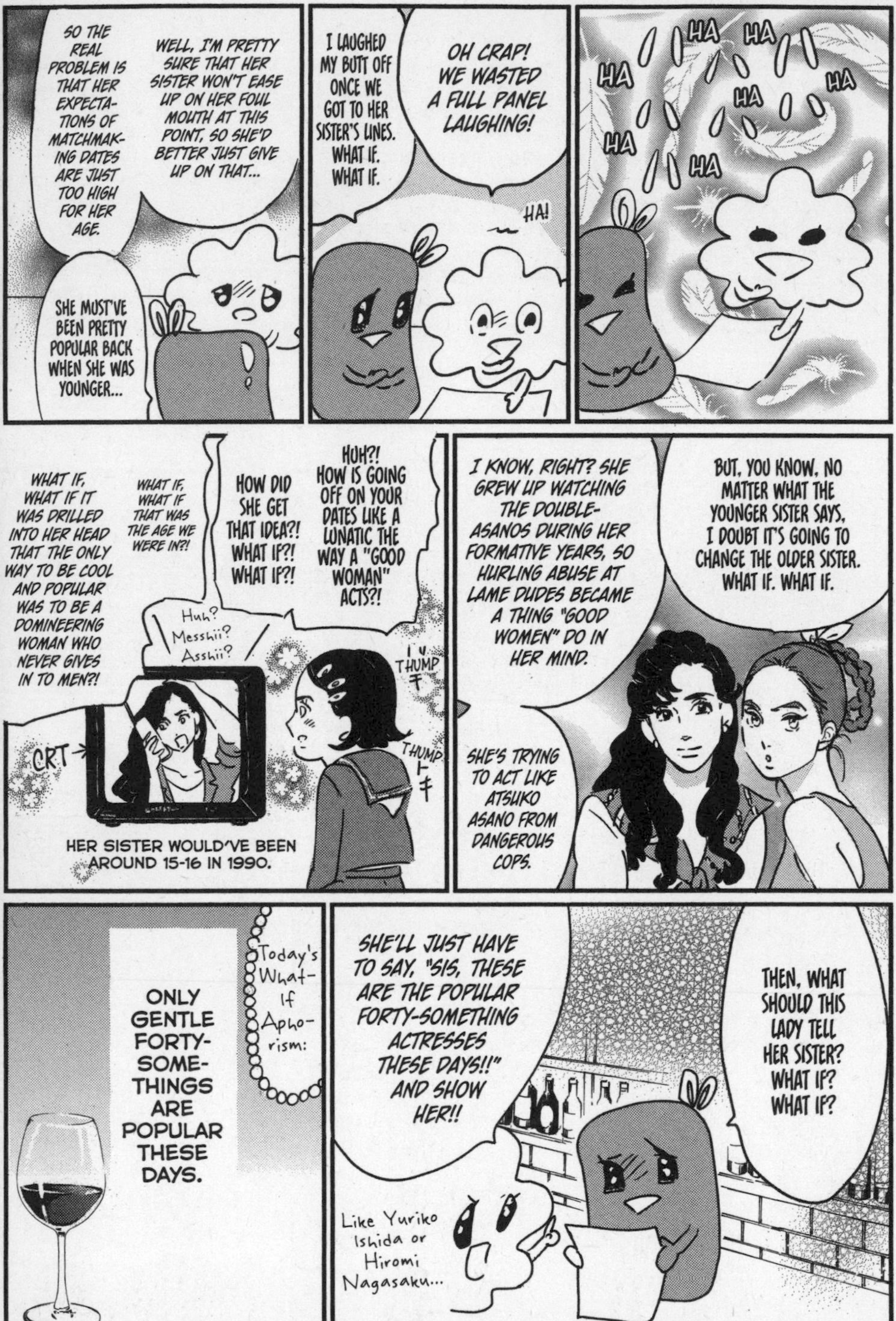
HA HA HA HA HA HA HA
OH CRAP! WE WASTED A FULL PANEL LAUGHING!
I LAUGHED MY BUTT OFF ONCE WE GOT TO HER SISTER'S LINES. WHAT IF. WHAT IF.
HA!
WELL, I'M PRETTY SURE THAT HER SISTER WON'T EASE UP ON HER FOUL MOUTH AT THIS POINT, SO SHE'D BETTER JUST GIVE UP ON THAT...
SO THE REAL PROBLEM IS THAT HER EXPECTATIONS OF MATCHMAKING DATES ARE JUST TOO HIGH FOR HER AGE.
SHE MUST'VE BEEN PRETTY POPULAR BACK WHEN SHE WAS YOUNGER...
BUT, YOU KNOW, NO MATTER WHAT THE YOUNGER SISTER SAYS, I DOUBT IT'S GOING TO CHANGE THE OLDER SISTER. WHAT IF. WHAT IF.
I KNOW, RIGHT? SHE GREW UP WATCHING THE DOUBLE-ASANOS DURING HER FORMATIVE YEARS, SO HURLING ABUSE AT LAME DUDES BECAME A THING "GOOD WOMEN" DO IN HER MIND.
SHE'S TRYING TO ACT LIKE ATSUKO ASANO FROM DANGEROUS COPS.
HUH?! HOW IS GOING OFF ON YOUR DATES LIKE A LUNATIC THE WAY A "GOOD WOMAN" ACTS?!
HOW DID SHE GET THAT IDEA?! WHAT IF?! WHAT IF?!
WHAT IF, WHAT IF THAT WAS THE AGE WE WERE IN?!
WHAT IF, WHAT IF IT WAS DRILLED INTO HER HEAD THAT THE ONLY WAY TO BE COOL AND POPULAR WAS TO BE A DOMINEERING WOMAN WHO NEVER GIVES IN TO MEN?!
THUMP
THUMP
Huh? Messhii? Asshii?
CRT
HER SISTER WOULD'VE BEEN AROUND 15-16 IN 1990.
THEN, WHAT SHOULD THIS LADY TELL HER SISTER? WHAT IF? WHAT IF?
SHE'LL JUST HAVE TO SAY, "SIS, THESE ARE THE POPULAR FORTY-SOMETHING ACTRESSES THESE DAYS!!" AND SHOW HER!!
Like Yuriko Ishida or Hiromi Nagasaku...
Today's What-If Aphorism:
ONLY GENTLE FORTY-SOMETHINGS ARE POPULAR THESE DAYS.

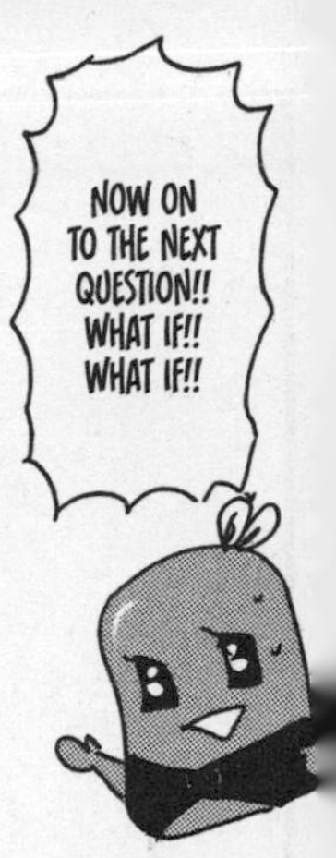
NOW ON TO THE NEXT QUESTION!! WHAT IF!! WHAT IF!!

AT 25 I MARRIED A MAN MY AGE THAT I MET AT A MIXER. SINCE HE MOVES AROUND A LOT FOR WORK, I QUIT MY JOB AND I'M NOW A HOUSEWIFE. MAYBE THIS IS THE KIND OF THING ALL THE TARAREBA GIRLS IN THE WORLD WOULD CONSIDER "SMOOTH SAILING" AND BE JEALOUS OF, BUT I'VE ALWAYS HAD A DRY PERSONALITY AND FIGURED IT WOULD BE SILLY TO ALWAYS BE SEARCHING FOR MR. RIGHT, SO I ENDED UP WITH MY CURRENT LIFESTYLE BY THINKING "I GUESS I'LL JUST GO WITH HIM." NOTHING MORE THAN THAT.
IT'S NOT LIKE I HAVE ANY REAL COMPLAINTS, BUT IT'S NOT LIKE MY LIFE IS SUPER HAPPY!! EITHER (MAYBE IT'S BECAUSE MY HOME LIFE WASN'T GREAT, BUT I DIDN'T HAVE HIGH HOPES OR WANT KIDS ANYWAY).
WHEN I THINK ABOUT LIVING THE NEXT SIXTY OR SO YEARS OF MY LIFE LIKE THIS, IT KIND OF SENDS SHIVERS UP MY SPINE. SHOULD I BE SATISFIED WITH MY CURRENT LIFE AND TRY TO BE SUPER HAPPY?

I'D LOVE TO HEAR YOUR SCATHING COMMENTS / ADVICE.

PN: SUPER DRY (26)

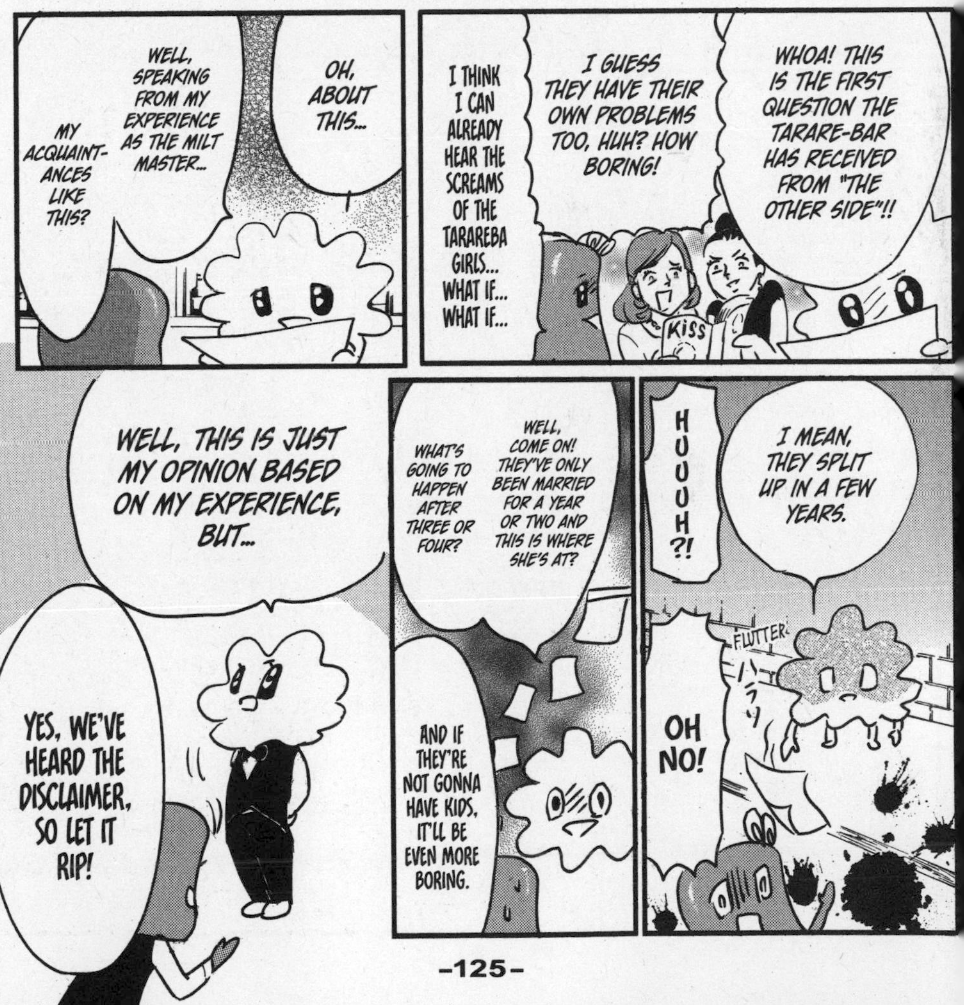
WHOA! THIS IS THE FIRST QUESTION THE TARARE-BAR HAS RECEIVED FROM "THE OTHER SIDE"!!
I GUESS THEY HAVE THEIR OWN PROBLEMS TOO, HUH? HOW BORING!
I THINK I CAN ALREADY HEAR THE SCREAMS OF THE TARAREBA GIRLS... WHAT IF... WHAT IF...
KISS
OH, ABOUT THIS...
WELL, SPEAKING FROM MY EXPERIENCE AS THE MILT MASTER...
MY ACQUAINT-ANCES LIKE THIS?
I MEAN, THEY SPLIT UP IN A FEW YEARS.
HUUUH?!
FLUTTER
OH NO!
WELL, COME ON! THEY'VE ONLY BEEN MARRIED FOR A YEAR OR TWO AND THIS IS WHERE SHE'S AT?
WHAT'S GOING TO HAPPEN AFTER THREE OR FOUR?
AND IF THEY'RE NOT GONNA HAVE KIDS, IT'LL BE EVEN MORE BORING.
WELL, THIS IS JUST MY OPINION BASED ON MY EXPERIENCE, BUT...
YES, WE'VE HEARD THE DISCLAIMER, SO LET IT RIP!

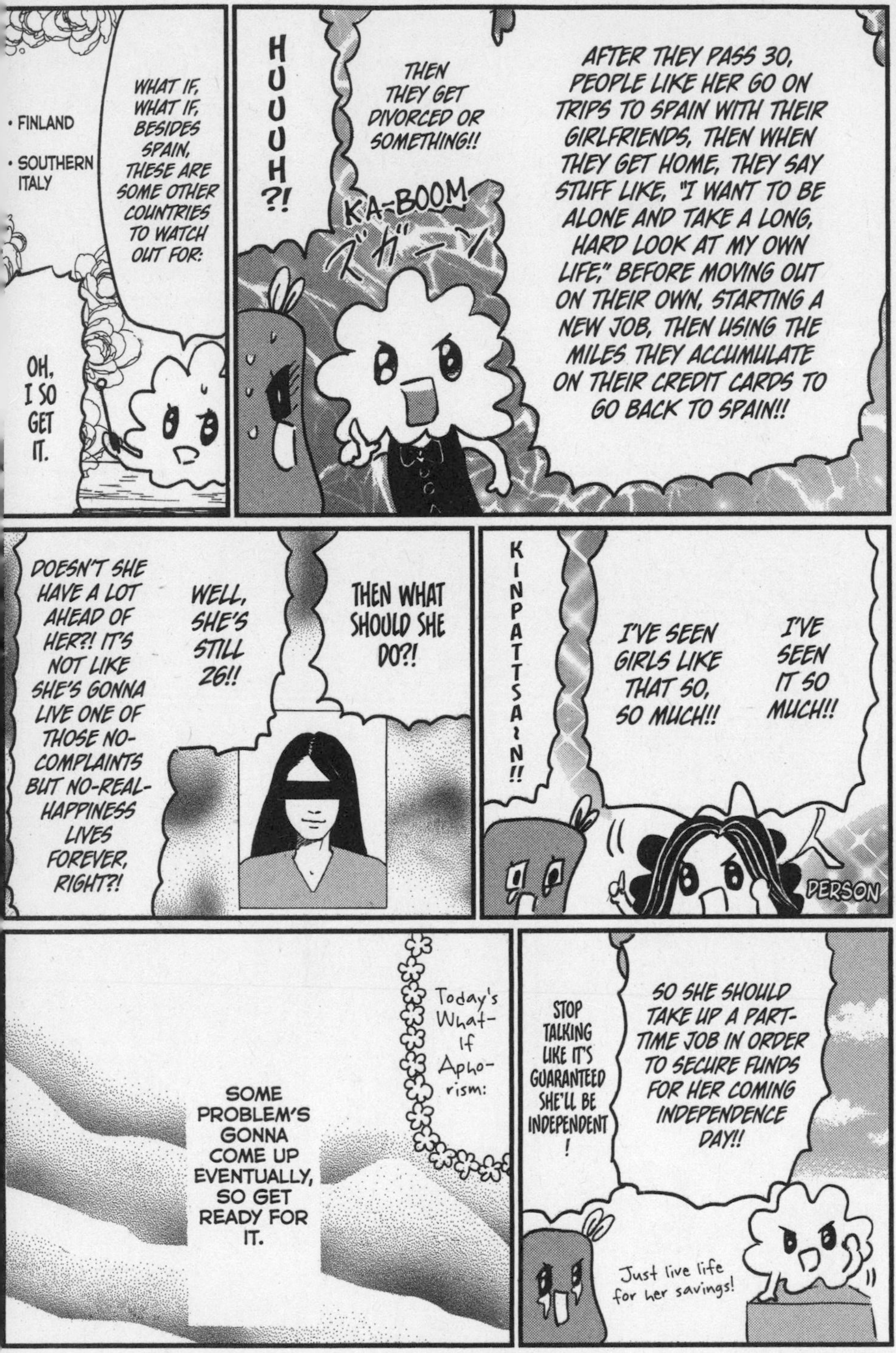
AFTER THEY PASS 30, PEOPLE LIKE HER GO ON TRIPS TO SPAIN WITH THEIR GIRLFRIENDS, THEN WHEN THEY GET HOME, THEY SAY STUFF LIKE, "I WANT TO BE ALONE AND TAKE A LONG, HARD LOOK AT MY OWN LIFE," BEFORE MOVING OUT ON THEIR OWN, STARTING A NEW JOB, THEN USING THE MILES THEY ACCUMULATE ON THEIR CREDIT CARDS TO GO BACK TO SPAIN!!
THEN THEY GET DIVORCED OR SOMETHING!!
HUUUUH?!
KA-BOOM
ズガーン
WHAT IF, WHAT IF, BESIDES SPAIN, THESE ARE SOME OTHER COUNTRIES TO WATCH OUT FOR:
• FINLAND
• SOUTHERN ITALY
OH, I SO GET IT.
I'VE SEEN IT SO MUCH!!
I'VE SEEN GIRLS LIKE THAT SO, SO MUCH!!
KINPATTSA~N!!
人
PERSON
THEN WHAT SHOULD SHE DO?!
WELL, SHE'S STILL 26!!
DOESN'T SHE HAVE A LOT AHEAD OF HER?! IT'S NOT LIKE SHE'S GONNA LIVE ONE OF THOSE NO-COMPLAINTS BUT NO-REAL-HAPPINESS LIVES FOREVER, RIGHT?!
SO SHE SHOULD TAKE UP A PART-TIME JOB IN ORDER TO SECURE FUNDS FOR HER COMING INDEPENDENCE DAY!!
STOP TALKING LIKE IT'S GUARANTEED SHE'LL BE INDEPENDENT!
Just live life for her savings!
Today's What-If Aphorism:
SOME PROBLEM'S GONNA COME UP EVENTUALLY, SO GET READY FOR IT.

TOKYO

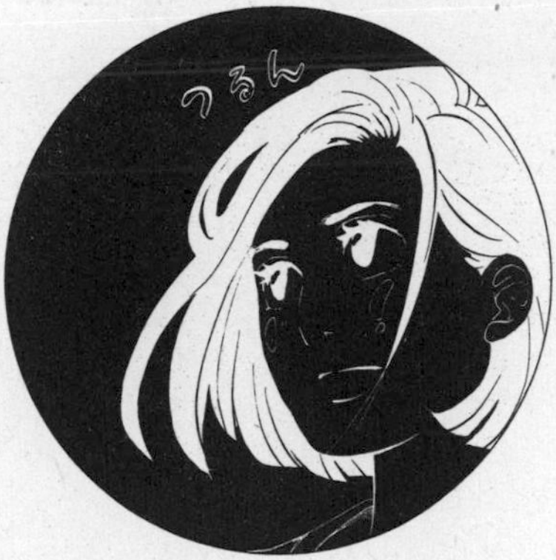
つるん

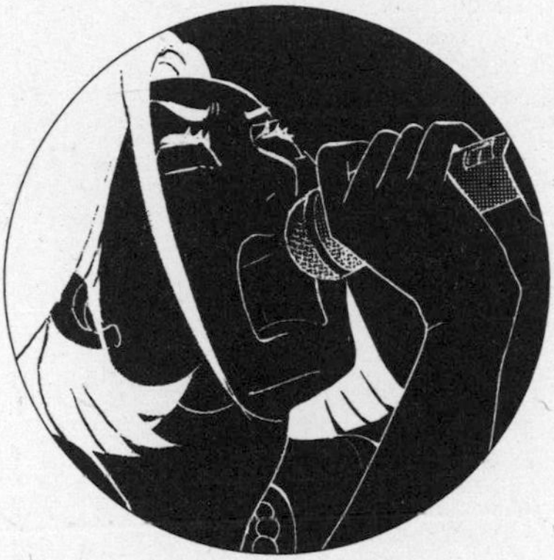

TARAREBA

GIRLS

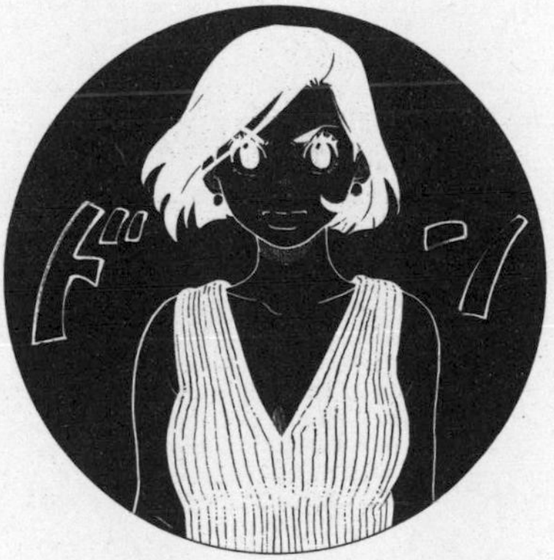

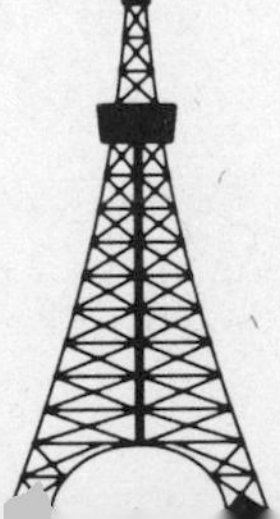

TOKYO

 TARAREBA

GIRLS

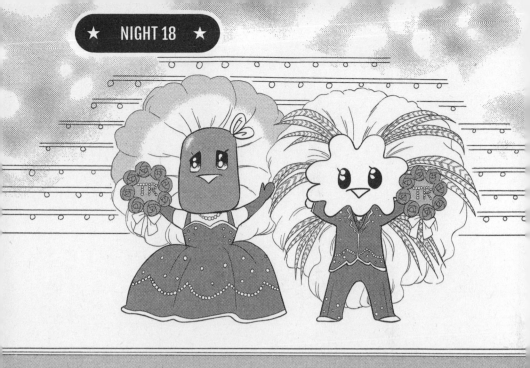

★ NIGHT 18 ★

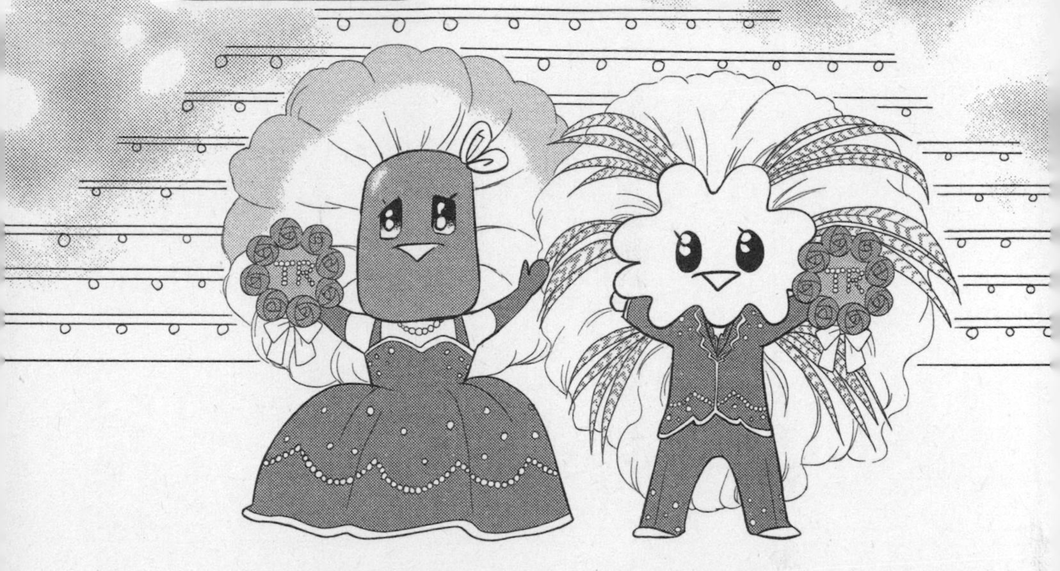

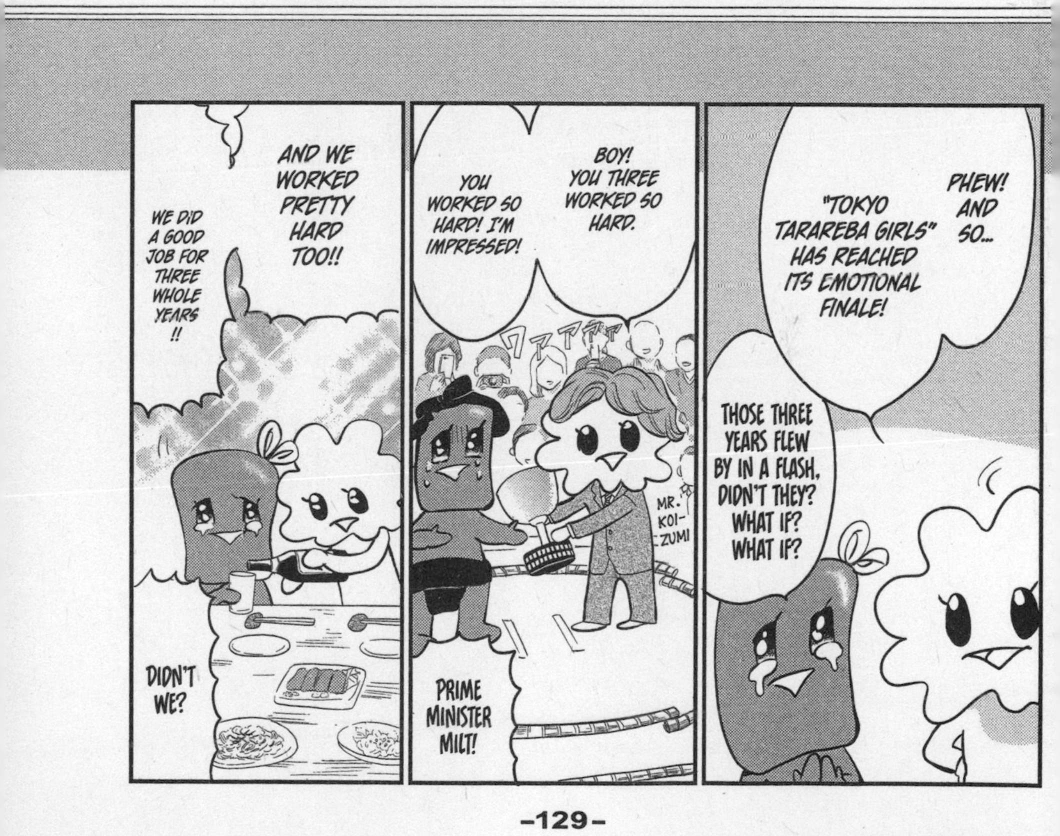
PHEW! AND SO...
"TOKYO TARAREBA GIRLS" HAS REACHED ITS EMOTIONAL FINALE!
THOSE THREE YEARS FLEW BY IN A FLASH, DIDN'T THEY? WHAT IF? WHAT IF?
BOY! YOU THREE WORKED SO HARD.
YOU WORKED SO HARD! I'M IMPRESSED!
MR. KOI-ZUMI
PRIME MINISTER MILT!
AND WE WORKED PRETTY HARD TOO!!
WE DID A GOOD JOB FOR THREE WHOLE YEARS!!
DIDN'T WE?

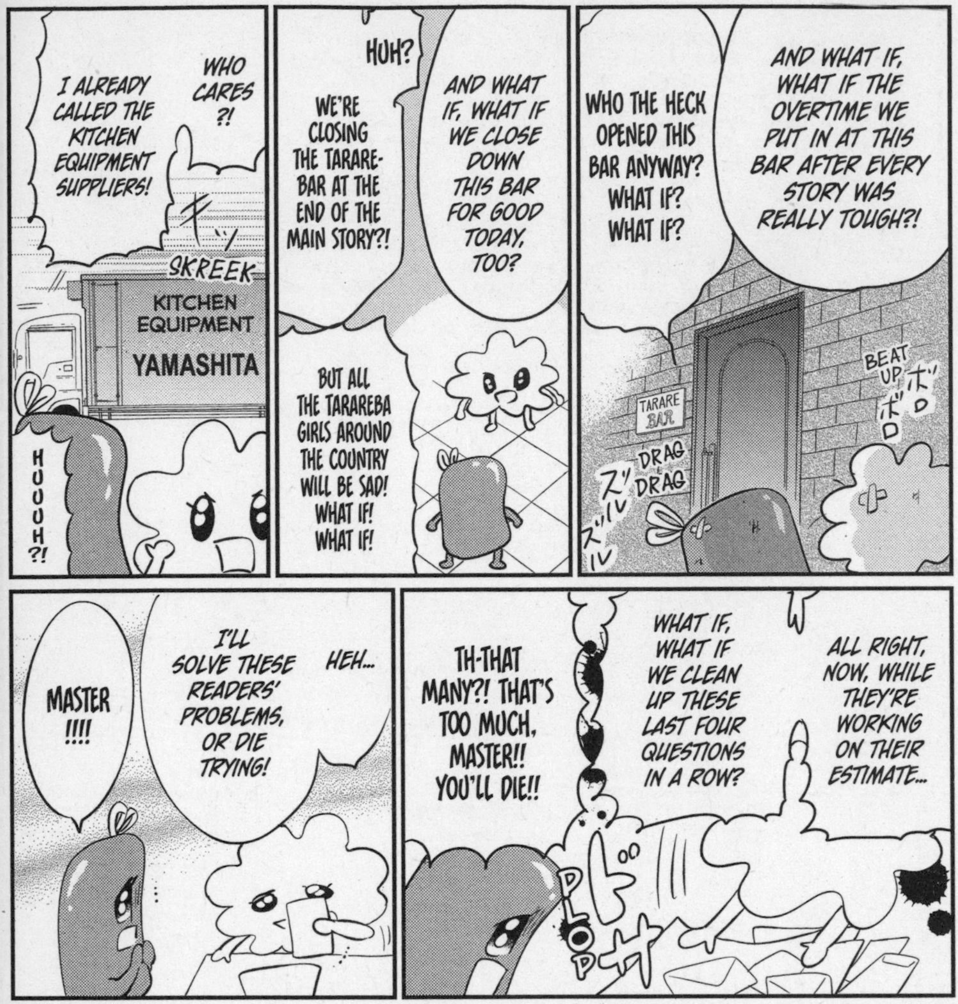
AND WHAT IF, WHAT IF THE OVERTIME WE PUT IN AT THIS BAR AFTER EVERY STORY WAS REALLY TOUGH?!
WHO THE HECK OPENED THIS BAR ANYWAY? WHAT IF? WHAT IF?
TARARE BAR
BEAT UP
DRAG DRAG
AND WHAT IF, WHAT IF WE CLOSE DOWN THIS BAR FOR GOOD TODAY, TOO?
HUH?
WE'RE CLOSING THE TARARE-BAR AT THE END OF THE MAIN STORY?!
BUT ALL THE TARAREBA GIRLS AROUND THE COUNTRY WILL BE SAD! WHAT IF! WHAT IF!
WHO CARES?!
I ALREADY CALLED THE KITCHEN EQUIPMENT SUPPLIERS!
SKREEK
KITCHEN EQUIPMENT
YAMASHITA
HUUUUH?!
ALL RIGHT, NOW, WHILE THEY'RE WORKING ON THEIR ESTIMATE...
WHAT IF, WHAT IF WE CLEAN UP THESE LAST FOUR QUESTIONS IN A ROW?
TH-THAT MANY?! THAT'S TOO MUCH, MASTER!! YOU'LL DIE!!
PLOP
HEH...
I'LL SOLVE THESE READERS' PROBLEMS, OR DIE TRYING!
MASTER!!!!

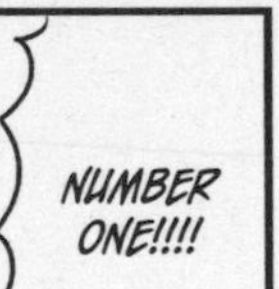
NUMBER ONE!!!!
FWIP

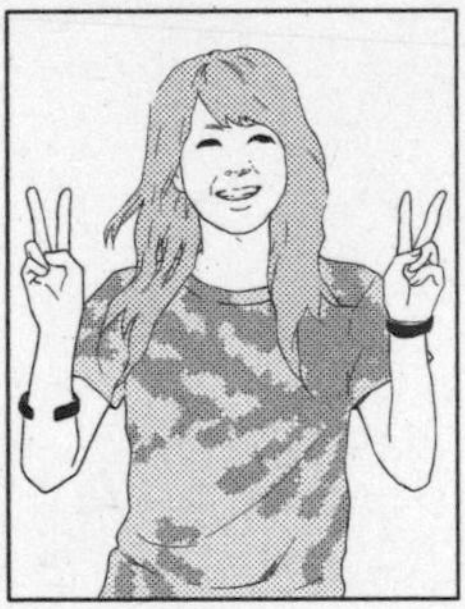

NICE TO MEET YOU.
HELLO. I AM A 35-YEAR-OLD SINGLE WOMAN LIVING IN OSAKA.
UM...FIRST OFF...
I FALL FOR, LIKE, EVERYONE. I HAVE ABSOLUTELY NO TYPE TO SPEAK OF, SO AS LONG AS THEY DON'T LOOK...WELL, UNFORTUNATE, I'LL FALL FOR MEN INSTANTLY (LOL). I'M ESPECIALLY WEAK TO BEING TREATED NICE AND BEING MADE TO FEEL SPECIAL, AND I CAN GET HAPPY JUST DAYDREAMING FROM THERE, GET COMPLACENT, AND END UP MAKING NO PROGRESS (SOB).
OR SOMETIMES I RUSH INTO A PHYSICAL RELATIONSHIP, WHICH IS THE WORST (SOB AGAIN)... WHEN THAT HAPPENED, I FELT REALLY ASHAMED OF MYSELF, SO I STOPPED. STILL, THERE HAVE BEEN TIMES WHEN I WENT HOME WITH A GUY AND EVEN THOUGH I KNEW I SHOULDN'T, I'D START THINKING HE MIGHT BE LIKE, "IS SHE HOLDING OUT ON ME?" OR "WHAT IS SHE EVEN HERE FOR?"...AND BECAUSE OF THAT, I'D END UP DOING IT ANYWAY.
AT THIS POINT, I DON'T EVEN KNOW WHAT MY DEAL IS EITHER, SO MAYBE I'M JUST DOING THIS STUFF WITHOUT EVEN THINKING...I GUESS? BUT I GUESS I KNOW IT'S "WEIRD" AND "STRANGE" (SWEAT).

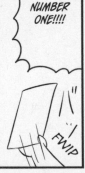

WHEN THE MAN IS A LOT YOUNGER THAN ME, IT DOESN'T FEEL REAL, SO I GET TO THINKING ABOUT THE FUTURE AND HOW "HE'S GONNA END UP DUMPING ME..." THEN, WHEN I TRY AN OLDER MAN, I START THINKING, "BUT HE'S SO MATURE..." EVEN AT MY AGE, I HAVE NO IDEA WHAT KIND OF GUY WOULD ACTUALLY "FIT" ME.
AT THE MOMENT, I'M AT THAT STAGE WHERE I FALL FOR GUYS THEN DO MY BEST TO GET THEM TO LIKE ME BACK...BUT WHEN I FINALLY "LAND" ONE, THE "CARNIVORE" INSIDE ME REVEALS ITSELF AND "FREAKS OUT" THE GUYS...
I CAN NEVER GET TO THE ACTUAL "DATING" STAGE, SO I'M JUST CRUSHING ON MULTIPLE GUYS AT THE MOMENT... (SOB)

#1 - MR. A (36)	FROM TOKYO, RESIDES IN GIFU OFFICE WORKER TALK ON THE PHONE, GO OUT FOR DRINKS WHEN HE COMES TO OSAKA, BUT THAT'S ALL. MET HIM AT A BAR NEAR HOME.
#2 - MR. S (40)	RESIDES IN OSAKA BARTENDER I GO TO DRINK AT HIS BAR, WE MEET AT MUTUAL ACQUAINTANCES' MUSIC EVENTS, WHEN HE GETS DRUNK (AND ONLY THEN) HE HUGS ME AND ACTS ALL CUTE AND NEEDY AND STUFF...

WRITING ALL THIS NOW HAS MADE ME SAD... YES, I'M A WOMAN WHO LOVES BOOZE AND MEETS ALL HER MEN AT BARS (SOB).
IN THE FUTURE...NO, IS THERE ANY WAY I CAN DATE BOTH OF THEM?
THERE ISN'T, RIGHT? WHAT IS REAL LOVE ANYWAY?

PN: CHAM (3♡)

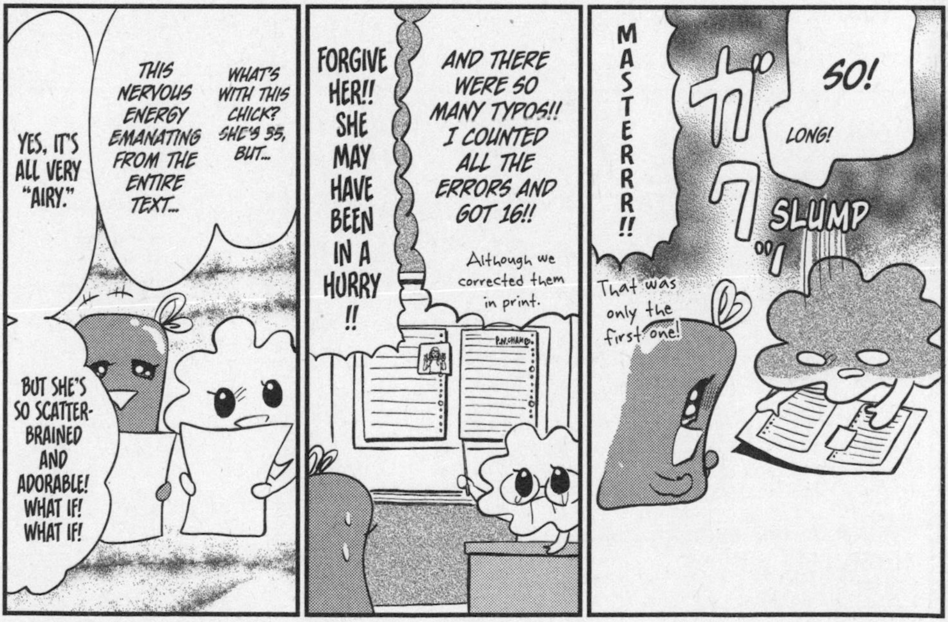
SO! LONG!
MASTERRR!!
ガク
SLUMP
That was only the first one!
AND THERE WERE SO MANY TYPOS!! I COUNTED ALL THE ERRORS AND GOT 16!!
Although we corrected them in print.
FORGIVE HER!! SHE MAY HAVE BEEN IN A HURRY!!
WHAT'S WITH THIS CHICK? SHE'S 35, BUT...
THIS NERVOUS ENERGY EMANATING FROM THE ENTIRE TEXT...
YES, IT'S ALL VERY "AIRY."
BUT SHE'S SO SCATTER-BRAINED AND ADORABLE! WHAT IF! WHAT IF!

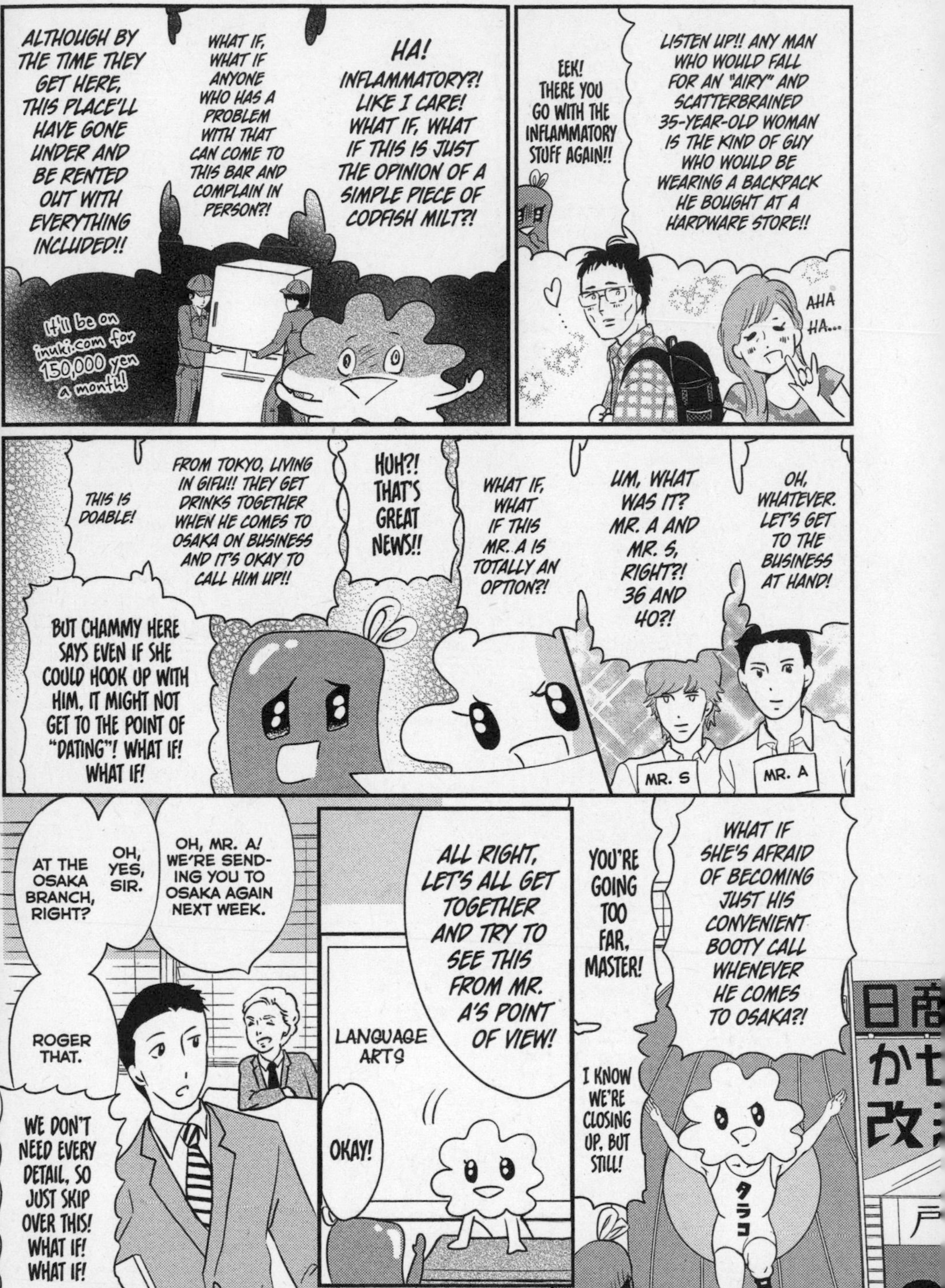
LISTEN UP!! ANY MAN WHO WOULD FALL FOR AN "AIRY" AND SCATTERBRAINED 35-YEAR-OLD WOMAN IS THE KIND OF GUY WHO WOULD BE WEARING A BACKPACK HE BOUGHT AT A HARDWARE STORE!!
EEK! THERE YOU GO WITH THE INFLAMMATORY STUFF AGAIN!!
AHA HA...
HA! INFLAMMATORY?! LIKE I CARE! WHAT IF, WHAT IF THIS IS JUST THE OPINION OF A SIMPLE PIECE OF CODFISH MILT?!
WHAT IF, WHAT IF ANYONE WHO HAS A PROBLEM WITH THAT CAN COME TO THIS BAR AND COMPLAIN IN PERSON?!
ALTHOUGH BY THE TIME THEY GET HERE, THIS PLACE'LL HAVE GONE UNDER AND BE RENTED OUT WITH EVERYTHING INCLUDED!!
It'll be on inuki.com for 150,000 yen a month!
OH, WHATEVER. LET'S GET TO THE BUSINESS AT HAND!
UM, WHAT WAS IT? MR. A AND MR. S, RIGHT?! 36 AND 40?!
WHAT IF, WHAT IF THIS MR. A IS TOTALLY AN OPTION?!
HUH?! THAT'S GREAT NEWS!!
FROM TOKYO, LIVING IN GIFU!! THEY GET DRINKS TOGETHER WHEN HE COMES TO OSAKA ON BUSINESS AND IT'S OKAY TO CALL HIM UP!!
THIS IS DOABLE!
BUT CHAMMY HERE SAYS EVEN IF SHE COULD HOOK UP WITH HIM, IT MIGHT NOT GET TO THE POINT OF "DATING"! WHAT IF! WHAT IF!
MR. A
MR. S
WHAT IF SHE'S AFRAID OF BECOMING JUST HIS CONVENIENT BOOTY CALL WHENEVER HE COMES TO OSAKA?!
YOU'RE GOING TOO FAR, MASTER!
I KNOW WE'RE CLOSING UP, BUT STILL!
タラコ
SHIRT: TARAKO
ALL RIGHT, LET'S ALL GET TOGETHER AND TRY TO SEE THIS FROM MR. A'S POINT OF VIEW!
LANGUAGE ARTS
OKAY!
OH, MR. A! WE'RE SENDING YOU TO OSAKA AGAIN NEXT WEEK.
OH, YES, SIR.
AT THE OSAKA BRANCH, RIGHT?
ROGER THAT.
WE DON'T NEED EVERY DETAIL, SO JUST SKIP OVER THIS! WHAT IF! WHAT IF!

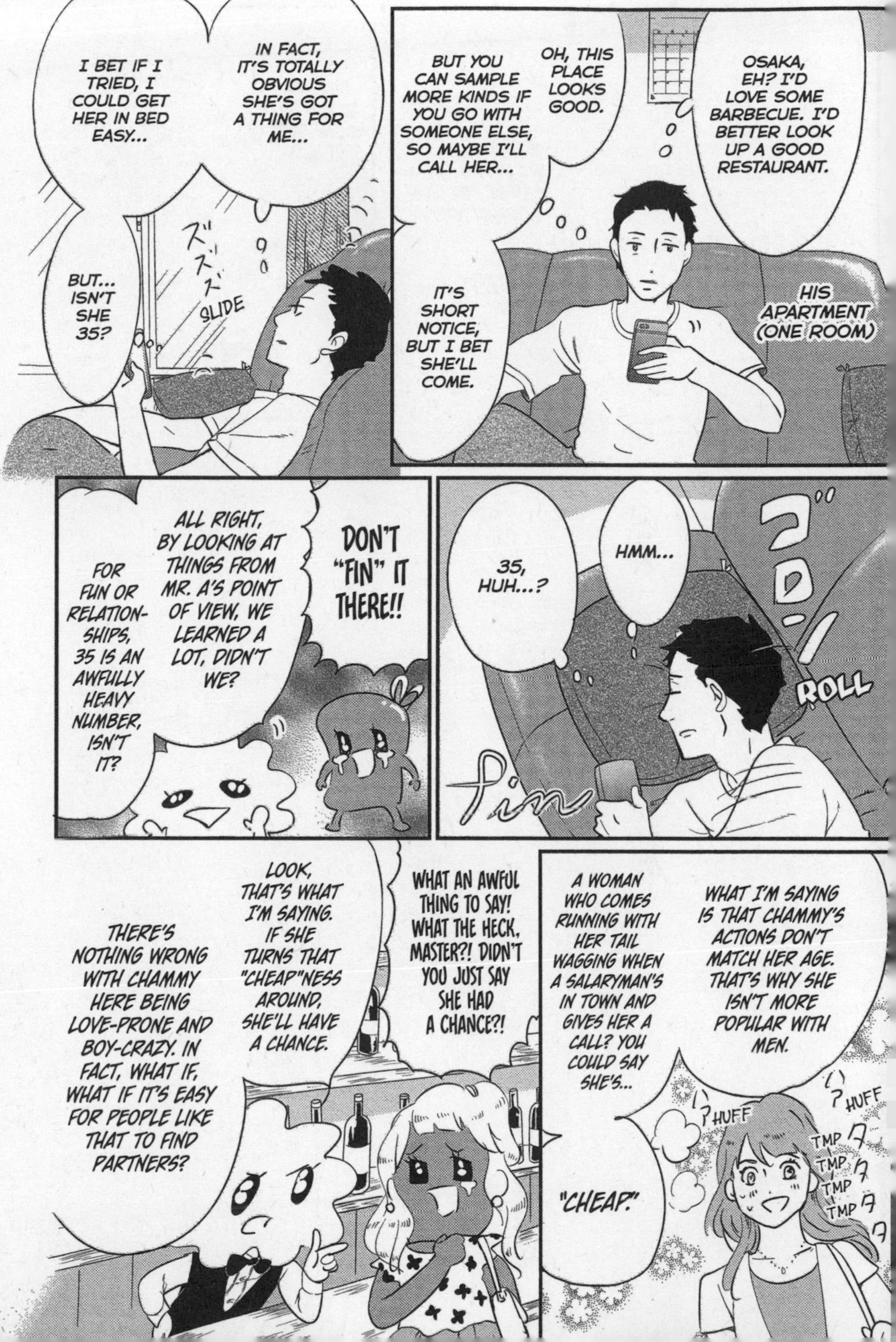
OSAKA, EH? I'D LOVE SOME BARBECUE. I'D BETTER LOOK UP A GOOD RESTAURANT.
HIS APARTMENT (ONE ROOM)
OH, THIS PLACE LOOKS GOOD.
BUT YOU CAN SAMPLE MORE KINDS IF YOU GO WITH SOMEONE ELSE, SO MAYBE I'LL CALL HER...
IT'S SHORT NOTICE, BUT I BET SHE'LL COME.
IN FACT, IT'S TOTALLY OBVIOUS SHE'S GOT A THING FOR ME...
I BET IF I TRIED, I COULD GET HER IN BED EASY...
SLIDE
BUT... ISN'T SHE 35?
HMM...
35, HUH...?
ROLL
fin
DON'T "FIN" IT THERE!!
ALL RIGHT, BY LOOKING AT THINGS FROM MR. A'S POINT OF VIEW, WE LEARNED A LOT, DIDN'T WE?
FOR FUN OR RELATION-SHIPS, 35 IS AN AWFULLY HEAVY NUMBER, ISN'T IT?
WHAT I'M SAYING IS THAT CHAMMY'S ACTIONS DON'T MATCH HER AGE. THAT'S WHY SHE ISN'T MORE POPULAR WITH MEN.
A WOMAN WHO COMES RUNNING WITH HER TAIL WAGGING WHEN A SALARYMAN'S IN TOWN AND GIVES HER A CALL? YOU COULD SAY SHE'S...
HUFF
HUFF
TMP
TMP
TMP
TMP
"CHEAP."
WHAT AN AWFUL THING TO SAY! WHAT THE HECK, MASTER?! DIDN'T YOU JUST SAY SHE HAD A CHANCE?!
LOOK, THAT'S WHAT I'M SAYING. IF SHE TURNS THAT "CHEAP"NESS AROUND, SHE'LL HAVE A CHANCE.
THERE'S NOTHING WRONG WITH CHAMMY HERE BEING LOVE-PRONE AND BOY-CRAZY. IN FACT, WHAT IF, WHAT IF IT'S EASY FOR PEOPLE LIKE THAT TO FIND PARTNERS?

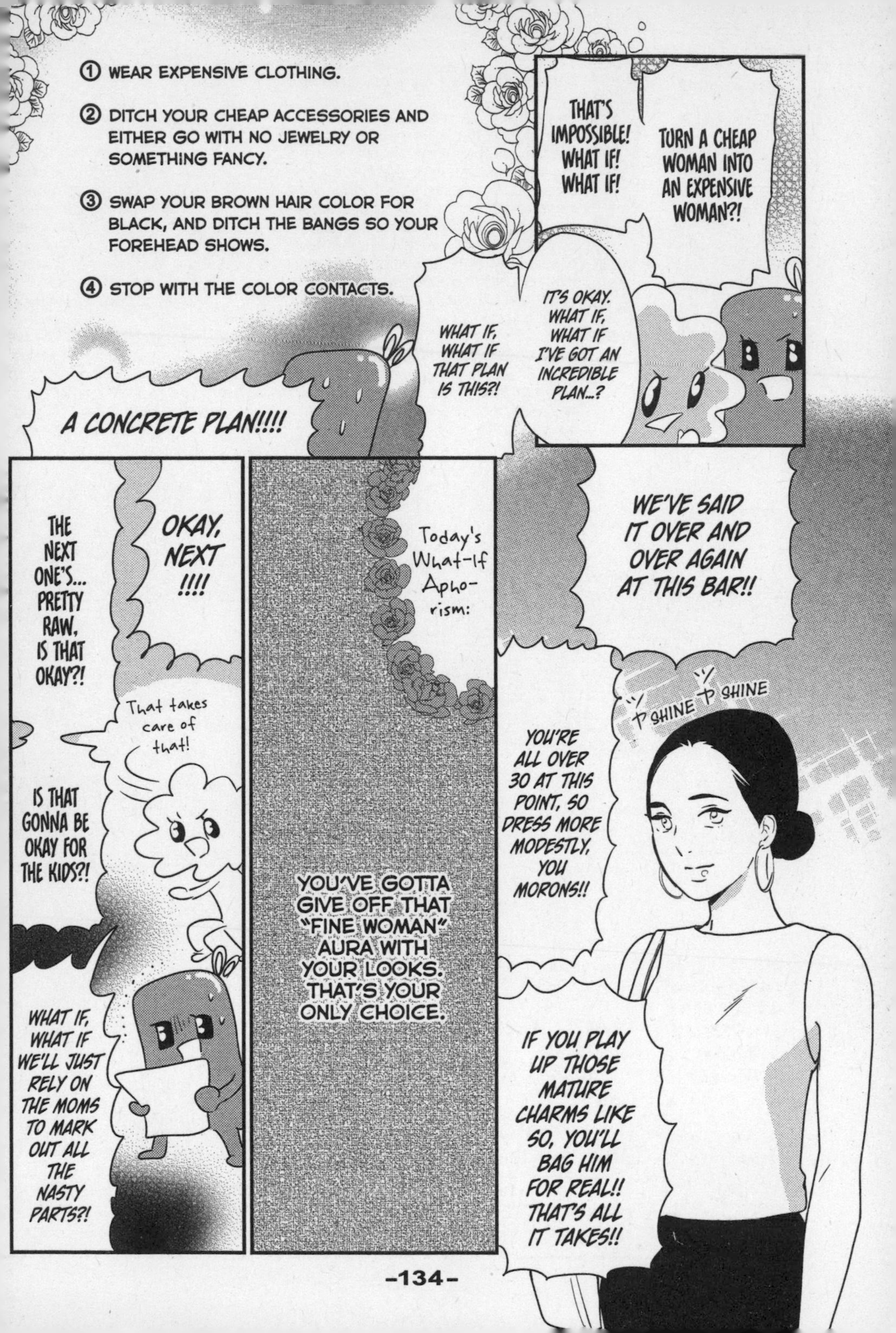

TURN A CHEAP WOMAN INTO AN EXPENSIVE WOMAN?!
THAT'S IMPOSSIBLE! WHAT IF! WHAT IF!
IT'S OKAY. WHAT IF, WHAT IF I'VE GOT AN INCREDIBLE PLAN...?
WHAT IF, WHAT IF THAT PLAN IS THIS?!
A CONCRETE PLAN!!!!
① WEAR EXPENSIVE CLOTHING.
② DITCH YOUR CHEAP ACCESSORIES AND EITHER GO WITH NO JEWELRY OR SOMETHING FANCY.
③ SWAP YOUR BROWN HAIR COLOR FOR BLACK, AND DITCH THE BANGS SO YOUR FOREHEAD SHOWS.
④ STOP WITH THE COLOR CONTACTS.
WE'VE SAID IT OVER AND OVER AGAIN AT THIS BAR!!
SHINE SHINE
YOU'RE ALL OVER 30 AT THIS POINT, SO DRESS MORE MODESTLY, YOU MORONS!!
IF YOU PLAY UP THOSE MATURE CHARMS LIKE SO, YOU'LL BAG HIM FOR REAL!! THAT'S ALL IT TAKES!!
Today's What-If Aphorism:
YOU'VE GOTTA GIVE OFF THAT "FINE WOMAN" AURA WITH YOUR LOOKS. THAT'S YOUR ONLY CHOICE.
OKAY, NEXT!!!!
THE NEXT ONE'S... PRETTY RAW, IS THAT OKAY?!
That takes care of that!
IS THAT GONNA BE OKAY FOR THE KIDS?!
WHAT IF, WHAT IF WE'LL JUST RELY ON THE MOMS TO MARK OUT ALL THE NASTY PARTS?!

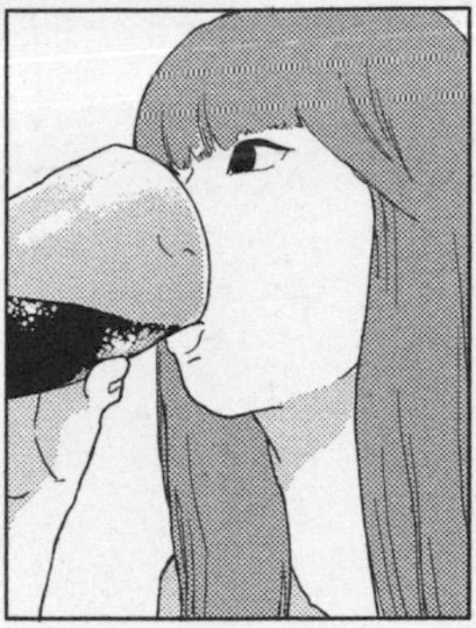

QUESTION: IS SEX MINUS THE WORDS "LET'S GO OUT" ALLOWED?

I'M 32. I SPENT MY TWENTIES CHASING AROUND IDOLS, SO NOW I'M A PANICKING TARAREBA GIRL. RECENTLY, I, A HUMBLE (ANIME, ETC.) OTAKU, FINALLY HAD A FATEFUL ENCOUNTER WITH A SUPER HIGH-SPEC MAN AT A MIXER. ON THE INSIDE, HE'S AN OTAKU (BASICALLY A SHUT-IN) LIKE ME, SO WE GET ALONG GREAT, BUT...ON THE OUTSIDE, HE'S AN ISEYA-STYLE* HUNK, OVER 180CM TALL, DOESN'T SMOKE, WENT TO A GOOD SCHOOL, DRIVES AN EXPENSIVE CAR, AND IS A FIREFIGHTER TWO YEARS MY JUNIOR. WE WENT ON SEVERAL DATES THAT I THOUGHT WENT WELL, THEN ON ONE OF OUR MOVIE DATES, WE MADE OUT BEGINNING TO END THERE IN THE DARKENED THEATER. ON THE WAY HOME, WE WERE KISSING THE WHOLE TIME TOO. DURING DINNER, HE TOLD ME HE WANTED TO "DO IT," BUT, OF COURSE, I'M AN OTAKU. I'M A VIRGIN WITH ABSOLUTELY NO EXPERIENCE WITH MEN, SO I NATURALLY DIDN'T TAKE HIM UP ON HIS OFFER, AND WAS EVEN A LITTLE FREAKED OUT BY HIS LACK OF COMMON SENSE IN SUCH A PUBLIC SPACE, SO I HAVEN'T CONTACTED HIM SINCE THAT NIGHT.
IF HE HAD ASKED ME TO GO OUT WITH HIM OR TOLD ME HE LOVES ME, MAYBE I WOULD HAVE UNDERSTOOD IT, BUT HE DIDN'T. I'VE GOT SO LITTLE CONFIDENCE IN MYSELF THAT I COULDN'T EVEN ASK HIM ABOUT OUR FUTURE PROSPECTS TOGETHER. I DON'T KNOW WHETHER I SHOULD HAVE JUST DONE AS THE TARAREBA GIRLS DO AND SLEPT WITH HIM, OR EVEN WHAT HIS FEELINGS ARE OR IF HE WAS JUST INTERESTED IN SEX. EVERYONE AROUND ME SAYS, "HE'S NO GOOD! MOVE ON TO THE NEXT ONE!" BUT NOW THAT IT'S OVER, I REALIZED I LOVE HIM AND DON'T THINK I'LL BE ABLE TO MOVE ON. I'M JUST LOOKING FOR THE NORMAL PROCESS OF "LOVE" > "GO OUT" > "THEN DO IT," BUT THIS IS SO HARD.
WHEN CONSIDERING THE HANDSOME OTAKU WITH A COMMON INTEREST PART, I DOUBT ANYONE LIKE HIM WILL APPEAR AGAIN. SHOULD I HAVE JUST "DONE IT" WITH HIM?

PN: MIDDLE SCHOOL DIARY (32)

*Yusuke Iseya: a famously handsome Japanese actor who has been active since the late '90s.

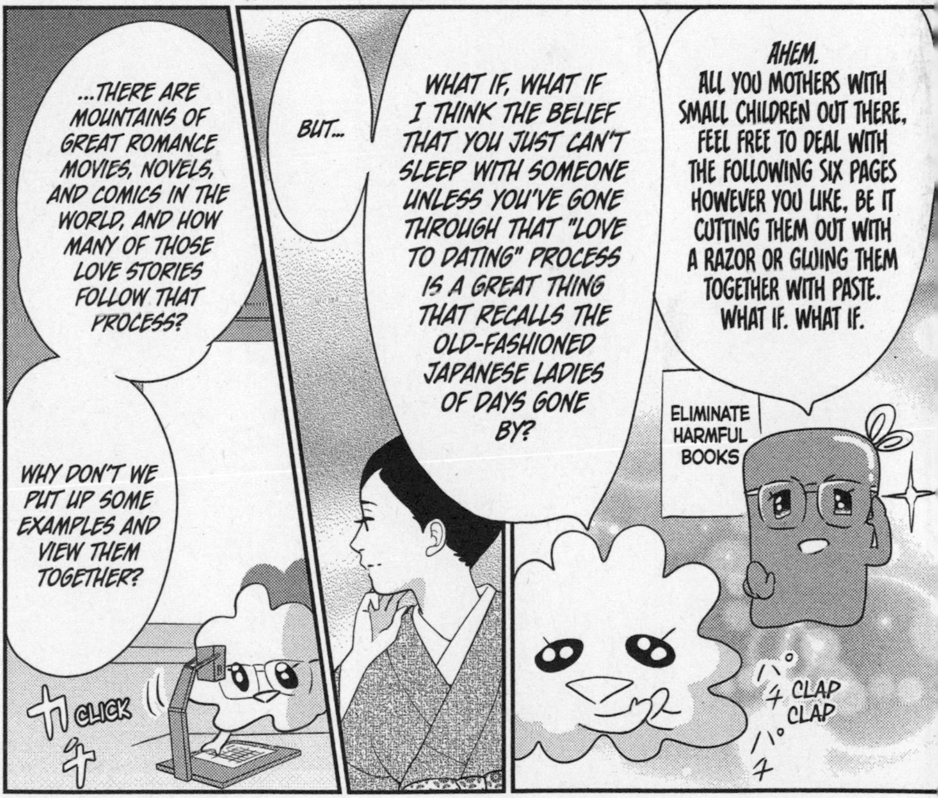
...THERE ARE MOUNTAINS OF GREAT ROMANCE MOVIES, NOVELS, AND COMICS IN THE WORLD, AND HOW MANY OF THOSE LOVE STORIES FOLLOW THAT PROCESS?
WHY DON'T WE PUT UP SOME EXAMPLES AND VIEW THEM TOGETHER?
カチ CLICK
BUT...
WHAT IF, WHAT IF I THINK THE BELIEF THAT YOU JUST CAN'T SLEEP WITH SOMEONE UNLESS YOU'VE GONE THROUGH THAT "LOVE TO DATING" PROCESS IS A GREAT THING THAT RECALLS THE OLD-FASHIONED JAPANESE LADIES OF DAYS GONE BY?
AHEM. ALL YOU MOTHERS WITH SMALL CHILDREN OUT THERE, FEEL FREE TO DEAL WITH THE FOLLOWING SIX PAGES HOWEVER YOU LIKE, BE IT CUTTING THEM OUT WITH A RAZOR OR GLUING THEM TOGETHER WITH PASTE. WHAT IF. WHAT IF.
ELIMINATE HARMFUL BOOKS
パチ CLAP
パチ CLAP

THE RESULTS OF WHETHER THAT PROCESS WAS FOLLOWED IN FAMOUS LOVE STORIES !!

TITLE	"I LOVE YOU"	"LET'S GO OUT"	RESULT
TITANIC	NOT SAID	NOT SAID	DID IT
BRIDGET JONES'S DIARY	NOT SAID	NOT SAID	DID IT
PRETTY WOMAN	NOT SAID	NOT SAID	DID IT
THE BODYGUARD	SAID WITH THE EYES	NOT SAID	DID IT
007 SERIES	NAH, NOT REALLY SAID	NEVER SAID	DID THE HELL OUT OF IT
BEFORE SUNSET	NOT SAID BUT PRAISE IS GIVEN	NOT SAID	DID IT
THE BALLAD OF NARAYAMA	NO CONCEPT	NO CONCEPT	DID IT

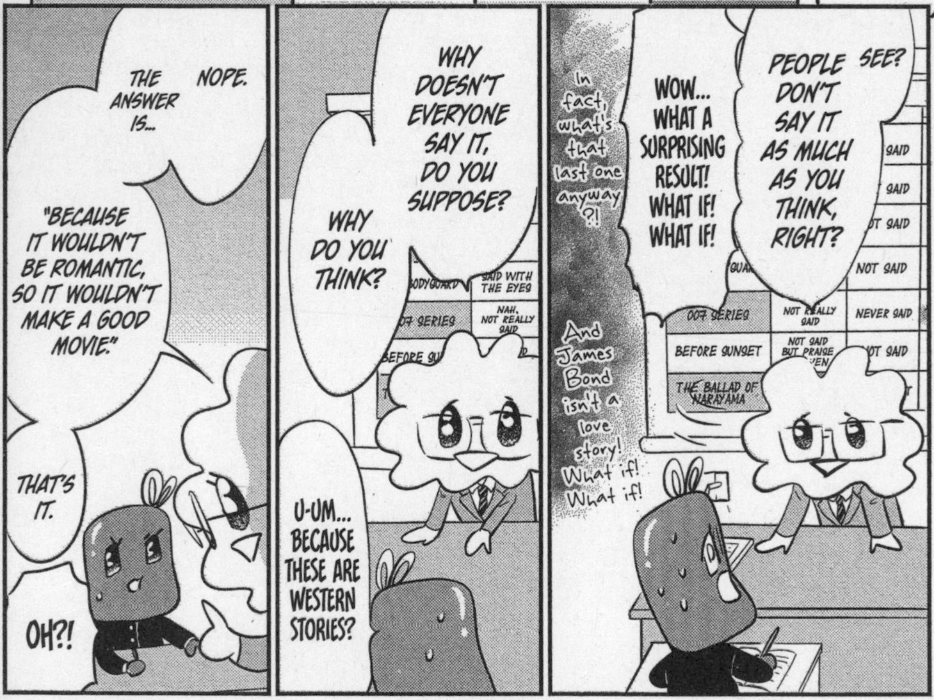
SEE?
PEOPLE DON'T SAY IT AS MUCH AS YOU THINK, RIGHT?
WOW... WHAT A SURPRISING RESULT! WHAT IF! WHAT IF!
In fact, what's that last one anyway?!
And James Bond isn't a love story! What if! What if!
WHY DOESN'T EVERYONE SAY IT, DO YOU SUPPOSE?
WHY DO YOU THINK?
U-UM... BECAUSE THESE ARE WESTERN STORIES?
NOPE.
THE ANSWER IS...
"BECAUSE IT WOULDN'T BE ROMANTIC, SO IT WOULDN'T MAKE A GOOD MOVIE."
THAT'S IT.
OH?!

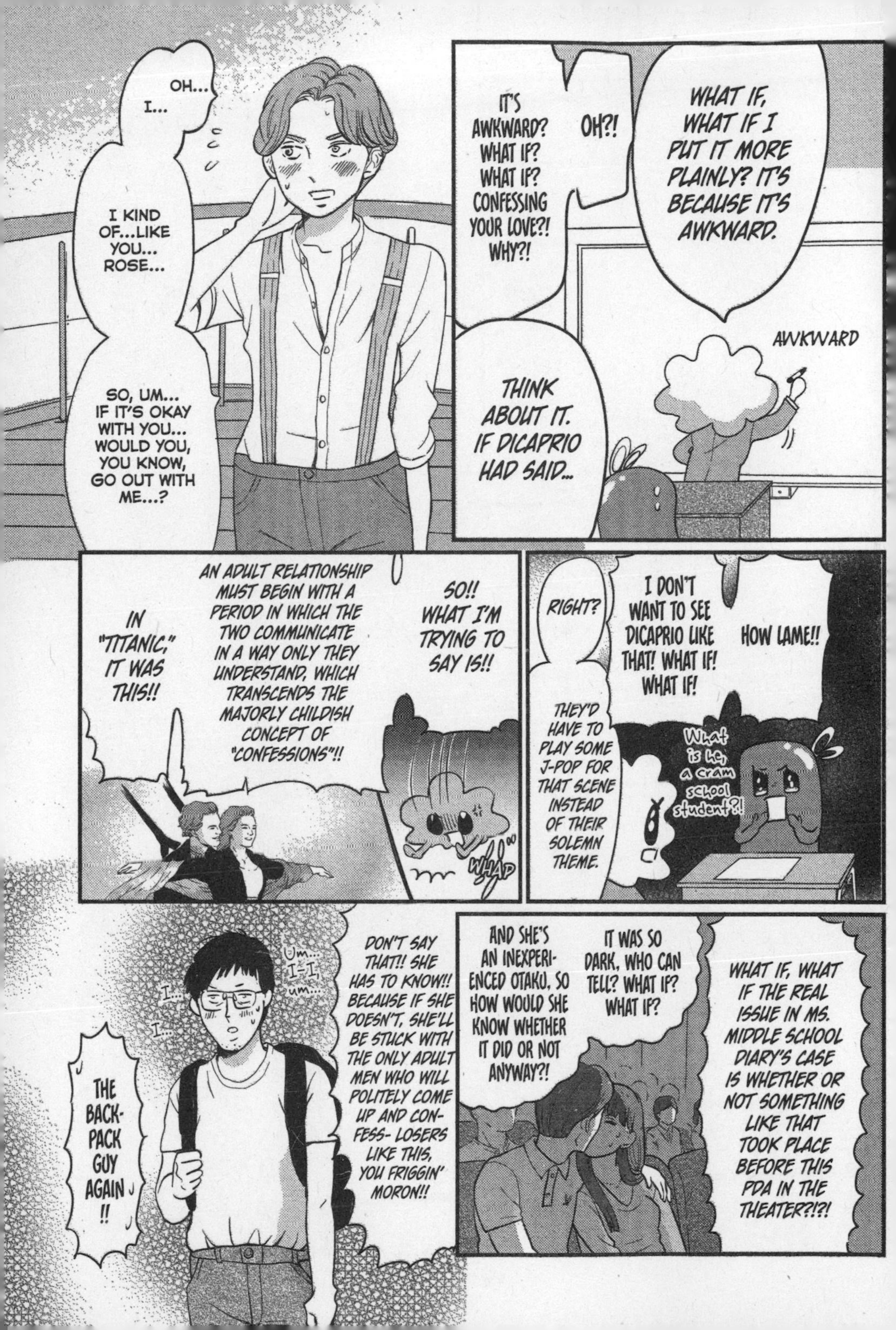
WHAT IF, WHAT IF I PUT IT MORE PLAINLY? IT'S BECAUSE IT'S AWKWARD.
OH?!
IT'S AWKWARD? WHAT IF? WHAT IF? CONFESSING YOUR LOVE?! WHY?!
AWKWARD
THINK ABOUT IT. IF DICAPRIO HAD SAID...
OH... I...
I KIND OF...LIKE YOU... ROSE...
SO, UM... IF IT'S OKAY WITH YOU... WOULD YOU, YOU KNOW, GO OUT WITH ME...?
HOW LAME!!
I DON'T WANT TO SEE DICAPRIO LIKE THAT! WHAT IF! WHAT IF!
RIGHT?
THEY'D HAVE TO PLAY SOME J-POP FOR THAT SCENE INSTEAD OF THEIR SOLEMN THEME.
What is he, a cram school student?!
SO!! WHAT I'M TRYING TO SAY IS!!
AN ADULT RELATIONSHIP MUST BEGIN WITH A PERIOD IN WHICH THE TWO COMMUNICATE IN A WAY ONLY THEY UNDERSTAND, WHICH TRANSCENDS THE MAJORLY CHILDISH CONCEPT OF "CONFESSIONS"!!
IN "TITANIC," IT WAS THIS!!
WHAP
WHAT IF, WHAT IF THE REAL ISSUE IN MS. MIDDLE SCHOOL DIARY'S CASE IS WHETHER OR NOT SOMETHING LIKE THAT TOOK PLACE BEFORE THIS PDA IN THE THEATER?!?!
IT WAS SO DARK, WHO CAN TELL? WHAT IF? WHAT IF?
AND SHE'S AN INEXPERI-ENCED OTAKU, SO HOW WOULD SHE KNOW WHETHER IT DID OR NOT ANYWAY?!
DON'T SAY THAT!! SHE HAS TO KNOW!! BECAUSE IF SHE DOESN'T, SHE'LL BE STUCK WITH THE ONLY ADULT MEN WHO WILL POLITELY COME UP AND CON-FESS- LOSERS LIKE THIS, YOU FRIGGIN' MORON!!
Um... I-I, um...
I... I...
THE BACK-PACK GUY AGAIN!!

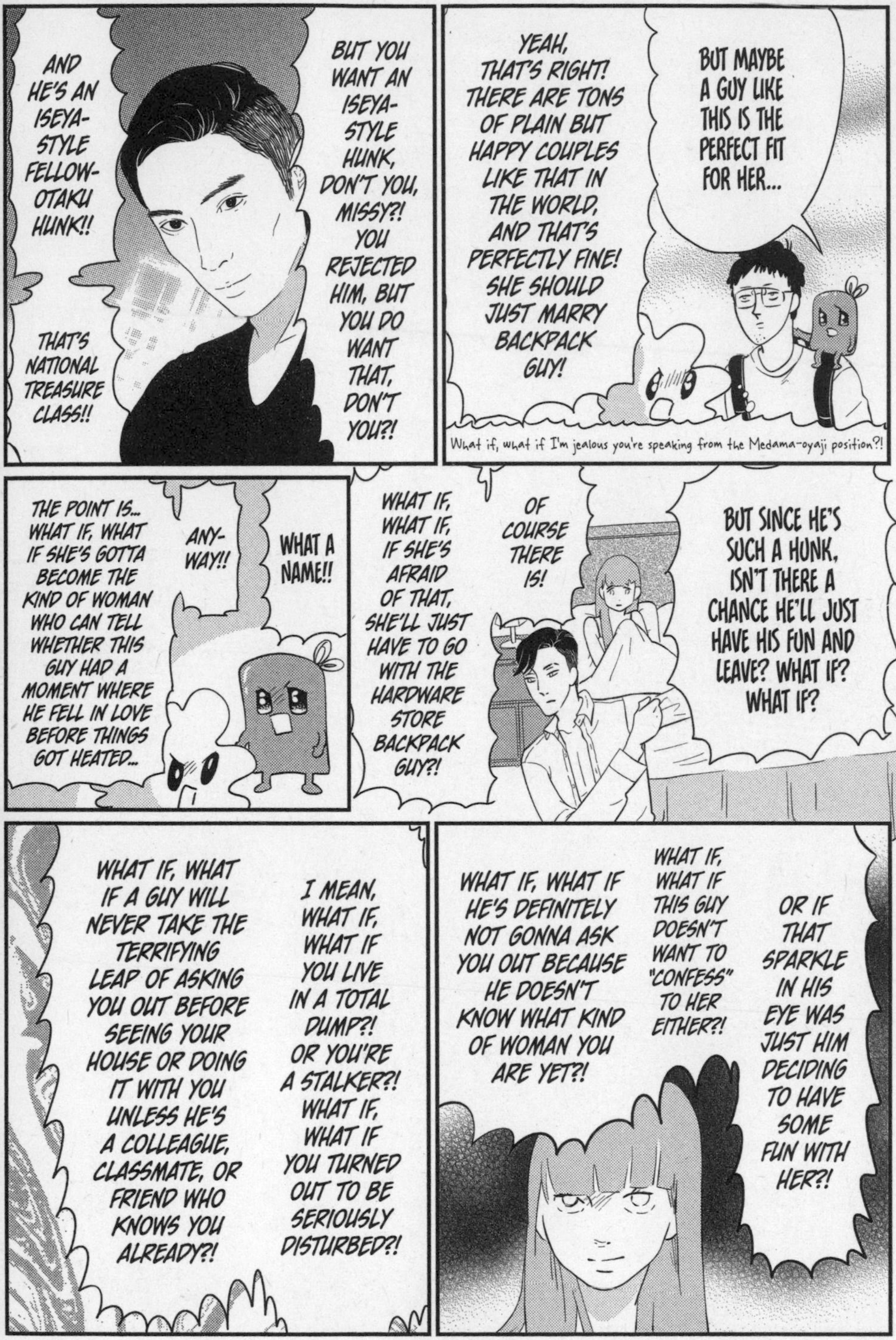
BUT MAYBE A GUY LIKE THIS IS THE PERFECT FIT FOR HER...
YEAH, THAT'S RIGHT! THERE ARE TONS OF PLAIN BUT HAPPY COUPLES LIKE THAT IN THE WORLD, AND THAT'S PERFECTLY FINE! SHE SHOULD JUST MARRY BACKPACK GUY!
What if, what if I'm jealous you're speaking from the Medama-oyaji position?!
BUT YOU WANT AN ISEYA-STYLE HUNK, DON'T YOU, MISSY?! YOU REJECTED HIM, BUT YOU DO WANT THAT, DON'T YOU?!
AND HE'S AN ISEYA-STYLE FELLOW-OTAKU HUNK!!
THAT'S NATIONAL TREASURE CLASS!!
BUT SINCE HE'S SUCH A HUNK, ISN'T THERE A CHANCE HE'LL JUST HAVE HIS FUN AND LEAVE? WHAT IF? WHAT IF?
OF COURSE THERE IS!
WHAT IF, WHAT IF, IF SHE'S AFRAID OF THAT, SHE'LL JUST HAVE TO GO WITH THE HARDWARE STORE BACKPACK GUY?!
WHAT A NAME!!
ANY-WAY!!
THE POINT IS... WHAT IF, WHAT IF SHE'S GOTTA BECOME THE KIND OF WOMAN WHO CAN TELL WHETHER THIS GUY HAD A MOMENT WHERE HE FELL IN LOVE BEFORE THINGS GOT HEATED...
OR IF THAT SPARKLE IN HIS EYE WAS JUST HIM DECIDING TO HAVE SOME FUN WITH HER?!
WHAT IF, WHAT IF THIS GUY DOESN'T WANT TO "CONFESS" TO HER EITHER?!
WHAT IF, WHAT IF HE'S DEFINITELY NOT GONNA ASK YOU OUT BECAUSE HE DOESN'T KNOW WHAT KIND OF WOMAN YOU ARE YET?!
I MEAN, WHAT IF, WHAT IF YOU LIVE IN A TOTAL DUMP?! OR YOU'RE A STALKER?! WHAT IF, WHAT IF YOU TURNED OUT TO BE SERIOUSLY DISTURBED?!
WHAT IF, WHAT IF A GUY WILL NEVER TAKE THE TERRIFYING LEAP OF ASKING YOU OUT BEFORE SEEING YOUR HOUSE OR DOING IT WITH YOU UNLESS HE'S A COLLEAGUE, CLASSMATE, OR FRIEND WHO KNOWS YOU ALREADY?!

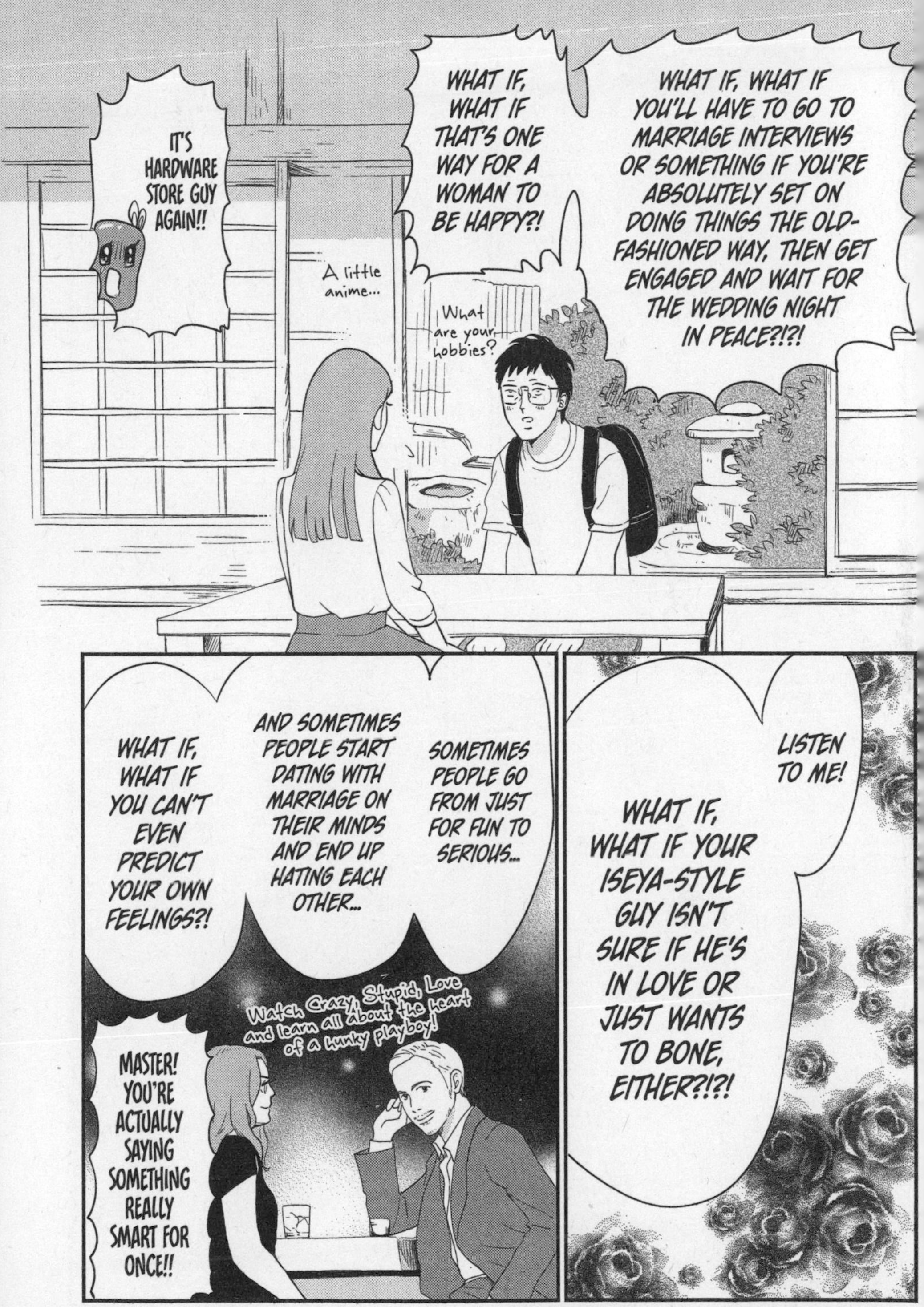
WHAT IF, WHAT IF YOU'LL HAVE TO GO TO MARRIAGE INTERVIEWS OR SOMETHING IF YOU'RE ABSOLUTELY SET ON DOING THINGS THE OLD-FASHIONED WAY, THEN GET ENGAGED AND WAIT FOR THE WEDDING NIGHT IN PEACE?!?!
WHAT IF, WHAT IF THAT'S ONE WAY FOR A WOMAN TO BE HAPPY?!
What are your hobbies?
A little anime...
IT'S HARDWARE STORE GUY AGAIN!!
LISTEN TO ME!
WHAT IF, WHAT IF YOUR ISEYA-STYLE GUY ISN'T SURE IF HE'S IN LOVE OR JUST WANTS TO BONE, EITHER?!?!
SOMETIMES PEOPLE GO FROM JUST FOR FUN TO SERIOUS...
AND SOMETIMES PEOPLE START DATING WITH MARRIAGE ON THEIR MINDS AND END UP HATING EACH OTHER...
WHAT IF, WHAT IF YOU CAN'T EVEN PREDICT YOUR OWN FEELINGS?!
Watch Crazy, Stupid, Love and learn all about the heart of a hunky playboy!
MASTER! YOU'RE ACTUALLY SAYING SOMETHING REALLY SMART FOR ONCE!!

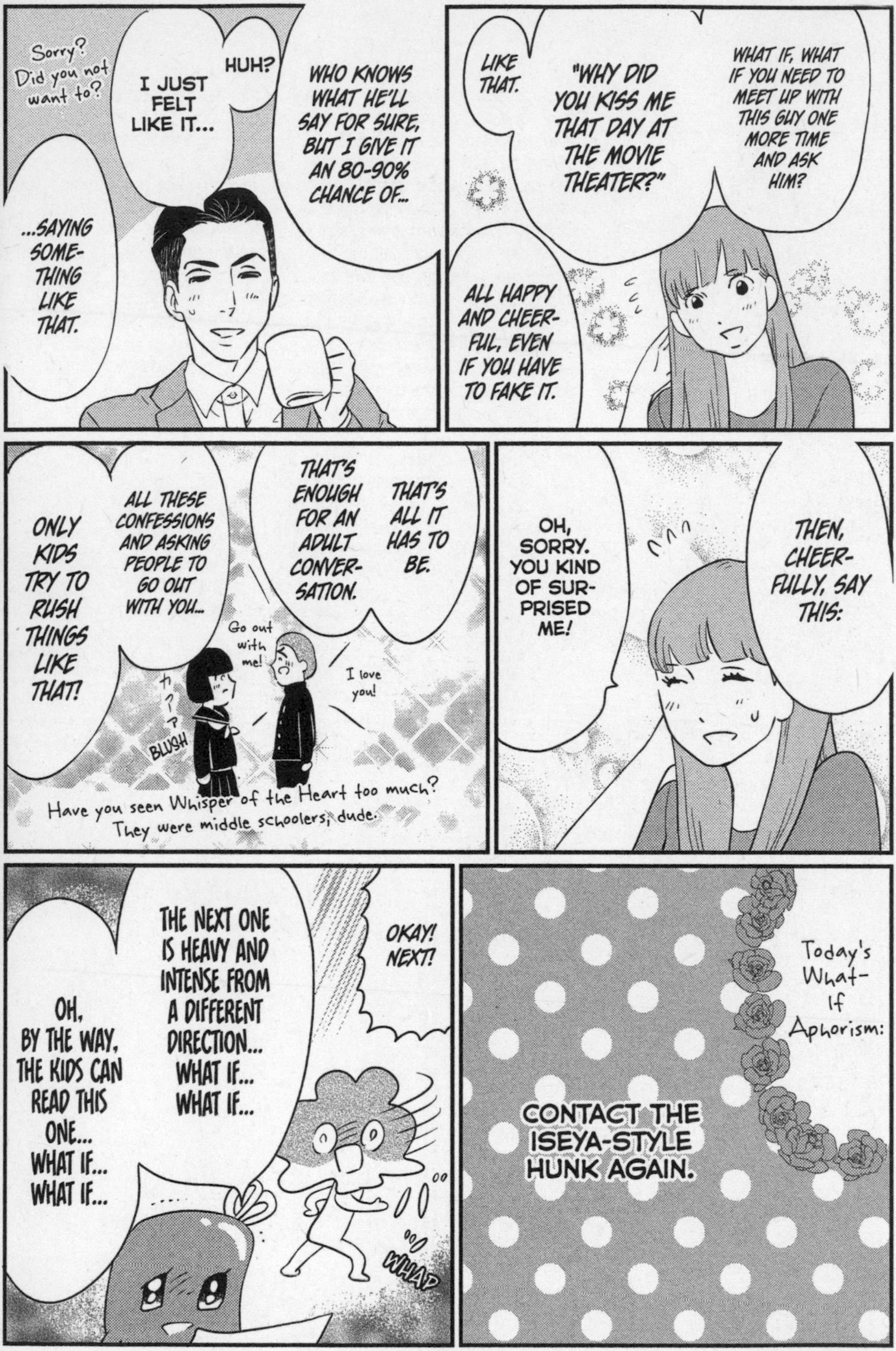
WHAT IF, WHAT IF YOU NEED TO MEET UP WITH THIS GUY ONE MORE TIME AND ASK HIM?
"WHY DID YOU KISS ME THAT DAY AT THE MOVIE THEATER?"
LIKE THAT.
ALL HAPPY AND CHEERFUL, EVEN IF YOU HAVE TO FAKE IT.
WHO KNOWS WHAT HE'LL SAY FOR SURE, BUT I GIVE IT AN 80-90% CHANCE OF...
HUH?
I JUST FELT LIKE IT...
Sorry? Did you not want to?
...SAYING SOMETHING LIKE THAT.
THEN, CHEERFULLY, SAY THIS:
OH, SORRY. YOU KIND OF SURPRISED ME!
THAT'S ALL IT HAS TO BE.
THAT'S ENOUGH FOR AN ADULT CONVERSATION.
ALL THESE CONFESSIONS AND ASKING PEOPLE TO GO OUT WITH YOU...
ONLY KIDS TRY TO RUSH THINGS LIKE THAT!
I love you!
Go out with me!
BLUSH
Have you seen Whisper of the Heart too much? They were middle schoolers, dude.
Today's What-If Aphorism:
CONTACT THE ISEYA-STYLE HUNK AGAIN.
OKAY! NEXT!
THE NEXT ONE IS HEAVY AND INTENSE FROM A DIFFERENT DIRECTION... WHAT IF... WHAT IF...
OH, BY THE WAY, THE KIDS CAN READ THIS ONE... WHAT IF... WHAT IF...
....
WHAP

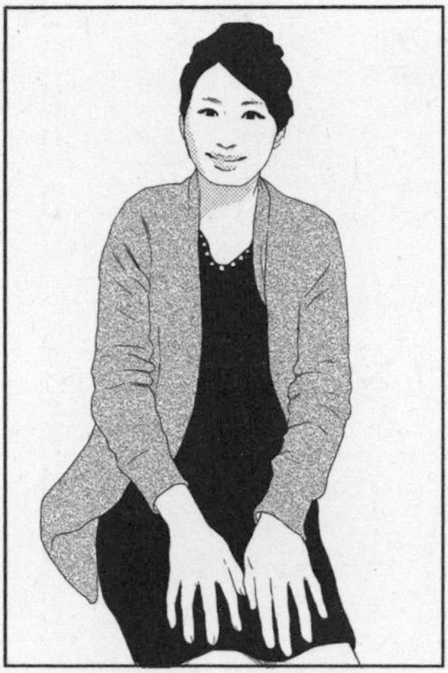

THIS YEAR, I TURN 33 JUST LIKE RINKO AND FRIENDS.

ACTUALLY, I'VE BEEN IN LOVE WITH THE SAME PERSON SINCE I WAS 14, BUT HE IS AN ANIME CHARACTER. IT'S NOT "MOE;" I TRULY LOVE HIM. I THOUGHT IT WAS WRONG, SO I NEVER TOLD ANYONE, BUT RECENTLY THIS SERIES REACHED ITS 20TH ANNIVERSARY (THE CHARACTER I LOVE APPEARED IN THE 3RD ANIME IN THE SERIES, SO I'M SORRY THE YEARS DON'T MATCH) SO I TOOK THAT OPPORTUNITY TO COME OUT TO MY FRIENDS AND COWORKERS. I TOLD MY FRIENDS WHO IT WAS, BUT I ONLY TOLD MY COWORKERS, "ACTUALLY, I LIKE 2D." THEY ASKED ME, "IS THIS CHARACTER KIND TO THE GIRLS IN THAT SHOW?" NO, HE'S NOT. HE'S THE KIND OF CHARACTER THAT SAYS STUFF LIKE, "I WILL UNLEASH A GOD OF DESTRUCTION UPON THIS WORLD."

I'VE ALREADY LOVED HIM FOR 18 YEARS, SO I THINK I'LL PROBABLY LOVE HIM FOREVER, BUT I'M AN ONLY CHILD, SO MY PARENTS WANT ME TO GET MARRIED. AND I'M A PART-TIME EMPLOYEE, SO, TO BE HONEST, I'M NOT GOING TO BE ABLE TO LIVE OFF JUST MY OWN INCOME.

I KNOW THE REALITY IS I NEED SOMEONE TO SUPPORT ME IN ORDER TO SURVIVE, BUT IT'S ALSO A REALITY THAT I'M IN LOVE WITH THIS CHARACTER. I'VE GONE TO MATCHMAKING PARTIES AND COMMUNITY MIXERS, BUT I ALWAYS JUST LOOK AT THE MEN THERE AND THINK, "HE'S NOT THE CHARACTER I LOVE." AS A RESULT, IT NEVER WORKS OUT.

WILL A MAN LIKE THIS ANIME CHARACTER EVER APPEAR TO ME IN REAL LIFE? OR SHOULD I COMPROMISE AND MARRY SOMEONE?

PN: AORINGO (32)

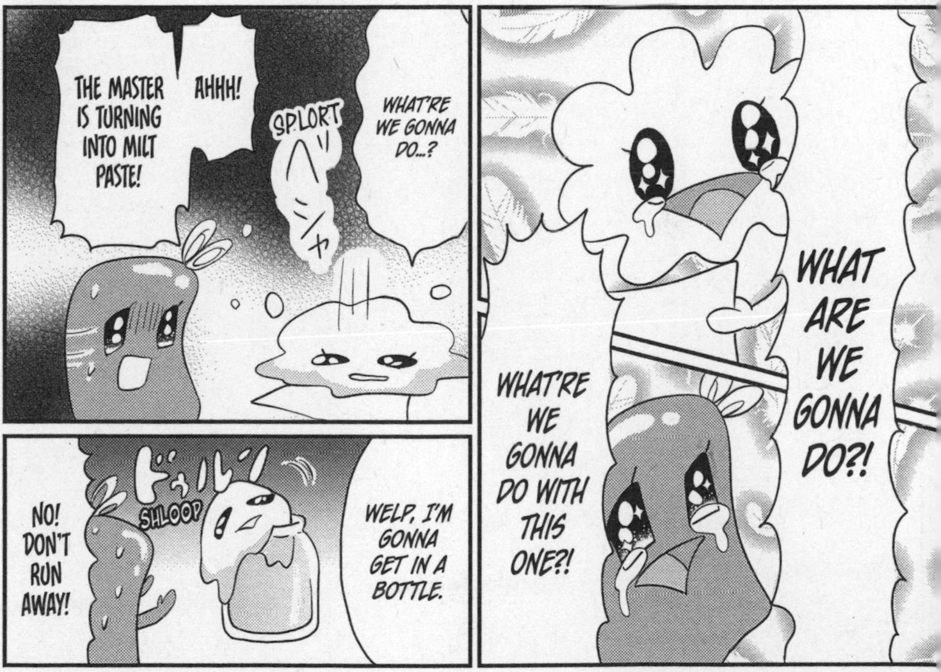
WHAT ARE WE GONNA DO?!
WHAT'RE WE GONNA DO WITH THIS ONE?!
WHAT'RE WE GONNA DO...?
SPLORT
AHHH!
THE MASTER IS TURNING INTO MILT PASTE!
WELP, I'M GONNA GET IN A BOTTLE.
SHLOOP
NO! DON'T RUN AWAY!

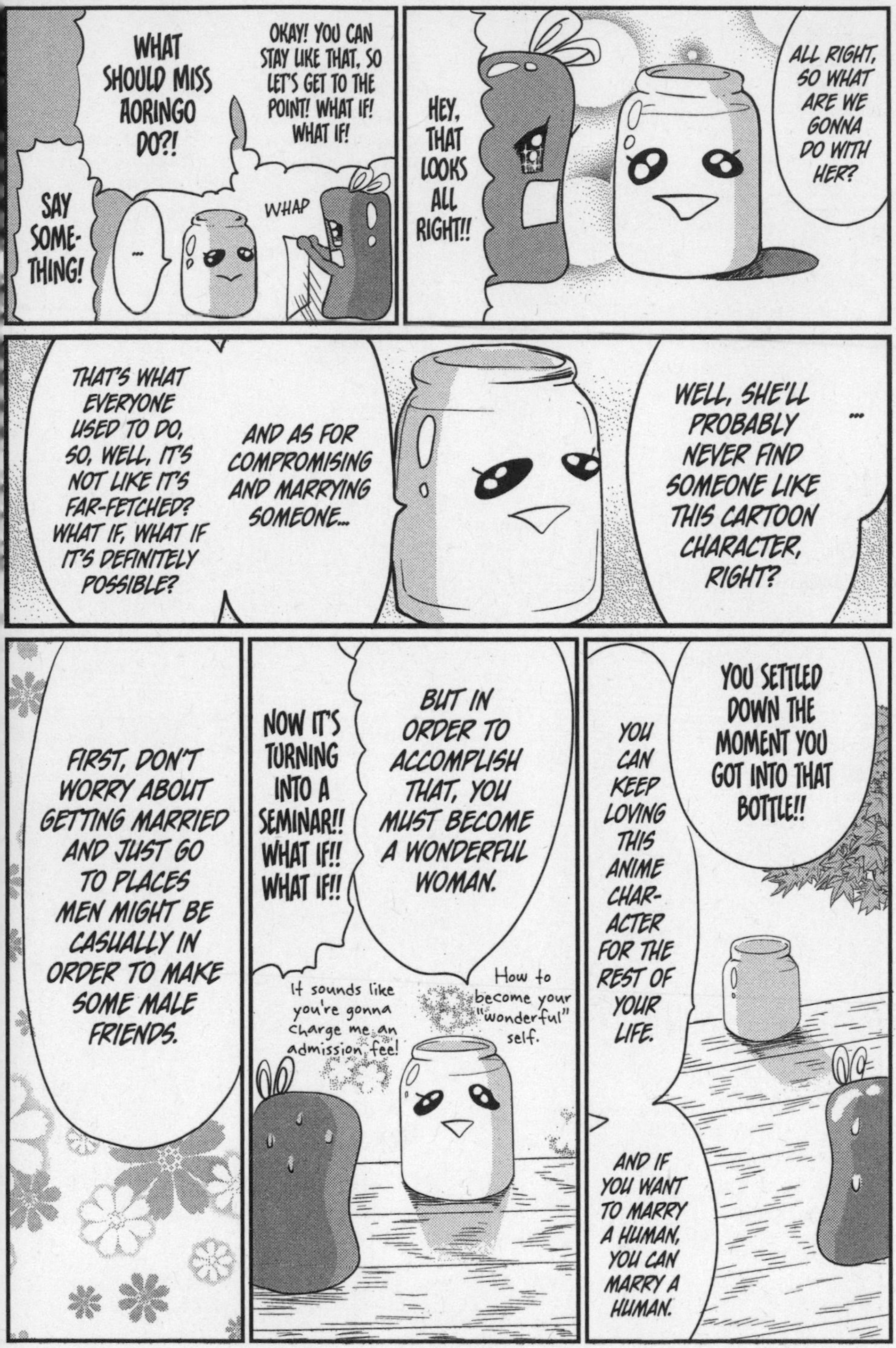
ALL RIGHT, SO WHAT ARE WE GONNA DO WITH HER?
HEY, THAT LOOKS ALL RIGHT!!
OKAY! YOU CAN STAY LIKE THAT, SO LET'S GET TO THE POINT! WHAT IF! WHAT IF!
WHAT SHOULD MISS AORINGO DO?!
WHAP
...
SAY SOME-THING!
...
WELL, SHE'LL PROBABLY NEVER FIND SOMEONE LIKE THIS CARTOON CHARACTER, RIGHT?
AND AS FOR COMPROMISING AND MARRYING SOMEONE...
THAT'S WHAT EVERYONE USED TO DO, SO, WELL, IT'S NOT LIKE IT'S FAR-FETCHED? WHAT IF, WHAT IF IT'S DEFINITELY POSSIBLE?
YOU SETTLED DOWN THE MOMENT YOU GOT INTO THAT BOTTLE!!
YOU CAN KEEP LOVING THIS ANIME CHAR-ACTER FOR THE REST OF YOUR LIFE.
AND IF YOU WANT TO MARRY A HUMAN, YOU CAN MARRY A HUMAN.
BUT IN ORDER TO ACCOMPLISH THAT, YOU MUST BECOME A WONDERFUL WOMAN.
NOW IT'S TURNING INTO A SEMINAR!! WHAT IF!! WHAT IF!!
How to become your "wonderful" self.
It sounds like you're gonna charge me an admission fee!
FIRST, DON'T WORRY ABOUT GETTING MARRIED AND JUST GO TO PLACES MEN MIGHT BE CASUALLY IN ORDER TO MAKE SOME MALE FRIENDS.

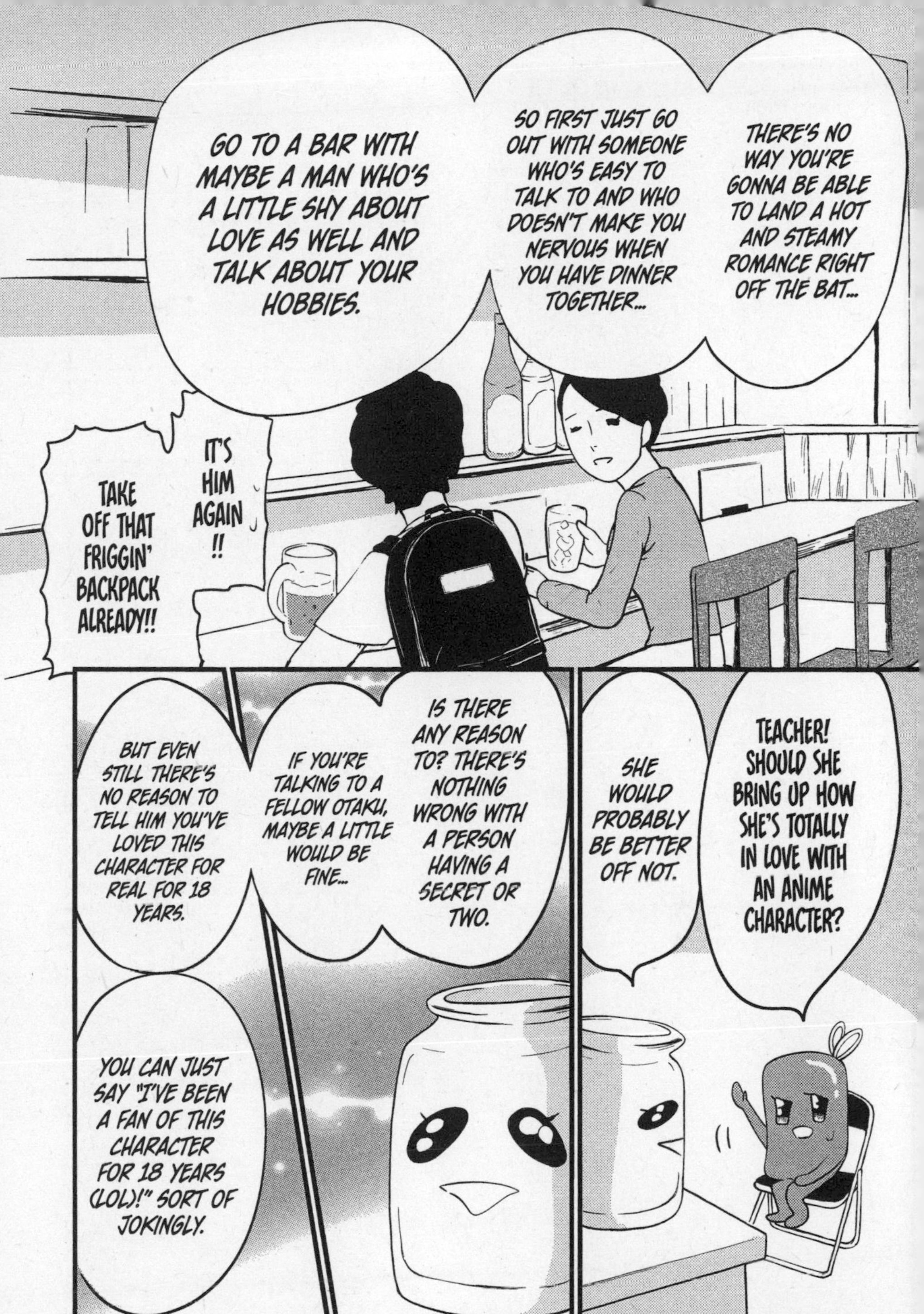
THERE'S NO WAY YOU'RE GONNA BE ABLE TO LAND A HOT AND STEAMY ROMANCE RIGHT OFF THE BAT...
SO FIRST JUST GO OUT WITH SOMEONE WHO'S EASY TO TALK TO AND WHO DOESN'T MAKE YOU NERVOUS WHEN YOU HAVE DINNER TOGETHER...
GO TO A BAR WITH MAYBE A MAN WHO'S A LITTLE SHY ABOUT LOVE AS WELL AND TALK ABOUT YOUR HOBBIES.
IT'S HIM AGAIN!!
TAKE OFF THAT FRIGGIN' BACKPACK ALREADY!!
TEACHER! SHOULD SHE BRING UP HOW SHE'S TOTALLY IN LOVE WITH AN ANIME CHARACTER?
SHE WOULD PROBABLY BE BETTER OFF NOT.
IS THERE ANY REASON TO? THERE'S NOTHING WRONG WITH A PERSON HAVING A SECRET OR TWO.
IF YOU'RE TALKING TO A FELLOW OTAKU, MAYBE A LITTLE WOULD BE FINE...
BUT EVEN STILL THERE'S NO REASON TO TELL HIM YOU'VE LOVED THIS CHARACTER FOR REAL FOR 18 YEARS.
YOU CAN JUST SAY "I'VE BEEN A FAN OF THIS CHARACTER FOR 18 YEARS (LOL)!" SORT OF JOKINGLY.

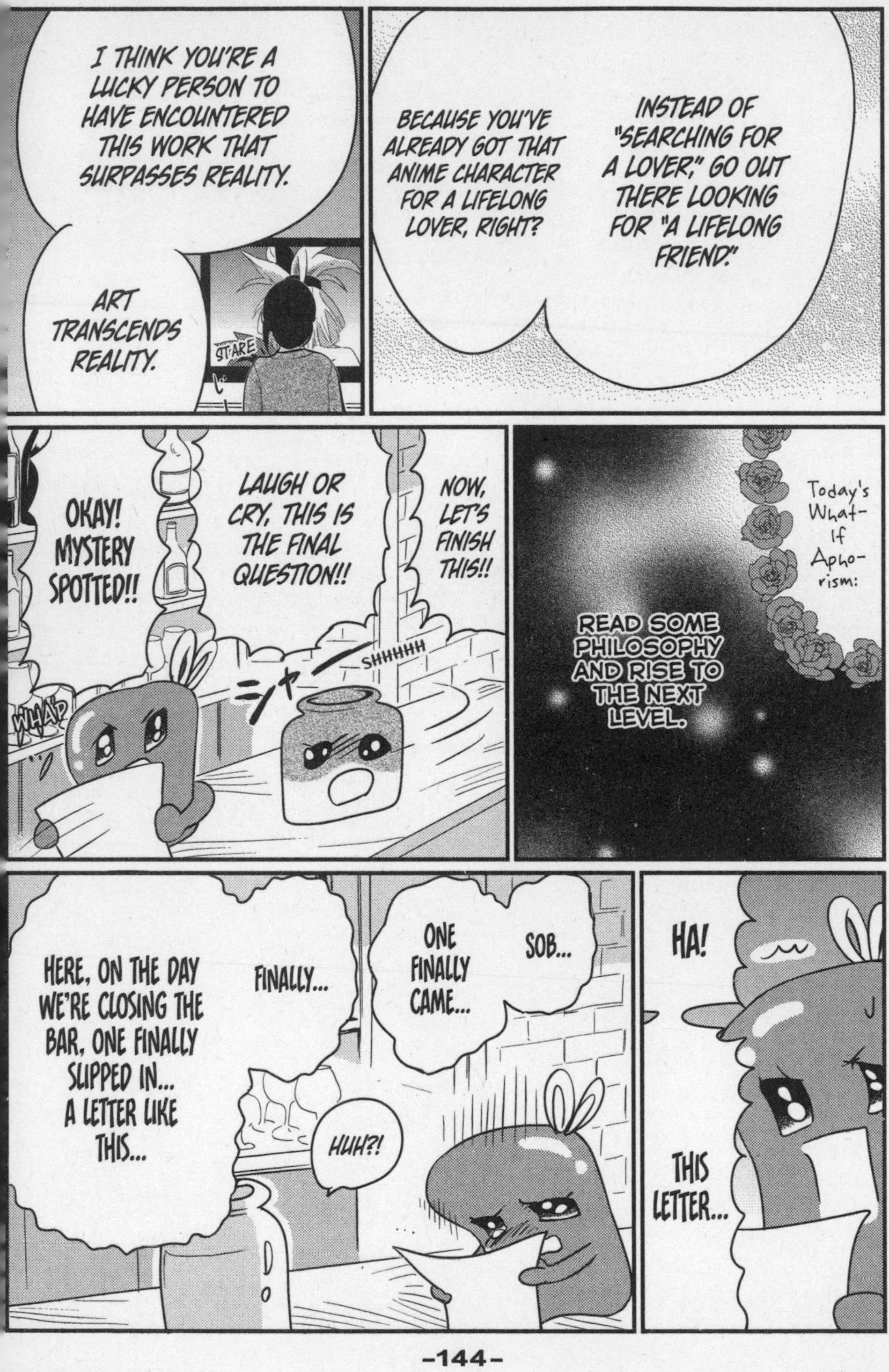
INSTEAD OF "SEARCHING FOR A LOVER," GO OUT THERE LOOKING FOR "A LIFELONG FRIEND."
BECAUSE YOU'VE ALREADY GOT THAT ANIME CHARACTER FOR A LIFELONG LOVER, RIGHT?
I THINK YOU'RE A LUCKY PERSON TO HAVE ENCOUNTERED THIS WORK THAT SURPASSES REALITY.
ART TRANSCENDS REALITY.
STARE
Today's What-If Aphorism:
READ SOME PHILOSOPHY AND RISE TO THE NEXT LEVEL.
NOW, LET'S FINISH THIS!!
LAUGH OR CRY, THIS IS THE FINAL QUESTION!!
OKAY! MYSTERY SPOTTED!!
SHHHHH
WHAP
HA!
THIS LETTER...
SOB...
ONE FINALLY CAME...
FINALLY...
HERE, ON THE DAY WE'RE CLOSING THE BAR, ONE FINALLY SLIPPED IN... A LETTER LIKE THIS...
HUH?!

I ALWAYS ENJOY READING "TOKYO TARAREBA GIRLS." THANKS TO THIS COMIC, I WAS ABLE TO GET MARRIED! I READ THE FIRST VOLUME IN DECEMBER OF 2015 AT AGE 30, AND IT HIT ME LIKE A TON OF BRICKS. IN MY TWENTIES, I BECAME DISTRUSTFUL OF MEN.

- I WENT OUT WITH A MAN FOR FOUR YEARS BEFORE WE BROKE UP, THEN WHEN WE GOT BACK TOGETHER, HE CHEATED ON ME, SO WE SPLIT UP AGAIN AFTER FOUR MONTHS. (WE HAD DISCUSSED MARRIAGE, AND I HAD ALREADY MET HIS PARENTS.)
- I HAD A CRUSH ON A MUSICIAN, THEN EVENTUALLY MANAGED TO BECOME FRIENDS WITH BENEFITS. THEN, SIX MONTHS LATER, HE TOLD ME WE SHOULD STOP. (HE DIDN'T HAVE A GIRLFRIEND, BUT THERE WAS SOMEONE HE HAD A CRUSH ON.)

EVERY MAN I THOUGHT I COULD TRUST TURNED OUT TO ALREADY HAVE A GIRLFRIEND OR WIFE, SO I ENDED MY TWENTIES WITHOUT EVER REALLY TRUSTING A MAN.
I THEN TURNED 30, THAT GLORIOUS TIME WHEN YOU HAVE TO START THINKING ABOUT OLD AGE AND PAYING [redacted]0,000 YEN A MONTH FOR WHOLE LIFE INSURANCE AND GETTING ALL SORTS OF USEFUL CERTIFICATIONS. I JUST SORT OF WONDERED "WILL I BE ABLE TO GET MARRIED SOMETIME?" (WILL I BE ABLE TO MEET A MAN I CAN TRUST?) WITHOUT ACTUALLY DOING ANYTHING ABOUT IT, WHILE THINKING ABOUT NOTHING BUT SHORING UP THE FOUNDATIONS FOR MY FUTURE.
BUT AFTER READING THIS COMIC, I STARTED LOOKING FOR A HUSBAND RIGHT AWAY.
AFTER STARTING THE SEARCH, I MET A MAN AT MY FIRST MIXER, AND AFTER OUR THIRD MEETING WE BEGAN DATING, THINGS PROGRESSED, AND SIX MONTHS LATER WE WERE MARRIED.
BECAUSE I DIDN'T TRUST MEN, NATURALLY, I SWORE I WOULDN'T SLEEP WITH HIM UNTIL WE WERE OFFICIALLY DATING. AFTER WE STARTED ACTUALLY DATING, WE NEVER ACTUALLY SLEPT TOGETHER UNTIL WE COULD GET THE SAME DAYS OFF TO STAY OVERNIGHT, SO I WAS SUPER PARANOID THAT HE HAD ANOTHER WOMAN (IT WAS ALL IN MY HEAD, OF COURSE!). THE MORE I FELL FOR HIM, THE MORE I JUST FLAILED AROUND ABOUT HOW TOUGH IT WAS TO FACE HIM AS JUST ONE PERSON TO ANOTHER. I CHUGGED A LOT OF BEER AT HOME AND RAN MYSELF IN CIRCLES FOR A WHILE, BUT AFTER HE WENT OUT WITH ME, PROPOSED SERIOUSLY, AND THEN MADE ME A FULL-FLEDGED HOUSEWIFE, I TRULY TRUST HIM. AT FIRST, I ONLY PRETENDED TO, BECAUSE EVEN IF I GOT HURT, I WANTED TO REDUCE THE DAMAGE.
I TOOK A STEP, FIGHTING MY WORRIES ALL THE WAY, HAD A ROMANCE, GOT MARRIED, SO NOW I'M HAPPY. I WON'T AVOID ANY HARD WORK IN THE FUTURE TO KEEP THIS LIFESTYLE GOING. BEING LOVED BY SOMEONE IMPORTANT TO YOU, SOMEONE YOU LOVE AS WELL, IS SUCH BLISS.

P.S. MY HUSBAND READS "TOKYO TARAREBA GIRLS" TOO. HE LAUGHS AND SAYS, "IT'S ALMOST LIKE YOU IN THE PAST!" AND HE'S RIGHT, SO ALL I CAN DO IS GRIN.

AFTER I STARTED LIVING WITH MY HUSBAND, MY EVENING DRINKING HAS GOTTEN MUCH LESS FREQUENT, SO I ONLY DRINK OUT MAYBE ONCE OR TWICE A MONTH. IN FACT, I CAN GO WITHOUT DRINKING AT ALL. I LOVE BEER, WINE, AND SAKE, SO I DIDN'T MIND GOING INTO BARS ALONE EITHER... PEOPLE REALLY CAN CHANGE. I'M GRATEFUL TO "TOKYO TARAREBA GIRLS."

PN: 98% OF MUSICIANS ARE TRASH (32)

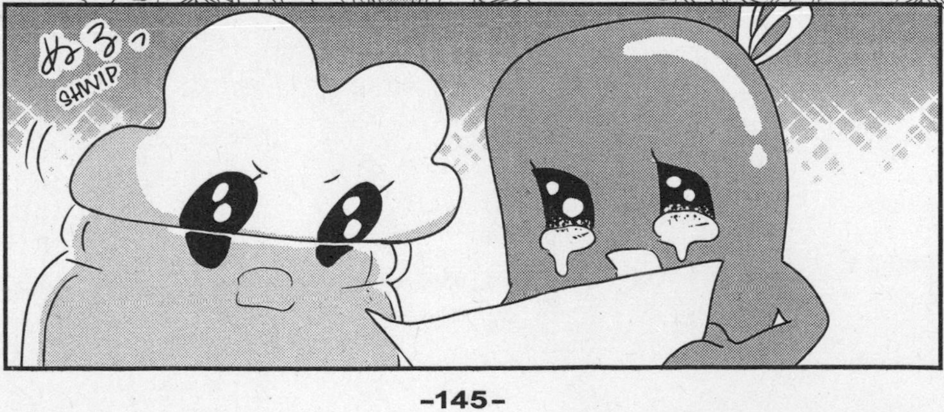
SHWIP

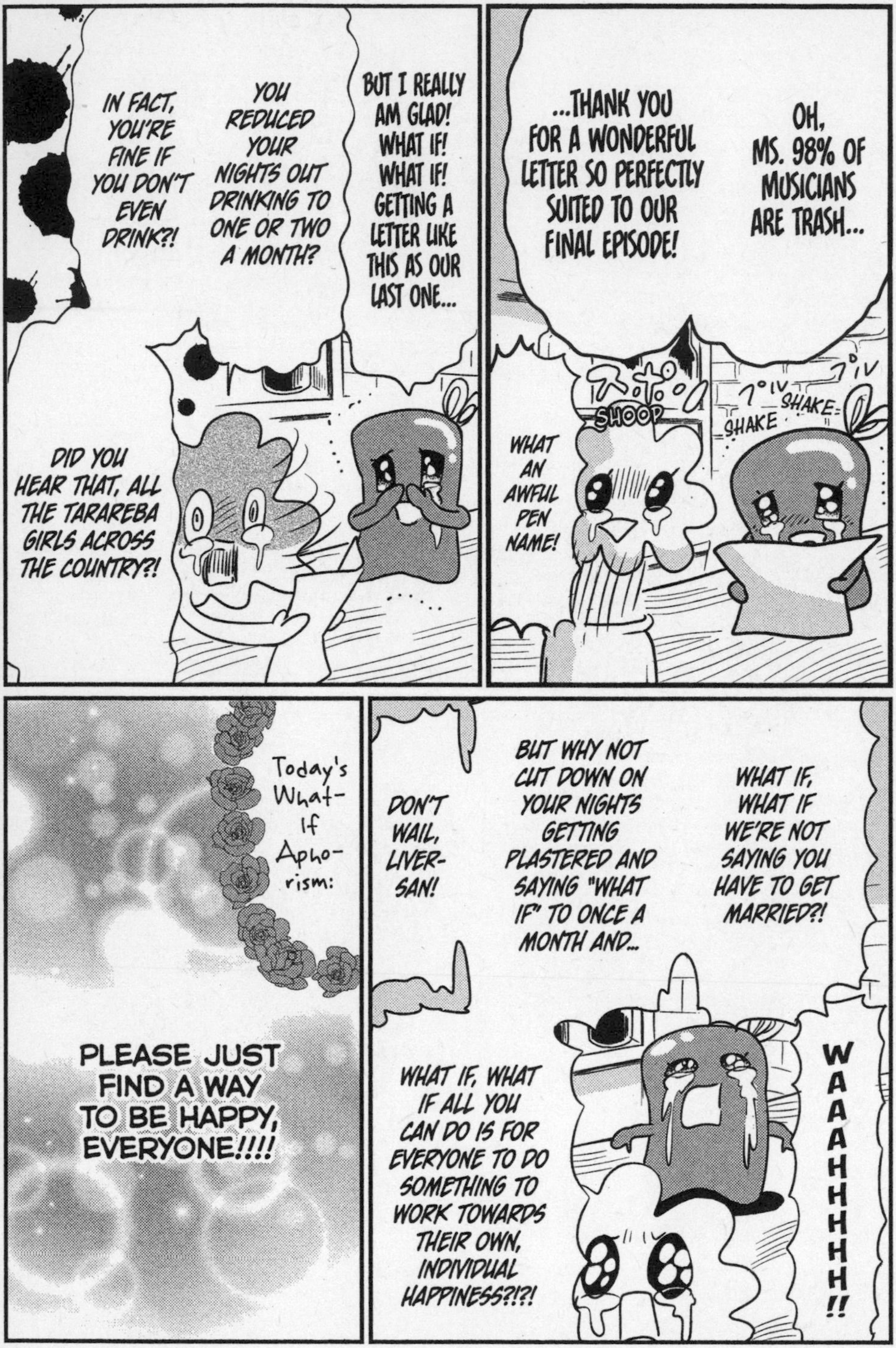
OH, MS. 98% OF MUSICIANS ARE TRASH...
...THANK YOU FOR A WONDERFUL LETTER SO PERFECTLY SUITED TO OUR FINAL EPISODE!
SHAKE SHAKE
SHOOP
WHAT AN AWFUL PEN NAME!
BUT I REALLY AM GLAD! WHAT IF! WHAT IF! GETTING A LETTER LIKE THIS AS OUR LAST ONE...
YOU REDUCED YOUR NIGHTS OUT DRINKING TO ONE OR TWO A MONTH?
IN FACT, YOU'RE FINE IF YOU DON'T EVEN DRINK?!
DID YOU HEAR THAT, ALL THE TARAREBA GIRLS ACROSS THE COUNTRY?!
WHAT IF, WHAT IF WE'RE NOT SAYING YOU HAVE TO GET MARRIED?!
BUT WHY NOT CUT DOWN ON YOUR NIGHTS GETTING PLASTERED AND SAYING "WHAT IF" TO ONCE A MONTH AND...
DON'T WAIL, LIVER-SAN!
WAAAAHHHHHH!!
WHAT IF, WHAT IF ALL YOU CAN DO IS FOR EVERYONE TO DO SOMETHING TO WORK TOWARDS THEIR OWN, INDIVIDUAL HAPPINESS?!?!
Today's What-If Aphorism:
PLEASE JUST FIND A WAY TO BE HAPPY, EVERYONE!!!!

TOKYO

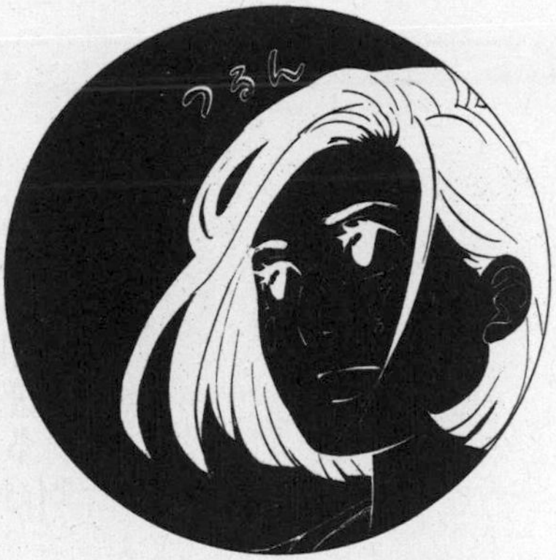
つるん

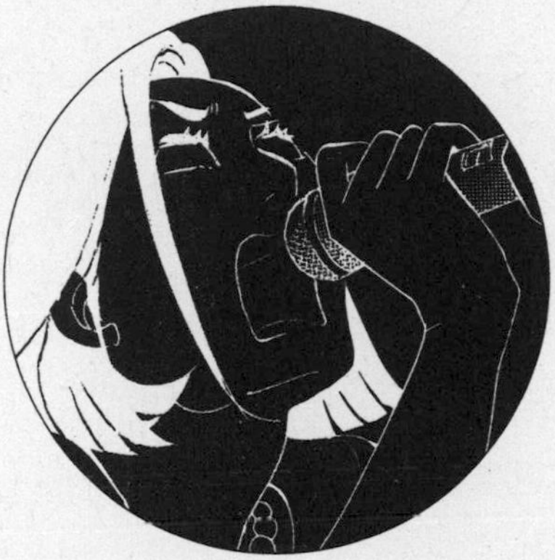

TARAREBA

GIRLS

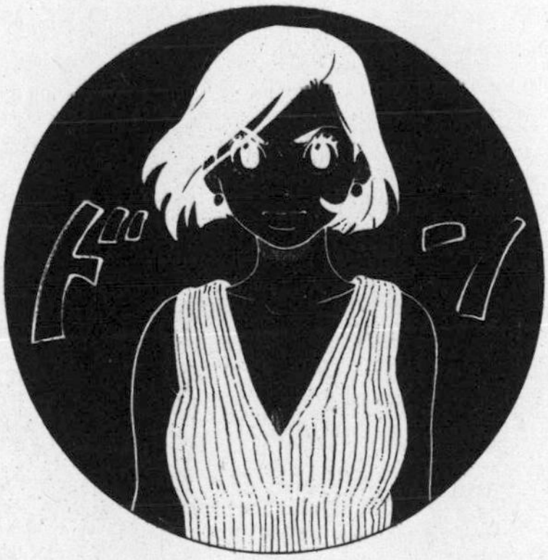

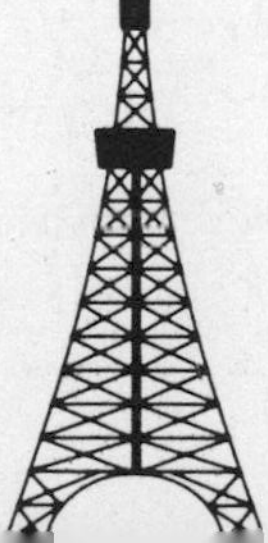

TOKYO

 **TARAREBA**

GIRLS

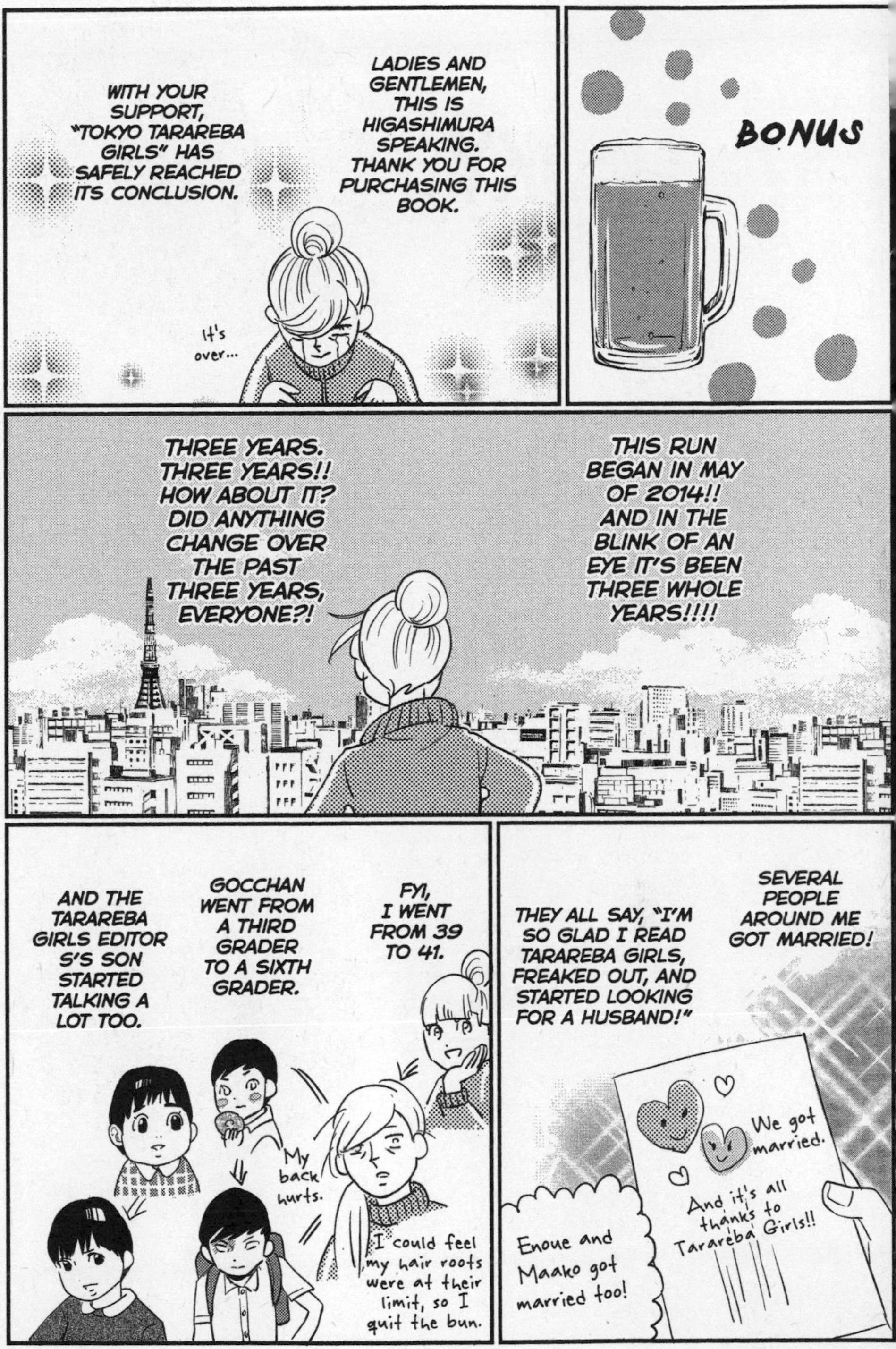

BONUS
LADIES AND GENTLEMEN, THIS IS HIGASHIMURA SPEAKING. THANK YOU FOR PURCHASING THIS BOOK.
WITH YOUR SUPPORT, "TOKYO TARAREBA GIRLS" HAS SAFELY REACHED ITS CONCLUSION.
It's over...
THIS RUN BEGAN IN MAY OF 2014!! AND IN THE BLINK OF AN EYE IT'S BEEN THREE WHOLE YEARS!!!!
THREE YEARS. THREE YEARS!! HOW ABOUT IT? DID ANYTHING CHANGE OVER THE PAST THREE YEARS, EVERYONE?!
SEVERAL PEOPLE AROUND ME GOT MARRIED!
THEY ALL SAY, "I'M SO GLAD I READ TARAREBA GIRLS, FREAKED OUT, AND STARTED LOOKING FOR A HUSBAND!"
We got married.
And it's all thanks to Tarareba Girls!!
Enoue and Maako got married too!
FYI, I WENT FROM 39 TO 41.
GOCCHAN WENT FROM A THIRD GRADER TO A SIXTH GRADER.
AND THE TARAREBA GIRLS EDITOR S'S SON STARTED TALKING A LOT TOO.
My back hurts.
I could feel my hair roots were at their limit, so I quit the bun.

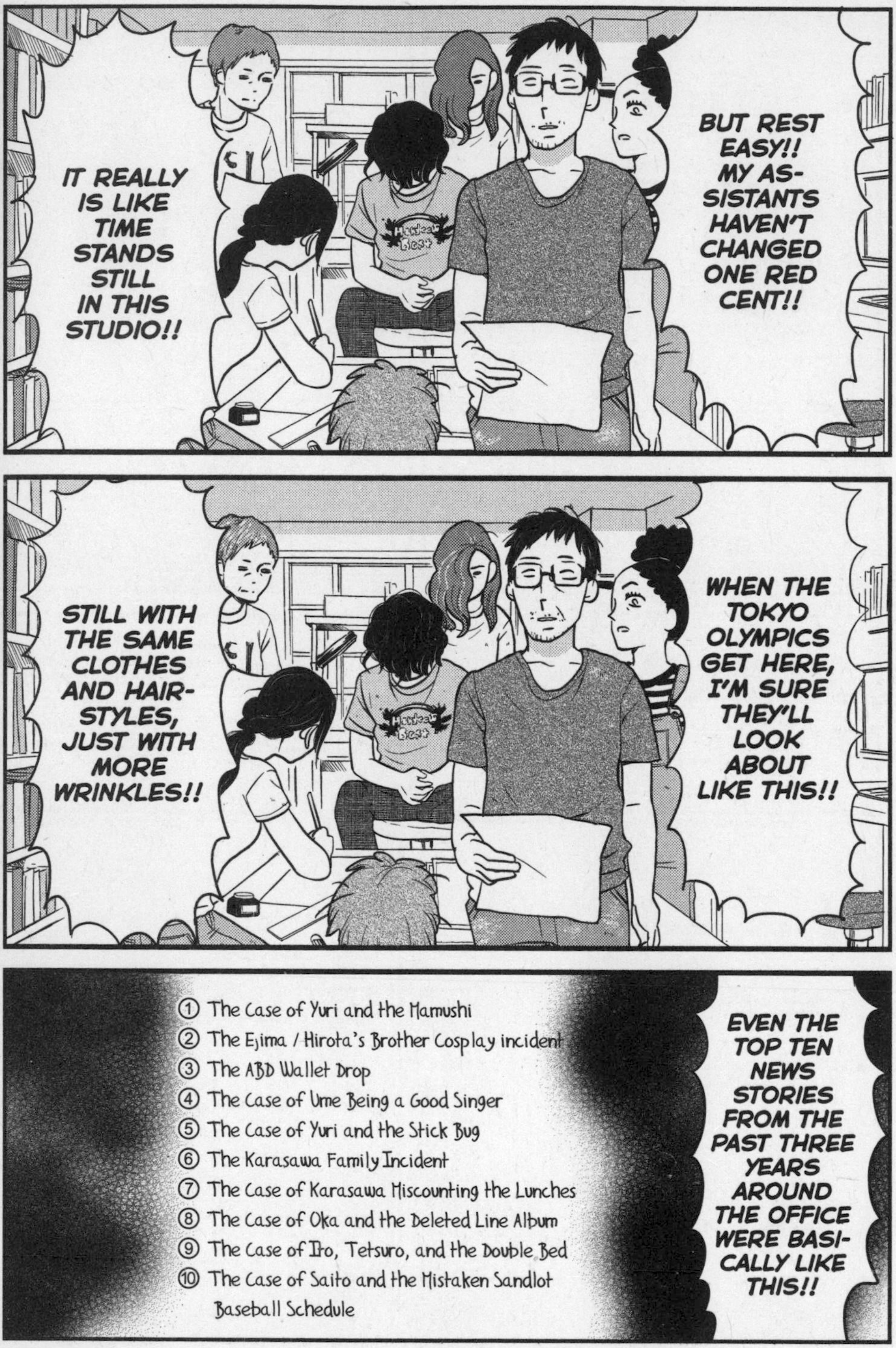
BUT REST EASY!! MY ASSISTANTS HAVEN'T CHANGED ONE RED CENT!!
IT REALLY IS LIKE TIME STANDS STILL IN THIS STUDIO!!
WHEN THE TOKYO OLYMPICS GET HERE, I'M SURE THEY'LL LOOK ABOUT LIKE THIS!!
STILL WITH THE SAME CLOTHES AND HAIRSTYLES, JUST WITH MORE WRINKLES!!
EVEN THE TOP TEN NEWS STORIES FROM THE PAST THREE YEARS AROUND THE OFFICE WERE BASICALLY LIKE THIS!!
① The Case of Yuri and the Mamushi
② The Ejima / Hirota's Brother Cosplay incident
③ The ABD Wallet Drop
④ The Case of Ume Being a Good Singer
⑤ The Case of Yuri and the Stick Bug
⑥ The Karasawa Family Incident
⑦ The Case of Karasawa Miscounting the Lunches
⑧ The Case of Oka and the Deleted Line Album
⑨ The Case of Ito, Tetsuro, and the Double Bed
⑩ The Case of Saito and the Mistaken Sandlot Baseball Schedule

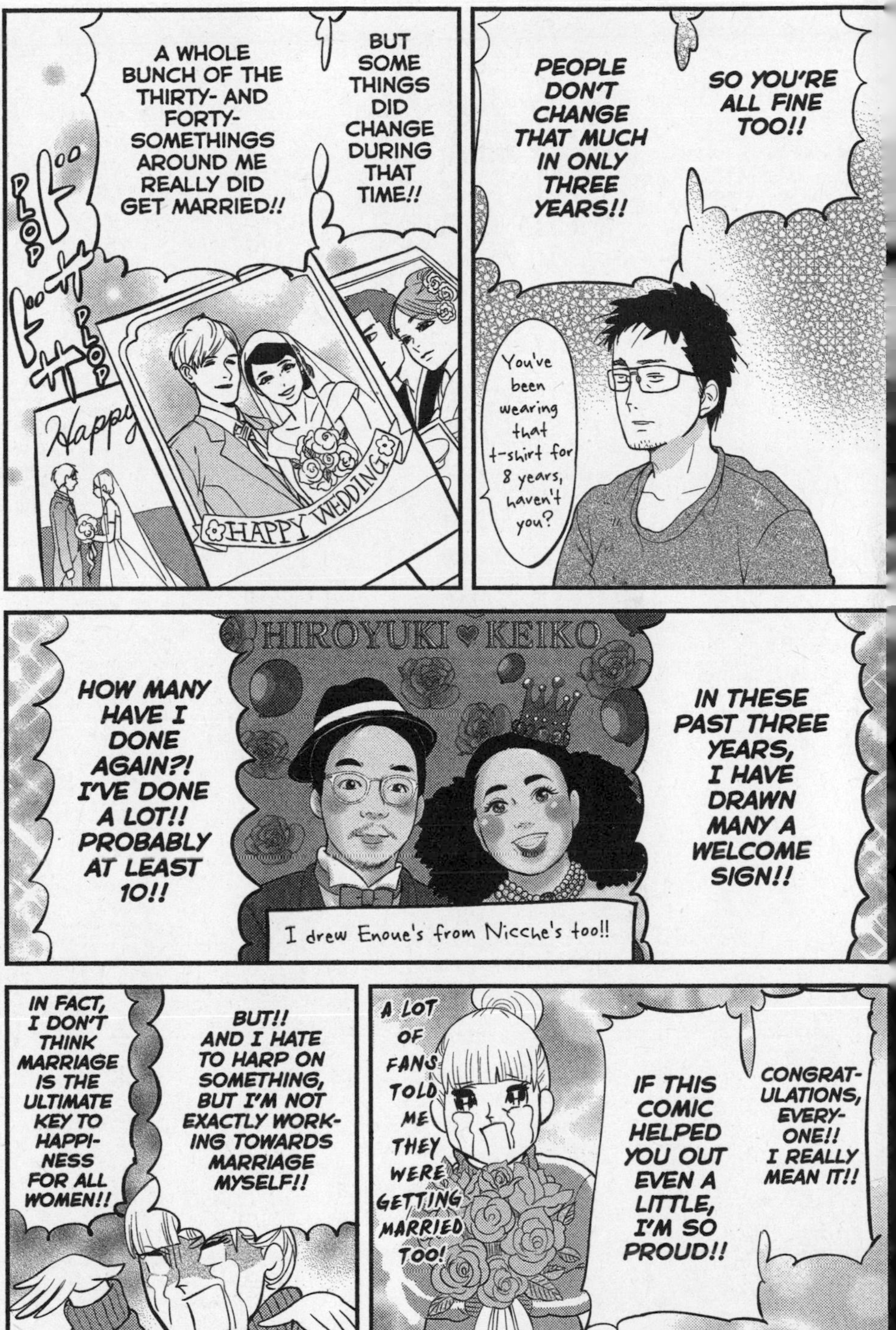

SO YOU'RE ALL FINE TOO!!
PEOPLE DON'T CHANGE THAT MUCH IN ONLY THREE YEARS!!
You've been wearing that t-shirt for 8 years, haven't you?
BUT SOME THINGS DID CHANGE DURING THAT TIME!!
A WHOLE BUNCH OF THE THIRTY- AND FORTY-SOMETHINGS AROUND ME REALLY DID GET MARRIED!!
PLOP
PLOP
HAPPY WEDDING
Happy
HIROYUKI♥KEIKO
IN THESE PAST THREE YEARS, I HAVE DRAWN MANY A WELCOME SIGN!!
HOW MANY HAVE I DONE AGAIN?! I'VE DONE A LOT!! PROBABLY AT LEAST 10!!
I drew Enoue's from Nicche's too!!
CONGRATULATIONS, EVERYONE!! I REALLY MEAN IT!!
IF THIS COMIC HELPED YOU OUT EVEN A LITTLE, I'M SO PROUD!!
A LOT OF FANS TOLD ME THEY WERE GETTING MARRIED TOO!
BUT!! AND I HATE TO HARP ON SOMETHING, BUT I'M NOT EXACTLY WORKING TOWARDS MARRIAGE MYSELF!!
IN FACT, I DON'T THINK MARRIAGE IS THE ULTIMATE KEY TO HAPPINESS FOR ALL WOMEN!!

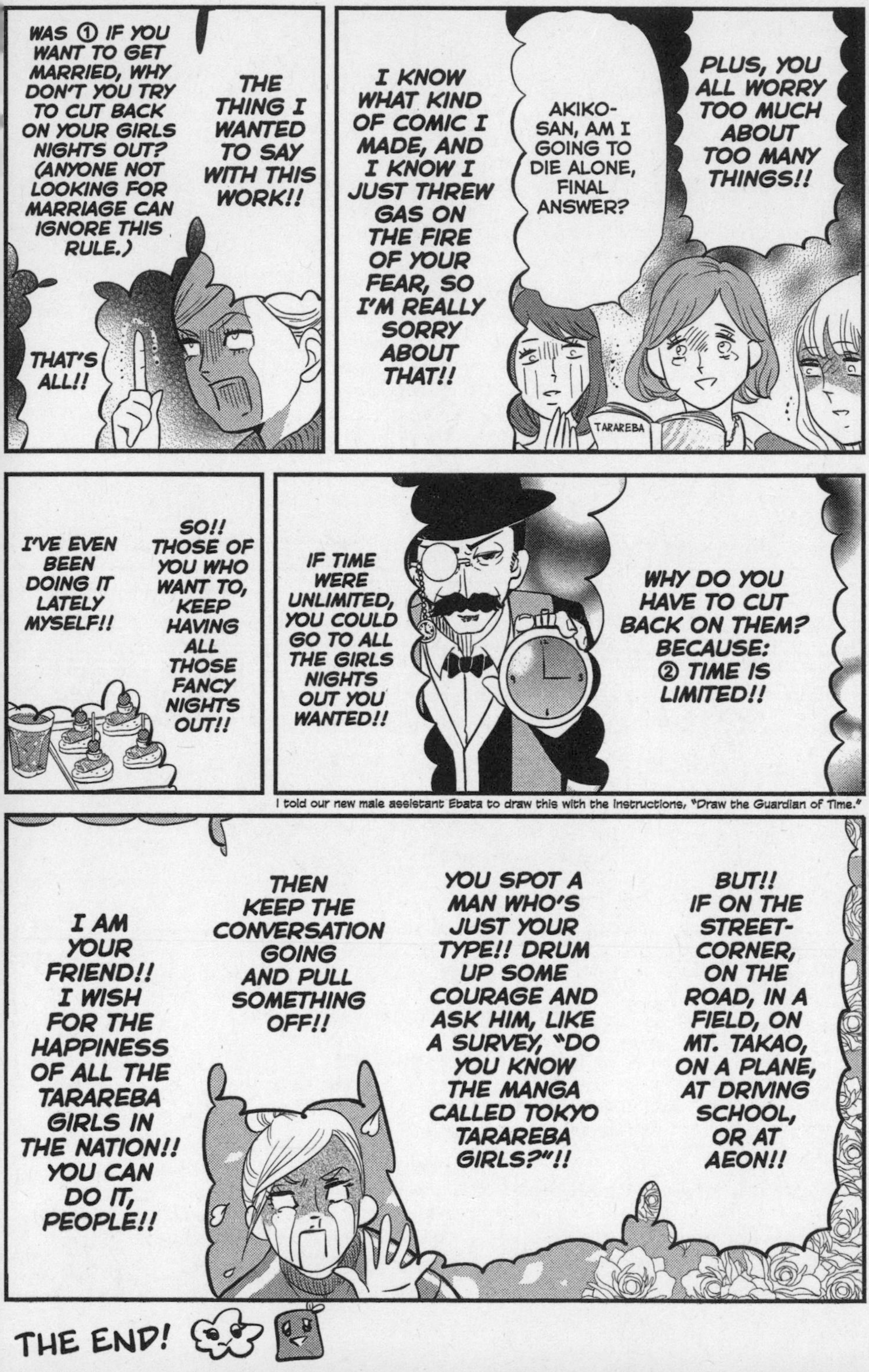
PLUS, YOU ALL WORRY TOO MUCH ABOUT TOO MANY THINGS!!
AKIKO-SAN, AM I GOING TO DIE ALONE, FINAL ANSWER?
I KNOW WHAT KIND OF COMIC I MADE, AND I KNOW I JUST THREW GAS ON THE FIRE OF YOUR FEAR, SO I'M REALLY SORRY ABOUT THAT!!
TARAREBA
THE THING I WANTED TO SAY WITH THIS WORK!!
WAS ① IF YOU WANT TO GET MARRIED, WHY DON'T YOU TRY TO CUT BACK ON YOUR GIRLS NIGHTS OUT? (ANYONE NOT LOOKING FOR MARRIAGE CAN IGNORE THIS RULE.)
THAT'S ALL!!
WHY DO YOU HAVE TO CUT BACK ON THEM? BECAUSE: ② TIME IS LIMITED!!
IF TIME WERE UNLIMITED, YOU COULD GO TO ALL THE GIRLS NIGHTS OUT YOU WANTED!!
SO!! THOSE OF YOU WHO WANT TO, KEEP HAVING ALL THOSE FANCY NIGHTS OUT!!
I'VE EVEN BEEN DOING IT LATELY MYSELF!!
I told our new male assistant Ebata to draw this with the instructions, "Draw the Guardian of Time."
BUT!! IF ON THE STREET-CORNER, ON THE ROAD, IN A FIELD, ON MT. TAKAO, ON A PLANE, AT DRIVING SCHOOL, OR AT AEON!!
YOU SPOT A MAN WHO'S JUST YOUR TYPE!! DRUM UP SOME COURAGE AND ASK HIM, LIKE A SURVEY, "DO YOU KNOW THE MANGA CALLED TOKYO TARAREBA GIRLS?"!!
THEN KEEP THE CONVERSATION GOING AND PULL SOMETHING OFF!!
I AM YOUR FRIEND!! I WISH FOR THE HAPPINESS OF ALL THE TARAREBA GIRLS IN THE NATION!! YOU CAN DO IT, PEOPLE!!
THE END!

Translation notes

Tokyo Tarareba Girls: *"Tarareba"* means "What-if," like the "What-if" stories you tell yourself about what could be or could have been. The name is also taken from the names of the two food characters in the series, *tara* (codfish milt) and *reba* (liver) who always say *"tara"* and *"reba"* respectively at the end of their sentences in Japanese, referencing the "what-if" meaning of *"tarareba."*

Suffixes (-san, -chan): In Japan, it is polite to use suffixes after a person's name or title. The most commonly used is "-san," which is akin to "Mr." or "Ms.". The other suffix used in this volume is "-chan," which is used to refer to someone younger than the speaker, and is mostly used for women and children (the male equivalent being "-kun").

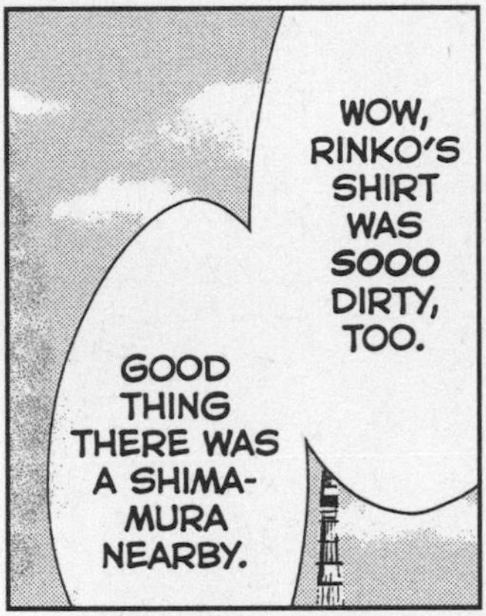
WOW, RINKO'S SHIRT WAS SOOO DIRTY, TOO.
GOOD THING THERE WAS A SHIMA- MURA NEARBY.

Shimamura, page 61
A mass-market fashion retail chain whose focus is on value and low prices. It would be a good place to buy a cheap item of clothing in an emergency like the one Rinko found herself in.

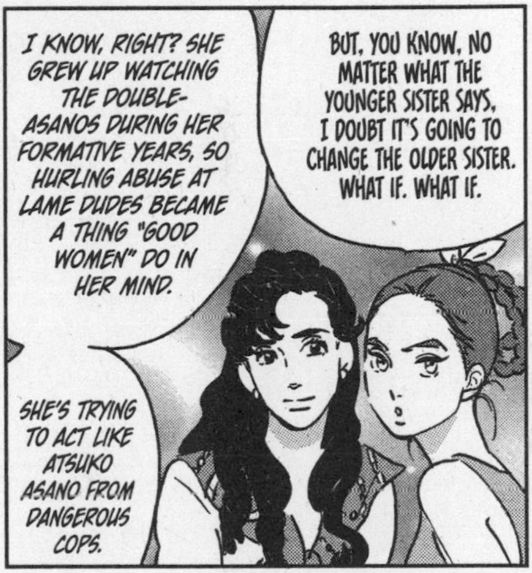
BUT, YOU KNOW, NO MATTER WHAT THE YOUNGER SISTER SAYS, I DOUBT IT'S GOING TO CHANGE THE OLDER SISTER. WHAT IF. WHAT IF.
I KNOW, RIGHT? SHE GREW UP WATCHING THE DOUBLE-ASANOS DURING HER FORMATIVE YEARS, SO HURLING ABUSE AT LAME DUDES BECAME A THING "GOOD WOMEN" DO IN HER MIND.
SHE'S TRYING TO ACT LIKE ATSUKO ASANO FROM DANGEROUS COPS.

Double Asanos, page 124
Atsuko Asano and Yuuko Asano were (unrelated) actresses who were double-billed in the hit 1988 drama series *Dakishimetai* (also known as *I Wanna Hold Your Hand!*), about two thirty-something women and their dating travails.

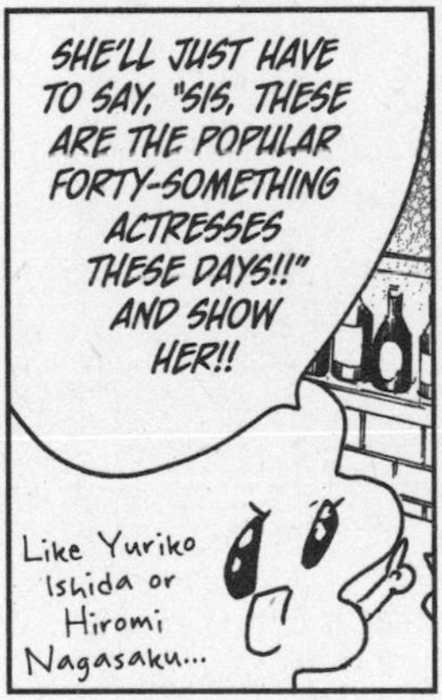
SHE'LL JUST HAVE TO SAY, "SIS, THESE ARE THE POPULAR FORTY-SOMETHING ACTRESSES THESE DAYS!!" AND SHOW HER!!
Like Yuriko Ishida or Hiromi Nagasaku...

Messhii / Asshii, page 124
Slang from the era for a man you can count on for a meal any time, and a man you can call up at anytime for a ride somewhere, respectively. The terms are derived the words for "food" (*meshi*) and "legs/feet" (*ashi*).

Yuriko Ishida and Hiromi Nagasaku, page 124
Yuriko Ishida and Hiromi Nagasaku are likewise actresses who got their starts in the late '80s / early '90s. Ishida is also an essayist, and Nagasaku is also a singer.

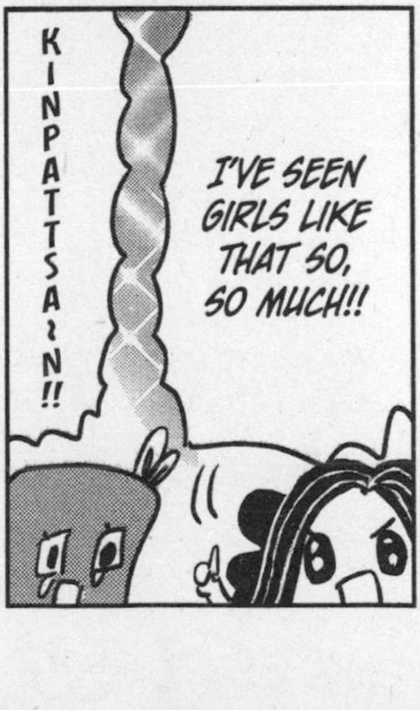
I'VE SEEN GIRLS LIKE THAT SO, SO MUCH!!
KINPATTSA~N!!

Kimpattsan, page 126
Reference to the long-running TV franchise "Kinpachi-Sensei" which is about an inspiring high school teacher who helps his students through difficulties based on a variety of social problems. The line Liver calls out as though asking for his help is a nickname for Kinpachi-sensei in the series.

Having lost his wife, high school teacher Kōhei Inuzuka is doing his best to raise his young daughter Tsumugi as a single father. He's pretty bad at cooking and doesn't have a huge appetite to begin with, but chance brings his little family together with one of his students, the lonely Kotori. The three of them are anything but comfortable in the kitchen, but the healing power of home cooking might just work on their grieving hearts.

"This season's number-one feel-good anime!" —Anime News Network

"A beautifully-drawn story about comfort food and family and grief. Recommended." —Otaku USA Magazine

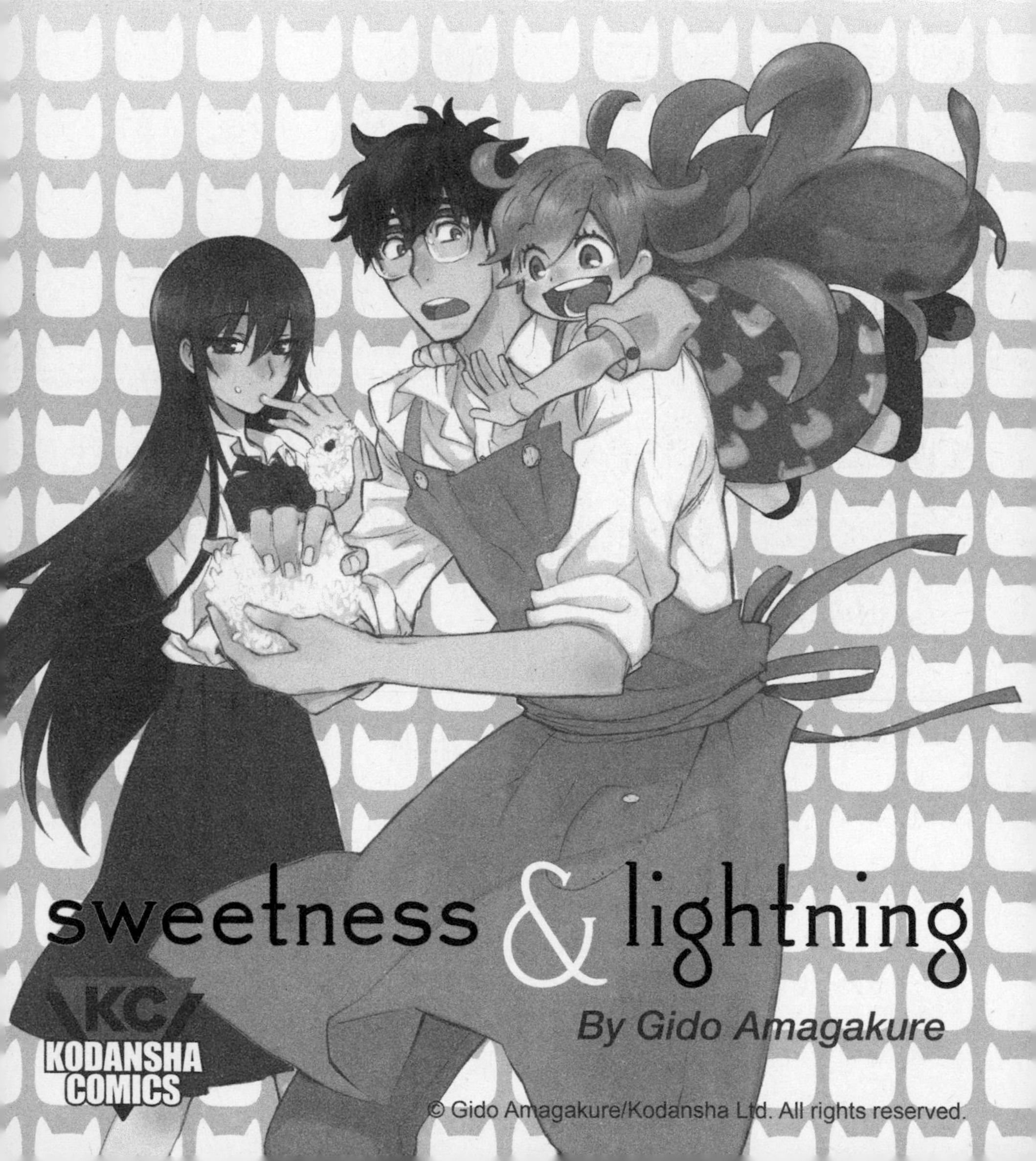
sweetness & lightning
By Gido Amagakure
KC
KODANSHA COMICS

In love, there are no save points.

ヲタクに恋は難しい

NOW AN ANIME!

WOTAKOI:
LOVE IS HARD FOR OTAKU
by FUJITA

Narumi has had it rough: Every boyfriend she's had dumped her once they found out she was an otaku, so she's gone to great lengths to hide it. At her new job, she bumps into Hirotaka, her childhood friend and fellow otaku. When Hirotaka almost gets her secret outed at work, she comes up with a plan to keep him quiet. But he comes up with a counter-proposal: Why doesn't she just date him instead?

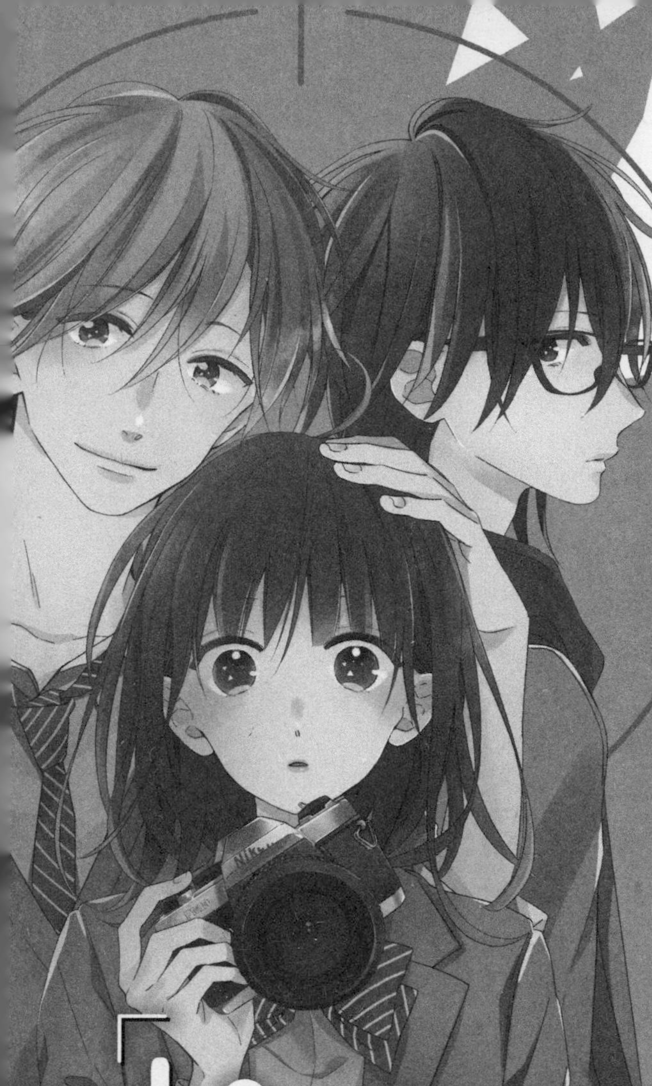

Acclaimed screenwriter and director Mari Okada (*Maquia*, *anohana*) teams up with manga artist Nao Emoto (*Forget Me Not*) in this moving, funny, so-true-it's-embarrassing coming-of-age series!

When Kazusa enters high school, she joins the Literature Club, and leaps from reading innocent fiction to diving into the literary classics. But these novels are a bit more...*adult* than she was prepared for. Between euphemisms like fresh dewy grass and pork stew, crushing on the boy next door, and knowing you want to do that *one thing* before you die—discovering your budding sexuality is no easy feat! As if puberty wasn't awkward enough, the club consists of a brooding writer, the prettiest girl in school, an agreeable comrade, and an outspoken prude. Fumbling over their own discomforts, these five teens get thrown into chaos over three little letters: S...E...X...!

Anime coming soon!

O Maidens in your Savage Season

Mari Okada   Nao Emoto

KC KODANSHA COMICS

◄ KAMOME ►
SHIRAHAMA

Witch Hat Atelier

A magical manga
adventure for
fans of Disney
and Studio
Ghibli!

Witch Hat Atelier © Kamome Shirahama/Kodansha Ltd.

The magical adventure that took Japan by storm is finally here, from acclaimed DC and Marvel cover artist Kamome Shirahama!

In a world where everyone takes wonders like magic spells
and dragons for granted, Coco is a girl with a simple dream:
She wants to be a witch. But everybody knows magicians
are born, not made, and Coco was not born with a gift for
magic. Resigned to her un-magical life, Coco is about to
give up on her dream to become a witch...until the day
she meets Qifrey, a mysterious, traveling magician. After
secretly seeing Qifrey perform magic in a way she's never
seen before, Coco soon learns what everybody "knows"
might not be the truth, and discovers that her magical
dream may not be as far away as it may seem...

KC
KODANSHA
COMICS

Yuri Is My Job!

miman

JOIN US FOR
AFTERNOON TEA
WITH EQUAL PARTS
YURI, ROM-COM,
AND DRAMA!

Hime is a picture-perfect high school princess, so when she accidentally injures a café manager named Mai, she's willing to cover some shifts to keep her façade intact. To Hime's surprise, the café is themed after a private school where the all-female staff always puts on their best act for their loyal customers. However, under the guidance of the most graceful girl there, Hime can't help but blush and blunder! Beneath all the frills and laughter, Hime feels tension brewing as she finds out more about her new job and her budding feelings...

"A quirky, fun comedy series... If you're a yuri fan, or perhaps interested in getting into it but not sure where to start, this book is worth picking up."
— Anime UK News

Tokyo Tarareba Girls volume 9 is a work of fiction. Names, characters, places, and incidents are the products of the author's imagination or are used fictitiously. Any resemblance to actual events, locales, or persons, living or dead, is entirely coincidental.

A Kodansha Comics Trade Paperback Original.

Tokyo Tarareba Girls volume 9 copyright © 2017 Akiko Higashimura
English translation copyright © 2019 Akiko Higashimura

Published in the United States by Kodansha Comics,
an imprint of Kodansha USA Publishing, LLC, New York.

Publication rights for this English edition arranged through Kodansha Ltd.,
Tokyo.

First published in Japan in 2017 by Kodansha Ltd., Tokyo, as *Tokyo Tarareba Musume* volume 9.

ISBN 978-1-63236-857-7

Printed in the United States of America.

www.kodanshacomics.com

9 8 7 6 5 4 3 2 1

Translation: Steven LeCroy
Lettering: Thea Willis and Paige Pumphrey
Editing: Sarah Tilson and Lauren Scanlan
YKS Services LLC/SKY Japan, INC.
Kodansha Comics Edition Cover Design: Phil Balsman